W9-DFG-002

DATE DUE

DEMCO, INC. 38-2931

SUPERVISION OF INSTRUCTION

A Developmental Approach

Second Edition

CARL D. GLICKMAN
The University of Georgia

Allyn and Bacon
Boston   London   Sydney   Toronto

Dedicated to Sam and Samantha

Copyright © 1990, 1985 by Allyn and Bacon
A Division of Simon & Schuster, Inc.
160 Gould Street
Needham Heights, Massachusetts 02194

Library of Congress Cataloging-in-Publication Data
Glickman, Carl D.
    Supervision of instruction : a developmental approach / Carl D. Glickman.—2nd ed.
    p.   cm.
    Includes bibliographies and index.
    ISBN 0-205-12153-5
    1. School supervision.   I. Title.
LB2806.4.G56   1989
371.2—dc20   89-35493
                                                                    CIP

Printed in the United States of America
10 9 8 7 6 5 4 3   93 92 91

Contents

Foreword

The school reform movement began in 1983 with the release of *A Nation at Risk*. Followed immediately by other reports on the status of education in the United States, *A Nation at Risk* focused attention on schools and schooling more than any other event since Sputnik.

At least three things have made an impact on the schools during the period since 1983. Information about the status of education was one. Another was the change that occurred in state government operations as a consequence of President Reagan's determined effort to devolve authority from the federal to the state level. The third was the revitalization of state legislatures as a consequence of the *Baker* v. *Carr* decision in the 1960s (the "one man, one vote" rule), which forced states to devise election procedures to make their legislatures truly representative. These factors produced a confluence of forces that affected public education in the 1980s.

Three things resulted: Expectations of the general public rose; more state laws directed at schools were passed; and morale and enthusiasm among professionals deteriorated.

Expectations of the public rose because gubernatorial candidates promised the public better schools. Legislatures of the states passed more laws directed at schools during the 1980s than they had passed since the turn of the century, and much of that legislation took the form of mandates. Because of promises made by governors to the public and mandates imposed upon schools by legislatures, many teachers became disillusioned and demoralized.

Teachers knew that promises made by candidates would not facilitate children's learning. They knew that state-mandated testing programs could not raise students' achievement levels. They knew that elaborate teacher evaluation programs would not improve teaching. They also knew that the laws of learning were not laws adopted by legislative bodies. Because teachers knew these things, they became discouraged.

Teachers want to do the right thing. They want to be law-abiding citizens; they want to do what the authorities say; they want to help young people learn. But teachers also know, intuitively at least, that authority rooted in knowledge and experience is different from authority rooted in the power of the state to coerce, even mildly, through the law.

The school reform movement has been a deliberate attempt to re-form—to form again—the schools we have. The emphasis on improving education has usually meant that change was imposed upon the schools by those outside the schools or by those inside the profession who were responding directly to demands from outside.

Many teachers felt "left out" or "put upon" by others. They were generally not even asked what they thought could or should be done to improve education for students in their classrooms. Those who were closest to where learning occurs were neither consulted nor heard. They were, in fact, almost always ignored. In many instances, "changing the schools" actually meant trying to get the teachers to change—their attitudes, their behavior, their very being—without their involvement. Only compliance was required.

Any change in human behavior is apt to come about very slowly, even if people want to change. Consider what happens when someone tries to stop smoking or lose weight. Even if a person really wants to change, it is often difficult—terribly difficult—to bring about a change in behavior that is significant and lasting. Changes that are "laid on" other people without their participation or consent are almost always doomed to failure. "A man convinced against his will is of the same opinion still."

Supervisors are confronted with these realities: The public expects more; there are more imposed restraints; and those who live and work in schools are unenthusiastic about changes imposed on them by others in attempts to improve the schools.

These are the challenges for supervisors today. This book is a response to those challenges. Rather than developing strategies to help supervisors implement state mandates, Carl Glickman outlines a concept of supervision in schools that is "bottom-up" rather than "top-down" in nature. He proposes ways of working that are aimed at helping teachers in the schools—ways that are predicated on a solid knowledge base and that build upon the commitments and intellectual capabilities of those directly involved with helping children learn.

Glickman seems to argue, albeit at an implicit level, that most educational policies and programs are one-dimensional solutions to multi-dimensional problems and therefore miss the essence of what is required in effective personal development, staff development, and curriculum development in schools. In one sense, he is "out of the mainstream" of thought regarding how to improve education. In another sense, he is articulating a "refreshing breath of fresh air" in a climate that is characterized more by ideological rhetoric than reflective professional discourse.

There is an ethical component to what Carl Glickman advocates. Ethics, in the professional sense, is directly related to how effective professionals are in helping other people. Physicians are ethical, for example, if they are effective in helping patients maintain or regain health; they are unethical if what they do causes damage or harm. The first requirement of the physician is "do no harm." In the same sense, teachers are ethical if they are effective in their efforts to help children learn. If they do anything that hinders or impedes learning, teachers are both unethical and ineffective.

In linguistics, the Whorf Thesis suggests that language shapes behavior. Words give shape to action. Legislators legislate. Administrators administer. Supervisors supervise.

How legislators define "legislation" in their own minds, however, has a profound impact on how and what they legislate. How administrators define "administration" affects their own activities. And how supervisors define "supervision" influences what they do and how they do it.

Carl Glickman is reshaping supervisory behavior by redefining supervision. He is helping people rethink what supervision is and what supervisors do by giving them a new language and new concepts with which to talk about supervision. Professor Glickman proposes a concept of supervision that invites supervisors to work with teachers in ways that will help teachers become the best people they can become, to help teachers devise approaches to the world of information and curriculum content that will assure student development and student learning and student growth, and to help teachers become more sensitive, more caring, and more helpful to the children they teach. Supervisors can help teachers become these kinds of people, not because states mandate particular programs or specific actions, but because the beliefs that supervisors hold and the language that supervisors use can lead to higher levels of expectation, higher levels of performance, and a better quality of life for those who live and work with children day after day.

Jack Frymier
Senior Fellow
Phi Delta Kappa

Preface

What is good teaching? What should be taught? What makes for a successful school? How do we educate all of our students? What do we want from our schools and how do we accomplish our goals? Why have so many educators devoted their professional (and personal) time to students, schools, and the future of American society? What knowledge, interpersonal skills, and technical skills will help us achieve our aspirations? What are the factors that slow, frustrate, and impede our desires? How should we operationalize supervision of instruction as instructional leadership so that we create rather than respond to the future of education? In essence, answering these questions for ourselves is the reason for this book.

Be forewarned that understanding the questions, knowing the possibilities, and choosing a course of action will be intellectually and emotionally taxing! The answers to instructional success are not simple; they do not exist in the collective wisdom of outside experts who can easily transfer their solutions to you. Rather, the responses are multifaceted—often contradictory—and may appear equally convincing, yet have far different consequences and outcomes. By understanding the consequences and outcomes behind our answers (not someone else's), we will take full moral responsibilities for our actions. A degree of vulnerability is involved once we accept that "experts" won't bail us out with easy solutions. Instead they can provide us with a slice of their own knowledge, combined with a greater slice of our own knowledge, to clarify choices, goals, paths, and decisions.

Excitement is building in education in the 1990s. Members of the education profession appear ready to step out from under the cloak of externally legislated, mandated, and centralized answers from "expert" panels, commissions, and state officials, emerging into the sunshine (and rain) of internal and local control over reform. The excitement must be tempered by the fear that without appropriate information, preparation, transitions, and accountability, we might achieve little in the 1990s. Such a failure could become the justification for future policy makers to tighten their cloak over schools, wrap us up tightly, and make the snaps secure. If we don't make good on the opportunity to chart our own destiny for improving student learning, we may see the eventual abandonment of public education.

The stakes are high, and the opportunities are emerging. In this book I present some of the research and theory as it applies to current and future practice of supervision of instruction.

The term *supervision*, as used in this book, refers to the school function that improves instruction through direct assistance to teachers, curriculum development, staff development, group development, and action research. The audience for this book includes those involved in school supervision from preschool through twelfth grade. Examples and research are drawn mainly from a substantial body of research on successful schools, teacher and adult development, and supervisory practice, as well as my own experiences as a public school teacher, supervisory principal, government education analyst, professor of supervision, and Director of the Program for School Improvement. Many public school supervisors in the United States and Canada (superintendents, central office directors, principals, lead teachers, department heads, and teachers) have worked with me in seminars, workshops, and courses to field-test, refine, and revise much of what follows. Many individual schools and school systems allowed me to see first-hand the reality of successful and unsuccessful supervisory practice.

This book is intended for use as a textbook for graduate students in educational supervision courses. It takes a broad field approach to the multiple skills, techniques, and tasks of supervision. Instructors in courses such as "Supervision of Instruction," "Supervision of Schools," and "Introduction to Supervision" will find this book interesting and valuable. Practicing supervisors, even without the benefit of taking a course, will find in this book practical applications to their real world of schools. They can use particular chapters to help them plan and implement direct assistance to teachers, staff development, program evaluation, and the like. Some of the more traditional content found in supervision textbooks, such as organizational arrangements, role descriptions, and history of supervision, has been compressed in order to keep this book focused on the relationship of supervision to teacher and adult development. I believe the key to successful supervision is thoughtful practice based on viewing teachers as developing adults.

This book is a straightforward presentation of positions, ideas, and practices, supported by research and theory only as it applies to the practical world of school. The concrete tools, techniques, and actions proposed in these chapters are not recipes to be followed blindly. The supervisor, as a professional with intelligence, knowledge, and awareness of his or her own situation, is asked to choose, revise, and adjust proposed actions according to his or her own judgment about the local school setting. There is no way I can know your situation, your staff, your relationship with your supervisors, or the outside constraints on your activities. I can write about what I believe will be successful; you must screen that information accordingly. I cannot offer any single correct action to be taken in a given situation, but I can suggest viable alternatives that are likely to succeed when adjusted for local conditions.

Jerome Bruner, the noted education psychologist who spearheaded the curriculum reform movement in the mid-1950s, made a cogent remark about education.* He stated that education involves *predicaments* rather than *problems*. Problems can be solved through correct solutions; in contrast, predicaments can be managed or improved on but cannot be solved once and for all. Predicaments, not problems, are the core of supervision. Improving a teacher's or a school's level of instruction is not a problem to which a single solution can be applied. It is a predicament that needs to be addressed in many ways. Ultimately, the job of supervision is to ensure that we find some of those ways.

Acknowledgments

It is impossible to recognize all those who have contributed to the development of this book. Former doctoral students such as Sherrie Gibney, Mary Phillips, Steve Gordon, Dale Rogers, Gale Rogers, Jeanie Jones, Emily Calhoun and John MacCrostie have made substantial research contributions. In particular, I want to single out Mary Guerke, Jim Kahrs, Barbara Lunsford, and Nancy Quintrell, who assisted in the establishment of the Program for School Improvement at the University of Georgia. Additionally, I have been aided by the numerous students in graduate courses who used and critiqued the first edition of *Supervision of Instruction*. Practicing supervisors in schools in Georgia, Vermont, Maine, Michigan, Nevada, California, Pennsylvania, Ohio, Saskatchewan, British Columbia, and Nova Scotia willingly provided settings for field-testing my developmental propositions about supervision. My colleagues (teachers and administrators) at Oglethorpe County High School and Fowler Drive Elementary School have been a constant source of intellectual excitement as they planned, implemented, and evaluated their own school improvements. My colleagues at the University of Georgia, most notably Professors Ray Bruce, Edith Grimsley, Ed Pajak, Tony Pellegrini, JoBeth Allen, and Terry Bey, have filled in considerable knowledge gaps of mine. (Not that I don't have a few left, but oh, how they tried!) The

* From F.M. Hechinger, Psychologist sees a key to learning in managing unsolvable problems, *New York Times*, August 18, 1981.

members of the Council of Professors of Instructional Supervision (COPIS) have provided me with resources, tolerance, and a forum for considering practice, research, and theory in supervision. I've grown with this organization, and the conflict of ideas among my productive colleagues has helped break new ground in thinking about the world of supervision. People from my first years of teaching, such as Martin Diggs, Art Sills, Dave Gaul, Geneva Woodruff, Roger Loring, Tom Condon, and Penny Condon, constantly reminded me of what schools could become—*if* we would trust the judgment of informed professionals.

Special mention needs to be made of Gerald Firth, Head of the Department of Curriculum and Supervision, and Alphonse Buccino, Dean of the College of Education, at the University of Georgia, who have provided me with opportunities and resources in my work with public schools far beyond the capabilities and priorities of most institutions of higher education.

The staff at Georgia who have worked with me through the years has been excellent. The bulk of the typing, editing, and diagramming fell to Donna Bell, Linda Edwards, and Ann Seagraves, who were ably assisted by Joan Towns and Harriet Elder. Putting up with my need to have everything done yesterday was a demanding job unto itself, one they endured with patience, tolerance, and humor.

My thanks to the staff of Allyn and Bacon, beginning with Hiram Howard and Paul Solaqua, later Susanne Canavan, and most recently Sean Wakely, and to David Hoyt and Elydia Davis for their excellent production work. I am grateful to the publisher's reviewers, whose names are unknown to me, for holding me to such high standards of precision.

I know there are others I have unwittingly left out; for that, I am sorry. Those who have helped me are not responsible for any faults and limitations of this book. Any errors are mine alone. Many have extended my vision about supervision and human development. All of you have helped to show me the light of school success and inspired me to devote my career to understanding the journey.

Finally, I wish to acknowledge my spouse and best friend, Sara, and our children, Jennifer and Rachel. They need no reason for acknowledgment other than that they are special to me.

To the Instructor

At the end of each chapter, you will find exercises that might be assigned to your graduate students. The first edition of this text has been used in universities and colleges throughout the United States and Canada. Based on the experience of many colleagues who have used the text with their supervision classes, I would like to offer some suggestions. The twenty-one chapters correspond roughly to the weeks of an academic semester. The first three chapters are relatively brief and can be read as one assignment. Students can then complete one or two chapters and one exercise for each subsequent week. For those who teach on a quarter system, it is recommended that the first three chapters be assigned the first week, and two chapters each subsequent week.

When reading more than one chapter at a time, the student should choose to do one exercise from any of the assigned chapters. Exercises are categorized as academic, field, and developmental. *Academic exercises* are those done primarily through library research, reading, writing, and constructing. *Field exercises* are those done in practice within school settings and with other professionals. Academic exercises are suitable for graduate students who do not hold supervisory positions and/or are seeking more knowledge of theory and research. Field exercises are suitable for practitioners who wish to make immediate improvements in their professional situations. Whether or not students are in supervisory positions, I suggest that a student do both field and academic exercises at a ratio of approximately 2 to 1 weighted toward their interest, situation, and needs. A short sharing session is useful at the beginning of each class, to give students an opportunity to discuss the results of their exercises.

Developmental exercises are done as sustained projects that can be used as a term or extra-credit project. Developmental exercises are written with the purpose of encouraging students to continue their professional growth. If used as a term assignment, please allow students during the first week of classes to scan *all* the developmental activities in each chapter before asking them to make a choice for the academic term.

The exercises (academic, field, and developmental) are numerous and provide students a wide arena of choice. Likewise, I encourage the instructor to make his or her own choices according to his or her own expertise and experience. The sequence of chapters is consistent with the proposed model of supervision, but an individual instructor might find another order more suitable. Similarly, the instructor might wish to adapt, revise, or discard suggestions for using chapter exercises. My purpose in writing this book was to increase supervisory success in schools. However an instructor can use this book to bring about such success will make my efforts worthwhile.

Carl D. Glickman

PART I

INTRODUCTION

Chapter 1

Supervision
for Successful Schools

Take a walk with me. First, let's step into Finnie Tyler High School, with a student body of twelve hundred, in a lower- to middle-class urban neighborhood. A sign by the entrance tells all visitors to report to the office. In the halls we see students milling around, boys and girls talking in groups, couples holding hands, one couple intertwined romantically in a corner. The bell rings and students scurry to the next class. We find the school office and introduce ourselves to the secretary and school principal, who are expecting our visit. They welcome us and assure us that we may move around the school and talk to students, teachers, and other staff. The school population have been notified of our visit and understand that we have come to see how Tyler High School operates. The principal tells us we will find Tyler a pleasant place. Equipped with a floor plan of classrooms and other facilities, we continue on our way.

The principal's description is accurate: Students seem happy and uninhibited, socializing easily with each other even during instruction time. Teachers joke with students. In the faculty lounge we hear laughter that rises, falls, and then rises again. Several teachers have told us about the traditional Friday afterschool gatherings at the local pizza parlor, where teachers and administrators socialize over a drink.

Classrooms vary considerably from each other; teachers tell us they can teach however they wish. Most teachers stand at the front of the room, lecturing, asking questions, and assigning seat work. Some, however, take a less structured approach, allowing students to work alone or in small groups. There is an unhurried atmosphere. Students move at a leisurely pace, and classes seldom start on time. Teachers of the same subjects use the same textbooks but otherwise seem to have discretion to function as they please. As one seven-year veteran teacher at this school sums it up: "We have an ideal situation. We like each other, and the administration leaves us alone. I am observed once a year. I have one faculty meeting a month to attend. I love the other teachers and we have a great time together. The kids are fine, not as academic as they should be, but this school is a nice place for them. I wouldn't want to teach anyplace else."

Now let's drive across town to Germando Elementary School, with six hundred students, located in a wealthy, suburban part of the city. Again, we follow the sign to the office. A few students are standing with their noses against the wall by their classroom doors. Otherwise the halls are vacant and still; all classroom doors are shut. In the principal's office sit two students with tears in their eyes, obviously fearful of their impending conference with the principal. The principal welcomes us and hands us a preplanned schedule of times to visit particular teachers. She tells us not to visit any classroom during instructional time. "I think you will find that I run a tight ship," she says. "Teachers and students know exactly what is expected of them and what the consequences are for ignoring those expectations. Teachers are here to teach, and I see to it that it happens."

Moving down the halls, we are struck by the similarity of the classrooms. The desks are in rows; the teacher is in front; the school rules are posted on the right of the chalkboard. At the first recess time, the students seem to erupt onto the playground. Expecting to find a group of teachers in the faculty lounge, we are surprised to find only two people. One is knitting, the other preparing a cup of coffee. All the other teachers have remained in the classrooms, either alone or with one other teacher.

Continuing our observation after recess, we find that teachers at each grade level not only work with the same textbooks but are on the same pages as well. When we ask about this, one teacher tells us the principal has standardized the entire curriculum and knows what is being taught in every classroom at each moment of the day. At the first faculty meeting in August, the principal lays out materials, schedules, and time lines developed by the central office. We ask how the principal can enforce such procedures, and the teacher replies, "She asks for weekly lesson plans, visits my room at least once every two weeks, and has other central office personnel visit and report back to her."

In the classrooms we visit, students are generally quiet but restless. They appear attentive; those who are not are disciplined. Teachers are mostly businesslike; some show warmth toward their students, others do not. We conclude our visit with three separate interviews of teachers. It seems that teaching in Germando is perceived as a job to do. Whether one likes them or not, the principal's rules are to be followed. Teachers mention that when they have attempted to make modest changes in their instruction, they have been told to drop the changes and return to the school plan. All three mention the teacher last year who refused to follow the reading textbook and was subsequently forced to resign.

Finnie Tyler High School and Germando Elementary School are examples of real schools. Which is the successful school? Which has better attendance, attitudes, and achievement? *Neither does!* Both are ineffective, mediocre schools. The successful schools in the same system are quite different from either. Our first conclusion might be that these schools are very different. Tyler High School appears to have little supervision of instruction, whereas Germando has too much. According to the definition of instructional supervision presented in this book, however, *neither* school has effective instructional supervision. It also might appear that Tyler meets teachers' individual needs, whereas Germando meets organizational goals set by the principal. In successful schools, however, individual needs are fulfilled only through organizational goals. In these two schools *neither* need is being met. Finally, the working environments in these two schools only appear to be dissimilar; soon we will see how similar they really are.

Supervisory Glue as a Metaphor for Success

We can think of supervision as the *glue* of a successful school. Supervision is the function in schools that draws together the discrete elements of instructional effectiveness into whole-school action. Research shows that those schools that link their instruction, classroom management, and discipline with staff development, direct assistance to teachers, curriculum development, group development, and action research under a common purpose *achieve their objectives* (MacKenzie 1983). In other words, when teachers accept common goals for students and therefore complement each other's teaching, and when supervisors work with teachers in a manner consistent with the way teachers are expected to work with students, then—and only then—does the school reach its goals. Regardless of a school's grade span, socioeconomic setting, or physical characteristics, successful schools have a common glue that keeps a faculty together and creates consistency among a school's various elements. The glue is the process by which some person or group of people is responsible for providing a link between individual teacher needs and organizational goals so that individuals within the school can work in harmony toward their vision of what the school *should* be.

This harmony does not happen by chance; those schools or systems in which the responsibility for applying the glue is not assigned to specific persons, through job descriptions and allocations of time, simply do not achieve. Unfortunately, there are more "glueless" than "glued" schools. Research findings on the effectiveness of schools paint a dismal picture. Most schools simply do not make much difference in their students' lives. Research focused on those rare schools that do make a difference, however, has much to tell us about how all schools could be changed for the better.

Thus the primary function of effective supervision is to take responsibility for putting more "glue" into the school. But before you run down to the nearest hardware store for buckets of glue to spill on your school floors and corridors (which, it's true, might cut down on student discipline problems and teacher absenteeism, particularly if the glue hardened during a recess period or between classes), let's caution that the adhesive under discussion is of a particular nature.

Effective supervision requires knowledge, interpersonal skills, and technical skills. These are applied through the supervisory tasks of direct assistance to teachers, curriculum development, staff development, group development, and action research. This adhesive pulls together organizational goals and teacher needs and provides for improved learning.

James McDonald (1981) talks about understanding a person's world view by the language and, particularly, the metaphors he or she uses. *Glue* is a good metaphor for effective, fully functioning school supervision. Glue is not glamorous; neither is supervision. When glue is doing its work properly—for example, by keeping a chair together—it goes largely unnoticed; so does supervision, when a school is functioning well. Glue does get attention when the legs of a chair collapse, just as supervision does when a school fragments and fails. With success, both glue and supervision are taken for granted; with failure they are both held responsible. This is as it should be: Teachers are in the forefront of successful instruction; supervision is in the background, providing the support, knowledge, and skills that enable teachers to succeed. When improved instruction and school success do not materialize, supervision should shoulder the responsibility for not permitting teachers to be successful.

Who Is Responsible for Supervision?

Anyone with direct responsibility for improving classroom and school instruction is referred to as a supervisor. Typical supervisors are school principals, assistant principals, instructional lead teachers, department heads, master teachers, teachers, program directors, central office consultants and coordinators, and associate or assistant superintendents. Supervision is viewed as a process and a function, not a particular position or person. Research on effective schools documents that such schools have in common staff members who attend to the function of improving instruction. The formal titles vary from school to school, however (Schneider 1982–1983; Purkey and Smith 1982). Therefore what is crucial is not a person's title but rather his or her responsibilities. Ben Harris (1975) clarifies the supervisor's role further by stating that supervision is related directly to helping teachers with instruction but only indirectly to instructing students. Supervision is not the act of instructing students—that is, teaching—but rather the actions that enable teachers to improve instruction for students.

The reason I emphasize the process and function of supervision rather than the title or position is that the titles *supervisor* and *administrator* are used indiscriminately in public schools. For example, a school system may have science supervisors, elementary supervisors, or high school supervisors who function mainly as record keepers, inventory clerks, and proposal writers and do not work directly to improve instruction. Despite the title of supervisor, they do not function in the realm of supervision. On the other hand, persons with titles such as principal, lead teacher, or superintendent may be heavily involved in supervision through direct assistance to teachers, curriculum development, staff development, group development, and action research. Of course, some titled supervisors do function in supervision, but the point is that what a person does in his or her job is the only key to whether or not he or she is involved in supervision. In this book the term *supervisor* will refer to any person involved with supervision, not to a particular title or position.

Schools vary with respect to who carries out supervisory responsibilities. Some schools assign responsibilities to department heads, assistant principals, guidance counselors, lead teachers, or central office personnel; in such schools the principal focuses on overall administration—the budget, community matters, schedules and reports, and physical plant. In other schools the principal might be largely responsible for supervision, with others attending to administrative matters. Again, a characteristic of successful schools is that someone, somewhere is responsible for and committed to the process, function, and tasks of supervision. Behind every successful school is an effective supervision program.

Organization of This Book

Figure 1-1 demonstrates the scope and organization of this book. For those in supervisory roles, the challenge to improving student learning is to apply certain knowledge, interpersonal skills, and technical skills to the tasks of direct assistance, curriculum development, staff development, group development, and action research that will enable teachers to teach in a collective, purposeful manner uniting organizational goals and teacher needs. As the supervisor allows teachers to take greater control over their own professional lives, a school becomes a dynamic setting for learning.

To facilitate such collective instructional improvement, those responsible for supervision must have certain prerequisites. The first is a *knowledge* base. Supervisors need to understand the exception—what teachers and schools can be—in contrast to the norm—what teachers and schools typically are. They need to understand how knowledge of adult and teacher development and alternative supervisory practices can help break the norm of mediocrity found in typical schools. Second, there is an *interpersonal skills* base. Supervisors must know how their own interpersonal behaviors affect individuals as well as groups of teachers and then study ranges of interpersonal behaviors that might be used to promote more positive and change-oriented relationships. Third, the supervisor must have *technical skills* in observing, planning, assessing, and evaluating instructional improvement. Knowledge, interpersonal skills, and technical competence are three complementary aspects of supervision as a developmental function.

Supervisors have certain educational tasks at their disposal that enable teachers to evaluate and modify their instruction. In planning each task the supervisor needs to plan specific ways of giving teachers a greater sense of professional power to teach students successfully. Those supervisory tasks that have such potential to affect teacher development are direct assistance, curriculum development, staff development, group development, and action research. Direct assistance (*A*) is the provision of personal, ongoing contact with the individual teacher to observe and assist in classroom instruction. Curriculum development (*B*) is the revision and modification of the content, plans, and materials of classroom instruction. Staff development (*C*) includes the legally sanctioned and

Figure 1-1 Supervision for successful schools

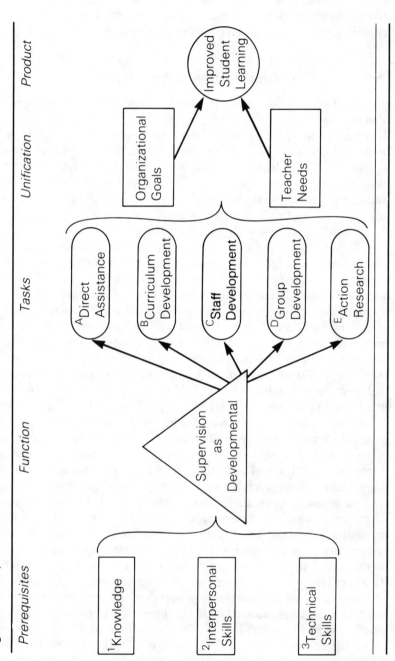

| Prerequisites | Function | Tasks | Unification | Product |

Knowledge

Interpersonal Skills

Technical Skills

Supervision as Developmental

A Direct Assistance

B Curriculum Development

C Staff Development

D Group Development

E Action Research

Organizational Goals

Teacher Needs

Improved Student Learning

supported learning opportunities provided to faculty by the school and school system. Group development (D) is the gathering together of teachers to make decisions on mutual instructional concerns. Action research (E) is the systematic study by a faculty of what is happening in the classroom and school with the aim of improving learning.

By understanding how teachers grow optimally in a supportive and challenging environment, the supervisor can plan the tasks of supervision to bring together organizational goals and teacher needs into a single fluid entity. The unification of individual teacher needs with organizational goals in "a cause beyond oneself" has been demonstrated to promote powerful instruction and improved student learning.

Figure 1-1, therefore, presents the organization of this textbook in a nutshell. Part II will be devoted to essential knowledge. Part III will deal with interpersonal skills. Part IV will explain technical skills the supervisor needs, and Part V will discuss the application of such knowledge and skills to the tasks of supervision. Finally, Part VI will suggest ways of applying knowledge, skills, and tasks to integrate individual needs with organizational goals to achieve instructional success.

The Agony of Thought and Feeling

This book promises to provide a deep and comprehensive understanding of supervision, instruction, and school improvement. Treatment of the knowledge, the technical and interpersonal skills, and the tasks of supervision will be explained from theoretical, philosophical, empirical, and experiential premises, from ideology to case studies. Such understandings, however, are mine, formed from my own beliefs about desirable goals of schools and supervision. The details of practice are not intended to be taken as scientific prescriptions to be learned and followed. I concur with Wiggins, who wrote (1979, p. 150):

> I entertain the unfriendly suspicion that [the reason some people]
> . . . want a scientific theory of rationality [is] . . . because they
> hope and desire, by some conceptual alchemy, to turn such a theory
> into . . . a system of rule by which to spare themselves some of
> the agony of thinking and all the torment of feeling and under-
> standing all that is involved.

You will not be spared! As you finish this first chapter, please be prepared to read and react with your own "agony of thinking" and "torment of feeling" in formulating your own theory of supervision.

EXERCISES

Academic

1. Compare this chapter's definition of *instructional supervision* with at least four definitions of educational supervision found in other supervision texts.
2. This chapter lists five tasks of instructional supervision. Rank these tasks according to what you consider their order of importance. Write a rationale for your ranking.
3. Several recent national studies have cited shortcomings in U.S. public education and have called for educational reforms. After reviewing one of these studies, discuss the major educational problems the study cites and the major reforms it recommends.
4. This chapter describes two schools, Finnie Tyler High School and Germando Elementary School. For both schools, discuss at least three instructional problems likely to result from the type of supervision practiced by the respective principals. Discuss how each probable instructional problem could be avoided or better managed through more appropriate supervision.
5. Review three journal articles that deal with the tasks, roles, and responsibilities of instructional supervision. Write a summary of each article.

Field

1. Prepare five questions to be asked during an interview with a school supervisor, focusing on problems the supervisor confronts in his or her attempts to facilitate instructional improvement and how he or she attempts to manage such problems. Conduct the interview and write a brief report on the supervisor's responses.
2. Arrange to visit a school that has a reputation for being exemplary. If possible, include visits to the school office, a few classrooms, the teachers' lounge, the cafeteria, and the school playground. Write a description of the learning climate of the school, including examples of how the type of supervision present in the school affects the learning climate.
3. Ask three supervisors and three teachers to list what they consider the five most important tasks of educational supervision. Write a report comparing supervisors' perceptions with teachers' perceptions with the five tasks of supervision outlined in Chapter 1.

4. Ask two supervisors, two teachers, two students, and two parents to write one or two paragraphs on "What Makes a Successful School." After reviewing the responses, write a report discussing and comparing the respondents' perceptions.
5. Arrange a panel interview of four persons on the topic "What Makes a Successful School." The panel might include supervisors, teachers, parents, students, and perhaps business and community leaders. Record the discussion on a tape recorder.

Developmental

1. Write down any questions concerning instructional supervision that you have raised while reading Chapter 1. Refer to these questions as you read appropriate chapters in the remainder of this book.
2. Review Figure 1-1 and the model of instructional supervision it implies. As you continue to explore this book and other readings in supervision, begin to formulate your own proposed model of educational supervision.
3. Begin a file (to be kept throughout your reading of this book) on knowledge, skills, and procedures gained from the text and related activities that can be used by you as a supervisor—either now or in the future—to help teachers improve their instructional performance.

REFERENCES

Harris, B.M. 1975. *Supervisory behavior in education,* 2nd ed. Englewood Cliffs, N.J.: Prentice-Hall.

MacKenzie, D.E. 1983. Research for school improvement: An appraisal of some recent trends. *Educational Researcher 12*(4):8.

McDonald, J. 1981. Hermeneutics and curriculum. Address to a meeting on curriculum development, Athens, Ga., May.

Purkey, S.C., and Smith, M.S. 1982. Too soon to cheer? Synthesis of research on effective schools. *Educational Leadership 40*(3):64–69.

Schneider, E.J. 1982–1983. Stop the bandwagon, we want to get off. *Educational R & D Report 5*(1):7–11.

Wiggins, D. 1979. Deliberation and practical reason. In J. Raz (Ed.), *Practical reasoning.* New York: Oxford University Press.

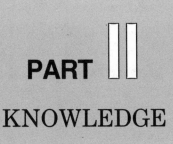

PART II

KNOWLEDGE

Introduction

Part II examines the prerequisite knowledge for supervision. Chapter 2 will explain the optimistic news found in school research on characteristics of successful schools, with particular attention to those work environment factors within the province of supervision. Chapter 3 will consider the pessimistic news—why schools are typically ineffective. The causes of ineffectiveness will be traced to the teaching career and the school environment. Chapter 4 will explain how optimal adult development contrasts with the teaching career. Chapter 5 will look at how supervisory practices might respond to helping teachers develop and eliminate the causes of ineffectiveness. While moving from optimism to pessimism to realism, we will be riding through highly explosive grounds. Reactions of delight, anger, chagrin, hope, and disagreement are to be expected as current research challenges us to rethink current supervisory practices.

Chapter 2

The Exception:
What Schools Can Be

At the most general level, the characteristic of a successful organization is apparent. Whether it be a school, potato-chip manufacturer, airline company, or civic club, there exists a certain commonality to their success. William James, the philosopher, once mentioned that characteristic when he wrote about his concern with men involved in war. During World War I, he was disturbed by his admiration for the qualities that war brought out in humans. As a Quaker and a pacifist, he could not condone the activities involved in waging war, yet he couldn't help but be impressed by the loyalty, support, and courage soldiers gave to their comrades, even to the point of sacrificing their own lives to advance the cause of their division (Stone 1986).

As James pondered his ambivalence, he rendered an observation that the challenge of our times was to find those domestic causes that are "the moral equivalent of war." In that statement, James identified what has been the essential point made by researchers and writers about successful organizations. Whether it be found in the best-selling book, *In Search of Excellence* (Peters and Waterman 1982), about corporate success, or in interpretive writings about effective schools (Rosenholtz 1985), what is conveyed is that successful organizations have a collection of individuals who work together on a common goal that transcends their own self-interest. As a result, they willingly sacrifice their own immediate gain in pursuit of the common goal because it is perceived as far more important. Later, the concept of educators being involved in a cause beyond themselves will be discussed in greater detail, from a moral, social, and cognitive developmental perspective.

The "common cause" and the "moral equivalent of war" are critical concepts for understanding school success. However, when we analyze the definitions of school success, we find great divergence in goals and practices. What do we mean by school success, and how do we measure it? Is the measure of school success short-

14

term—higher achievement scores on standardized basic-skills tests? Is school success measured by improved student attitudes toward learning, social behavior, displays of creative work, critical writing or thinking, attendance, grades, promotion, retention, or community or extracurricular participation? The instructional goals that a school sets and how these goals are measured reflect how the staff members collectively understand and prioritize their beliefs about education. A successful school is foremost an organization that defines good education for itself, through its goals and desired practices, and then engages in the "moral equivalent of war" in achieving that vision (Glickman 1987).

Background to School Effectiveness Studies

The research of the late 1960s and 1970s reported that most schools are not effective. James Coleman's assessment of equality in 1966 was the second-largest school study ever done in the United States. He and his staff canvassed schools across the country in rural, urban, and suburban settings. He considered the contributions to school quality of a wide range of characteristics—teacher academic credentials, district per-pupil expenditures, instructional materials, socioeconomic background of students, racial mix of students, structure and age of physical plant, and size of school. He found that most school variables had little or no relationship to student achievement. Performance on standardized tests was not affected by teacher credentials, per-pupil cost, materials, or curriculum. Instead, the variable that had the greatest relationship with student achievement was the composition of the student population. Students from low-income populations did significantly better when they attended schools where a majority of students came from middle- or upper-income populations. When school composition was mostly low-income, students did not perform as well. Coleman concluded that the strongest variable accounting for student achievement was parents' socioeconomic class. He observed further that this variable was beyond the control of the school. Children of middle- or upper-income families entered schools substantially ahead of students of low-income families; as they continued in school, the achievement gap between socioeconomic levels grew larger. Wealthy students stayed ahead, and poor students fell further behind. Regardless of the school's physical plant, teachers, materials, or finances, the gap enlarged. Most interpretations of Coleman's study indicate that schools made no difference in student achievement.

In 1972 Christopher Jencks and colleagues reanalyzed Coleman's data and issued a report entitled *Inequality: A Reassessment of the Effect of Family and Schooling in America.* Instead of using achievement test results to measure school effectiveness, Jencks looked at what employment students secured after leaving public school. He studied factors that contributed to students going into different careers or vocations, such as higher education, white-collar work, or blue-collar work, or remaining unemployed. First, the reassessment of Coleman's data reaffirmed that school success was largely a result of socioeconomic status, not of teachers or schools. Second, a student's job success in terms of status and pay was similar to the parents' occupational status. Those who obtained high-status jobs were children of parents with high-status jobs. Finding a specific job was a matter of chance and included being at the right place at the right time. It was socioeconomic background, however, that influenced students to use behavior, language, and manners appropriate for specific job opportunities. Students of low-income parents usually mirrored the conditions of their parents and either secured low-status and low-paying jobs or went onto the unemployment and welfare rolls. Jencks concluded that public schools not only did not help alleviate inequality in the United States but, in fact, contributed to such inequality. He concluded that the solutions to unequal opportunity in adult life were not to be found in the schools, but rather in the redistribution of wealth in the larger society.

During the time of these studies, another distinguished researcher was moving across the country, visiting schools to observe classrooms and interview teachers, principals, and administrators. He and his staff were studying classroom practices and what students were learning. In his 1971 book, *Crisis in the Classroom,* Charles Silberman concluded from his lengthy studies that schools were not only ineffective but mindless as well. When he asked teachers and principals to articulate the reasons they organized their schools or classes in certain ways, used particular instructional materials, or grouped their students as they did, the reply was more often than not an incredulous "I don't know, we've always done it this way." When he sought to establish the priorities or objectives of each school, Silberman found little consistency between the response and what actually transpired in the classrooms. He found schools were operating in a confused manner, without specific purpose, commitment, understanding, or shared belief.

Silberman's study, together with those of Coleman and Jencks, left a haze over the landscape of public education—one that has yet to lift. Popular books on education such as Jonathan Kozol's

Death at an Early Age and Ivan Illich's *Deschooling Society* have further weakened confidence in school effectiveness. The media have focused on declining achievement scores and the continued erosion of public confidence. The National Commission on Excellence in Education, in its "Open Letter to the American People" (1983), reported that U.S. students rank considerably below those of other nations on achievement tests, that twenty-three million Americans are functionally illiterate, that average achievement scores of students are lower than those of 1957, that only 20 percent of seventeen-year-olds can write a persuasive essay, and that only a third can solve multistep problems in mathematics.

What Makes Schools Successful?

Researchers, including Edmonds and Brookover and colleagues, have demonstrated that there *are* effective schools and school systems. The large normative studies of the mid-1960s and early 1970s were concerned with schools as monolithic institutions. A researcher who pulls together data from many schools looks for the overall influences schools have on students. If the overwhelming majority of schools are ineffective, the group results would wash out those individual schools that might have results to the contrary. The research of the mid-1970s and 1980s focused on individual schools that are exceptional, that consistently achieve results far superior to those of schools in general. In composition of student body, location, socioeconomic setting, and per-pupil expenditure, these schools do not differ from schools in general. Yet whether they are in poor urban areas or in wealthy suburbs, they succeed while others fail.

Ronald Edmonds, after discovering that the results of his own research were consistent with those of other independent investigations, has been confident enough to predict that *all schools could be effective.* In his words (1979, p. 22):

> It seems to me, therefore, that what is left of this discussion are three declarative statements: (a) We can, whenever and wherever we choose, successfully teach all children whose schooling is of interest to us; (b) We already know more than we need to do that; and (c) Whether or not we do it must finally depend on how we feel about the fact that we haven't so far.

How can one make such bold statements? What are these findings that so contradict the gloomy assessments of Coleman, Jencks, Silberman, and the National Commission on Excellence in Education? Effective schools have faculties with a clear, collective purpose toward which they work. They believe in "a cause beyond oneself." Let's look at how such a phrase has been derived from the research. Edmonds conducted three different studies. His first study was of two inner-city schools in Detroit; the second was of fifty-five effective schools in the Northeast (discovered by reanalyzing the Coleman study); and the third included twenty schools in inner-city New York. He found that effective schools were distinguished by the presence of:

- Strong leadership
- A climate of expectation
- An orderly but not rigid atmosphere
- Communication to students of the school's priority on learning the basics
- Diversion of school energy and resources when necessary to maintain priorities
- Means of monitoring student (and teacher) achievement (Edmonds 1979)

Brookover's research on six improving Michigan elementary schools, as contrasted with two declining schools, contained similar results. Improving schools were distinguished by:

- An emphasis on academics
- Teachers' belief that students could master the subjects
- Less satisfaction on the part of teachers in the effective schools with their instruction (Brookover et al. 1979)

Fifteen Thousand Hours by Rutter et al. (1979) is a study of twelve inner-city London high schools. Successful schools were defined by high levels of student achievement, attitudes, and attendance and low rates of delinquency. Some of their findings were as follows:

> the teachers in the schools which were more successful . . . were much less likely to report that they had absolute freedom in planning their course [1979, p. 112].

> . . . children's behavior is most likely to be good in school when there is an agreed discipline approach, but not too much actual use of punishment [1979, p. 122].

> It was striking, however, that in the less successful schools teachers were often left completely alone to plan what to teach, with little guidance or supervision from their senior colleagues and little coordination with other teachers to ensure a coherent course from year to year [1979, p. 136].

"A Study of Schooling" by John Goodlad and associates was concluded in December, 1981 (see Goodlad 1984). Goodlad studied thirteen triples (a *triple* consists of an elementary, middle, and senior high school that pass the same students on to each other). The triples, selected as a representative sample of schools in the United States, were taken from seven regions. After surveying 1,350 teachers, 18,000 students, 8,600 parents, and all the principals, superintendents, and school board members in these schools—and after 5,000 classroom observations—Goodlad (1982) drew several strong conclusions:

- The greatest predictor of school success was goal congruence among teachers, administrators, students, and parents.
- The staff in successful schools had little concern about violence, discipline, and management; instead, their concern was with the school's educational priorities.
- Effective schools were perceived as workplaces that provided autonomy as well as involvement in educational decisions.
- Teachers in successful schools spent more time on instruction, and students spent more time on learning tasks.
- There was little difference in actual techniques and methods of teaching between successful and unsuccessful schools.

Stedman (1987) studied two groups of effective elementary schools: the highest-achieving schools in one state, and then a subsequent case study of the best examples of effective schools in the United States. Contrary to the results of previous research on effective schools, he found that emphasis on basic skills and time-on-task had little impact. Instead, he concluded that there were nine broad categories related to effectiveness (1987, p. 218):

1. Emphasis on ethnic and racial pluralism
2. Parent participation
3. Shared governance with teachers and parents
4. Academically rich programs
5. Skilled use and training of teachers
6. Personal attention to students
7. Student responsibility for school affairs
8. An accepting and supportive environment
9. Teaching aimed at preventing academic problems

Other studies have pointed out that a successful school can vary considerably from other successful schools in the degree of community involvement, school leadership, and change initiation (Hallinger and Murphy 1987; Purkey and Smith 1983). As Stringfield and Teddlie noted (1987, p. 7):

> In the last ten years School Effectiveness researchers and practitioners have occasionally behaved as if there was one best prescription . . . .

The writers then go on to explain the differences in practices among equally effective schools. There is ample research on school improvement to inform us of the different paths, factors, and actors of school success. We can say with some confidence that participants in successful schools show a remarkable tendency to see themselves as being involved in "a moral equivalent of war" or "a cause beyond oneself."

A Cause beyond Oneself

Later chapters on observation, direct assistance, staff development, and curriculum development will explain how a supervisor can use the research on effective classroom practice with teachers. For now, however, the outside-the-classroom but within-the-school factors that correlate with or predict school success provide the more significant issue. All the research on successful schools has cited a particular type of social organization, which Edmonds referred to as a "climate of expectation." Brookover called it "teacher belief that students could learn and not being satisfied with less," and Goodlad cited it as "goal participation and agreement." Rutter et al. (1979, p. 184) identified this social organization as a "concept of ethos . . . the well-nigh universal tendency for individuals in common circumstances to form social groups with their own rules, values and standards of behavior." Where ethos was developed around a clear educational purpose, an effective school emerged:

> It should be emphasized that the more successful schools were not unduly regimented. Rather, good morale and the routine of people working harmoniously together as part of an efficient system meant that both supervision and support were available to teachers in a way which was absent in less successful schools [Rutter et al. 1979, p. 184].

Every major research study on successful schools has noted the organizational phenomenon of collective action, agreed-on purpose, and belief in attainment (Pratzner 1984, Rosenholtz, 1985). On the other hand, every major research study on ineffective schools has noted an absence of such purpose. Effective schools do not happen by accident: Supervision is the force that shapes the organization into a productive unit.

Clearly, one characteristic of successful schools is that each teacher has what I refer to as "a cause beyond oneself." Teachers do not view their work as simply what they carry out within their own four walls. In successful schools, teachers see themselves as part of the larger enterprise of complementing and working with each other to educate students. For successful schools, education is a collective rather than an individual enterprise.

Chapter 1 introduced two schools, Finnie Tyler High School and Germando Elementary School. Neither was a successful school because both lacked "a cause beyond oneself." Teachers in one school, forced to do as they were told, therefore did not participate in formulating or working toward a common cause. In the other school teachers could do whatever they liked, and therefore they did not participate in a common cause either. Unless the individual needs of staff members are linked with collective school goals, a school cannot be successful.

Successful schools are characterized by teachers who enjoy working with each other *as* they accomplish school tasks. In many schools teachers enjoy being with each other, but the task dimension is missing. They laugh, they party, but they don't get anything done. In other schools, accomplishing tasks (writing curriculum, revising schedules, filling out forms, following the text) predominates over individual and social needs. People are busy, but their tension is evident in gossip, sidelong glances, and frowns. As a result, tasks are accomplished in a forced, hurried manner; the participants feel neither kinship with each other nor commitment to each other in carrying out the tasks. They may even resist carrying out the tasks because of the impersonal manner in which these tasks are chosen. Neither type of school is truly professional or effective. A successful school balances both dimensions so that people enjoy each other's company when they are accomplishing school goals.

What to Do with Successful School Research: Some Propositions

Based on research, certain propositions can be made concerning teachers' attitude, confidence, awareness, stimulation, and thoughtfulness that can be promoted via supervision.

- Proposition 1: *Supervision can enhance teacher belief in a cause beyond oneself.* Teachers can see themselves not just as individuals separated by classroom walls, but as a body of people complementing and strengthening each other.
- Proposition 2: *Supervision can promote teachers' sense of efficacy.* Teachers can see themselves as being able to instruct students successfully, regardless of influences outside of school. Within the school they can learn to believe they do have control over management and instruction. They have power to reach students.
- Proposition 3: *Supervision can make teachers aware of how they complement each other in striving for common goals.* Teachers can observe each other at work, share materials, pick up techniques from each other, and learn how to support each other.
- Proposition 4: *Supervision can stimulate teachers to plan common purpose and actions.* Teachers can be given responsibilities to guide and assist others, to make decisions about school-wide instruction, to plan staff development, to develop curriculum, and to engage in action research. Such involvement shows respect and trust in teachers and strengthens collective action.
- Proposition 5: *Supervision can challenge teachers to think abstractly about their work.* Teachers can be given feedback, questioned, and confronted to appraise, reflect, and adapt their current practices to future instruction. More varied practice and abstract thinking are the results.

In summary, supervision must be viewed as developmental if schools are to become more successful. Supervision must not only respond to current teacher performance but also encourage greater involvement, autonomous thinking, and collective action by teachers. The first order of business for a supervisor is to build the staff into a team. In order to improve school instruction, a supervisor has to work with staff to create a professional togetherness. They must share a common purpose for their instruction. They must have confidence that their collective action will make a difference in their students' lives.

Gaining knowledge of successful schools and effective classrooms is only the first step in improving schools. Using such knowledge in one's own school demands skill and practice. Skill and practice flow from knowledge. We have seen that the research on school success converges on the concept of a cause beyond oneself or a belief in collective action. To use that knowledge, a supervisor needs further understanding about teaching and the teaching profession to understand why such a cause beyond oneself does not occur naturally in schools.

EXERCISES

Academic

1. Write a personal reaction to this chapter's summary of the Coleman study, in which you support or criticize its major conclusions. Base your reaction on your own experience and/or observation of public education.

2. The chapter summarizes the results of several studies of successful schools but also suggests that the majority of schools are not successful. Prepare a report expressing your agreement or disagreement.

3. Review three journal articles that deal with research on successful schools. Based on these readings and your reading of the text, compile a composite list of probable characteristics of a successful school.

4. Read single chapters dealing with the same topic from two books listed as references for Chapter 2. Write a paper comparing and contrasting the two authors' conclusions concerning the chosen topic.

5. For each of the chapter's five propositions based on successful-school research, write a description of a related supervisory activity that you believe could improve the effectiveness of teachers in a typical school setting. Write rationales to support the relationship between each proposition and corresponding supervisory activity.

Field

1. The chapter asserts that effective supervision must provide for both completing tasks and meeting individual and social needs. Observe an administrator or supervisor who is able to balance task and human needs effectively. Write a report on your observations, including a description of the knowledge, skills, and procedures the supervisor draws on in meeting both organizational goals and teacher needs.

2. Present the chapter's five propositions based on successful-school research to a group of educators. The group may include teachers, supervisors, or both. After presenting each proposition, ask for reactions from the educators, including their opinions as to whether each proposition is or can become a reality in their own educational setting. Record the interviews in writing or on audiotape.

3. Prepare a slide or transparency presentation on a summary of successful-school research. Make your presentation to a group of educators. Ask for and record reactions to your presentation.

4. Visit a school that is perceived to be a successful school by both educators and community members. Seek and observe examples of effective leadership, communication, instruction, and other factors that researchers have found to be present in successful schools. Take photographs representative of the effective characteristics observed. Mount selected photographs on poster board, along with brief written descriptions of how the scene in each photograph relates to effective education. Display your photo essay to interested parties.

5. Conduct an interview with a supervisor or administrator in a business, industrial, government, or military setting, focusing on how he or she attempts to integrate organizational goals (task emphasis) with employees' individual and social needs (human emphasis). Write a summary of his or her attitudes, strategies, and methods and your opinion about whether they can be applied to a school setting.

Developmental

1. Maintain an ongoing review of prominent educational journals for reports on future successful-school research. With each new research study, look for (a) findings not already indicated in the review of research in Chapter 2, and (b) any findings that tend to contradict the research cited in Chapter 2.

2. Monitor any major changes in leadership style, curriculum, staff development, or instruction within a local school system over the next few months. Examine such changes to determine which are at least partially based on recent research on successful schools.

3. Over the next few months, examine statements made by prominent educational, political, and civic leaders which include pro-

posals for educational reform. To what extent do such proposals reflect what we have learned from research on successful schools?

REFERENCES

Brookover, W., Beady, C., Flood, P., Schweiter, J., and Wisenbaker, J. 1979. School social systems and students' achievement. *Schools can make a difference.* New York: Praeger.

Coleman, J.S., Campbell, E.Q., Hobson, C.J., McPartland, J., Mood, A.M., Weinfield, F.D., and York, R.L. 1966. *Equality of educational opportunity.* Washington, D.C.: U.S. Government Printing Office.

Edmonds, R. 1979. Effective schools for the urban poor. *Educational Leadership 37*(1):15–24.

Glickman, C.D. 1987. Good and/or effective schools: What do we want? *Kappan 68*(8):622–624.

Goodlad, J.I. 1982. A study of schooling. Paper presented to the Stanford Teacher Education Project, Stanford, Calif., January 28.

————. 1984. *A place called school: Prospects for the future.* New York: McGraw-Hill.

Hallinger, P., and Murphy, J. 1987. Social context on school effects. Paper presented at the annual meeting of the American Educational Association, Washington, D.C., April.

Illich, I.D. 1972. *Deschooling society.* New York: Harrow Books.

James, William, as cited in Stone, R. 1986. A higher horror of the whiteness. *Harper's 273*(1639):54.

Jencks, C. 1972. *Inequality: A reassessment of the effect of family and schooling in America.* New York: Basic Books.

Kozol, J. 1967. *Death at an early age.* Boston: Houghton Mifflin.

National Commission on Education. 1983. An open letter to the American people. A nation at risk: The imperative for educational reform. *Education Week 2*(31):12.

Peters, T.J., and Waterman, R.H. 1982. *In search of excellence.* New York: Harper and Row.

Pratzner, F.C. 1984. Quality of school life: Foundations for improvement. *Educational Researcher 13*(3):20–25.

Purkey, S.C., and Smith, M.S. 1983. Effective schools: A review. *Elementary School Journal 83*, 427–452.

Rosenholtz, S.J. 1985. Effective schools: Interpreting the evidence. *American Journal of Education 93*(3):352–388.

Rutter, M., Maughan, B., Mortimore, P., Ouston, J., and Smith, A. 1979. *Fifteen thousand hours: Secondary schools and their effects on children*. Cambridge, Mass.: Harvard University Press.

Silberman, C.E. 1971. *Crisis in the classroom: The remaking of American education*. New York: Random House.

Stedman, L.C. 1987. It's time we change the effective schools formula. *Kappan 69*(3):215–224.

Stone, R. 1986. A higher horror of the whiteness. *Harper's 273*(1639):49–54.

Stringfield, S., and Teddlie, C. 1987. A time to summarize: Six years and three phases of the Louisiana School Effectiveness Study. Paper presented at the annual meeting of the American Educational Research Association, Washington, D.C., April, p. 7.

Chapter 3

The Norm:
Why Schools Are as They Are

Dan Lortie (1986) wrote about the concept of structural strain, describing teachers of today who still work under school conditions of long ago. (See Kottkamp, Provenzo, and Cohn 1986.) He and others have studied the work environment of schools and how work conditions promote or inhibit teacher development and instructional improvement. Our eyes must be wide open as we examine historical aspects of schools, teachers, and leadership. We must acknowledge that schools cannot be left alone, to do business as usual, if we are serious about lasting instructional improvement.

The Work Environment or Culture of Schools

The study of values, beliefs, myths, rituals, symbols, heroes, shamans, and storytellers in organizations is well documented in the literature (Deal 1985). It may seem technically incorrect to apply the term *culture* to professional settings; the term is appropriated from the anthropological studies of largely intact and isolated communities of people. However, the concept of culture helps us reexamine schools as places of human community with peculiar histories and stories. When we grasp the underlying values of our particular school as a work environment, we can consciously act to reshape the organization into a purposeful collection of individuals who believe that schools are for students, for learning, and for improvement rather than for insularity, self-protection, and complacency.

How does it happen that in the same school district, teachers in two schools view their work so differently from each other? In Meadow Valley Middle School, teachers come to school within fifteen minutes of the required arrival time and leave school fifteen minutes after the last bell. If a teacher arrives earlier or stays later, other teachers' questions and glances make that teacher feel as if he or she shouldn't be working more than the required time. To do so is to violate an unspoken norm that teachers have come to accept about the proper amount of time to spend in school. Yet one and a half miles across town, at the other middle school in the same district, the norms about proper time are different. At Mountain View Middle, teachers are in their classrooms forty-five minutes ahead of time, sharing coffee with each other, organizing materials, and conferring with individual students. One hour after school each day, the majority of staff are still there, working industriously in their own rooms, conducting tutorials, calling parents, and checking on tomorrow's plans. If a teacher arrives later or leaves earlier, the questions and glances of other teachers make him or her feel that a taboo is being violated. Teachers in both schools work under the same district regulations, yet their expectations about work in their particular school are quite different. Why is this so? How does this come about? What have been the enduring norms of schools and how have they been established? The answers to these questions are quite important if we are to know how to intervene in our own schools so as to minimize resistance and capitalize on school beliefs that give impetus to student learning.

The Legacy of the One-Room Schoolhouse

Discussing the present work environment of schools without discussing the one-room schoolhouse would be comparable to talking about issues in Western democracies without acknowledging the Magna Carta. Much of what exists in beliefs and expectations about schools can be traced to the idyllic-looking, clapboard, one-room schoolhouses of pioneer times. The teacher was responsible for the total instruction of all students, the maintenance of the building, keeping the stove filled with wood, and cleaning the floors. Our first schoolteachers were seen as working in an honorable but menial profession, poorly paid but second only to the preacher in prestige (Lortie 1975). Many readers who currently teach may think of hall and bus duty, taking attendance, and straightening venetian blinds and immediately identify with the honorable but menial status of their predecessors. In the one-room schoolhouse, the teacher was responsible for all that transpired within its four walls; therefore, collective action in a school was automatic. What the teacher wanted to do about curriculum and instruction was what the school did! This legacy of independence, isolation, and privatization of teaching remains alive and well in many schools today. Instead of having physically separated one-room schoolhouses, we often see the one-room schoolhouses repeated every few yards down a school corridor. Each teacher sees his or her students, within the four walls, as his or her own school. Although the old one-room school is physically gone, it still holds a pervasive grip on the minds and actions of many teachers and schools. The sense of classrooms as being private places is in direct contrast to the research on norms of improving schools.

Research suggests that the schools with the greatest student learning going on are those which do not isolate teachers, but instead encourage professional dialogue and collaboration. Teaching in effective schools is a collective, rather than individual enterprise [Freiberg and Knight 1987, p. 3].

However, as Willower and Smith (1986) observed in a study of two secondary schools,

Many of the features of the typical school organization appear to be stacked against the formation of a peculiar school culture devoted to educational aims. . . . A number of the norms in the teacher group such as that for autonomy and non-interference in a colleague's teaching activities encourage the kind of fragmentation we found [p. 15].

The one-room schoolhouse of pioneer times has spawned a deep-seated institutional belief among educators that is characterized by isolation, psychological dilemmas, routine, inverted beginner responsibilities, lack of career stages, lack of professional dialogue, and lack of involvement in school decisions. Many educators accept that these characteristics are simply part of a school culture, and there is little doubt that they pervade the minds and beliefs of most teachers and administrators. However, instructional leaders question whether beliefs and practices acceptable in the past are appropriate for the present, when we need to initiate a new culture based on purposeful and collective beliefs about school, students, and teaching. Let's look at the characteristics of today's education that are derived from the one-room schoolhouse of bygone days.

Isolation

The isolation and individualism of teachers has been observed in all major studies of their work environment. As an example of this isolation, Dreeben (1973) has noted that

perhaps the most important single property of classrooms, viewed from a school-wide perspective, is their spatial scattering and isolation throughout school buildings; and because teachers work in different places at the same time, they do not observe each other working . . . . the implications of this spatial isolation are far reaching [p. 468].

He further wrote:

> Unlike hospitals and law firms, for example, where new recruits to medicine and law learn their trade as apprentices by performing work tasks of gradually increasing difficulty under close supervision, schools provide a less adequate setting—the classroom—for work and training activities to occur simultaneously [p. 470].

As Dreeben points out, classrooms are set up structurally in such a way that teachers are difficult to supervise, do not receive feedback from others, and cannot work collaboratively. During a typical work day a teacher will talk to only a few other adults—on the way to the classroom in the morning, for twenty minutes or so at lunch and recess, and at the end of the day on the way out of the building.

While teaching, teachers in most schools are invisible to each other and lack any concrete knowledge of what other teachers are doing in their classrooms. (To see just how strong this tradition of classroom isolation is, think of schools built in the 1970s according to an open-space design. Within a few years, in almost every school, portable partitions were erected to wall off each classroom.) It is little wonder, then, that most school faculties do not work well together on common goals that transcend their individual self-interests. They do not talk with each other about professional matters, and they seldom see what others are doing.

Suppose members of a surgical staff were given separate cubicles to perform their specific parts of the common function of saving a patient. The patient would be wheeled first into the anesthesiologist's cubicle for drugs, then into the technician's room for monitoring of vital signs, then to the surgeon's room for the first incision, back to the technician's room for monitoring vital signs, to the surgeon's assistant's room for cleaning the incision, to the surgeon's room for the second incision . . . an absurd notion of how to save the patient! This is the work environment of teaching—more comparable to that of a piecework garment factory, where no one except top management needs to know what each person is doing. In high-status professions, by contrast, success depends on professionals working together to combine, review, and share their knowledge, skills, and practices.

Psychological Dilemma

The teacher's work environment is marked by incessant psychological encounters. In just a few minutes of observation, one might see a teacher ask a question, reply with a smile to a student's answer, frown at an inattentive student, ask a student to be quiet, put a hand on a student's shoulder, and begin to lecture. Teachers have thousands of such psychological encounters in a normal school day (Jackson 1968). A look, a shrug, and a word all have intended meanings between teacher and students.

Each day an elementary teacher meets with twenty-five to thirty-five students for six and one-half hours. A secondary teacher meets with a hundred to a hundred and fifty students for five to seven fifty-minute periods. All this human interaction takes place in a nine-hundred-square-foot room, where a teacher must instruct, manage, discipline, reinforce, socialize, and attend to multiple occurrences. This crowded professional life makes teachers wish for smaller classes to reduce the psychological demand of constant decision making. Sarason (1971) described this incessant demand as a psychological dilemma:

> . . . the teacher feels, and is made to feel, that her worth as a teacher will be judged by how much her class learns in a given period of time. The strong feeling that teachers have about the complexity of their tasks stems from the awareness that they are expected to bring their children (if not all, most) to a certain academic level by a time criterion in regard to which they have no say. Faced with numbers and diversity of children and the pressure to adhere to a time schedule presents the teacher not with a difficult task but an impossible one. *I say impossible because I have never met a teacher who was not aware of and disturbed by the fact that she had not the time to give to some children in the class the kind of help they needed* [p. 152; emphasis in original].

To maintain their own sanity in the face of an overload of psychological encounters and an inability to attend to the psychological needs of each student in a confined and regulated workplace, teachers often cope by routinizing classroom activity. The classroom routine for students becomes similar to the outside routine for teachers. For example, a science teacher might have students listen to a twenty-minute presentation, followed by a ten-minute question and answer period and then by twenty minutes of seat work. An elementary teacher might have three reading groups who rotate to him or her for fifteen minutes each; each group reads aloud, responds to teacher questions, and then does worksheets. By routinizing what happens within the classroom, a teacher avoids making hundreds of decisions. The routinization of teaching allows the teacher to avoid the inherent conflict between being overwhelmed psychologically by the responsibility for teaching a large number of students, and being aware of neglecting the personal needs of individual students. In interpersonal terms, teaching closely resembles clinical psychology, but it takes place in an environment more like that of factory production.

Routine

The routine of the teaching day is imposed by administrative fiat, school board policy, and state guidelines. Every classroom teacher is required to be at school before students enter and to remain until they have departed. In primary or elementary schools, a teacher has specific times for recess and lunch and approximate time allocations for teaching a given subject (for example, forty-five minutes for reading, thirty minutes for mathematics, thirty minutes twice a week for social studies). The teacher is assigned a certain number of students and has responsibility for them for the entire day and school year. He or she is expected to remain physically in the assigned classroom for the entire school day, with the exception of recess, lunch, or special classes. Outside the classroom, teachers also have scheduled responsibilities for lunch, recess, and dismissal. In middle schools, junior high schools, and senior high schools, the school day is different from that of elementary schools but still has a set routine. A secondary teacher will have four to seven different classes of students meeting at specific times each day for an extended period (eleven, eighteen, or thirty-six weeks). Again, the teacher begins and dismisses each class at a prescribed time and has regular duties outside the classroom (for example, monitoring the lunchroom, halls, or bathrooms).

Regardless of grade level, teachers do not schedule their own time or determine the number or type of students. Unlike more autonomous professionals, teachers do not put up a shingle on the door, ask clients to arrange for appointments, or take Wednesday mornings off. Teachers do not have the right to make changes in their schedule. Imagine a teacher asking the school secretary to clear his or her schedule for several hours so he or she can attend to other business. School goes on, students keep coming, the bells keep ringing, and teachers cannot make individual readjustments of their professional time.

Of course, elementary and secondary teachers often do make readjustments within the assigned time, within their four walls, with their assigned students, and with instruction. School time, however, is imposed. Starting and ending times, numbers of students, physical locations for teaching, and extra duties are set for the duration, and a teacher has little control. The routines the school as a workplace imposes are more like those of the factory than like those of high-status professions. The punch-in, punch-out clock may not be visible in the entering hallway of the school, but nonetheless it exists.

Inverted Beginner Responsibilities

Teaching has been a career in which the greatest challenge and most difficult responsibilities are faced by those with the least experience—a strange state of affairs indeed! If a teacher makes known that he or she will not be returning in the fall, after the last day of school, other teachers will often descend upon the vacant classroom and remove materials that will be useful to them. Not only are instructional materials removed, but also tables and chairs! In their place are put those discarded items and furniture that no one else wants. Additionally, teachers may jockey around for the more spacious, better lighted classrooms. To compound matters, when it comes time for student and class placements for the following year, the current staff and administration will often arrange for the "problem" and/or lowest-achieving groups of students to be taken by the newest teacher. So for the incoming year, the neophyte teacher with the least amount of experience often steps into the physically least desirable classroom in the school, with discards for furniture and equipment, and with the most difficult students to teach. Those with the greatest experience have the better rooms, the most abundant materials, and the "best" students. The message to the newcomers (if not verbally then at least symbolically) when they enter their rooms, look around, and see their students is: "Welcome to teaching, now let's see if you can make it!" When the new teacher encounters the predicted first-year difficulties, without help or support from senior faculty or administration, he or she learns that teaching in this school really is an isolated act. When he or she can't take it any longer and finally blurts out that "teaching is not what I'm cut out to do," a sympathetic colleague will reassure him or her with "Oh, don't worry, we all went through this our first year. It really is rough, but following years will be much better." Why will this be so? Because, at the end of the year, the teacher will be able to take better materials and furniture and easier-to-teach students, leaving next year's rookie with the same baptism rites that he or she endured.

Is there truth in the above depiction? Many of us, looking back at our first year, would concur that it was the most difficult teaching experience we ever encountered. Many of us also need to admit, sheepishly, that teaching did improve in following years because we could use seniority to our benefit by creating a better teaching situation—to the distinct detriment of new teachers. We didn't see the norms of our work as creating "a cause beyond oneself" in looking at a common good—which would mean giving the first-year teachers the least-difficult students and best physical and material conditions. Instead, we saw the norms of teaching as protecting us, in our four walls, so as to keep our one-room schoolhouse intact.

The message conveyed by such actions is that teaching is not a supportive career that eases neophytes into graduated responsibilities; rather, it's a case of "do unto others as they've done unto you."

Unstaged Career

More prestigious professions avoid such an abrupt transition from student to full professional. Physicians, lawyers, engineers, and scientists all experience several transition years of apprenticeship, internship, and junior membership on the job before they qualify for full rights and responsibilities in the profession.

This set of circumstances leads to the negative characteristic of the teaching profession that perhaps most significantly differentiates it from others—an unstaged career ladder. More prestigious occupations have rigorous screening and requirements. Furthermore, they have a transitional or proving-ground stage; only when an aspirant has been judged competent by senior members does the junior member step into the next stage of the career, which provides high visibility, greater challenge, a substantial increase in salary, and responsibility for monitoring and judging the next wave of junior members. For example, a law school graduate must pass the bar exam and then serve as a clerk, as a legal aide, or as a junior member of a law firm. He or she works behind the scenes on writing and research that are credited to his or her superior. After proving competence over time, however, the lawyer then becomes a partner in a firm, a public prosecutor or defender, or an independent attorney. This movement brings visibility and stature in the profession and the right to have one's own apprentices to do the less challenging, less exciting work.

This apprenticeship period has persisted because aides, interns, or assistants are willing to endure the long hours and hard work in view of the ultimate benefits. It is not unusual for the salary of a legal assistant, a medical intern, a junior engineer, or a graduate assistant to double upon promotion to full membership in the profession. The public appears to recognize and approve this long, arduous, and selective process as a requirement for membership in a high-status profession.

Teaching, on the other hand, has been unstaged from entry to exit. Education majors take courses, spend time in schools, perform as student teachers, and then graduate from college into their own classrooms as teachers. After that, no matter how many years they continue to teach, they do not move into another stage. The twenty-year veteran teacher has the same classroom space, number of students, and requirements as the first-year teacher. Furthermore, for each year of experience a teacher realizes a salary increase identical to that received by all others of comparable experience.

Lack of Dialogue about Instruction

Generally, people in schools do not talk about their work, teaching, with each other. DeSanctis and Blumberg (1979) found the mode length of instruction-related discussion among teachers in a typical school day in a high school in New York was two minutes. Little's (1982) study of schools, Rosenholtz's (1985) review of effective schools, and Pajak and Glickman's (1987) study of fifteen exemplary elementary and secondary schools in three improving districts pointed to one essential dimension of successful schools: Professionals constantly talk with each other, in a problem-solving, action-oriented way, about teaching. This talk is generated through faculty and committee meetings, in-service workshops, observations and conferences, faculty lounge contacts, and other informal occasions. This talk is of a specific nature: teaching and learning of students. Of course, teachers talk with each other in all schools, but the talk is of a more social nature—telling stories about students, parents, administrators, community, and school events.

For teachers to talk often and seriously with each other about the core of their job, instruction and curriculum, is a rarity in many schools. Time is not planned for it to occur. Faculty meetings are information-giving, and when school concerns are raised, they are often deflected to noninstructional matters such as schedules, district policies, extracurricular responsibilities, and building maintenance.

The public school as a work institution is unique in that a collection of adults can be employed as professionals within the same physical setting, with a common responsibility for providing their particular services to the same group of clients (students), and not be frequently and intensively engaged with each other in discussions on how to improve their services. Again, the lack of such dialogue is related to the one-room schoolhouse legacy, which accepts isolation, privacy, inverse responsibility, and lack of career stages as the norms of teaching.

Lack of Involvement in School-Wide Curriculum and Instructional Decisions

If teachers don't see each other at work, don't talk with each other about their work, and see teaching as what goes on within their own four walls, it is not surprising that they are not given the opportunity, time, or expectations to be involved in decisions about curriculum and instruction beyond their four walls. Goodlad's (1984) study of schooling found that teachers' involvement in decisions about curriculum and instruction was virtually nil. Blumberg (1987) has referred to one of the basic problems with public schools as "Institutions premised on having mature, competent adults as employees, yet treating these same adults as children when it comes to deciding and operationalizing their work." Boyer (1983) has been even more adamant, referring to schools as impoverished intellectual climates for adults. The norm in most schools is that teachers are not expected to contribute experience, knowledge, and wisdom to decisions about the common good of educating students.

Blaming the Victim and Structural Strain

A Nation at Risk (National Commission on Education 1983) intensified a long era of legislated school reform that enforced more rigorous teacher selection, teacher evaluation, standardization of curriculum, and testing of students. Arthur Wise (1988) noted that the previous sixteen years of school reform had been predicated on the assumption that teachers are the problem or reason for mediocre school performance and therefore need to be carefully controlled and monitored. Lee Shulman (1987) has referred to this sixteen-year period as one of "teacher bashing," in which the wrongs of education were attributed to incompetent, inconsiderate, and self-serving teachers and administrators.

Myriad critical reports on the status of teaching have been published. For example, Schlechty and Vance (1981) wrote of a longitudinal seven-year study of teachers in North Carolina. They concluded:

> There is considerable evidence that those who choose to major in teacher education are, as a group, less academically able than most other college majors. There is some strong evidence that graduates of teacher education institutions are not as academically proficient as most other categories of college graduates [p. 106].

Their study of characteristics of teachers who remain in the profession, compared with those who decide to leave the profession, concluded:

> There is a strong negative relationship between measured academic ability and retention in teaching. . . . Year after year, those North Carolina teachers who scored highest on a test of academic ability (the NTE) are the most likely to leave education [pp. 110, 112].

In the same year, Milton Goldberg, director of the National Institute of Education, after reviewing national statistics about teachers, reported to the U.S. House Subcommittee on Post Secondary Education that those entering teaching were not terribly promising and that those leaving were among the best in the profession. Teaching seemed to be attracting, in his words, "the least academically able students."

The result of such criticisms of teachers has been the establishment of more rigorous, liberal-arts-based teacher education programs; many required five-year teacher education degree programs (Holmes Group 1986); a National Center for Teacher Licensing (Carnegie Task Force 1986); the development of career ladders that pay teachers more for experience combined with increased responsibility; merit pay to reward those who attain higher teacher evaluation rankings; scholarship incentives to attract more academically proficient students into teaching; and general pay scale increases to be competitive with pay scales in comparable private professions, in order to attract and retain competent teachers. (A dramatic example of competitiveness is a new pay scale in Rochester, New York, which has a ceiling of $70,000.) Although some of these attempts to retain, attract, and reverse the loss of bright and capable teachers are worthwhile, laudable, and essential, they do not deal directly with the school as a culture or a workplace. It is the workplace of teaching that supports or stifles intellectual vitality and is a major factor in the ability of public schools to retain the "best and brightest."

The studies of Barbara Tye (1987) and Linda McNeil (1986, 1988) have shown that most school environments are predicated on control—control of students and control of teachers. The feminist literature helps us to understand why schools as controlling workplaces have been resistant to change. Historically, teachers' work has been equated with a sexist view of women's work—servile yet smiling. Administrators' work has been equated with a similar prejudiced view of men's work—controlling and paternalistic. As

Grambs (1986) wrote, "Men have organized the structure of the school environment which suits their perceptions of what is appropriate. Yet, since most teachers are women, the lack of fit has been ignored. . . ." The parallels are clear. Administrators prize conformity, privacy, dependency, quietness, and routine in their teachers and consider unconventionality, public attention, creativity, assertiveness, spontaneity, and collective action among teachers to be threatening and "unschool-like." As a result, teachers are rewarded for conforming and penalized for being intellectually critical. Critics then bemoan the statistics that show the majority of teachers to be conformist, dependent, and not of the highest academic caliber as compared to those who do not choose to enter or who decide to leave teaching. It takes no great insight to know that inquisitive and thoughtful people are drawn to work cultures that value, reward, and encourage inquisitiveness and thoughtfulness. Those who are less inquisitive and thoughtful about their work are not the villains of school improvement, but the victims of institutional work environments that demand compliance and conformity. We then blame teachers for being what most schools force them to be. What if we changed the work culture of schools?

Ted Sizer (1984) poignantly argued that the fine high school teacher named Horace could never become a great teacher under the existing structure of schools. Neither he nor his colleagues are encouraged to rethink and restructure how students could learn in their schools. As a result, Horace has learned to compromise his beliefs about how students should receive instruction in English against the realities of the work environment.

> Horace is a gentle man. He reads the frequent criticism of his profession in the press with compassion. Johnny can't read. Teachers have low Graduate Record Examination scores. We must vary our teaching to the learning styles of our pupils. We must relate to the community. We must be scholarly, keeping up with our fields. English teachers should be practicing, published writers. If they aren't all these things, it is obvious that they don't care. Horace is a trouper; he hides his bitterness.
>
> Nothing can be gained by showing it. The critics do not really want to hear him or to face facts. He will go with the flow. What alternative is there? [Sizer, 1984, p. 19]

We have, I believe, quickly reached the point of structural strain with the Horaces of public education. Either the work environment of schools must be altered, or we must accept that regardless of extrinsic rewards, schools are not the place for our best teachers and thinkers. Supervision of instruction can play a strong role in reshaping the work environment to promote norms of collegiality and collective action, or supervision can remain another control apparatus "to keep teachers in their place." We can then continue to blame the victims for not shaking the institutional chains that shackle every attempt to work together in the instructional interest of all students.

To Qualify, Summarize, and Propose

If supervision is to improve instruction in a school, then it must be an active force that provides focus, structure, and time for matters of curriculum and instruction. Supervision is intended to reduce the norms of the one-room schoolhouse—isolation, psychological dilemma, routine, inverted beginner responsibilities, and lack of career stages—and increase the norms of public dialogue and action for the benefit of all students. If supervision is to improve instruction, it must reshape norms and beliefs about the work culture of schools, as in the following propositions:

- Proposition 1: *Supervision cannot rely on the existing work environment of schools to stimulate instructional improvement.* Since the work environments of schools are routinized, isolated, and psychologically tense, teachers become private and regulated in their work rather than open to improvement.

- Proposition 2: *Supervisors cannot assume that teachers will be reflective, autonomous, and responsible for their own development.* Since teachers as a group have been conditioned to conform rather than to be involved as initiators of change, change will not automatically occur if left solely to teacher initiative.

- Proposition 3: *Supervisors who hold formal leadership roles will have to redefine their responsibilities—from controllers of teachers' instruction to involvers of teachers in decisions about school instruction.* Since successful schools are communities of professional colleagues rather than hierarchies of power and status, formal supervisors will need to view teachers as worthy of making decisions about their work.

These three bold propositions have a basis in research but nevertheless need further qualification. For the most part, I have portrayed schools as operating in a culture of fragmentation and control and teachers as operating in a professional world of isolation and dependency. Obviously, this is more true of some schools than others. Historically, this has been the state of affairs, but there have always been teachers and schools that do not fit such portrayals.

In fact, there are increasing numbers of teachers and schools that have established autonomous, collective, and intellectually challenging work environments. That is the very point of this book. *Those schools whose staff members knowingly combat the inertia of their profession and environment are most successful. In the most successful schools, supervision works to break up the routine, lack of career stages, and isolation of teaching and to promote intelligent, autonomous, and collective reason in order to establish a cause beyond oneself and to shape a purposeful and productive body of professionals achieving common goals for students.*

The best response to structural strain today is to move away from patching and reinforcing the old school vessel and instead remake it with a broader base, greater flexibility, and more adaptations so as to challenge teachers to take an increasing intellectual and active role. However, rejuvenation of the school environment might be a disastrous undertaking if we fail to acknowledge the need to plan and act according to knowledge of optimal adult development and life-span transitions and how they may conflict with what is known about teacher and occupational development. The discrepancies will lead us to several more propositions about the information needed for transitions in supervision for the rejuvenation of schools.

EXERCISES

Academic

1. Choose a period of American history (for example, the colonial period or the early twentieth century) and research the state of teaching as a profession during that era. Prepare a report comparing the role, functions, working conditions, and status of teachers in the selected era and the current era.

2. Research the state of teaching as a profession in an industrialized nation other than the United States. Prepare a report comparing the role, functions, working conditions, and status of teachers from the selected nation with those of U.S. public school teachers.

3. The chapter lists routine, psychological dilemma, and isolation as three factors associated with the work environment of teach-

ers. Interview a supervisor about the work environment of teachers in his or her school. How does he or she attempt to improve conditions? Write a summary of your interview.

4. In most public school systems, a teacher's career is unstaged. Outline a plan for a staged teaching career. Include recommended entry requirements, screening methods, a description of an apprenticeship period (other than student teaching), and suggested requirements and rewards for promotion to full membership in the teaching profession. Suggest ways in which teachers who have attained full professional status can be presented with new challenges and rewarded for meeting such challenges.

5. Write an autobiographical essay in which you discuss your experiences with the daily routine, psychological encounters, and isolation you have confronted as a teacher or observed as a visitor in a public school.

Field

1. Interview three public school teachers of various experience levels about why they chose teaching as a career. Write a report that includes a brief description of each teacher, a summary of his or her reasons for becoming an educator, and comparison of the various teachers' responses.

2. Conduct interviews with a veteran and a first-year public school teacher in which you ask them to compare their written job descriptions with the duties they actually carry out. During both interviews, write out a list of duties the teacher carries out that are not listed on the formal job description. Prepare a report summarizing your findings and drawing conclusions.

3. Interview a member of a graded profession (physician, attorney, college professor, scientist, engineer, or the like) who has reached full professional status. Ask the professional about the stages and challenges he or she had to pass through to attain such status, the extent to which having to pass through these grades increased his or her professional performance, and the rewards of reaching full professional status. Prepare a report summarizing the interviewer's responses and giving your opinion of whether aspects of such a graded career could be adapted to the teaching profession.

4. Interview a veteran instructor or supervisor in a teacher preparation program. Ask him or her to compare students who are preparing for a career in education today with teacher candidates

of ten years ago in terms of academic preparation, performance, and commitment to a teaching career. If the interviewee perceives significant differences between present and past teacher candidates, ask for his or her perceptions of why such differences exist and how they are likely to affect the future of public education. Prepare a report summarizing the interview and drawing your own conclusions.

5. Interview an individual who was a teacher for at least five years and voluntarily left teaching for a new career. Request (a) his or her reasons for entering the teaching field, (b) his or her reasons for leaving teaching, and (c) a comparison of the teaching profession with his or her present career. Prepare a written report on the interview.

Developmental

1. As you read the remainder of this book, note the propositions on page 39. Examine the remaining chapters for proposals, implicit in the propositions, for dealing with instructional problems. Keep a written journal of major propositions, proposals, and actions you would take to change your own school.

2. Begin a diary of how the major characteristics of your work environment affect your job performance over a period of time.

3. Begin a notebook of ideas for breaking up the inertia of the teaching profession and environment. Over time, note your own ideas and also record the ideas and actions of teachers and supervisors you observe attempting to counter the routine, psychological dilemma, and isolation of the teaching environment. Include ideas for promoting teacher autonomy and encouraging teachers and supervisors to focus on a cause beyond oneself.

REFERENCES

Blumberg, A. 1987. A discussion on the effects of local, state, and federal mandates on supervisory practices. Annual conference of the Council of Professors of Instructional Supervision, Philadelphia, November.

Boyer, E.L. 1983. *High School: A report on secondary education in America.* New York: Harper & Row.

Carnegie Task Force on Teaching as a Profession. 1986. *A nation prepared: Teachers for the 21st century.* New York: Carnegie Forum on Education and the Economy.

Deal, T.E. 1985. The symbolism of effective schools. *Elementary School Journal 85*(5):601–620.

DeSanctis, M., and Blumberg, A. 1979. An exploratory study into the nature of teacher interactions with other adults in the schools. Paper presented at the annual meeting of the American Educational Research Association, San Francisco, April.

Dreeben, R. 1973. The school as a workplace. In R.M. Travers (Ed.), *Second handbook of research on teaching.* Chicago: Rand McNally, pp. 450–473.

Freiberg, H.J., and Knight, S. 1987. External influences of school climate. Paper presented at the annual meeting of the American Educational Research Association, Washington, D.C., April.

Goodlad, J.I. 1984. *A place called school.* New York: McGraw-Hill.

Grambs, J.D. 1986. Are older women teachers different? Paper presented at the annual meeting of the American Educational Research Association, Washington, D.C., April, p. 24.

The Holmes Group. 1986. *Tomorrow's teachers: A report of the Holmes Group.* East Lansing, Mich.: Holmes Group.

Jackson, P.W. 1968. *Life in classrooms.* New York: Holt, Rinehart & Winston.

Kottkamp, R.B., Provenzo, E.F., Jr., and Cohn, M.M. 1986. Stability and change in a profession: Two decades of teacher attitudes. 1964–1984. *Kappan 67*(8):559–567.

Little, J.W. 1982. Norms of collegiality and experimentation: Workplace conditions of school success. *American Educational Research Journal 19*(3):325–340.

Lortie, D.C. 1986. Teacher status in Dade County: A case of structural strain. *Kappan 67*(8):568–575.

Lortie, D.C. 1975. *School teacher: A sociological study.* Chicago: University of Chicago Press.

McNeil, L.M. 1986. *Contradictions of control: School structure and knowledge.* New York: Methuen/Routledge and Kegan Paul.

————. 1988. Contradictions of reform, Part I: Administrators and teachers. *Kappan 69*(5):333–339.

National Commission on Education. 1983. An open letter to the American people. A nation at risk: The imperative for educational reform. *Education Week 2*(31):12.

Pajak, E., and Glickman, C. 1987. Dimensions of improving school districts. Presentation to the annual conference of the Association for Supervision and Curriculum Development, New Orleans, March. '

Rosenholtz, S.J. 1985. Effective schools: Interpreting the evidence. *American Journal of Education* 93(3):352–388.

Sarason, S. 1971. *The culture of the school and the problem of change.* Boston: Allyn and Bacon.

Schlechty, P.C., and Vance, V.S. 1981. Do academically able teachers leave education? The North Carolina case. *Kappan* 63(2):106–112.

Shulman, L.S. 1987. Teaching alone, learning together: Needed agendas for the new reforms. Paper presented at the Conference on Restructuring Schooling for Quality Education, San Antonio, August.

Sizer, T. 1984. *Horace's Compromise.* Boston: Houghton Mifflin.

Tye, B.T. 1987. The deep structure of schooling. *Kappan* 69(4):281–284.

Willower, D.J., and Smith, J.P. 1986. Organizational culture in schools: Myth and creation. Paper presented at the annual meeting of the American Educational Research Association, San Francisco, April.

Wise, A.E. 1988. The two conflicting trends in school reform: Legislated learning revisited. *Kappan* 69(5):328–333.

Chapter 4

Contrasting Optimal Adult Development with Actual Teacher Development: Clues for Supervisory Practice

This chapter will serve as a core for thinking and practicing supervision in a developmental framework. So far, I have defined "a cause beyond oneself" as a demarcation between the collective, thoughtful, autonomous, and effective staffs of successful schools and the isolated, unreflective, and powerless staffs of unsuccessful schools. Knowledge of how teachers can grow as competent adults is the guiding principle for supervisors in finding ways to return wisdom, power, and control to both the individuals and the collective staff in order for them to become true professionals. With understanding of how teachers change, the supervisor can plan direct assistance, staff development, curriculum development, group development, and action research at an appropriate level to stimulate professional growth and instructional improvement.

The research on adult development has been prolific (Belenky, Clinchy, Goldberger, and Tarule 1986; Loevinger 1976; Levinson 1977; Harvey, Hunt, and Schroeder 1961; Neugarten 1977; Whitbourne 1986), and the research in teacher development is advancing (McNergney and Carrier 1981; Sprinthall and Thies-Sprinthall 1982; Oja 1979; Burden 1982; Burke, Christensen, Fessler, McDonnell, and Price 1987; Levine 1989). I have attempted to distill the knowledge of adult and teacher development that has direct applications for supervision and supervisors. Readers who desire more detail should refer to the references at the end of the chapter. The use of such readily available and potentially rich knowledge about human growth can be extremely valuable to those who work with adults. If schools are to be successful, supervision must respond to teachers as changing adults.

What Is Known about Adult Development

What is known about adults, of course, cannot be summarized in a few pages, an entire book, or even a number of books. Instead, it can only be hoped that this section will provide an abbreviated outline of what is known about adults with regard to hierarchies of thought and occupational transitions. The distinction between research on adult development and research on life-span transitions needs to be made. Adult development is the study of adults' capabilities to improve over time. Research on life-span transitions focuses on typical events and experiences that people encounter as they age.

Adult development studies have built on some of the findings of research on children. Adults change in predictable ways according to age, individual characteristics, and the demands of the environment. One major finding of adult research is that cognitive, social, and language development do not solidify at adolescence or early adulthood but continue throughout life. In childhood, changes are dramatic, as when a child changes from uttering sounds to speaking in full sentences or, within two years, goes from lying on his or her back to crawling, to walking, to running. Changes in adults are usually not so dramatic or so rapid. An adult's thinking, attitudes toward work, and social relationships change in subtle ways; differences become apparent only after many years. Keeping gradual change in mind, however, the principles of development uncovered for children appear to apply equally to adults:

1. There are common stages of growth through which all humans are capable of passing.
2. The stages are in order, in that one stage precedes the next.
3. The rate of passage from one stage to the next varies from individual to individual.

In considering stage theory, some caution is necessary. Life is a complex mix of person and environment, and not all of life is growth-oriented. For example, an individual's neurological and visual capacities become less responsive over time. Each of us knows firsthand that we cannot sustain physical activity or react as quickly to stimuli as we were able to do in younger years. On the other hand, decision making, information processing, and understanding can improve with age. In some ways individuals have the capability to improve; in other ways they begin to degenerate. Research on adult development focuses on the improvement, and school supervisors can apply such knowledge to help educators improve.

Cognitive, Conceptual, and Personality Development

The areas of research in adult development most applicable to educational supervision are cognitition, conceptual attainment, and personality. Havighurst (1980, p. 6), in his review of life-span counseling, wrote about findings in cognition: "Research studies of the relation of aging to learning during the past 20 years have found that there are two brands or categories of intelligence, one which increases during adulthood, while the other decreases." The work of Horn and Cattell (1967), Long and Mirza (1980), and others has labeled these two categories of learning *fluid* and *crystallized*. Fluid learning depends on physiological and neurological capacities. Given similar tasks in inductive reasoning, figure matching, memory span, and perceptual speed, those below the age of thirty consistently outperform those over thirty. (Comedian and educator Bill Cosby relates that upon turning fifty, it has become more common for the inexplicable to happen. Often, while sitting in his living-room chair, he will get up to find something in the next room. Once on his feet, he forgets why he stood up, where he was going, or what he was planning to do. Only after sitting back down again does he remember why he was getting up! This is a clear case of the decline of short-term memory and fluid learning! Now where was I?)

The decline of the nervous system accounts for the slowing of abilities to handle instant and visual information. Yet the reverse appears to be true for crystallized learning, which is predicated on relations between experiences. Older people naturally have more experience and knowledge to draw on in processing new information and solving familiar tasks. Experiments show that performance on tasks of verbal comprehension, mechanical knowledge, arithmetic ability, fluency of ideas, experiential evaluation, and general information continues to improve throughout much of the life span. The rate of increase gradually slows and, for inactive persons over sixty, eventually comes to a halt. To generalize, intelligence or the ability to solve new problems becomes a slower but more thorough process with age. An older person cannot respond as quickly but can relate more experience to understanding new problems.

In the field of conceptual development, the same type of movement is apparent. *Concept formation* might be defined as the acquisition of symbols or abstractions that accommodate particular events into an integrated, larger category. For example, the concept of justice is formed on the basis of multiple discrete events such as stealing, rewards, courts, trials, laws, and punishment. The research of Kohlberg and Turiel (1971) presents the idea of a hierarchy of concepts related to morality. People in stage 1 of moral reasoning think that morality (reasoning what is right or wrong) is based on whether the individual is caught and punished. If a person is going to be caught, then he or she shouldn't steal. If he or she won't be caught, then it's all right. Stage 1 is called *punishment and obedience orientation.* In stage 2 people reason according to parental and societal rules. Something is judged as right or wrong according to external standards determined by authority. This is labeled the *good boy/good girl orientation.* However, persons in the highest stage (stage 6) decide what is right or wrong according to universal criteria. They consider the consequences of the act of stealing on the basis of the best interest of all people, not according to prescribed law. This orientation is labeled *individual principles of conscience.* Kohlberg found that moral reasoning is age-related and that the majority of persons do not move beyond stage 4, *conventional reasoning according to rules of authority.*

Belenky, Clinchy, Goldberger, and Tarule, in their book *Women's Ways of Knowing* (1986), suggest that developmental trends found in studies of men might be somewhat different from what has been found in their interviews of women. They posit that women at highest stages might reason "not by invoking a logical hierarch of abstract principles but through trying to understand the conflict in the context of each person's perspective, needs, and goals—and doing the best possible for everyone that is involved" (1986, p. 149). The importance of their work and that of their predecessor Carol Gilligan (1982) is to point out that gender might be an influence in the development of reasoning abilities. At higher stages of thought, men might tend to reason according to objective principles that stand apart from the immediate or long-term effects on individuals, in contrast to women, who might tend to see the personal consequences for individuals as the core of what is a moral and correct action. However, Greeno and Maccoby (1986) caution that basic developmental research on sex difference has not uncovered definitive differences.

> We can only sound a warning: Women have been trapped for generations by people's willingness to accept their intuitions about the truth of gender stereotypes. To us, there seems no alternative to the slow, painful, and sometimes dull accumulation of quantitative data to show whether the almost infinite variations in the way human beings think, feel, and act are actually linked to gender [1986, p. 312].

David Hunt's (1966) work on how people form concepts appears to parallel both the work of Kohlberg and Turiel and that of Belenky et al. According to Hunt, the normal course of conceptual development "leads to more orientations towards the environment and the interpersonal world" (Sullivan, McCullough, and Stager 1970). Stage 1 is characterized by concepts based on learning the rules or cultural standards of one's group. Stage 2 is marked by learning how the individual is distinct from the cultural standards of the group. In stage 3 one learns to empathize with others. Stage 4 is characterized by learning to see oneself both apart from and in relation to others. Concept development, as moral and crystallized learning, is the natural tendency to acquire more information about oneself, one's situation, and one's relationship with others before making judgments.

Jane Loevinger's research at the Institute for Social Science has been concerned with ego or personality development, which she defines as broader than concept or moral development. The scheme accounts for four domains: (1) impulse control or character development, (2) interpersonal style, (3) conscious preoccupations, and (4) cognitive style (Witherell and Erickson 1978). Her research on adults has resulted in definitions of ten stages and transitional levels the adult uses to make sense out of the complexity of life. Her developmental theory moves from *symbiotic* and *impulsive* thinking (where the individual is dependent on others deciding for him or her) to *conformist* levels (where thinking is conceptually simple, conforming to socially approved codes with little awareness of inner choice) to *autonomous* thinking (where a person is a "synthesizer—able to integrate conceptually ideas that appear unrelated or even oppositional to those at lower stages") (Witherell and Erickson 1978, p. 231).

Cognitive, moral, conceptual, and ego development research and theory are of use to the practicing supervisor who needs to be able to determine teacher levels when planning for direct assistance, staff development, curriculum development, group development, and action research. Let's conclude with the statement that the findings of adult research reinforce the child development research findings of Piaget (1955) and Bruner (1960) in underscoring human development from simplistic, concrete thinking to multi-informational and abstract thinking. Soon we will look at what schools and supervisors can do to support or negate such thinking among teachers.

Life Transition

The last area of adult studies to be discussed is research on life-span transitions or critical events in adults' lives. These studies are drawn from the pioneering work of Charlotte Buhler (1956) and Erik Erikson (1950). They have been refined by the work of Bernice L. Neugarten (1977) in her studies of men and women between the ages of forty and seventy; by Daniel Levinson's study (1977) of forty men of various occupational levels from their mid-thirties to mid-forties; and by Blum and Meyer's (1981) study of twenty-five heart attack patients ranging in age from thirty-one to seventy-two.

Some conclusions about life adaptations and transitions can be made. Buhler found that adults between the ages of eighteen and twenty-five are dominated by the issue of occupation and life dreams. For the next twenty years, from twenty-five to forty-five, the adult is concerned with "creative expansion" and realization of possibilities in regard to occupation, marriage, and home. The years from forty-five to sixty-five are characterized by the "establishment of inner order," with a reassessment of priorities.

Neugarten studied the timing of events such as childbearing, occupational advancement and peaking, children leaving home, retirement, personal illness, and death of a spouse or close friend. Many of these events are common to all adults; the time of their occurrence, according to Neugarten, influences how the person responds and continues with life. For example, the Blum and Meyer (1981) study of the recovery of adult men from severe heart attacks highlights the difference in timing of critical events. Young men were bitter and hostile toward their heart attack and couldn't wait to resume their previous lives. Middle-aged men were reflective about the heart attack and seriously weighed whether they wanted to continue to live as they had before. They contemplated changes in family relations, job, and living environments. Older men were accepting and grateful that the heart attack had left them alive with the opportunity to finish some of their desired retirement plans. As one can see, the same event—a heart attack—resulted in quite different reactions, depending on the time and age of the adult.

Levinson's work (1977) is a coherent treatment of changes in a person's life but has limitations in that the subjects were all male, middle-class, and white-collar. However, his findings suggest some commonalities with other men and women in various occupations and might be particularly helpful in understanding the life transitions of teachers. The beginning years of adulthood are marked by active mastery of the outer world. As one approaches mid-life, the issue of making it becomes important. One sees advancement to higher status and responsibility as important not only in itself but also as a sign of how high one might aspire. If promotion or advancement does not occur, the individual sees younger people move ahead while he or she remains on a plateau. With such an occurrence, the person can either accept the plateau, move to another organization within the same profession, or attempt to change careers. Becker (1971) has singled out a critical element in career success within the same organization and profession: Conforming to the social norms of the organization is imperative for career success. Advancing in a career is often tied to one's degree of assimilation to the conventions, standards, and rules of the organization. Levinson mentions that a young adult has an advantage in an organization if he or she finds a mentor. A senior executive or other established person takes the young adult under his or her wing and cautions, advises, and protects. Through the mentor, the young adult learns how to behave for later success.

Young adulthood is often a time of feelings of omnipotence, when all one's dreams seem attainable. Middle adulthood is ushered in by a loss of such feelings of omnipotence, with the realization of one's limitations. It occasions a period of reexamination of self and a revision of plans. The mentor relationship becomes less important as the young adult continues to move toward his or her goals and the middle-aged mentor no longer appears so exalted or wise. On the one hand, the middle-aged adult becomes more autonomous in deciding his or her priorities; on the other hand, he or she confronts the limits to what he or she can ultimately hope to accomplish. This dilemma often results in so-called mid-life crisis—a groping to find a consistent meaning to one's life. In older age, people accept their life and affiliations and focus on concluding important activities.

Human reactions to crucial life events can be extremely complex and idiosyncratic. We have already seen how the timing of an event such as a heart attack can alter a person's response. Besides timing, there are other influences on a person's choices. Let's take an example. Based on our temperament, intelligence, attractiveness, and based on the environment in which we grew up (cold, friendly, lonely, secure, aggressive, or warm), you and I may have chosen very different careers and lifestyles. For example, from the age of twenty-five to thirty, we both thought about making a career move in education. Because of my own limited intelligence and the perceived attractiveness and friendliness of a rural environment, I decided to become a teacher, writer, and self-styled farmer. You, because of your higher intelligence and the excitement of living in a city, aspired to be a school principal or director in an urban, sophisticated area. Now I spend my Sunday mornings chasing escaped cows; you (ah! the road not taken) spend yours reading the *Times,* listening to baroque music, and dining on smoked salmon and French pastries. In young adulthood we both passed through a stage of sorting out aspirations, but our choices differed. Adult life-span research focuses on common or predictable experiences rather than the variety of ways individuals respond to those experiences.

Placing Adult Development with Life Transition

We now can summarize and relate the two areas of adult studies. In adult development there is an improvement of thinking, concept formation, and ego development that is characterized as crystallized (using more information), complex, and autonomous. Also, it has been shown that adult transitions encompass a life span moving developmentally through initial feelings of omnipotence, greater reflection and reordering of reality, and finally consolidation and acceptance of life. The interaction of crucial life events and individual characteristics influences the scope and intensity of transitions.

Adult development does *not* mean that *all* people become more autonomous, abstract, and accepting. Folklore says the opposite: "You can't teach an old dog new tricks." There's probably some truth to this adage, but research on adult development suggests that adults *are* capable of learning new tricks and becoming more flexible. The capacity to improve and become a more integrative problem solver exists in humans. Its occurrence or failure to occur is a significant matter—one that is fundamental to successful or unsuccessful instructional supervision.

Figure 4-1 shows the relation of adult development and life transitions. The young adult is marked by limited experience, simple standards of reasoning about concepts, egocentricity, and dependence on authority during a period of unbounded dreams and feelings of omnipotence. The middle-aged adult has had a variety of experiences, has developed the ability to draw relationships between self and others, and possesses an awareness of his or her own abilities. This happens during a period of reflection, reordering of priorities, and setting of limited goals. Finally, the older adult has had many experiences, can understand more easily the plight of others, and can make decisions that take into account more of the total situation. This is done during a time of acceptance, consolidation, and planning for future tasks.

Critical influences on development are individual traits, environmental characteristics, timing of life events, and the interpersonal mentor-disciple relationship. The next section will jux-

Figure 4-1   Adult development and life transitions

Age	21	40	65
Crystallized intelligence	⟶ New information more easily related to old ⟶		
Concept formation	⟶ More comparisons and relations between self ⟶ and others		
Ego state	⟶ More autonomous and integrated outlook ⟶		
Life transitions	Omnipotence; aspirations for family, occupation, and life-styles	Reflection; reordering of priorities	Acceptance; consolidating; finalizing

tapose what is known about optimal adult development with what is known about teacher development.

Effective Teachers Are Thoughtful Adults

The apparently self-evident statement that teachers are adults takes on new meaning when knowledge of the adult as learner is contrasted with the treatment of teachers. Supervisors treat teachers as if they were all the same, rather than individuals in various stages of adult growth. In most schools, teachers receive the same in-service workshops, the same observations, and the same assessments. It is as if teachers were stamped out of teacher-training institutes as identical and thereafter have no further need to be viewed as individual learners. The research on adults shows the lack of wisdom of such assumptions (Mathis 1987). A discussion of how stages of adult development apply to teacher development and how life transitions apply to teaching transitions will follow.

Results of research on stages of ego, conceptual, and moral development of teachers are similar to findings for the population of all adults. Most teachers have been found to be in the conformist to conscientious stages of Loevinger's ego development scale (Oja and Pine 1981; Glickman and Tamashiro 1982). According to Oja and Pine (1981, p. 112),

> These levels indicate ego stages which are characterized by con-
> formist behavior to external standards, little self-awareness. . . .
> *Conventional moral adjustments* based upon often unquestioned

conformity to peer, social, and legal norms, with few self evaluated standards . . . and *conceptual levels* indicating thinking in terms of stereotypes and cliches with dawning recognition of individual differences . . . [emphasis in original].

On conceptual development, according to Harvey (1970), teachers were found to be mostly in stage 1 of a four-stage system—that is, in the unilateral-dependence state. Unilateral dependence describes a stage in which concepts are undifferentiated and do not account for ambiguity. Thought is absolute and concrete, with dependence on authority. Harvey's (1970) study shows that a higher proportion of undergraduate education majors than of liberal arts majors are in lower stages of conceptual thinking. Furthermore, there are more practicing or experienced teachers than preservice teachers in the lower stages of conceptual thinking.

Research on moral reasoning of teachers is consistent with ego and conceptual studies of teachers. Wilkins (1980), in comparing Australian preservice teachers with U.S. preservice teachers, concluded that the majority of teachers were in the conventional-reasoning stage. Morality in that stage is governed by adherence to external rules of a group. More recent work by Rest (1986) indicates that teachers are largely in moderate levels of principled reasoning.

The majority of teachers appear to be in relatively moderate to low stages of ego, conceptual, and moral development—probably no different from the adult population at large. So what? What difference does it make that many teachers are not complex or autonomous? Perhaps one does not need higher-ordered thinking to teach? One could argue that if teaching is a simple enterprise with no need for decision making, then it would make little difference. In fact, if most teachers were autonomous and abstract, then trying to do a simple job would create great tension, resentment, and noncompliance. If teaching is a simple activity, schools need people who can reason simply. If teaching is complex and ever-changing, however, then higher levels of reasoning are necessary. A simple thinker in a dynamic and difficult enterprise would be subjected to overwhelming pressures.

Sociologists have documented the environmental demands posed by making thousands of decisions daily, by constant psychological pressure, and by expectations that the teacher must do the job alone—unwatched and unaided. A teacher daily faces up to 150 students of various backgrounds, abilities, and interests, some of whom succeed while others fail. Concrete, rigid thinking on the part of the teacher cannot possibly improve instruction. As Madeline Hunter (1986) has noted, "Teaching . . . is a relativistic situational profession where *there are no absolutes*" (italics in original). Researcher David Berliner (see Brandt 1986) has studied expert teachers and has reported, "we keep finding the behavior of these expert teachers unstable from day to day. . . ."

Teacher improvement can only come from abstract, multiinformational thought that can generate new responses toward new situations. Glassberg's (1979) review of research on teachers' cognitive development as related to instructional improvement concluded:

> in summary these studies suggest that high stage teachers tend to be adaptive in teaching style, flexible, and tolerant, and able to employ a wide range of teaching models. . . . effective teaching in almost any view is a most complex form of human behavior. Teachers at higher, more complex stages of human development appear as more effective in classrooms than their peers at lower stages.

The problem with the need for high-stage teachers is that, although the work by its nature demands autonomous and flexible thinking, teachers in most schools are not supported in ways to improve their thinking. *The only alternative for a teacher in a complex environment who cannot adjust to multiple demands and is not being helped to acquire the abilities to think abstractly and autonomously is to simplify and deaden the instructional environment.* Teachers make the environment less complex by disregarding differences among students, by establishing routines and instructional practices that remain the same day after day and year after year. Research on effective instruction (Berman and McLaughlin 1975; Porter and Brophy 1988; Rutter et al. 1979) indicates that effective instruction is based on adaptation of curriculum and materials to local settings and particular learning goals. In other words, effective teachers think about what they are currently doing, assess the results of their practice, and explore with each other new possibilities for teaching students. Effective teaching has been misunderstood and misapplied as a set and sequence of certain teaching behaviors (review previous day's objectives, present objectives, explain, demonstrate, guided practice, check for understanding, etc.). This explanation of effectiveness is simply untrue, as can be seen in the prior references to Hunter (1986) and Berliner (quoted in Brandt 1986). Rather, successful teachers are thoughtful teachers (Porter and Brophy 1988).

Evidence of the relationship between high-stage attainment of conceptual and ego development and effective instructional practice can be found in several research studies. Harvey (1967) found high-concept teachers to have students with higher achievement, less nurturance, more cooperation, and more involvement in their work than low-concept teachers. Hunt and Joyce (1967) found correlations between teacher conceptual level and ability to use learners' needs as a basis for planning and evaluation. High-concept teachers used a greater range of learning environments and teaching methods. Murphy and Brown (1970) found that high-stage teachers could help students theorize and express, could ask precise questions, and could encourage exploration and group involvement significantly more effectively than low-stage teachers. Parkay (1979), in a study of inner-city high school teachers, found that high-concept teachers stimulated positive student attitudes and student achievement gains and were less susceptible to professional stress. A study of 52 teachers by Calhoun (1985) found that teachers with high conceptual thought provided more corrective feedback to students, gave more praise, and were less negative and punitive. These teachers were more varied in their instructional strategies and were able to elicit more higher-order conceptual responses from their students than teachers of moderate and lower levels of conceptual thought. Witherell and Erickson (1978) found in case studies of teachers that the teachers of highest levels of ego development demonstrated

> greater complexity and commitment to the individual (student) in the following areas: (a) analytic self-reflection and "explanatory power" . . . (b) philosophy of education . . . (c) constructs relating to children and the capacity to take the child's perspective, (d) the generation and use of varieties of data in teaching, and (e) understandings and practices relating to rules, authority, and moral development . . . [1978, p. 232].

Thies-Sprinthall's study of teachers showed that as teachers acquired higher conceptual levels, their indirect teaching increased. Indirect teaching (the use of less lecture, more praise, and more acceptance of student ideas) has been positively associated with pupil achievement gain (Gage 1978).

The works of Thies-Sprinthall and Sprinthall (1987), Macrostie (in process), Phillips (1989), Oja and Pine (1981), and Parker (1983) are particularly important because they suggest that teachers, when provided with a stimulating and supportive environment, can increase their levels of cognitive complexity. Research on adults shows that crystallized learning does increase over time. However, some studies on teachers (Schlechty and Vance 1981; Glickman and Tamashiro 1982) indicate that teachers' capacity to integrate new information related to previous experience does not increase.

Why, if optimal adult learning suggests a continued capability to learn, are teachers characterized by a lack of such cognitive growth? Sociologists have even suggested that problem-solving ability of teachers *decreases* over time. Phillip Jackson, in *Life in Classrooms* (1968), has noted the common pattern of nontechnical language and regulated responses among teachers. Judith Little, on the other hand, found that teachers in successful schools used precise, technical language in discussing instructional concerns (Little 1982). Teachers in successful schools do continue to think and are challenged to extend the use of their mental abilities. If a supervisor could promote thinking among the school staff, school effectiveness might not be far behind. Thinking improves when people interact with each other, when they break routine by experimenting, when they observe others at work, and when they assess and revise their own actions. A cause beyond oneself becomes the norm, and the school becomes successful.

Teachers who are isolated in their classrooms, receive no systematic feedback, attend monthly faculty meetings only to listen to monologues of announcements, and spend a few minutes each day chatting idly in the lounge may be viewed as remarkable specimens of survival. Such teachers, however, are not contributors to a successful school.

Life Transitions of Teachers

Research by Adams, Hutchinson, and Martray (1980) in Kentucky and by Ayers (1980) in Tennessee has shown that the third year of teaching is a crucial transition time. Both studies found that ratings of teacher effectiveness, as measured by principal evaluation, student surveys, and classroom observations, rose for the first three years of teaching and then dramatically dropped off. Why do teachers continue to improve their instruction for the first three years but not afterwards? Ayers, addressing this point, speculated that:

1. At the end of the third year of teaching, individuals receive tenure in the schools. It was felt that many teachers after this point may relax their teaching style since they feel that the pressure to achieve a stable position has been eased.

2. Initially, most individuals who enter the teaching profession have high ideals and expectations. It was felt that after several years, these ideals and expectations give way to an attitude that reflects the climate of the school. Acceptance of the norms of the school becomes more commonplace and the level of teaching may be reduced.

3. After several years of teaching it was felt that subjects may be losing enthusiasm for the profession . . . [p. 31].

The loss of enthusiasm mentioned by Adams also has been studied by Nathalie Gehrke (1979) with teachers in Arizona. She wrote that "most teachers do not become aware of feelings of boredom and waning enthusiasm until they have taught at least two years. First year teachers seldom remark about the repetitive nature of the job, with good reason. First year teachers are overwhelmed by new experiences." In the third year, however, teachers perceive the job as basically unchanging. They grow bored as a result of "inflexible scheduling and housekeeping duties, the relatively unchanging nature of the content they taught, or the shallowness of the peers or students with whom they worked" (p. 190).

Teaching becomes largely a personal issue of making it through the day. Since there exists little uncertainty or challenge in the work itself (the materials, the classroom, the loneliness, and the schedule), only the students are unusual. Therefore, many of those who remain in teaching appear to establish their procedures in the first three years and then resign themselves to a monotonous existence. Many who leave simply cannot endure the sameness of existence (Scriven 1979; Ellison 1981).

It may be an oversimplification to depict teaching as a rush of excitement for three years followed by increased boredom and dissatisfaction. Many experienced teachers continue to find excitement in their work, to vary their environment, and to seek out new challenges. Some continue to improve for over thirty years. On the other hand, many teachers leave the profession within the first three years, others never show improvement, and still others finally begin to improve after ten years of repetitive teaching. The exceptions point out the wonderful complexities of human behavior, but too often the general course of teaching is characterized as initial excitement and growth followed by a leveling off into a monotony of procedures by those who choose to remain, or by abandonment of the profession by those who seek more varied work.

Interestingly enough, state reform in education in the past few years, intended to improve education and teaching, has had the unintended result of demoralizing some of our most dedicated and enthusiastic teachers. As Linda McNeil's (1986) studies of magnet high schools have shown, reforms that standardize curriculum, testing of students, and evaluation of teachers for contract renewal and merit pay have cramped the creativity and judgment of outstanding teachers:

Many of the best teachers in these magnet schools are talking about leaving . . . they love to teach but will return to industry rather than go through the motions of teaching without being able to incorporate their considerable knowledge of the field into their courses [p. 23].

One teacher expressed his frustration with new evaluation policies this way: "I'm not a teacher anymore. I'm just a worker now" (p. 11).

The work environment of magnet schools has been characterized as more amenable to teacher reflection and judgment than that of traditional schools. Yet the loss of enthusiasm is probably less related to years of teaching than to a teacher's realization that the school does not accommodate his or her professional and personal development. In most schools, this loss of enthusiasm occurs rather quickly.

Occupational development of teachers appears to run counter to the needs of adults in critical transition times. The work of Levinson (1977) and Neugarten (1977) points to early adulthood as a period of bravado, romance, and the pursuit of dreams. The young adult aged twenty to thirty-five is on an exciting search for status, comfort, and happiness in work, family, and friends. The middle years, thirty-five to fifty-five, provide a transition into some disillusionment, reflection, and reordering of priorities according to a reassessment of one's capabilities and opportunities. In teaching, however, the young adulthood period, which should be one of romance, quickly becomes one of disillusionment. The young person of twenty-four or twenty-five who has entered teaching to pursue his or her dreams often finds after three years that work life is going nowhere. The job does not excite; the advancements do not exist; and the variety of work is nonexistent. The result can be intense boredom, leading to resignation—either *from* the job or *on* the job. What does it mean to education when a young teacher's natural inclination toward excitement and idealism is bound by a straitjacket of repetition?

Let's ask the next question. What happens when the natural inclination of the middle-aged teacher to reflect and reorder his or her teaching priorities confronts the same six periods of thirty students that he or she has faced for the past twenty years? One might expect a further despair of any impulse to change and to improve. Finally, what about the older teacher who is perceived by many as an anomaly, a relic who has remained in teaching because of inability to advance into administration or supervision. The acquisition of thirty years of experience coincides with the natural time for consolidating achievements and identifying one's remaining career objectives. Instead, there is only the same job—the same job as that of the new teacher down the hall, who might be the age of the older teacher's grandchild. Where is the sense of responsibility, generativity, and accomplishment in seniority? Old and new teachers are treated the same, accorded the same status, and expected to conform to the same routines.

Teaching appears to be a topsy-turvy occupation, running against the needs of life transition periods. Those who continue to make lasting improvement and enhance their students' educational lives should have our utmost respect. If not fortunate enough to be in a school that responds and supports change in teachers according to principles of adult learning and transitions, the effective teacher truly transcends the system and educates in spite of, not because of, the school.

Optimal Teacher Development

Optimal development is a matter of what the individual is capable of becoming. There are mitigating factors that impede the growth of adults and teachers. Studying how outstanding teachers change may give us guidance for altering conditions for those teachers who are not improving. We have already seen how teachers judged outstanding on measures of flexibility, adaptability, and improvement in student achievement and attitudes have in common the ability to think at high abstract levels.

Abstraction

The normal development of thinking moves from concrete to abstract (see Figure 4-2). Learners' initial interaction with objects is determined by the singular physical dimension of the objects being present. With development, however, a learner's interaction is independent of the objects' presence. The learner can hold a mental image of the object and categorize its dimensions in multiple ways (Piaget 1955; Flavell 1977). The vehicle for movement of a person's thinking toward greater abstraction is provision of a concrete learner with familiar experiences and information that are embedded in the actual physical context. Gradually, unfamiliar experiences are provided by introducing uncommon or novel information that asks the learner to hold onto a mental image. At the end of the continuum, the abstract learner can seek unfamiliar experiences by mentally imagining novel information and thus thinking of truly new ways of acting.

Abstract thought is the ability to determine relationships, to make comparisons and contrasts between information and expe-

Figure 4-2   Development of abstract thought

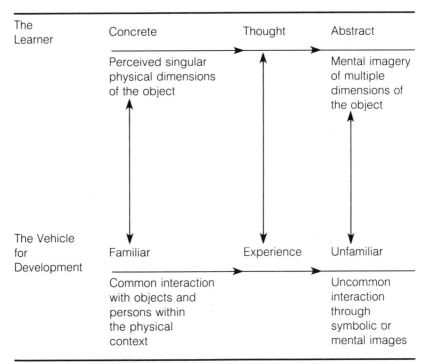

rience, and to use these to generate multiple possibilities in formulating a decision. Therefore, as experience (with objects and persons) increases from the familiar to the unfamiliar, so does abstract thought.

Teachers (like any learner) can be helped to think more abstractly by being given information and experience that are slightly novel. If we begin to assess teachers on a continuum of abstract thinking, clues to the type and delivery of information and experience emerge. As in Table 4-1 (Glickman 1981), we can classify the abstract thinking of teachers as low, moderate, or high.

Teachers with low levels of abstract thinking have difficulty in determining whether changes in their classroom are necessary. Often they do not see the relationship of their own behavior to the problem; they may say, "The students are lazy," or "The parents don't care." If they do perceive a need for changes, they often expect someone else to tell them exactly what to do. Left to themselves, they often respond to a dilemma by making a decision that is either habitual ("Whenever a student misbehaves, I give him more home

Table 4-1   Levels of abstract thinking

Low	Moderate	High
Confusion about situation	Can define situation by focusing on one dimension	Can define the situation by drawing relationships between several sources of information
Doesn't know what can be done	Can think of several responses	Can relate the information to change in classroom practice
Asks to be shown	Has difficulty in thinking of consequences of changing the situation	Can generate many alternative responses
Has habitual responses to varying situations		Can evaluate the consequences of each response and choose the one most likely to succeed

work") or impulsive ("I changed the assignments because I felt like it").

Teachers with moderate levels of abstract thinking realize that improvement is needed but have difficulty deciding what actions to take or what the consequences of certain actions would be. They believe that when students are failing or misbehaving, it relates in some way to what the teacher is doing. However, they are limited in determining the relationships between their teaching practice, materials, organization, and student needs. They often choose a change in the curriculum, grouping, or instruction that contains unexpected consequences, which in turn create further problems. Inadequate definition of the problem often leads to further difficulties.

Highly abstract teachers can use a rational process of problem solving by incorporating several sources of information and applying their own knowledge and experience. For example, a particular student's learning difficulty will be considered against knowledge of the student's previous work, her peers, her work with other teachers in other situations, her family and out-of-school time, current instruction, materials, student level of achievement, and student attitude toward work. This is all considered *before* the teacher generates possible changes such as regrouping, changing materials, holding a conference with the student, or setting rewards. This might appear to be a lengthy process, but highly abstract teachers can think and respond to a problem rapidly and decisively (Parker 1983).

Concern

In the 1960s and early 1970s, Frances Fuller conducted pioneer studies of teacher concerns. In analyzing both her own studies and six others, she found that the responses by hundreds of teachers at various stages of experience showed different concerns. Beginning teachers were concerned mainly about their own survival. They wanted to know how the school principal, other supervisors, and other teachers perceived them—how adequate they were and whether they could maintain control over the classroom. Older teachers identified as superior were not concerned with mere adequacy but instead with the impact that they were having on students. In Fuller's words (1969, p. 221), "When concerns are 'mature,' i.e., characteristic of experienced teachers, concerns seem to focus on pupil gain and self evaluation as opposed to personal gain and evaluation by others." Superior teachers, as identified by principals and fellow teachers, were distinct from other teachers in that pupil progress was of overriding importance. On the other hand, many experienced teachers *not* identified as superior had concerns about their own adequacy, similar to those of beginners. Later work on teachers' concerns by Hall and Loucks (1978), Adams and Martray (1981), Demarte and Mahood (1981), and others has refined Fuller's work into three developmental substages of concerns: (1) self concerns, (2) task concerns, and (3) impact concerns. The general direction of concerns has remained consistent from study to study. I believe the trend from self (or egocentric) to student (or altruistic) concerns is similar to the ego-development progression of Loevinger and the moral reasoning stages of Kohlberg (see Figure 4-3).

Beginning teachers are concerned with their own survival—whether or not they can make it as teachers. Their concern corresponds to the ego state of fearfulness and the moral state of avoidance of punishment. They want to know if they can avoid being driven out by students, ostracized by peers, or fired by superiors. Such concerns can be classified as an *egocentric motivation to teaching*; they revolve around the person's survival and security. With survival and security assured, teachers think less of their own needs and begin to address the tasks of teaching. They begin to think about altering or enriching the classroom schedule, the teaching materials, and their instructional methodology. The beginning teacher is concerned with learning *any* system that will enable him or her to survive. The more experienced teacher, assured

Figure 4-3   Development of teacher concerns, ego, and moral development

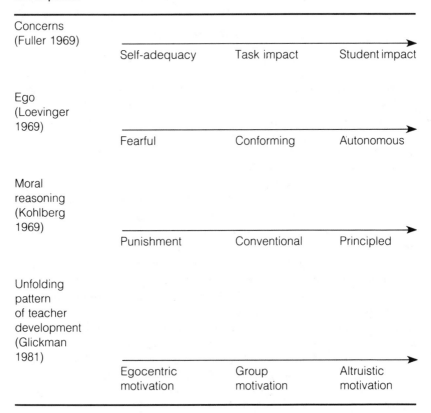

Concerns
(Fuller 1969)

| Self-adequacy | Task impact | Student impact |

Ego
(Loevinger
1969)

| Fearful | Conforming | Autonomous |

Moral
reasoning
(Kohlberg
1969)

| Punishment | Conventional | Principled |

Unfolding
pattern
of teacher
development
(Glickman
1981)

| Egocentric motivation | Group motivation | Altruistic motivation |

that his or her teaching practice is adequate for survival, still doubts its adequacy for all students. The experienced teacher is concerned with *adapting* the instructional system to improve learning for students. Note that the shift in the nature of teachers' concerns corresponds to the shift in moral reasoning based on learning other conventional practices that are available and accepted in the school and that will improve teaching tasks. The teacher is now concerned about his or her class as a group, and thus can be identified as having progressed to the teacher development pattern of *group motivation.* The concern of superior teachers for individual student impact is correlated with the ego state of autonomy and the moral state of principled reasoning. Superior teachers mature beyond the group and conventional orientation to teaching; they seek help for individual students that may be outside the accepted norms of the school. The autonomous teacher wants to succeed with every student, even at the risk of being different. His or her thinking is altruistic in that actions are motivated by the needs of others and not of self. The autonomous teacher is willing to help other teachers, to work on school-wide change, and to address larger issues of education and the profession. When a teacher's underlying concern is with improving education for all, that teacher has progressed to the development pattern of *altruistic motivation*. The unfolding of teacher concerns occurs on a continuum, beginning with *I* concerns to concern for *my group* to concerns for *all students*.

This characterization of teachers' concerns does not mean that certain specific types of instructional practice are superior—for example, "The best teachers use a direct instruction model and begin with an anticipatory set and end their lessons with a summary and closure." It is not the particular classroom practice but the reasoning *behind* the teacher's practice that marks the level of maturity of the teacher. An autonomous teacher might teach at times in a very spontaneous and activity-centered manner, as a response to the individual needs of students and the particular learning goal. As Berliner reminds us, the behaviors of expert teachers are highly unstable "from day to day and year to year" (quoted in Brandt 1986).

Finally, if we accept that there is optimal teacher development, which moves from egocentric to altruistic motivation, and that there is optimal teacher thinking, which moves from concrete to abstract, then we can begin to assess teachers as developing adults. The lack of such movement becomes apparent and ultimately may be traced to conditions of the work environment and the occupation.

Development: Ebb and Flow

There may be a tendency to view the career cycle as a linear process, with an individual . . . progressing through the various stages. While there is a certain logic to this view . . . It is more likely to be an ebb and flow, with teachers moving in and out of stages in response to both personal and organizational influences [Burke, Christensen, Fessler, McDonnell, and Price 1987, p. 13].

Not only is development likely to be an ebb and flow; there are also different paths within the same individual, depending on the particular context or subject. Previous developmental stage theory has often implied a lock-step progression of stages. More recently, cognitive researchers have shown that stages of thinking vary according to the domain or topic (Gardner, 1983, Case, 1986, Sternberg, 1988). The same can be said for motivation.

Perhaps a few examples will establish the point. Recently, an outstanding science teacher of advanced physics (a winner of state and national awards) was asked to teach an introductory biology class. Her level of thinking about physics was at a generative, flexible, and abstract stage, yet her thinking about general biology was, at least at the beginning of the year, at a concrete, imitative stage of needing to follow the teacher manual. Her motivation to succeed in both classes may have been equally high, but her operational level of thinking was quite different. The same can be seen in the case of a teacher who has a high level of abstract thinking about the subject matter he or she teaches and a lower level of abstraction about the method of teaching (or vice-versa).

Motivation has the same variation for an individual. Fred loves to teach art to his second-grade youngsters. He's constantly looking for ideas, finding materials, and expending energy to improve his art program. Yet when it comes to teaching mathematics, he puts in the required time, uses the worksheets, and muddles through the material. He never liked mathematics as a student and doesn't care to spend extra time on it. (The same variation can be seen in anyone's level of motivation when it comes to fixing a special meal versus cleaning the pots and pans afterwards.) Suffice it to say that teachers, like all humans, are not static in their levels of thinking and motivation about all endeavors.

Furthermore, development can regress, recycle, or become blocked. Because one has reached a high level of development in one arena does not mean the stage is consolidated eternally. Experience is a relative term—a teacher (or supervisor) with thirty years of teaching (or supervising) can still be inexperienced in many ways. Change the expectations of the jobs and/or change the clientele served, and suddenly there is an inexperienced person trying to figure out how to survive. Likewise, a first-year teacher may, after only a few months, be experienced and able to reason according to concerns beyond his or her own survival.

Alterations to a person's personal or professional situation can usher in regression in stages of thinking and stages of motivation. A highly committed and thoughtful faculty, who had made their school an exciting and successful place, was jolted when negotiations between the teachers' union and the school board resulted in a bitter strike. The immediate result on the school was that teachers retreated within their four walls, carrying out the letter of their contract and removing themselves from involvement in school curriculum and instruction issues. Most teachers retreated to a self-survival stage.

Teacher or adult development is not monolithic, linear, or eternal. The research on developmental stages provides lenses for viewing teachers individually and collectively as to their current levels of thinking and motivation about instructional improvement. Through such lenses, we can explore possible interventions to assist teachers individually and collectively to move into higher stages of development.

Considering Teacher Development within the Context of the School

One theme of this book is that teacher development, according to levels of motivation and levels of thought, is crucial for deciding approaches and skills to help teachers become more abstract and altruistic. The ideal teacher is committed to the needs of all students and has the cognitive skills to improve his or her own instruction. In helping teachers grow, supervisors must consider characteristics of the teacher as a client. For example, one would not work with a highly abstract teacher in the same way as with a concrete and rigid teacher. Nor would one work the same way with a teacher who is highly motivated about one aspect of teaching and indifferent about another aspect. The approaches and skills used in direct assistance, staff development, curriculum development, group development, and action research will differ according to the level of motivation and level of thought of teachers. A supervisor must be able to choose those skills and techniques that will enable teachers to develop individually and collectively to create a cause beyond oneself. A commitment to that cause is essential for school success.

This chapter has been intentionally theoretical and research-based. It provides the basis for choosing supervisory skills and strategies for working with individuals or groups of teachers. We can view teacher development against the background of adult development, life transitions, the work environment of the school, and characteristics of the teaching profession. The context of teacher development is illustrated in Figure 4-4. Imagine a large felt board representing the context of a teacher's life. At the center is the individual with his or her unique development and life transitions embedded into the work environment of the school, which is in turn embedded into characteristics of the teaching profession. When viewing a teacher's growth (or lack of growth), we must consider both the characteristics of the individual and the influences of the work environment and the teaching profession. For example, a teacher may be resistant because of previous negative experiences within the work environment of the school. Perhaps at

Figure 4-4   The context of teacher development

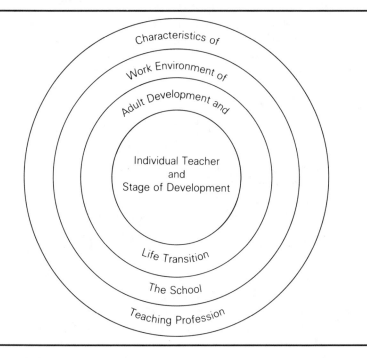

one time the teacher was concerned with improving her class and used abstract thought to implement a new classroom design. Perhaps other teachers or a supervisor frowned on such experimentation and threatened the teacher with the loss of her job. This teacher, needing to keep the job for financial reasons, therefore gave up trying to change. She retreated from improvement because of adverse pressure. This teacher might now be resistant, but she still has the ability to improve. Improvement will not occur, however, until changes occur in her immediate work environment. Another example might be a willing teacher who has found a satisfactory, maintenance level of group instruction and can live comfortably with the school norms. The reasons he does not demonstrate further improvement might be traced to characteristics of the teaching profession. The teacher may see no future prospects for increased status, income, or responsibility. Without any prospects for career advancement, he may rationally decide to remain adequate but nothing more. The supervisor must develop ways to provide advancement, recognition, and/or status in this teacher's career in order to realize further growth. The point is that characteristics of the individual teacher may not be fixed, but rather functions of the teacher's perceptions of the larger environment. Research on adults has demonstrated that teachers can become more motivated and more thoughtful about their work. Every person has the potential to improve: *Such potential might be blocked, slowed down, or even reversed, but it still exists.* The challenge for the supervisor is to treat teachers as individual adult learners to enable them to use their potential.

Summary, Conclusions, and Propositions

This chapter has contrasted the research on optimal adult development with teacher development. Adults were examined according to cognitive, conceptual, and personality development. Research on learning as a process that moves from simplistic, concrete thinking to multi-informational, abstract thinking was cited. Critical life transitions of adults were shown—from the young adult's feelings of omnipotence to the middle-aged person's need to reflect and reorder, to the older adult's needs to accept and consolidate. When comparing research on teachers with that on optimal development of adults, it becomes apparent that teachers' thinking does not automatically become more abstract. Furthermore, the teaching career does not coincide appropriately with adult life transitions. Teaching responsibilities are not increased, mentor relationships are not provided, and—usually after the third year of teaching—there is a general loss of enthusiasm for the occupation. Propositions for supervision that emerge from the contrasting of adult and teacher development are as follows:

- Proposition 1: *Supervision, to be effective, must be a function that responds to the developmental stages of teachers.* Teachers are not all alike in their thinking or their motivation for teaching. They should not be treated as a homogeneous group.

- Proposition 2: *Supervision, to be effective, must be a function that responds to adult life transitions of teachers.* Initial enthusiasm should be encouraged by gradually increasing responsibilities through mid-career. Late in their careers, teachers should be given reduced responsibilities so they may pursue their remaining educational goals.

These two propositions provide the general developmental *principles of action* that will serve as the core of supervisory thought and practice. The supervisory goal is to improve classroom and school instruction by enabling teachers to become more adaptive, more thoughtful, and more cohesive in their work. In the next chapter on prerequisite knowledge for developmental supervision, a supervisor's present platform of practice will be examined to determine its fit in the developmental framework.

EXERCISES

Academic

1. Review the theories of a major author on adult development or adult life-span transitions, as found in the list of references that follows these exercises. Write a paper summarizing the author's theories and any research on which those theories are based.

2. Review the research of a prominent investigator of teacher development or teacher life-span transitions, as found in the References list. Write a paper summarizing the major conclusions that researcher has drawn from his or her studies.

3. Review literature and/or research on adult learning. On the basis of your review, list at least eight generally accepted principles of adult learning. For each principle, infer and list an implication for supervision.

4. Read *Women's Ways of Knowing* by Belenky, Clinchy, Goldberger, and Tarule. Write a summary of your findings and a personal response to the book.

5. The chapter reports that teachers' enthusiasm and performance appear to improve for the first three years of teaching but not afterward. Possible reasons for the dropoff are cited. Write a reaction in which you (a) put forward your own proposal of why enthusiasm appears to wane and (b) offer possible solutions to the problem.

Field

1. Visit the classrooms of a teacher you perceive to be a highly abstract thinker and one you perceive to be a highly concrete thinker. Write a report comparing the teachers in terms of teaching methods, interaction with students, classroom management, attention to individual student needs, and general teaching effectiveness. (Use fictitious names in your report.)

2. On the basis of observations of leader-teacher, teacher-teacher, and teacher-student interactions, faculty meeting activities,

posted communications, and the like, infer a group of *social norms* that prevail at a selected school. Write a paper stating your perceptions of the school's social norms and your opinion of whether those norms are positive or negative influences on teachers' conceptual development.

3. Interview a veteran teacher who is nearing retirement. Ask the teacher to discuss the major transitions that have taken place during his or her career. Summarize the interview in writing.

4. Reflect on your own career and the major transitions that have taken place during your career. Choose an artifact that symbolizes each major transition. Prepare a display of your artifacts and a verbal or written report explaining the relationship between your career transitions and these artifacts.

5. Ask a first-year teacher, a third-year teacher, and a teacher with at least ten years of experience to list their concerns about teaching. Prepare a report comparing the various responses and drawing relevant conclusions.

Developmental

1. For the time that you will be reading the book, keep a diary of weekly decisions you have made. You might want to include the possible choices for each decision, the factors important in resolving your problems and the success with which you carried out your decisions. Review your diary after six weeks or more. Do you see any trends? What appear to be the most important considerations you use in making your decisions?

2. Begin a career scrapbook with the purpose of documenting your own professional development.

3. Begin an in-depth study of a major topic discussed in Chapter 4 (for example, adult life-span transitions, adult cognitive development, adult conceptual development, adult ego development, adult moral reasoning, or adult learning).

REFERENCES

Adams, R.D., Hutchinson, S., and Martray, C. 1980. A developmental study of teacher concerns across time. Paper presented at the annual meeting of the American Educational Research Association, Boston, April.

Adams, R.D., and Martray, C. 1981. Teacher development: A study of factors related to teacher concerns for pre, beginning, and experienced teachers. Paper presented at the annual meeting of the American Educational Research Association, Los Angeles, April.

Ayers, J.B. 1980. A longitudinal study of teachers. Paper presented at the annual meeting of the American Educational Research Association, Boston, April.

Becker, H.S. 1971. Personal change in adult life. In H.S. Becker (Ed.), *Sociological work: Method and substance*. London: Allen Lane.

Belenky, M.F., Clinchy, B.M., Goldberger, N.R., and Tarule, J.M. 1986. *Women's ways of knowing. The development of self, voice, and mind*. New York: Basic Books.

Blum, L.S. and Meyer, R. 1981. Developmental implications of myocardial infarction for mid-life adults. Paper presented at the annual meeting of the American Educational Research Association, Los Angeles, April.

Brandt, R.S. 1986. On the expert teacher: A conversation with David Berliner. *Educational Leadership 44*(2):4–9.

Bruner, J.S. 1960. *The process of education*. Cambridge, Mass.: Harvard University Press.

Buhler, C. 1956. *From childhood to maturity*. London: Routledge and Kegan Paul.

Burden, P.R. 1982. Developmental supervision: Reducing teacher stress at different career stages. Paper presented at the annual conference of the Association of Teacher Educators, Phoenix, Ariz., February.

Burke, P.J., Christensen, J.C., Fessler, R., McDonnell, J.H., and Price, J.R. 1987. The teacher career cycle: Model development and research report. Paper presented to the annual meeting of the American Educational Research Association, Washington, D.C., April.

Calhoun, E.F. 1985. Relationship of teachers' conceptual level to the utilization of supervisory services and to a description of the classroom instructional improvement. Paper presented at the annual meeting of the American Educational Research Association, Chicago, April.

Case, R. 1986. The new stage theories in intellectual development. In M. Perlmutter (Ed.), *Perspectives on intellectual development*, Vol. 19. Hillsdale, N.J.: Lawrence Erlbaum.

Demarte, P.J., and Mahood, R.W. 1981. The concerns of teachers in rural, urban, and suburban school settings. Paper presented at the annual meeting of the American Educational Research Association, Los Angeles, April.

Ellison, E. 1981. Survey here cites high teacher stress. *Atlanta* (Georgia) *Constitution*, February 26, p. 8B.

Erikson, E.L. 1950. *Childhood and society.* New York: Norton.

Flavell, J.H. 1977. *Cognitive development.* Englewood Cliffs, N.J.: Prentice-Hall.

Fuller, F.F. 1969. Concerns of teachers: A developmental conceptualization. *American Educational Research Journal* 6(2):207–266.

Gage, N.L. 1978. *The scientific basis of the art of teaching.* New York: Teachers College Press.

Gardner, H. 1983. *Frames of mind: The theory of multiple intelligences.* New York: Basic Books.

Gehrke, N.J. 1979. Renewing teacher enthusiasm: A professional dilemma. *Theory into Practice* 18(3):188–193.

Gilligan, C. 1982. *In a different voice.* Cambridge, Mass.: Harvard University Press.

Glassberg, S. 1979. *Developing models of teacher development.* ERIC document ED 171 685, March.

Glickman, C.D. 1981. *Developmental supervision: Alternative approaches for helping teachers to improve instruction.* Alexandria, Va.: Association for Supervision and Curriculum Development.

Glickman, C.D., and Tamashiro, R.T. 1982. A comparison of first year, fifth year, and former teachers on efficacy, ego development and problem solving. *Psychology in the Schools* 19(4):558–562.

Greeno, C.G., and Maccoby, E.E. 1986. How different is the "different voice"? *Signs: Journal of Women in Culture and Society* 11(2):310–316.

Hall, G.E., and Loucks, S. 1978. Teacher concerns as a basis for facilitating and personalizing staff development. *Teachers College Record* 80(September):36–53.

Harvey, O.J. 1967. Conceptual systems and attitude change. In C. Sherif and M. Sheif (Eds.), *Attitude, ego involvement and change.* New York: Wiley.

————. 1970. Beliefs and behavior: Some implications for education. *The Science Teacher* 37(December):10–14, 73.

Harvey, O.J., Hunt, D.E., and Schroeder, H.M. 1961. *Conceptual systems and personality organization.* New York: Wiley.

Havighurst, R.J. 1980. Life-span developmental psychology and education. *Educational Researcher* 9(10):3–8.

Horn, J.L., and Cattell, R.B. 1967. Age differences in fluid and crystallized intelligence. *Acta Psychologica* 26:107–129.

Hunt, D.E. 1966. A conceptual systems change model and its application to education. In O.J. Harvey (Ed.), *Experience, structure, and adaptability.* New York: Springer-Verlag, pp. 277–302.

Hunt, D.E., and Joyce, B.R. 1967. Teacher trainee personality and initial teaching style. *American Educational Research Journal* 4(3):253–255.

Hunter, M. 1986. To be or not to be—Hunterized. *Tennessee Educational Leadership* 12:70.

Jackson, P. 1968. *Life in classrooms.* New York: Holt, Rinehart and Winston.

Kohlberg, L., and Turiel, E. 1971. Moral development and moral education. In G. Lessor (Ed.), *Psychology and educational practice.* Chicago: Scott Foresman.

Levine, S.L. 1989. *Promoting adult growth in schools.* Boston: Allyn and Bacon.

Levinson, D.J. 1977. The seasons in a man's life. New York: Knopf.

Little, J.W. 1982. Norms of collegiality and experimentation: Workplace conditions of school success. *American Educational Research Journal* 19(3):325–340.

Loevinger, J. 1976. *Ego development.* San Francisco: Jossey-Bass.

Long, H.B., and Mirza, M.S. 1980. Some qualitative performance characteristics of adults at the formal operations stage. *Journal of Research and Development in Education* 13(3):21–24.

Macrostie, J. In process. A study of the teacher direct assistance program. Ph.D. dissertation, University of Tasmania, Australia.

Mathis, C. 1987. Educational reform, the aging society, and the teaching profession. Paper presented to the annual meeting of the American Educational Research Association, Washington, D.C., April.

McNeil, L.M. 1986. Exit, voice and community: Magnet teachers' responses to standardization. Presentation to the annual meeting of the American Educational Research Association, San Francisco, April.

McNergney, R.F., and Carrier, C.A. 1981. *Teacher development.* New York: Macmillan.

Murphy, P., and Brown, M. 1970. Conceptual systems and teaching styles. *American Educational Research Journal* 7(November): 529–540.

Neugarten, B.L. 1977. Personality and aging. In J.E. Birren and K.W. Schaie (Eds.), *Handbook of the psychology of aging.* New York: Van Nostrand Reinhold.

Oja, S.N. 1979. A cognitive-structural approach to adult ego, moral, and conceptual development through in-service education. Paper presented at the annual meeting of the American Educational Research Association, San Francisco, April.

Oja, S.N., and Pine, G.J. 1981. Toward a theory of staff development. Paper presented at the annual meeting of the American Educational Research Association, Los Angeles, April.

Parkay, F.W. 1979. Inner-city high school teachers: The relationship of personality traits and teaching style to environmental stress. Paper presented to the Southwest Educational Research Association, Houston.

Parker, W.C. 1983. The effect of guided reflection and role-taking on the interactive decision making of teachers. Paper presented at the annual meeting of the American Educational Research Association, Montreal, April.

Phillips, M. 1989. A case study evaluation of the impact on teachers of a peer coaching program in an elementary school. Ed.D. dissertation, University of Georgia.

Porter, A.C., and Brophy, J. 1988. Synthesis of research on good teaching. Insights from the work of the Institute for Research on Teaching. *Educational Leadership* 45(7):78–85.

Piaget, J. 1955. *The language and thought of the child.* New York: World Publishing.

Rest, J. 1986. *Moral development: Advances in research and theory.* New York: Praeger.

Rutter, M., Maughan, B., Mortimore, P., Ouston, J., and Smith, A. 1979. *Fifteen thousand hours. Secondary schools and their effects on children.* Cambridge, Mass.: Harvard University Press.

Schlechty, P.C., and Vance, V.S. 1981. Do academically able teachers leave education? The North Carolina case. *Kappan* 63(2):106–112.

Scriven, R. 1979. The big click. *Today's Education* 68(4):34–36.

Sprinthall, N.A., and Thies-Sprinthall, L. 1982. Career development of teachers: A cognitive developmental perspective. In H. Mitzel (Ed.), *Encyclopedia of educational research*, 5th ed. New York: Free Press.

Sternberg, R.J. 1988. *Triachic mind: A new theory of human intelligence*. New York: Viking.

Sullivan, E.V., McCullough, G., and Stager, M.A. 1970. Developmental study of the relationship between conceptual, ego, and moral development. *Child Development 41*:399–411.

Thies-Sprinthall, L., and Sprinthall, N.A. 1987. Experienced teachers: Agents for revitalization and renewal as mentors and teacher educators. Presentation to the annual meeting of the American Educational Research Association, Washington, D.C., April.

Whitbourne, S.K. 1986. *Adult development*, 2nd ed. New York: Praeger.

Wilkins, R.A. 1980. If the moral reasoning of teachers is deficient, what hope for pupils. *Kappan 61*(8):548–549.

Witherell, C.S., and Erickson, V.L. 1978. Teacher education as adult development. *Theory and Practice 17*(June):229–238.

Chapter 5

Reflections on Schools, Teaching, and Supervision

As we seek ways to improve school and classroom instruction, we need to understand how present thinking, beliefs, and practices in the field of supervision interact with instruction and the assumptions about students and teachers as learners. This chapter will show how issues of school and teaching effectiveness are not clearly answered by research but instead must be resolved by human judgments about goals and purposes. Next, we will look at how supervisory beliefs are related to a particular educational philosophy or platform. An instrument will then be provided to help clarify each person's own supervisory belief, and we will examine how one's own supervisory belief fits along a control continuum. Finally, some propositions about supervisory belief and consequences for teacher development will be presented.

How do we reconcile the uncertainties of supervision, teaching, and instructional improvement? How do we know whether we are progressing in the desired direction? Unless we reflect on our own beliefs, there is little to steer us.

Sergiovanni and Starrat (1983, pp. 226–227) note the importance of understanding one's own supervisory beliefs:

> What is needed is some firm footing in principle. Some have called our often unexpressed constellation of principles a platform. Just as a political party is supposed to base its decisions and actions on a party platform upon which it seeks election, so, too, supervisory personnel need a platform upon which, and in the light of which, they can carry on their work. With a clearly defined platform, they can begin to take a position relative to edu ...onal practices, looking beyond the surface behavior to probe for the real consequences of a variety of school practices.

Knowing oneself as a supervisor is necessary before considering alternative practices and procedures. To move from a platform, we must first know where we are standing. Let's look at the human decisions that a supervisor must make about school improvement, teaching effectiveness, and one's purpose in working with teachers.

The Coast of Britain

Correct answers to questions about even physical matters are human decisions. Answers about social and educative matters are even more clearly human judgments (see Glickman 1987b). An example from geometry is illustrative. To the question, "How long is the coast of Britain?" the geometer Benoit Mandelbrot answered that the coast has no real length apart from human judgment (Hardison 1986). If one uses a measurement scale of 100 miles to an inch to draw the British coastline, that coastline has large bays and capes. If one uses a scale of 10 miles to an inch, then new inlets and promontories appear. The coast becomes longer or shorter, depending on the scale used. Furthermore, what happens when measurement of the coast begins when the tide is coming in? Each incoming wave reduces the coast, and each outgoing wave lengthens the coast. Therefore, how does one find the length of the British coast? The question can be answered only by agreeing on the purpose of the measurement, the perspective and the unit of measurement to be used, and the particular time at which the measurement is to be made. The length of the coast is a mathematical fiction created so that humans can find a representation that will accomplish their purpose.

Effective and Good Schools: The Same?

In discussing questions about supervision, teaching, and school improvement, as in measuring the coast of Britain, there is no certainty about how to arrive at an answer. The issue of effective schools highlights the human values that drive school decisions and actions (Glickman 1987a).

Many of the clarion calls for school reform cite the findings from recent research on effective teaching and effective schools as examples of how schools and classrooms should change. The reformers tell us that the goal of all schools should be effectiveness—as measured by such factors as students' scores on tests of basic skills, their attendance rates, and their performance on the Scholastic Aptitude Test (SAT). Furthermore, we ought to narrow the academic focus of the curriculum, test students more frequently, raise standards for promotion, and have teachers state specific, measurable objectives and follow a prescribed instructional approach that involves reviewing, explaining, demonstrating, guiding practice, checking for understanding, and summarizing. The findings of the recent research on effective teaching and effective schools are treated as scientific laws that apply to *all* teachers and *all* schools.

The findings of the research on effective teaching and effective schools are too often equated with what is desirable or good. By failing to distinguish between *effectiveness* and *goodness*, we avoid two central questions in education. The first question with which schools and school systems must deal is, "What is good?" Only after that question has been answered should we deal with the second question: "How do we become effective?" The current fascination with findings from the research on effectiveness has blinded schools and school systems to the more basic question of goodness.

Do higher SAT scores justify labeling a school "good," if the price for those higher scores has been an increase in the dropout rate? Are higher scores in reading and mathematics "good" if students gain them at the expense of time spent in studying science, social studies, art, or music? Is an average gain of eight points on reading test scores worth the increased allocation of time and resources to direct instruction in reading? Is that gain more desirable than maintaining current achievement levels in reading but devoting a greater proportion of class time to a whole-language approach that emphasizes creative writing or critical thinking? The research on effective schools and effective teaching does not answer these questions for us. The research is neutral: It does not choose our goals but simply tells us how to accomplish certain things (which may or may not be among our goals). Educators who care about the fate of all children must define *goodness* before they worry about *effectiveness;* as supervisors we must first clarify our own definitions.

Instructional Improvement and Effective Teaching

Let's continue this reflection on practice by taking an innocuous statement about supervision that virtually no one would take issue with: "The goal of supervision is to improve instruction." It sounds nice, until we ask for a definition of what type of instruction we wish to improve. Do we wish to improve instruction for short-term basic-skill acquisition, or do we wish to improve instruction for cooperative learning, for critical thinking, for inductive reasoning, for intrinsic learning, for individualized learning? Do we agree with a single definition of desired instruction? Those who have researched and theorized about effective instruction have uniformly disclaimed any single definition (Council of Professors of Instructional Supervision 1988).

Barak Rosenshine, the synthesizer of what has become commonly termed "effective instruction," says now that the body of research on instruction that results in short-term basic-skill acquisition should be more aptly referred to as "teachers' effects" research.

> My main point is that it is difficult to apply some of the major findings which we have learned from the teaching of skills to lessons which teach content. Some of these findings include checking for student understanding, providing for active student participation, providing for a high success rate, correcting errors, and providing for guided practice and independent practice. But such findings do not, and will not, transfer easily to the teaching of content, and we haven't faced this problem [1986a, p. 14].

Furthermore, Rosenshine has written that explicit teaching is "less relevant for teaching compositions, writing of term papers, reading comprehension, analyzing literature, historical trends . . . discussion of social issues, or for teaching entangled concepts. . . ." (1986a, p. 60). He has openly expressed the opinion that teaching specific skills and factual knowledge, in which explicit direct instruction is appropriate, accounts for 40 percent of teaching at most. Other instructional goals account for the other 60 percent. To muddy the waters even further, there are recent studies of elementary and secondary schools where teachers were trained and observed using "effective" teaching skills. It was found that their students had lower basic-skills achievement gains than students with teachers who had not been trained (Stalling 1987; Gersten, Gall, Grace, Erickson, and Stieber 1987). Therefore it is inappropriate to view explicit, direct instruction as the model for effective teaching, valid for the majority of instruction in a classroom. Yet many school districts and states use this very misapplication of research in evaluating teachers against a template of "effective" instruction.

Jere Brophy, the noted pioneer of process-product research, stated the distinction succinctly. "In short, information about teachers' effects [in fostering students' achievement of academic knowledge and skills] is not the same as information about teachers' effectiveness" (1986, p. 2). Lest this explanation be seen as a polemic against explicit or direct instruction, remember that the critics of its overgeneralization and prescriptive applications are the researchers who conducted the actual studies and developed the instructional theory.

Joyce, Showers, and Rolheiser-Bennett (1987), in their review of research on various instructional models that have been experimentally tested in schools and classrooms over the past ten years, found high effect sizes (magnitude of the potential of the instructional model to affect student learning by analyzing the statistical significance and standard deviation of gains between experimental and control groups). The highlights of their findings were as follows (p. 13):

- Cooperative learning approaches, representing social models of teaching, yield effect sizes from modest to high. The more complex the outcomes—higher-order thinking, problem solving, social skills and attitudes—the greater are the effects.

- Information-processing models, especially the use of advance organizers and mnemonics, yield modest to substantial effect sizes; and the effects are long-lasting.

- Synectics and nondirective teaching, exemplifying personal models of teaching, attain their model-relevant purposes and affect student achievement in such basic areas as recall of information.

- DISTAR, an example of the behavioral family of models, yields modest effect sizes in achievement and, further, influences aptitude to learn.

- When these models and strategies are combined, they have even greater potential for improving student learning.

Finally, let's return to the question: "How do we define the instruction that supervision intends to improve?" Should supervision emphasize one or two instructional models, should it emphasize all, should it emphasize a particular model first and then add others later? These are not easy questions. Regardless of what we decide as to the focus of supervision, as Mandelbrot reminds us, we are still making a human judgment with competing consequences.

My resolution is first to clarify what our goals as a school are (which will be reflected in the educational philosophy, curriculum, view of knowledge, and view of the learner) and clarify with individual teachers their particular classroom instructional goals. Next, the supervisor focuses on assisting teachers to make decisions as to the most appropriate instructional model to use for a particular learning goal and the most appropriate instructional models to emphasize in the context of the school's priorities. Then, as teachers become proficient in the use of a model of instruction, supervision assists them to identify further learning goals and the use of an increased repertoire of models (see Joyce and Weil 1986). With such a supervision emphasis, effective instruction is seen as the teachers' ability to use various ways of teaching according to a variety of learning goals and outcomes. As Porter and Brophy (1988) wrote,

> Effective teachers are clear about what they intend to accomplish through their instruction, and they keep these goals in mind both in designing the instruction and in communicating its purposes to the students. . . .
>
> Effective teachers create learning situations in which their students are expected not just to learn facts and solve given problems but to organize information in new ways and formulate problems for themselves. Such learning situations include creative writing opportunities in language arts, problem-formulation activities in mathematics, and independent projects in science, social studies, and literature. Such learning situations are intrinsically more demanding for both teachers and students than expository instruction followed by drill-and-practice exercises, but they must be included along with these more familiar learning situations if instruction is to address higher-level cognitive objectives in addition to lower-level ones. . . .
>
> Finally, effective teachers are thoughtful about their practice: They take time for reflection and self-evaluation, monitor their instruction to make sure that worthwhile content is being taught to all students, and accept responsibility for guiding student learning and behavior [1988, pp. 81–82].

Instructional improvement can be defined as helping teachers acquire teaching strategies that increase the capabilities of students to make wise decisions in varying contexts (with regard to peers, adults, academics, and life). Effective teaching consists therefore of those teaching decisions about actions, routines, and techniques that increase the decision-making capabilities of students.

Supervision Beliefs

Issues central to both supervision and instruction are those of control, knowledge, and ultimately philosophy. The central question behind educational goals and curriculum is the source of knowledge. Where does it come from? What does it look like? Who possesses it? Clearly, teachers appear to be able to detect a supervisor's philosophy. Let's look at four descriptions of central office supervisors as described by teachers (Glickman, in progress):

> The supervisor is viewed as a detached person who has little concern with the everyday problems of teachers in the field. His main concern is with "numbers." Are the teachers meeting their goals? As long as goals are being met and no individuals are

causing problems, not many teachers will hear from the supervisor.

(From a rehabilitation counselor)

The supervisor is viewed as exceptionally competent. His ability to get teachers to strive for excellence stems from their recognition that he accepts nothing less from himself and treats teachers as professionally able and willing to do their very best. He seeks the assistance of teachers and values their opinions and ideas.

(From a high school teacher)

The typical supervisor is a vivacious, interested person who periodically observes my teaching. She gives positive feedback. She takes the initiative to organize after school meetings within our school system of all elementary physical education teachers for us to share problems and ideas for solution. She has limited knowledge of our field and gives us much freedom.

(From an elementary physical education teacher)

The supervisor is good at politicking and P.R. words. She knows how to say the right things and knows whose a—— to kiss.

(From a high school teacher)

From the four descriptions of central office supervisors, underlying philosophies can be surmised. In description 1 the supervisor might be seen to have an *essentialist* philosophy, concerned with monitoring imposed results. In description 2 the supervisor has an *experimentalist* philosophy, concerned with shared participation. In description 3 the supervisor might be said to have an *existentialist* philosophy, concerned with human freedom. In description 4 the supervisor probably has no philosophy; *expediency* is the goal. You might think about or write a description that teachers would use to describe you as a supervisor. The next section deals with the development and implications of each philosophy.

Supervisory Platform
as Related to Educational Philosophy

Most supervisors, of course, are former teachers. As a result, their views about learning, the nature of the learner, knowledge, and the role of the teacher in the classroom influence their view of supervision. After all, supervision is in many respects analogous to teaching. Teachers wish to improve students' behavior, achievement, and attitudes. Supervisors similarly wish to improve teachers' behavior, achievement, and attitudes. A definition of *improvement* merges teaching and supervision. (Scratch the surface of a supervisor, and underneath one is likely to find a teacher.)

Many different philosophies exist. Some, such as idealism and realism, date back to ancient times. Others, such as pragmatism and behaviorism, have been developed within the last century. Even more recent has been the emergence of progressivism, reconstructionism, and existentialism. Philosophies are numerous and overlapping, and many have historical roots in each other. To unravel the major philosophical trends in education, one must decipher how philosophies differ from each other and then build overriding conceptual categories. Each conceptual category or superphilosophy is created by grouping various philosophies that have central agreement on the type and scope of education. In other words, there may be disagreement on the specific nature of knowledge, truth, and reality; yet they hang together as a general educational philosophy because they are in agreement on the purpose and treatment of education.[1]

With educational application in mind, divergent philosophies can be simplified and classified. Three major educational superphilosophies have direct relevance to supervision. These categories have been labeled, according to Johnson et al. (1973), as essentialism, progressivism, and existentialism. We would like to substitute for progressivism the more general term *experimentalism,* as described by Van Cleve Morris (1961).

Essentialism

Essentialism as a philosophy is derived from idealism and realism. *Idealism,* which dates back to Plato, espouses a belief in absolutes: The world we live in is merely a reflection of reality. Reality, truth, and standards of morality exist beyond our common ways of knowing. Only by training the mind do we glimpse the ultimates. Yet training the mind is not sufficient in itself; it only brings the mind nearer to grasping reality. Divine revelation, insight, and faith are the necessary elements for ultimate knowledge of what exists. Therefore idealism emphasizes truth and reality existing outside of people. It is absolute and unchanging. Realism, developed at the onset of the industrial age, places a similar emphasis on truth and reality being outside of people. Instead of humankind and the outer environment being separated from each other, realism maintains that humanity is part and parcel of that environment. The world is a preordained, mechanistic reality. All of existence operates according to scientific, cause-and-effect relations. It is as if existence is a clock that always runs according to mechanical principles governing levers, gauges, and gears. Humans have no existence apart from this clock; they are a part of the predetermined machine. Knowledge is learning how the machine works; truths are the scientific laws of regulation. Nothing exists outside the principles of nature. The purpose of education is to condition the mind to think in a natural, logical way. The mind should be trained to become consciously aware of the predetermined nature of the world.

Essentialism, created by William L. Bagley in 1938, encompassed the educational philosophies of idealism and realism. He took the ideas of knowledge being eternal and outside of humankind (idealism—absolutes; realism—natural laws) to form pedagogy. Essentialists emphasize that there is a body of timeless knowledge, both historical and contemporary, that is of value to the living.

Essentialism in terms of supervision emphasizes the supervisor as the person who teaches truths about teaching to teachers. Supervisors are those most knowledgeable about those absolute standards. Teachers are then handled mechanistically to systematize and feed content to students. As teachers digest these teaching truths, they move closer to being good teachers.

Experimentalism

As Western society became more industrialized, optimism and confidence in human ability to control nature emerged. The philosophy of pragmatism developed by Charles S. Pierce and William James emphasized what people can do to nature rather than what nature does to humankind. John Dewey, circa 1920, further expanded on the writings of James by putting the individual squarely in the context of society. Humans can both reform and be reformed by society. Dewey's philosophy is, of course, the well-known school of progressive thought. Reconstructionism is a further offshoot of both pragmatism and progressivism. Richard Pratte (1971) cites the pamphlet *Dare the Schools Build a New Social Order,* written by George S. Counts in 1932, as a guiding document for the then-radical notion that schools and students were the reformers of society.

Experimentalism emerges from the philosophies of pragmatism, progressivism, and reconstructionism. They hold in common a historical break from the more traditional philosophies of realism and idealism. The essentialist idea that knowledge, truth, and morality exist as absolute and outside of humans was rejected. The emerging faith in the scientific method, the ability of humans to create their own laws, principles, and machines, and the fact that such man-made inventions would work for them demanded an accompanying philosophy. Experimentalism provided that philosophy.

Reality was what worked. If a person could form a hypothesis, test it, and find it to work, then it was regarded as tentatively true. On repeated experimentation with the same results, it became real. Yet experimentalists would never claim an absolute truth. The human environment was believed to be constantly changing, so that what one can do and prove today may not be probable tomorrow. A new situation and a different approach may alter yesterday's reality. Experimentalists point to the historical evidence of Newton's law of gravity as a past truth that has given way to Einstein's theory of relativity; they believe that in time a new theory will replace Einstein's.

Morality is also viewed in relation to what works for humanity and human society. Morality is that behavior which promotes one's working with the group to achieve greater ends. To be wise is to understand how the environment (of things and people) affects oneself and how one might affect it. Whether action is moral or not is determined by the degree of progress that has been achieved by the group. The use of trial and error in a laboratory setting is the key to evaluating the outcome of action. Therefore experimentalists do not view knowledge as absolute or external to human capabilities. Rather, knowledge is a result of the interaction between the scientific person and the environment.

The educational application of experimentalist thinking to supervision is well documented in the writing of Dewey. Teachers (as students) need to learn what are the truths of their time, but they should not rest content with that parcel of knowledge. Supervisors view schools as laboratories for working with teachers to test old hypotheses and to try new ones. Supervisors work democratically with teachers to achieve collective ends that will help everyone. Supervisors are not solely conveyors of age-old wisdom, they are both the conveyors of the rudimentary knowledge of the time and the guiders of trial-and-error, exploratory learning.

Existentialism

Existentialism as a school of thought is derived from the rejection of the other philosophies encompassed in essentialism and experimentalism. As such, it is a large category for many diverse philosophers. They have in common a scorn for rational, empirical, and systematic thinking as the way of knowing reality. As previously mentioned, the essentialists believe in rational thinking to help elevate the mind to uncover the absolutes of the universe. Experimentalists believe in rational, scientific thinking to explore and frame the relevant knowledge of the times. However, the existentialists believe that this same rational thinking restricts humans from discovering existence and therefore keeps them ignorant.

This philosophy has roots in the writings of Sören Kierkegaard in the mid-nineteenth century. It has been popularized in drama and literature by such exponents as Albert Camus and Jean-Paul Sartre. The current popular cults of transcendental thinking, meditation, and introspection (knowing oneself) have a kinship with existentialism. The basic tenet of the philosophy is that the individual is the source of all reality. All that exists in the world is the meaning the individual puts on his or her own experiences. There is no absolute knowledge, no mechanical working of the universe, and no preordained logic. To believe in such inventions is merely the narrow, incorrect way humans interpret their own experiences.

Beyond the individual exists only chaos. The only reality that exists is one's own existence. Only by looking within oneself can one discern the truth of the outside disorder. Humanity is paramount. Human dignity and worth are of greatest importance; they are the source and dispenser of all truth. With this realization one acquires a profound respect for all human beings and their uniqueness. Human relations become very important, affirming individual worth and protecting the individual's right to discover his or her own truth. Morality is the process of knowing oneself and allowing others the freedom to do likewise. Faith, intuition, mysticism, imagery, and transcendental experiences are all acceptable ways of discovery. Humans are totally free, not shaped by others or restricted by the flux of the times. They hold within themselves the capacity to form their own destiny.

This philosophy of education, applied to supervision, means a full commitment to individual teacher choice. The supervisor provides an environment that enables the teacher to explore his or her own physical and mental capabilities. Teachers must learn for themselves. The supervisor does not dispense information and shies away from intrusively guiding a teacher. Supervisors help when needed, protect the rights of others to self-discovery, and encounter the teacher as a person of full importance.

Checking Your Own Educational Philosophy and Supervisory Beliefs

Here are two instruments to test whether or not your supervisory beliefs have a relationship to your educational philosophy. The first, developed by Patricia D. Jersin and entitled "What is Your Educational Philosophy?" is found in Appendix A. The second, developed by Glickman and Tamashiro (1981) and entitled "Determining One's Beliefs Regarding Teacher Supervision," helps the reader look at supervisor practices in school settings as reflective of three predominate systems. Those belief systems correspond to the philosophies of essentialism, experimentalism, and existentialism, and are labeled *directive* supervision, *collaborative* supervision, and *nondirective* supervision. Glickman and Tamashiro (1980) wrote:

> *Directive Supervision* is an approach based on the belief that teaching consists of technical skills with known standards and competencies for all teachers to be effective. The supervisor's role is to inform, direct, model, and assess those competencies.
>
> *Collaborative Supervision* is based on the belief that teaching is primarily problem solving, whereby two or more persons jointly pose hypotheses to a problem, experiment, and implement those teaching strategies that appear to be most relevant in their own surroundings. The supervisor's role is to guide the problem-solving process, be an active member of the interaction, and keep the teacher(s) focused on their common problems.
>
> *Non-Directive Supervision* has as its premise that learning is primarily a private experience in which individuals must come up with their own solutions to improving the classroom experience for students. The supervisor's role is to listen, be nonjudgmental, and provide self-awareness and clarification experiences for teachers [p. 76].

The inventory is as follows.

The Supervisory Beliefs Inventory

This inventory is designed for supervisors to assess their own beliefs about teacher supervision and staff development. The inventory assumes that supervisors believe and act according to all three of the orientations of supervision, but that one usually dominates. The inventory is designed to be self-administered and self-scored. Supervisors are asked to choose one of two options. A scoring key follows.

Instructions: Circle either A or B for each item. You may not completely agree with either choice, but choose the one that is closest to how you feel.

1. A. Supervisors should give teachers a large degree of autonomy and initiative within broadly defined limits.
   B. Supervisors should give teachers directions about methods that will help them improve their teaching.

2. A. It is important for teachers to set their own goals and objectives for professional growth.
   B. It is important for supervisors to help teachers reconcile their personalities and teaching styles with the philosophy and direction of the school.

3. A. Teachers are likely to feel uncomfortable and anxious if the objectives on which they will be evaluated are not clearly defined by the supervisor.
   B. Evaluations of teachers are meaningless if teachers are not able to define with their supervisors the objectives for evaluation.

4. A. An open, trusting, warm, and personal relationship with teachers is the most important ingredient in supervising teachers.
   B. A supervisor who is too intimate with teachers risks being less effective and less respected than a supervisor who keeps a certain degree of professional distance from teachers.

5. A. My role during supervisory conferences is to make the interaction positive, to share realistic information, and to help teachers plan their own solutions to problems.
   B. The methods and strategies I use with teachers in a conference are aimed at our reaching agreement over the needs for future improvement.

6. In the initial phase of working with a teacher:
   A. I develop objectives with each teacher that will help accomplish school goals.
   B. I try to identify the talents and goals of individual teachers so they can work on their own improvement.

7. When several teachers have a similar classroom problem, I prefer to:
   A. Have the teachers form an ad hoc group and help them work together to solve the problem.
   B. Help teachers on an individual basis find their strengths, abilities, and resources so that each one finds his or her own solution to the problem.

8. The most important clue that an in-service workshop is needed occurs when:
   A. The supervisor perceives that several teachers lack knowledge or skill in a specific area, which is resulting in low morale, undue stress, and less effective teaching.
   B. Several teachers perceive the need to strengthen their abilities in the same instructional area.

9. A. The supervisory staff should decide the objectives of an in-service workshop since they have a broad perspective on the teachers' abilities and the school's needs.
   B. Teachers and supervisory staff should reach consensus about the objectives of an in-service workshop before the workshop is held.

10. A. Teachers who feel they are growing personally will be more effective than teachers who are not experiencing personal growth.
    B. The knowledge and ability of teaching strategies and methods that have been proved over the years should be taught and practiced by all teachers to be effective in their classrooms.

11. When I perceive that a teacher might be scolding a student unnecessarily:
    A. I explain, during a conference with the teacher, why the scolding was excessive.
    B. I ask the teacher about the incident, but do not interject my judgments.

12. A. One effective way to improve teacher performance is to formulate clear behavioral objectives and create meaningful incentives for achieving them.
    B. Behavioral objectives are rewarding and helpful to some teachers but stifling to others; some teachers benefit from behavioral objectives in some situations but not in others.

13. During a preobservation conference:
    A. I suggest to the teacher what I could observe, but I let the teacher make the final decision about the objectives and methods of observation.
    B. The teacher and I mutually decide the objectives and methods of observation.

14. A. Improvement occurs very slowly if teachers are left on their own; but when a group of teachers work together on a specific problem, they learn rapidly and their morale remains high.
    B. Group activities may be enjoyable, but I find that individual, open discussion with a teacher about a problem and its possible solutions leads to more sustained results.

15. When an in-service or staff development workshop is scheduled:
    A. All teachers who participated in the decision to hold the workshop should be expected to attend it.
    B. Teachers, regardless of their role in forming a workshop, should be able to decide if the workshop is relevant to

their personal or professional growth and, if not, should not be expected to attend.

Scoring Key

Step 1. Circle your answer from Part II of the inventory in the following columns:

Column I	Column II	Column III
1B	1A	
	2B	2A
3A	3B	
4B		4A
	5B	5A
6A		6B
	7A	7B
8A		8B
9A	9B	
10B		10A
11A		11B
12A	12B	
	13B	13A
14B	14A	
	15A	15B

Step 2. Tally the number of circled items in each column and multiply by 6.7.

2.1 Total response in column I _____ × 6.7 = ____
2.2 Total response in column II _____ × 6.7 = ____
2.3 Total response in column III _____ × 6.7 = ____

Step 3. Interpretation: The product you obtained in step 2.1 is an approximate percentage of how often you take a directive approach to supervision, rather than either of the other two approaches. The product you obtained in step 2.2 is an approximate percentage of how often you take a collaborative approach, and that in step 2.3 an approximate percentage of how often you take a nondirective approach.

From Carl D. Glickman, *Developmental Supervision: Alternative Approaches for Helping Teachers Improve Instruction,* pp. 13–15. Reprinted by permission of the Association for Supervision and Curriculum Development, Alexandria, Va. Copyright © 1981 by the Association for Supervision and Curriculum Development. All rights reserved. This instrument has been field-tested six times with ninety supervisors and supervisor trainees. Response between the options indicated "good" item discrimination. The items were also critiqued by teachers, curriculum specialists, and college professors in education for theoretical consistency. Dr. Roy T. Tamashiro of Webster College, St. Louis, Missouri, developed this inventory with me.

What Does Your Belief Mean
in Terms of Teacher Control?

Beliefs about supervision and educational philosophy can be thought of in terms of control (see Table 5-1). An essentialist philosophy is premised on the supervisor being the expert on instruction and therefore having major control over the teacher. A situation of high supervisor control and low teacher control is labeled *directive supervision*. An experimentalist philosophy is premised on the supervisor and teachers being equal partners in instructional improvement; equal supervisor and teacher control is labeled *collaborative supervision*. Existentialist philosophy is premised on teachers discovering their own capacities for instructional improvement. Low supervisor control and high teacher control is labeled *nondirective supervision*. As we clarify our own educational philosophy and supervisory beliefs, we rarely find a pure ideological position. Therefore, Sergiovanni's idea of a supervisory platform becomes helpful. What combination of various philosophies and beliefs do we consider important? Perhaps our beliefs are mainly essentialist and directive yet contain parts of experimentalism and collaboration; or perhaps we have another combination of beliefs. A particular platform is not right or wrong; rather, it is an assessment of the bits and pieces we use to create the floor we stand on.

Developmental Supervision

My own supervisory platform is based on the premise that human development is the aim of education. Therefore, supervision should be *eclectic* in practice, directed toward the goal of nondirective, existentialist supervision. My goal as a supervisor is even-

Table 5-1 Relationship of philosophy, control, and supervisory belief

Educational Philosophy	Control	Supervisory Belief
Essentialism	Supervisor high, teacher low	Directive
Experimentalism	Supervisor equal, teacher equal supervisor low	Collaborative
Existentialism	Supervisor low, teacher high	Nondirective

tually to return control to the teaching faculty to decide on collective, instructional improvements. Such an ideal cannot be achieved suddenly, if at all. Instead, the supervisor at times might use behaviors that come from an essentialist-directive belief structure as a point of entry, or might use behaviors that come from an experimentalist-collaborative belief structure as another point of entry. Regardless of the entry point, the supervisor should always strive to shift control to teachers. The supervisor may never allow total autonomy, but moving in that direction is worth the effort. My platform is, therefore, one of collaborative experimentalism striving toward nondirective existentialism.

Here are some examples of why I believe a purposeful, developmental supervision should be employed for the improvement of instruction. Research on reading effectiveness shows the merits of different supervisory orientations when matched to the particular characteristics of the teaching staff. Reading effectiveness occurred in previously failure-prone schools and classrooms when teachers with little experience, competency, or desire to improve their instruction were monitored, evaluated, and directed by the supervisor (principal) to use a new, systematic reading program (Vanezky 1982). The results speak clearly for a directive orientation when the teaching force is unskilled and unmotivated. In still other schools, which had had several years of successful reading improvement, researchers noted frequent group problem-solving meetings and mutual adaptation of the curriculum (Humphries 1981; McLaughlin and Marsh 1978). For a staff that has successfully developed competency and motivation, a collaborative approach to future improvement appears to be in order. Finally, a staff with extensive background, competency, and motivation, who know how to work both together and alone, should find ways to improve student performance informally and independently. A nondirective orientation is most appropriate here.

Summary, Conclusion, and Propositions

We have examined the relationship of educational philosophy to supervisory belief and practice. The reader was asked to define what is meant by good and effective schools and teaching effectiveness and then to determine his or her own supervisory platform by responding to two instruments. I revealed my platform of supervision as collaborative experimentalism striving toward nondirective existentialism within a developmental framework. I believe teachers will become collectively purposeful as they gain greater control over decisions for instructional improvement.

The following propositions about supervision that will enhance collective teacher actions are now possible:

- Proposition 1: *Supervisors should use a variety of practices that emanate from various philosophies and belief structures with developmental directionality in mind.* Directive, collaborative, and nondirective supervisory approaches are all valid as long as they aim to increase teacher self-control.

- Proposition 2: *As supervisors gradually increase teacher choice and control over instructional improvement, teachers will become more abstract and committed to improvement, and a sense of ethos or of a cause beyond oneself will emerge.*

Allowing for gradual choice will increase teacher abstraction and autonomy and lead to more altruistic, collective faculty action.

EXERCISES

Academic

1. Write your own educational platform. Your platform need not exclusively reflect any of the three major philosophies discussed in the chapter.

2. Design a chart comparing the three major philosophies discussed in the chapter in terms of what each philosophy assumes about:

   a. Human nature.

   b. What constitutes reality.

   c. The human relationship to the environment.

   d. The human relationship to fellow humans.

   Design a second chart comparing *implications* of the three philosophies in terms of:

   a. How people best learn.

   b. The proper goal(s) of education.

   c. The appropriate role of the teacher.

   d. The appropriate role of the educational supervisor.

3. Prepare a report in which you identify one of the three major philosophies discussed in the chapter (essentialism, experimentalism, existentialism) as the one most clearly reflected in U.S. public education today. Provide a rationale for your choice.

4. Read at least one chapter from another text on educational supervision. Prepare a report identifying one of three major philosophies discussed in the text (essentialism, experimentalism, existentialism) as having the greatest influence on the author. Include quotations from the text that support your position.

5. Write a reaction to the author's supervisory platform. Include your perceptions of problems that might be encountered by a supervisor attempting to make the author's platform a reality within a public school setting.

Field

1. Ask five teachers from different school districts for single-paragraph descriptions of central office supervisors. Assuming each teacher has given an accurate description of at least one central office supervisor, classify each described supervisor according to his or her probable philosophy (experimentalist, essentialist, existentialist, or other). Summarize your study and conclusions in writing. (Supervisors and school districts should remain anonymous in the teacher descriptions; responding teachers should remain anonymous in your written summary.)

2. Ask five adults to list improvements that should be made in U.S. public education. On the basis of the lists, attempt to relate each respondent to one of the major philosophies described in the chapter (essentialism, experimentalism, existentialism). Summarize your study and conclusions in writing.

3. Ask five teachers each to write one or two paragraphs on "What Makes an Effective Supervisor." On the basis of the teachers' responses, predict which supervisory approach each teacher would prefer during classroom supervision or staff development activities.

4. Ask five students to write one or two paragraphs on "What Makes a Good School?" Attempt to relate each student response to one of the three major philosophies described in the chapter (essentialism, experimentalism, existentialism). Write a report reviewing the students' responses and showing whether and/or how each response relates to one of the three philosophies.

5. Visit or recall the organization and climate of a selected school. On the basis of your observations or recollections, which of the three major philosophies described in the chapter (essentialism, experimentalism, existentialism) does the school's organization and climate most clearly reflect? Prepare a report discussing the

school's organizational and climate characteristics and supporting your philosophical classification of the school.

Developmental

1. Begin an in-depth study of one of the philosophies described in Chapter 5. As you carry out the study, continue to relate your inquiry to education and educational supervision.
2. Plan to retake the Supervisory Beliefs Inventory after finishing this book in order to detect and interpret any changes in your attitude toward supervision.
3. Begin a review of the works of popular authors who present what they consider successful approaches to management, leadership, or interpersonal communication. For each author, consider whether his or her recommended approach or system most nearly resembles a directive, collaborative, nondirective, or eclectic approach. Make a personal evaluation of each author's proposals.

NOTE

1. The descriptions of philosophy in Chapter 5 are taken from C.D. Glickman and J.P. Esposito, *Leadership Guide for Elementary School Improvement: Procedures for Assessment and Change* (Boston: Allyn and Bacon, 1979), p. 20.

REFERENCES

Brophy, J. 1986. Synthesizing the results of research linking teacher behavior to student achievement. Paper presented at the annual meeting of the American Educational Research Association, San Francisco, April.

Council of Professors of Instructional Supervision. 1988. Resolution on effective teaching. Annual meeting, San Antonio, Texas, November.

Gersten, R., Gall, M., Grace, D., Erickson, D., and Stieber, S. 1987. The differential effects of teacher behavior on high-ability and low-ability students in algebra classes. Paper presented at annual meeting of the American Educational Research Association, Washington, D.C., April 7.

Glickman, C.D. 1987a. Good and/or effective schools: What do we want? *Kappan 68*(8), 622–624.

————. 1987b. Unlocking school reform: Uncertainty as a condition of professionalism. *Kappan 69*(2):120–122.

————. In progress. An informal study of teachers' perceptions of typical central office supervisors. (Descriptions collected in 1983.)

Glickman, C.D., and Tamashiro, R.T. 1980. Determining one's beliefs regarding teacher supervision. *Bulletin 64*(440):74–81.

————. 1981. The supervisory beliefs inventory. In C.D. Glickman, *Developmental supervision: Alternative practices for helping teachers to improve instruction.* Alexandria, Va.: Association for Supervision and Curriculum Development, pp. 12–16.

Hardison, O.B., Jr. 1986. A tree, a streamlined fish, and a self-squared dragon: Science as a form of culture. *Georgia Review* (Summer):394–403.

Humphries, J.D. 1981. Factors affecting the impact of curriculum innovation on classroom practice. Unpublished Ph.D. dissertation, University of Georgia.

Johnson, J.A., Collins, H.W., Dupuis, V.L., and Johansen, J.H. 1973. *Foundations of American education.* Boston: Allyn and Bacon.

Joyce, B., Showers, B., and Rolheiser-Bennett, C. 1987. Staff development and student learning: A synthesis of research on models of teaching. *Educational Leadership 45*(2):11–23.

Joyce, B., and Weil, M. 1986. *Models of teaching.* Englewood Cliffs, N.J.: Prentice-Hall.

McLaughlin, M.W., and Marsh, D.D. 1978. Staff development and school change. *Teacher College Record 80*(1):69–74.

Morris, V.C. 1961. *Philosophy and the American school.* Boston: Houghton Mifflin.

Porter, A.C., and Brophy, J. 1988. Synthesis of research on good teaching: Insights from the work of the Institute for Research on Teaching. *Educational Leadership 45*(8):74–85.

Pratte, R. 1971. *Contemporary theories of education.* Scranton, Pa.: T.Y. Crowell.

Rosenshine, B.V. 1986a. Unsolved issues in teaching content: A critique of a lesson on Federalist Paper No. 10. Paper presented at the annual meeting of the American Educational Research Association, San Francisco, April.

————. 1986b. A synthesis of research on explicit teaching. *Educational Leadership* 43(7):60–69.

Sergiovanni, T.J., and Starrat, R.J. 1983. *Supervision: Human perspectives*, 3rd ed. New York: McGraw-Hill, pp. 226–227.

Stalling, J. 1987. For whom and how long is the Hunter-based model appropriate? Response to Robbins and Wolfe. *Educational Leadership* 44(5):62–63.

Vanezky, R.L. 1982. Effective schools for reading instructions. Address to the California (Calfee) Reading Project, Stanford University, January 22.

PART II CONCLUSION

Part II reviewed the prerequisite knowledge for supervision as the developmental function for effective schools. You have read about "The Exception: What Schools Can Be" (Chapter 2); "The Norm: Why Schools Are As They Are" (Chapter 3); "Contrasting Optimal Adult Development with Actual Teacher Development: Some Clues for Supervisory Practices" (Chapter 4); and "Supervisory Beliefs and Reflections on Practice" (Chapter 5). A number of propositions were constructed from each chapter to set the framework for supervision being viewed as a developmental function. Those propositions are placed together as general, guiding principles to review.

What Can Be

- Proposition 1: Supervision can strengthen teachers' belief in a cause beyond oneself.
- Proposition 2: Supervision can promote teachers' sense of efficacy.
- Proposition 3: Supervision can make teachers aware of how they complement each other in striving for common goals.
- Proposition 4: Supervision can stimulate teachers to appraise, reflect, and adapt their instruction.
- Proposition 5: Supervision can challenge teachers toward more varied, abstract thought.

What Is

- Proposition 1: Supervision cannot rely on the existing work environment of schools to stimulate instructional improvement.
- Proposition 2: Supervisors cannot assume that teachers are reflective, autonomous, and responsible for their own development.
- Proposition 3: Supervisors will have to redefine their responsibilities—from controllers of teachers' instruction to involvers of teachers in decisions about school instruction.

Figure II-1 Supervision for successful schools

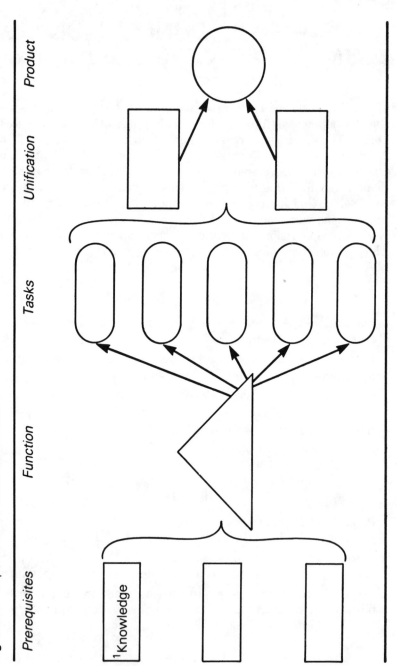

Prerequisites   Function   Tasks   Unification   Product

[1]Knowledge

Implications of Contrasting Adult and Teacher Development

- Proposition 1: Supervision, to be effective, must be a function that responds to the developmental stage of teachers.
- Proposition 2: Supervision, to be effective, must be a function that responds to the adult life transitions of teachers.

Supervisory Belief to Move from What Is to What Can Be

- Proposition 1: Supervisors should use a variety of practices that emanate from various philosophical and belief structures, with a developmental directionality in mind.
- Proposition 2: As supervisors gradually increase teacher choice and control over instructional improvement, teachers will become more abstract and committed to improvement, and a sense of ethos or cause beyond oneself will emerge.

At the end of each of the book's remaining parts, you will be reminded of the organization of effective supervision as a developmental function. See Figure II-1, in which the knowledge prerequisite has been filled in but many geometric figures remain empty. The next section will deal with the prerequisite of interpersonal skills.

PART III
INTERPERSONAL SKILLS

Introduction

The organization of this book was outlined in Figure 1-1 in Chapter 1. The prerequisites for supervision as a developmental function are knowledge, interpersonal skills, and technical skills. Part II examined the critical knowledge base. Part III will describe interpersonal skills. Chapter 6 will introduce the supervisory behavior continuum, Chapter 7 will detail the use of nondirective behaviors, Chapter 8 will detail the use of collaborative behaviors, and Chapter 9 will detail the use of directive behaviors. Chapter 10 will discuss application of alternative interpersonal skills according to characteristics of individuals and groups of teachers.

Knowledge of what needs to be done for teacher growth and school success is the base of a triangle for supervisory action (see Figure III-1). Knowledge needs to be accompanied by interpersonal skills for communicating with teachers and technical skills for planning, assessing, observing, and evaluating instructional improvement. We will now turn to the interpersonal skill dimension.

Figure III-1 Prerequisite dimensions for a supervisor

Chapter 6

Supervisory Behavior Continuum: Know Thyself

This chapter looks at the range of interpersonal behaviors available to a supervisor who is working with individuals and groups of teachers. It will assess how supervisors typically behave with staff in school settings and then determine other behaviors that might be used skillfully and effectively. Later chapters will provide training in each of three clusters of interpersonal skills.

What are the categories of behaviors? After many years of collecting supervisors' observations in meetings with individuals and groups of teachers for purposes of making classroom or school decisions, broad categories of supervisory behaviors have been derived (Glickman 1981; Wolfgang and Glickman 1980). These categories encompass almost all observed supervisor behaviors that are deemed purposeful. A *purposeful* behavior is defined as one that contributes to the decision being made at the conference or meeting. The derived categories of supervisory behaviors are listening, clarifying, encouraging, reflecting, presenting, problem solving, negotiating, directing, standardizing, and reinforcing. Definitions of each category are as follows:

Listening: The supervisor sits and looks at the speaker and nods his or her head to show understanding. Gutteral utterances ("uh-huh," "umm . . .") also indicate listening.

Clarifying: The supervisor asks questions and statements to clarify the speaker's point of view: "Do you mean that?" "Would you explain this further?" "I'm confused about this." "I lost you on . . . ."

Encouraging: The supervisor provides acknowledgment responses that help the speaker continue to explain his or her positions: "Yes, I'm following you." "Continue on." "Ah, I see what you're saying; tell me more."

Reflecting: The supervisor summarizes and paraphrases the speaker's message for verification of accuracy: "I understand that you mean . . . ." "So, the issue is . . . ." "I hear you saying . . . ."

Presenting: The supervisor gives his or her own ideas about the issue being discussed: "This is how I see it." "What can be done is . . . ." "I'd like us to consider . . . ." "I believe that . . . ."

Problem Solving: The supervisor takes the initiative, usually after a preliminary discussion of the issue or problem, in pressing all those involved to generate a list of possible solutions. This is usually done through statements such as "Let's stop and each write down what can be done." "What ideas do we have to solve this problem?" "Let's think of all possible actions we can take."

Negotiating: The supervisor moves the discussion from possible to probable solutions by discussing the consequences of each proposed action, exploring conflict or priorities, and narrowing down choices with questions such as "Where do we agree?" "How can we change that action to be acceptable to all?" "Can we find a compromise that will give each of us part of what we want?"

Directing: The supervisor tells the participant(s) either what the choices are: "As I see it, these are the alternatives: You could do A . . . , B . . . , or C . . . . Which of these make the most sense to you and which will you use?" *Or* the supervisor tells the participants what is to be done: "I've decided that we will do . . . ." "I want you to do . . . ." "The policy will be . . . ." "This is how it is going to be." "We will then proceed as follows."

Standardizing: The supervisor sets the expected criteria and time for the decision to be implemented. Target objectives are set. Expectations are conveyed with words, such as: "By next Monday, we want to see . . . ." "Report back to me on this change by . . . ." "Have the first two activities carried out by . . . ." "I want an improvement of 25 percent involvement by the next meeting." "We have agreed that all tasks will be done before the next observation."

Reinforcing: The supervisor strengthens the directive and the criteria to be met by telling of possible consequences. Possible consequences can be positive, in the form of praise: "I know you can do it!" "I have confidence in your ability!" "I want to show others what you've done!" Consequences also can be negative: "If it's not done on time, we'll lose the support of . . . ." or "It must be understood that failure to get this done on time will result in . . . ."

Figure 6-1 The supervisory behavior continuum

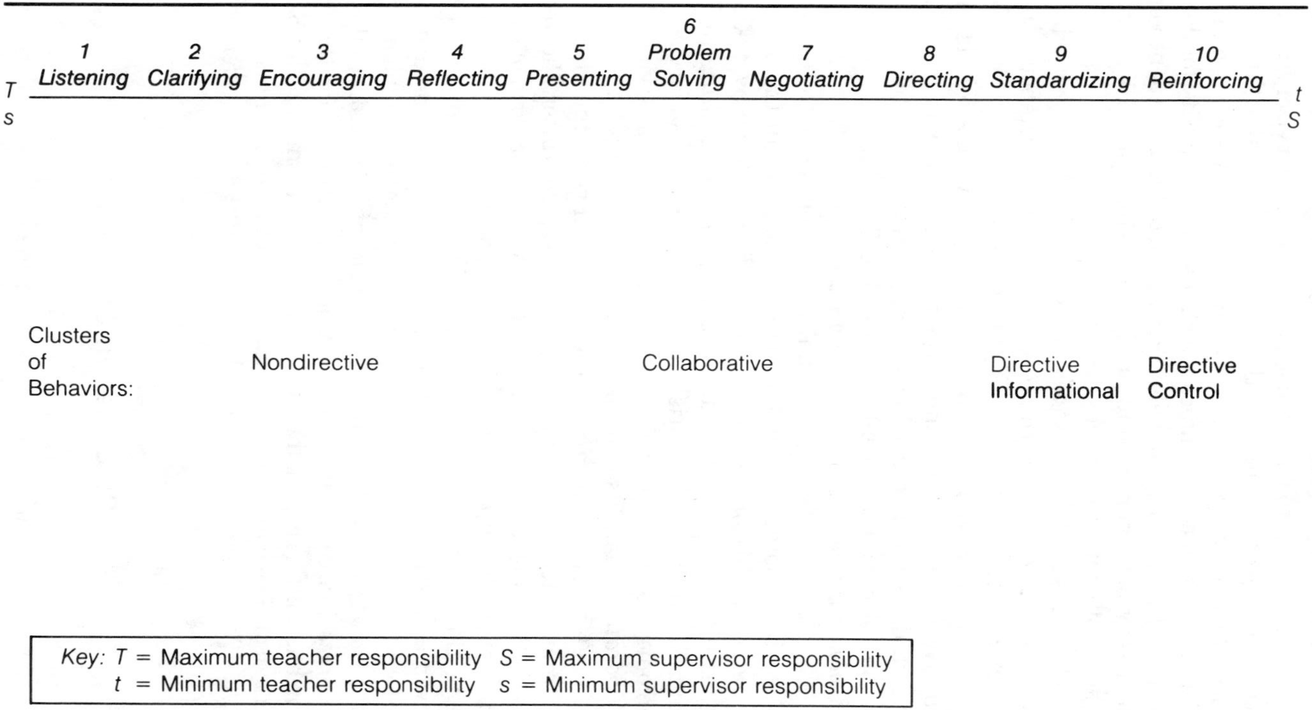

T
s

1	2	3	4	5	6	7	8	9	10
Listening	Clarifying	Encouraging	Reflecting	Presenting	Problem Solving	Negotiating	Directing	Standardizing	Reinforcing

t
S

Clusters
of
Behaviors:

Nondirective

Collaborative

Directive
Informational

Directive
Control

Key: T = Maximum teacher responsibility   S = Maximum supervisor responsibility
     t = Minimum teacher responsibility   s = Minimum supervisor responsibility

The foregoing categories of interpersonal supervisory behavior move participants toward a decision. Some supervisory behaviors place more responsibility on the teacher(s) to make the decision, others place more responsibility on the supervisor to make the decision, and still others indicate a shared responsibility for decision making. The categories of behaviors are listed in a sequence on the supervisory behavior continuum (Figure 6-1 on page 107) to reflect the scale of control or power.

When a supervisor *listens* to the teacher, *clarifies* what the teacher says, *encourages* the teacher to speak more about the concern, and *reflects* by verifying the teacher's perceptions, then clearly it is the teacher who is in control. The supervisor's role is that of an active prober or sounding board for the teacher to make his or her own decision. The teacher has high control and the supervisor low control over the actual decision (big *T*, small *s*). This is seen as a *nondirective interpersonal approach*.

When a supervisor uses nondirective behaviors to understand the teacher's point of view but then participates in the discussion by *presenting* his or her own ideas, *problem solving* by asking all parties to propose possible actions, and then *negotiating* to find a common course of action satisfactory to teacher and supervisor, then the control over the decision is shared by all. This is viewed as a *collaborative interpersonal approach*.

When a supervisor *directs* the teacher in what the alternatives are from which the teacher might choose, and after the teacher selects, the supervisor *standardizes* the time and criteria of expected result, then the supervisor is the major source of information, providing the teacher with restricted choice (small *t*, big *S*). This is viewed as a *directive informational, interpersonal approach*.

Finally, when a supervisor *directs* the teacher in what will be done, *standardizes* the time and criteria of expected results, and *reinforces* the consequences of action or inaction, then the supervisor has taken responsibility for the decision (small *t*, big *S*). The supervisor is clearly determining the actions for the teacher to follow. These behaviors are called a *directive control interpersonal approach*.

Outcomes of Conference

Another way of clarifying the distinctions among supervisory approaches is by looking at the outcomes of the conference and determining who controls the final decision for instructional improvement.

Approach	Outcome
Nondirective	Teacher self-plan
Collaborative	Mutual plan
Directive informational	Supervisor-suggested plan
Directive control	Supervisor-assigned plan

In the nondirective approach the supervisor facilitates the teacher's thinking in developing a self-plan. In the collaborative approach both supervisor and teacher share information and possible practices as equals in arriving at a mutual plan. In the directive informational approach the supervisor provides the focus and the parameters of possible actions, and the teacher is asked to choose within the supervisor's suggestions. In the directive control approach the supervisor tells the teacher what is to be done. Nondirective provides maximum teacher choice; collaborative, mutual choice; directive informational, selected choice; and directive control, no choice in the outcome of the conference.

Your Own Interpersonal Behavior Approach

Chapter 5 dealt with supervisory beliefs and practicing beliefs. Now let's step back and watch ourselves at work. First watch how we act with individual teachers and then with groups. Read the Supervisory Interpersonal Behavior Questionnaire for Working with Individuals, and select the approach you most often take.

Supervisory Interpersonal Behavior Questionnaire for Working with Individuals: A Scenario*

The school day has just ended for students at Whichway School. Just as the teacher sits down at the desk, you the supervisor appear at the door and the teacher invites you in. "How is everything going?" you ask. Looking at the large stack of papers to correct, the teacher predicts a number of them will reflect that the students did not understand the work. "It's very frustrating working with this class. They have such a wide range of ability!" Then the teacher mentions another source of frustration: "Some of the students are discipline problems and their behavior results in class disruption."

After further discussion, the teacher and you agree that you

---

will come into the classroom to observe what is going on, followed by a conference to discuss the classroom visit.

A few days later, after you have observed in the classroom and carefully analyzed the collected information, you begin to plan for the conference. You consider a number of approaches to use in the conference to help the teacher.

Approach A. Present what you saw in the classroom and ask for the teacher's perceptions. Listen to each other's responses. After clarifying the problem, each of you can propose ideas. Finally, you will agree on what is to be done in the classroom. You will mutually identify an objective and agree to an action plan that both of you will work together to carry out. The plan is for both of you to make.

Approach B. Listen to the teacher discuss what is going on in the classroom. If asked, offer your perceptions regarding what you observed. Encourage the teacher to analyze the problem further, and ask questions to make sure the teacher is clear about his or her view of the problem. If the teacher requests your views on how to proceed, respond, but only if asked. Finally, ask the teacher to determine and detail the actions he or she will take and find out if you might be of further help. The plan is the teacher's to make.

Approach C. Share your observations with the teacher and tell the teacher what you believe to be the major focus for improvement. Ask the teacher for input into your observations and interpretations. Based on your own experience and knowledge, carefully delineate what you believe are alternative actions to improve the classroom and ask the teacher to consider and select from these options. The plan to follow is chosen by the teacher from the supervisor's suggestions.

Approach D. Present your beliefs about the situation and ask the teacher to confirm or revise the interpretation. After identifying the problem, offer directions to the teacher on what should be done and how to proceed. You can go into the classroom to demonstrate what you are telling the teacher to do, or tell the teacher to observe another teacher who does well in this particular area. Praise and reward the teacher for following the given assignment. The plan is for you the supervisor to make.

Response. Most often, I use Approach _____.

Interpretation.

Approach A: A cluster of *collaborative behaviors* in which the supervisor and teacher share the decision making about future improvement.

Approach B: A cluster of *nondirective behaviors* in which the supervisor helps the teacher formulate his or her own decision about future improvement.

Approach C: A cluster of directive informational behaviors in which the supervisor frames the teacher's choices about future improvement.

Approach D: A cluster of *directive control behaviors* in which the supervisor makes the decision for the teacher.

Next take a look at the interpersonal behaviors you typically use when meeting with groups of teachers. Please respond to the Supervisory Interpersonal Behavior Questionnaire for Working with Groups.

The Supervisory Interpersonal Behavior Questionnaire for Working with Groups

You have just called upon the science teachers to decide on a policy for allowing students to use laboratory equipment after school. Many students have complained about not having enough class time for doing their experiments. The issue is how and when to free up more laboratory time for students (before school, at lunchtime, during study hall, after school) under the supervision of certified teachers. How would you work with the science teachers to make a decision?

Approach A.   Meet with the staff and explain that they need to decide what to do about this issue. Present the information you have about the problem and ask for clarification. Paraphrase what they say and, once the teachers verify your summary, ask them to decide among themselves what they are going to do. Remain in the meeting, helping to move the discussion along by calling on people, asking questions, and paraphrasing, but do not become involved in making your own position known or influencing the outcome in any conscious way.

Approach B.   Meet with the staff by first explaining that you have to make a decision that will meet the needs of students, teachers, and supervisor. Either by consensus or, if not, then by majority vote, make a decision. You should listen, encourage, clarify, and reflect on each staff member's perception. Afterwards, ask each member including yourself to suggest possible solutions. Discuss each solution; prioritize the list; and, if no consensus emerges, call for a vote. Argue for your own solution, but go along with the group's decision.

Approach C. Meet with the staff and explain to them that there are several permissible actions that you have thought about that could remedy this situation. You would like them to discuss and agree upon which of these actions or combinations of actions they would like to implement. Lay out the alternatives, explain the advantages and disadvantages of each, and then allow the group to discuss and decide among your alternatives.

Approach D. Meet with the staff and tell them you want their feedback before you make a decision about the issue. Make it clear that the staff's involvement is to be advisory. Ask for their suggestions, listen, encourage, clarify, and paraphrase their ideas. After everyone has had a chance to speak, decide what changes should be made. Tell them what you are going to do, when the changes will be made, and that you expect them to carry out the plan.

Response. Most often, I would use Approach _____.

Interpretation.

Approach A: A cluster of *nondirective behaviors* in which the supervisor assists the group to make its own decision.

Approach B: A cluster of *collaborative behaviors* in which the supervisor works as part of the group in making a group decision.

Approach C: A cluster of directive informafional behaviors in which the supervisor works as the framer of choices among which the group is to decide.

Approach D: A cluster of *directive control behaviors* in which the supervisor makes the decision for the group.

---

*Adapted from an instrument developed by Katherine C. Ginkel, 1983. "An Overview of a Study Which Examined the Relationship between Elementary School Teachers' Preference for Supervisory Conferencing Approach and Conceptual Level of Development," a paper presented at the annual meeting of the American Educational Research Association, Montreal, April. Used with permission of Katherine C. Ginkel.

Valid Assessment of Self

After assessing our own approach to individuals and groups, we need to make sure that how we perceive ourselves is consistent with how others perceive us. For example, if we checked that we typically use a collaborative approach with individuals and a nondirective approach with groups, then we need further information to know whether that is true. If not, then later in this chapter we might recommend a continuation, refinement, or discontinuation with a cluster of behaviors that simply do not exist in anyone's mind but our own. As an example, let me give a personal instance of erroneous self-perception.

As a school principal in New Hampshire, I regarded myself as operating a successful school and being accessible to teachers. I could document my success by external evidence—state and national recognition the school had received and complimentary letters from numerous visitors. I documented my accessibility through casual discussions with teachers in the lounge and by having an open-office policy for every staff member who wished to speak with me. In my third year as a principal at this particular school, the superintendent asked all principals in the school system to allow teachers to evaluate principal performance. One item on the evaluation form was "Ability to Listen to Others," followed by a numerical scale of responses from 1 ("rarely listens") to 7 ("almost always listens"). Before giving the form to teachers, I filled out the same evaluation form according to my own perception of my performance. I confidently circled the number 7 on "ability to listen." Once the teachers' responses were collected and results were received, I was amazed to find that the lowest teacher rating on the entire survey was on that very item on which I had rated myself highest. To my chagrin, there was an obvious discrepancy between my own perception of performance and staff perceptions. I will refer again to this painful recollection as we look at perceptions of supervisory behavior.

Johari Window

The Johari window (Luft 1970) provides a graphic way to look at what we know and do not know about our behavior (see Figure 6-2). Visualize a window with four windowpanes. In this scheme there are four windowpanes of the self in which behaviors are either known or not known by self (the supervisor) and others (the teachers). In windowpane I there are behaviors that both supervisor and

Figure 6-2   Adaptation of Johari window

	Known to Supervisor	Not Known to Supervisor
Known to Teachers	1. Public self	2. Blind self
Not Known to Teachers	3. Private self	4. Unknown self

Source: Adapted from Joseph Luft, *Group Processes: An Introduction to Group Dynamics* (New York: National Press Books, 1970).

teachers know the supervisor uses. This is the *public self.* For example, the supervisor knows that when he or she is anxious, speech will become halting and hesitant; teachers are also aware of what such speech indicates.

In windowpane II is the *blind self*—behaviors the supervisor practices that are unknown to the self but are known to teachers. For example, as a school principal I was displaying behaviors toward teachers that I thought were listening behaviors, but teachers saw the same behaviors as a failure to listen. Of course, once one becomes aware of teachers' perceptions of those behaviors, the blind self becomes the public self.

In windowpane III is the *private self*—behaviors the supervisor has knowledge about but that teachers do not know. For instance, in new situations a supervisor might mask his or her unsureness by being extroverted in greeting others. Only the supervisor knows that this behavior is covering up insecurity. Once the supervisor discloses this perception to others, the private self becomes public.

Finally, there is windowpane IV, the *unknown self.* There are actions a supervisor takes of which both supervisors and teachers are unaware. From time to time the supervisor might rapidly shift his legs while speaking behind a table. Neither supervisor or teachers are aware of this leg movement. Perhaps a supervisor becomes irritated while a certain teacher is speaking. The supervisor may not know why she is irritated or even that she feels this way, and the teacher may not know either. The unknown self is unconscious to all; it becomes private, blind, or public only by circumstances that create a new awareness.

What does the Johari window have to do with supervision? We cannot become more effective as supervisors unless we know what we are doing. We may, at our discretion, decide to keep parts of ourselves private. (For example, we may not want teachers to know all the details of our life and personality.) Yet we need to understand that by remaining largely private and not sharing the experiences that bind us as humans, we are creating a distance when we work with teachers. We may prefer formality and distance and may be able to document that such privateness accomplishes certain results. On the other hand, we must also accept that our privateness will be reciprocal, and that staff may not easily discuss personal situations that may affect teaching performance. First we must be aware of how private or public we are with our staff and determine if we desire teachers to be the same way with us. Second, as supervisors, we cannot afford to be blind to our own behaviors and the effect of those behaviors on others. We can improve only what we know; to believe only our own self-perceptions is to court disaster.

My perception of my listening behavior as a principal is a case in point. As long as I saw myself as a wonderful, accessible listener, it did not seem probable that teachers were not coming to me with instructional problems. However, I discovered that on two different occasions teachers had gone to the superintendent about instructional problems of which I was unaware. After the superintendent had told me that teachers were going over my head, I angrily confronted the teachers with their "unprofessional" behavior. It did not occur to me that I might have been the one at fault. After the staff evaluations, I could no longer delude myself. Many teachers were not telling me their concerns because they did not believe that I would really listen. I had to face the fact that the staff did not see me as accessible. I might have avoided collecting such information, continued with my euphoric self-perception, and then been devastated as the school fell apart.

We need to check the validity of our own perceptions. Try this: Photocopy the Supervision Belief Inventory (Chapter 5), the Supervisory Interpersonal Behavior Questionnaire for Working with Individuals, and the Supervisory Interpersonal Behavior Questionnaire for Working with Groups. Let the copies be distributed and collected by a staff member who is trusted by the other teachers. Instructions to teachers should be that no names are to be written on the pages; only circles or checks need to be made on the response sheets. Confidentiality will increase the honesty of the responses. Teachers should know that only summarized results, prepared by the designated teacher, will be given to the supervisor. Therefore a teacher's individual responses cannot be identified or used against him or her. The supervisor can see which of his or her supervisory beliefs and practices are public (consistent between his or her own perception and others') and which are blind (inconsistent between his or her own perception and others'). With such information the supervisor can determine which are valid perceptions and which are invalid. With the invalid perceptions we can attempt to move from the blind to the public self via a program of behavior change.

Cognitive Dissonance

Invalidity of perceptions creates *cognitive dissonance,* according to a model of motivation by psychologist Leon Festinger (1957). The model is based on the premise that a person cannot live with contradictory psychological evidence—that is, thinking of himself or herself in one way while other sources of information indicate that he or she is different. When my perception of my listening abilities were contradicted by teacher perceptions, mental turmoil or cognitive dissonance was created. For example, if you believe that you are a collaborative supervisor and then you receive feedback from teachers that you are a directive supervisor, this will cause cognitive dissonance. We must wrestle with disparent perceptions and reconcile them. If not, the two differing sources of information will continue to bother us. This mental anguish strives to resolve the question of what is it that we really do. The resolution can come about in three alternative ways (Hyman 1975).

First, we can dismiss the source of contrary evidence as biased and untrue. For example, the principal might rationalize, "I really am a good listener; teachers marked me low because they didn't like the way I scheduled bus duties." Or the supervisor might think he or she really is collaborative: "Teachers simply don't understand what collaboration is." By dismissing the other source of information as erroneous, we can continue to believe that we are what we originally thought. No further change is necessary.

Second, we can change our own self-perception to conform to the other source of information and can then live with the new perception of ourselves. We accept that they are right and we are wrong; thus our perception will now be theirs. For example, "I really was wrong about my listening abilities, and I now reconcile myself to being a poor listener," or, "The supervisor is really not collaborative but instead is, as the teachers say, directive." Accepting the other source of information makes dissonance vanish so that no further change is necessary.

Third, we can accept our original self-perception as how we wish to be perceived, use the other source of information as an indicator of how we are currently perceived, and then change our behaviors to be more similar to our wish. In other words, our perception was not accurate, but it still represents what we want to be. I thought I was a good listener, but others say that I was not; so I attempt to change my listening behaviors in order to become a good listener. The supervisor thought he or she was collaborative but others say that he or she was directive; so he or she changes behavior to become more collaborative.

The third alternative to resolving cognitive dissonance creates behavioral change. Whenever we have an idea of how we desire to be matched against the reality of how others see us, there exist conditions for individual change. The acknowledged gap between what is and what should be becomes a powerful stimulus to change.

We change our behaviors and gather feedback from others to determine whether others are forming new perceptions of us and more positive results are forthcoming.

Summary, Conclusions, and Preview

This chapter outlined the supervisory behavior continuum and the clustering of interpersonal behaviors into nondirective, collaborative, directive informational, and directive control approaches. Several assessment instruments were provided. A discourse on the Johari window and cognitive dissonance was given so that we might check the perception of our own beliefs and behaviors by those who are recipients of our behaviors. To assess our own perceptions, supervisory beliefs, and interpersonal behavior with those of teachers is believed to be important in refining and changing behaviors.

What information do we have from those we supervise to confirm or reject our perceptions? What if we find inconsistency in the ways we believe, the ways we work with individuals, and the ways we work with groups? In fact, in real life we may not be consistent in the ways we work with one individual as opposed to another individual, or with one group and another. Neither consistency nor inconsistency is being advocated here. A particular approach is not necessarily better than others. However, there is research evidence that the effectiveness of different supervisory behaviors and approaches is dependent on characteristics of individuals and groups of teachers. The last chapter of this section will discuss how one might vary one's approach according to those characteristics to help staff become more self-reliant and cohesive. For now, however, you should assess your own beliefs and practices as predominantly nondirective, collaborative, directive informational, directive control, or some combination thereof. We will next examine and practice the skills of each supervisory approach in terms of actual conferencing and meeting behaviors. Understanding how we behave as supervisors and then refining our present behaviors are the first steps toward acquiring new interpersonal behaviors.

Each of the next four chapters begins with a scenario of an idealized conference, followed by a discussion of the supervisory responses. These chapters are meant for practical skill building in each of the three approaches. As a result, involvement and role playing are expected of the reader.

EXERCISES

Academic

1. After reviewing the ten categories of supervision defined in the chapter, list specific behaviors your supervisor has exhibited while supervising you. For each example, write a brief description of your feelings toward the supervisor while he or she was using the given behavior, as well as your behavioral response to the situation. What does a review of your feelings and responses tell you about the supervisory approach you most prefer? Least prefer?

2. The chapter proposes three possible ways of resolving the mental conflict brought about by cognitive dissonance. Prepare a report in which you cite examples of cognitive dissonance you have personally experienced and your reaction to each resulting dilemma. Based on your recollections, which of the three possible responses to cognitive dissonance has been your typical mode of resolution?

3. Label the left-hand column of a sheet of paper "Public Self" and the right-hand column "Private Self." Think of personality or other characteristics that you intentionally disguise in your work setting. For each characteristic, describe in a few words the image you consciously present to others (left-hand column) and the real you that your public behavior conceals (right-hand column).

4. Locate a research study on the effectiveness of one or more of the following supervisor approaches to supervisor-teacher conferences: (1) directive control, (2) directive informational, (3)

collaborative, (4) nondirective. Summarize the purpose, methods, results, and conclusions of the study in writing.

5. Chapter 6 relates an experience in which a discrepancy between my blind self and public self led to communication problems with subordinates. Discuss in writing three other situations in which conflicts between a supervisor's blind self and public self might eventually lead to leadership problems.

Field

1. Arrange to visit a teacher's class for a postobservation conference with that teacher. The postobservation conference should include an analysis of the teacher's instructional performance, the setting of instructional improvement goals, and planning a strategy for meeting those goals. Record the postobservation on audiotape. Refer to the categories of supervisor behavior in this book as you listen to the tape. Write a paper in which you state whether you used a primarily directive, collaborative, or nondirective approach during the postobservation conference. Cite examples of specific behaviors you exhibited during the postobservation conference. Compare those behaviors with your results on the Supervisor Beliefs Inventory and the Supervisory Interpersonal Behavior Questionnaire for Working with Individuals.

2. Carry out the exercise suggested in the chapter. Prepare a written report on the results of the exercise and your reaction to those results.

3. Rewrite the Supervisory Interpersonal Behavior Questionnaire for Working with Individuals or the Supervisory Interpersonal Behavior Questionnaire for Working with Groups so that the rewritten instrument asks *teachers* which type of interpersonal behavior they would prefer a supervisor to exhibit during supervisor-teacher interaction relative to the situation described in the chosen questionnaire. Report on your collected data and conclusions in writing.

4. Put yourself in the shoes of an individual you supervise or have supervised. (Even those not in formal supervisory roles have at one time or another been responsible for supervising others.) Write a description of your supervisory style; be careful to describe your supervisory style as the other person would, not as you would. Compare this description of your supervisory style with your results on the Supervisor Beliefs Inventory, the Supervisory Interpersonal Behavior Questionnaire for Working

with Individuals, and the Supervisory Interpersonal Behavior Questionnaire for Working with Groups.

5. Draw a two-frame cartoon for each of the following themes: (1) public self–private self, (2) my message–their perception, (3) cognitive dissonance. Base your cartoons on personal experiences or observations in a school setting.

Developmental

1. Begin to make mental notes on behaviors you use when supervising others. Look for patterns of behavior that can be related to an orientation toward supervision (directive, collaborative, nondirective, eclectic) of which you may not now be conscious.

2. Informally observe others in leadership roles. Do their behaviors tend to cluster toward a directive, collaborative, or nondirective approach?

3. Begin to examine discrepancies between your public self and your private self, and consider possible reasons for such discrepancies.

REFERENCES

Festinger, L. 1957. *A theory of cognitive dissonance.* Stanford, Calif.: Stanford University Press.

Ginkel, K.C. 1983. An overview of a study which examined the relationship between elementary school teachers' preference for supervisory conferencing approach and conceptual level of development. Paper presented at the annual meeting of the American Educational Research Association, Montreal, April.

Glickman, C.D. 1981. *Developmental supervision: Alternative practices for helping teachers improve instruction.* Alexandria, Va.: Association for Supervision and Curriculum Development.

Hyman, R.T. 1975. *School administrator's handbook of teacher supervision and evaluation methods.* Englewood Cliffs, N.J.: Prentice-Hall, pp. 46–47.

Luft, J. 1970. *Group processes: An introduction to group dynamics.* New York: National Press Books.

Wolfgang, C.H., and Glickman, C.D. 1980. *Solving discipline problems: Alternative strategies for teachers.* Boston: Allyn and Bacon.

Chapter 7

Nondirective Behaviors

Teacher (barging into supervisor's office): This damn place is a zoo! I can't stand it any longer. These kids are a bunch of ingrates! I've had it.

Supervisor (looking at the teacher): Wow, you are angry! Tell me what's going on? Have a seat.

Teacher (refusing to sit): I get no help around here from you or the administration. The students know that they can act any way they damn please and get away with it. I'm not going to put up with it anymore.

Supervisor: What have they been doing?

Teacher: Just now, I went back into the class after being called out for a message and they were jumping all over the place, running around, throwing papers and being totally obnoxious. I can't leave them for a minute.

Supervisor: What did you do?

Teacher: What do you think? I screamed my bloody head off at them and after it all, Terence had the nerve to laugh at me.

Supervisor: Terence laughed at you?

Teacher: Yeah, that little snot! He always has the last word. He's so defiant it drives me mad!

Supervisor: Is he always like that?

Teacher: He sure is. Terence is my number one problem; if I could get him to behave and learn, the rest of the class would be no problem.

Supervisor: So the main problem is Terence. What do you do when he misbehaves?

Teacher: I've been sending him out of the room but that doesn't work. He could care less about school and will only work when forced to. He really gets to me.

Supervisor: He's a lot to handle.

Teacher: He sure is! That kid is a bundle of jumping nerves. He doesn't pay any attention to what goes on in class.

Supervisor: He must really keep you hopping! Does Terence do anything right in class?

Teacher: Hardly! He's just not excited about anything in school. If he could live in a world of rock videos and football games, he'd be just fine.

Supervisor: (joking): Well, maybe we need a flashing movie room of video and football highlights to keep him entertained!

Teacher: (laughing and calming down): Oh, I don't know. He just drives me nuts. He's not a bad kid.

Supervisor: Could we capitalize on his interests to improve his classroom behavior?

Teacher: I need to sit down with him and talk to him one on one. I really want to find something in class that would interest him and keep him out of my hair.

Supervisor: What might that be?

Teacher: Students get to do special history projects in class. Maybe I could tie his love for music or sports into a history project, or maybe make a contract with him about his good behavior so that he could earn time to listen to music? Let me talk to him.

Supervisor: Sorry about your class today. It sounds to me as if Terence is the key and you have some ideas. Are there ways that I could help?

Nondirective Behaviors with Individuals

Nondirective supervision is based on the assumption that an individual teacher knows best what instructional changes need to be made and has the ability to think and act on his or her own. The decision belongs to the teacher. The role of the supervisor is to assist the teacher in the process of thinking through his or her actions.

As the foregoing hypothetical script shows, the supervisor behaves in ways that keep the teacher's thinking focused on observation, interpretation, problem identification, and problem solutions. Notice how in the example the nondirective approach allowed the teacher to move from an angry outburst about the entire class to an analytical focus on Terence's behavior. Rarely will a teacher move this rapidly from anger to reflection, but the pattern of supervisor helping teacher come to his or her own conclusions is characteristic of a nondirective approach. The supervisor does not interject his or her own ideas into the discussion unless specifically asked. All verbalizations by the supervisor are intended as feedback or to extend the teacher's thinking; they do not influence the actual design.

Refer to the supervisory behavior continuum to understand how nondirective behaviors are used. Read carefully, because the misuse of listening, clarifying, encouraging, reflecting, problem-solving, and presenting behaviors can result in a decision that is not really the teacher's.

Figure 7-1 shows a typical pattern of supervisory interpersonal behaviors used in a nondirective conference. They begin with listening and end with asking the teacher to present his or her decision. The sequence of behaviors between start and finish can vary, but the end should be the same—a noninfluenced teacher decision.

1. Listening: *Wait until the teacher's initial statement is made.* Face and look at the teacher; concentrate on what is being said. Avoid thinking about how you see the problem or what you think should be done. It is not easy to restrain your mind from galloping ahead, but your job is to understand what the teacher initially has said.

2. Reflecting: *Verbalize your understanding of the initial problem.* Include in your statement the teacher's feelings and perceived situation: "You're angry because students don't pay attention." Wait for an acknowledgment of accuracy from the teacher: "Yes, I am, but . . . ." Do not offer your own opinion; your job is to capture what the teacher is saying.

3. Clarifying: *Probe for underlying problem and/or additional information.* You now ask the teacher to look at the problem in some different ways and to consider new information that might be contributing to the problem. Clarifying is done to help the teacher further identify, not solve, the problem. Questions such as "Do you mean that you are really fed up with school?" "Is it a particular student who is getting to you?" or "When has this happened before?" are appropriate information-seeking questions. Avoid questions that are really solutions in disguise. Such questions as "Have you thought about taking up yoga to relax?" or "Maybe you could suspend that student for a few days, what do you think?" are inappropriate. Such leading or suggestive questions are attempts to influence the teacher's final decision.

4. Encouraging: *Show willingness to listen further as the teacher begins to identify the real problems.* Show that you will continue to assist and not leave the discussion incomplete. Statements such as "I'm following what you're saying, continue on," or "Run that

Figure 7-1 The supervisory behavior continuum: nondirective behaviors

T	1	2	3	4	5	6	7	8	9	10	t
s	Listening	Clarifying	Encouraging	Reflecting	Presenting	Problem Solving	Negotiating	Directing	Standardizing	Reinforcing	s

1. Wait until the immediate message is finished

2. Verbalize initial problem— feeling and situation

3. Probe for underlying problem and/ or additional information

4. Show willingness to listen further

5. Constantly paraphrase understanding of teacher's message

6. Ask teacher to think of possible actions

124

7. Ask teacher to consider consequences of various actions

8. Ask teacher for commitment to a decision

9. Ask teacher to set time and criteria for action

10. Restate the teacher's plan

Key: *T* = Maximum teacher responsibility   *S* = Maximum supervisor responsibility
     t = Minimum teacher responsibility   *s* = Minimum supervisor responsibility

by me again," or "I'm following you" are correct. Saying, "I like that idea," "Yes, that will work," "Ah, I agree with that," are, even unintentionally, influencing behaviors. A teacher, like any other person, cannot help but be influenced by the judgments a supervisor is making on what he or she says. Encouraging keeps the teacher thinking; praise, on the other hand, influences the final decision.

5. Reflecting: *Constantly paraphrase understanding of teacher's message.* Throughout the discussion, check on the accuracy of what you understand the teacher to be saying. When the teacher adds more information to the perceived problem, or explains different sources of the problem, considers the possible actions, and finally makes a decision, the supervisor should paraphrase. First, whenever you are uncertain of what the teacher is saying, you should paraphrase with statements such as "I think you're saying . . . " or "I'm not sure but do you mean . . . ." Then you can sit back and allow the teacher to affirm or reject your understanding. Second, when the teacher has come to a halt in thinking about the problem, the paraphrase should be used to jog the teacher's mind to reflect on what has already been said and what more needs to be done. For example, after a considerable pause in the teacher's talk, the supervisor might say, "Well, let me see if I can summarize what has been said so far . . . " or "So this is where you are—you're angry because. . . . " Comprehensive summarizing allows the teacher to rest, mentally stand off from himself or herself, and think about what has been said. Usually such paraphrasing will stimulate the teacher to interject, add, and continue. Reflecting should not become mechanical or artificial, with the supervisor paraphrasing every teacher statement. Instead it should be used judiciously when the supervisor is not completely clear about what has been said or when there is a long pause in the conversation. Incessant interjections of "I hear you saying . . . ", without aid or purpose, make teachers skeptical about the supervisor's concern.

6. Problem solving: *Ask teacher to think of possible actions.* After the teacher has finished identifying the problem and you are clear about his or her perception of the problem, your responsibility shifts to helping the teacher generate possible solutions. You can do this by asking straightforward questions: "What can you do about this?" "What else could be done?" "Think hard about actions that might help." "Let me see if you can come up with four to six possible solutions." It is helpful to allow the teacher to think for a minute or two about possible actions before verbalizing them. After actions have been proposed, you should reflect on the proposals, check on their accuracy, and probe for others. Regardless of whether the

teacher proposes only a few or many possibilities, if further probing is not successful, then you should move the conference on.

7. Problem solving: *Ask teacher to consider consequences of various actions.* The moment of truth is almost at hand. Your emphasis is on having the teacher move from possible to probable solutions. Taking each solution in order, ask: "What would happen if you did . . . ?" "Would it work?" "What problems would be associated with it?" Finally, after having the teacher explore the advantages and disadvantages of each action, he or she should be asked to compare the various actions: "Which would work best?" "Why do you think so?" "How would that be better than the others?"

8. Presenting: *Ask teacher for commitment to a decision.* After you have explored possible actions and the teacher has compared their likelihood of success, you must emphasize that the teacher should select actions that are within his or her resources (*do-able*), can be implemented in a short period of time (*feasible*), and are concrete (*accountable*). A simple question—"Well, what will you do now that is likely to improve the situation?"—should cut quickly to the heart of the matter.

9. Standardizing: *Ask teacher to set time and criteria for action.* The teacher is assisted in monitoring his or her own decision about future improvement by specifying the time period during which the action will be implemented, when various parts of the plan will be done, what resources are needed, and how the teacher will know the decision is working. A further series of supervisor questions to accomplish this purpose would be: "Now tell me what you are going to do." "What will be done first, next, last?" "What do you need in order to do it?" "How will you know it's working?" "When will it be done?" When the teacher can answer these questions, the conference is near completion.

10. Reflecting: *Restate the teacher's plan.* Before leaving, repeat the teacher's entire plan with "So you're going to do . . . ." After the teacher verifies the restated plan, the session is over.

Nondirective Behaviors with Groups

It would be redundant to explain step by step each behavior a supervisor should use in being nondirective in a meeting with a group. As noted in the scenario presented in Figure 7-2, whether the meeting is about bus schedules or textbook adoptions, the supervisory behaviors and sequence of steps are comparable to those of an individual conference. The supervisor would begin such a

Figure 7-2 Scenario: nondirective supervision

During fifth period planning time, Supervisor Eldredge sits down with the sixth-grade middle school team of Mrs. Murdock, English teacher; Mr. Holtz, social studies teacher; Ms. Elright, mathematics teacher; and Mrs. Patrick, science teacher. The supervisor begins by asking, "Well, what's on your minds this week?" Mrs. Murdock replies: "I have a real problem with Mr. Handwright the custodian. Twice in the last week, I've sent kids on errands and he has stopped them and started yelling at them for not being in the classroom."

Supervisor Eldredge listens until Mrs. Murdock finishes her account and then asks the team, "Has this occurred often with Mr. Handwright?" Mrs. Patrick replies, "Yes, it has, his voice just booms all over and he scares the kids to death." Mr. Holtz adds: "He's even yelled at students when they have been seated in my classroom. He talks through the open door and tells them not to scuff the floors or drop papers. I don't think it's right."

The supervisor responds: "Let me summarize; you are finding that Mr. Handwright is disciplining students in a loud and abusive way for things that they have not done or for things that are not his responsibility. You believe it is not the custodian's job to discipline?" Ms. Elright answers: "Yes, that's right! His job is to clean, our job is to discipline. He's putting his nose into things that are none of his business. He's upsetting our students and us."

Supervisor Eldredge now presses the team, "O.K., I understand the problem; now what do you think should be done?" "That's easy," says Mrs. Patrick. "Someone needs to tell him what is and what is not his job. The principal should do that." "I disagree," says Mr. Holtz. "I think that before we report him to the principal, we should talk with him. Maybe we are being remiss in cleaning up or we are doing some things that are bothering him."

Supervisor Eldredge listens to the discussion and asks Mrs. Patrick, "What do you think of Mr. Holtz's suggestion?" Mrs. Patrick replies to Mr. Holtz: "I don't object; let's sit down with Mr. Handwright and straighten this out. Should we do it as a team or as individuals?" Ms. Elright says: "It would be less threatening if only one of us talked to him. John [Holtz], since you know him best, could you?" Mr. Holtz replies, "Sure I'll talk to him this afternoon."

The supervisor interjects: "You've agreed to talk to the custodian this afternoon, and John will be the representative. What should the topics be, and when will he report back?" Mr. Holtz answers: "I'm going to tell him that we don't want him to yell at students. If there's a problem, he's to come to the teacher and the teacher will handle discipline. I'm also going to see if there are ways that we can make his job easier. I'll give a progress report to all of you tomorrow morning. . . ."

meeting by asking and *listening* to group members discuss their perceptions of the group issue. The supervisor would encourage all the members to express themselves and would constantly *clarify* and *reflect* on what they were saying. Once the problem had been discussed, the supervisor would ask the group to *problem solve* by asking each member to propose possible new actions. After compiling a list of possible actions generated by the group, he or she would ask members to discuss the consequences of each action on the list and would make sure that each proposed action was understood by the group. If not, the supervisor would ask for further clarification and then paraphrase the meaning so that the proposer of the action could verify accuracy. After the list of actions was understood, the supervisor would ask for a discussion of the merits of each proposed action and then ask for a comparison of actions most likely to succeed. After problem solving, the supervisor would ask if there was a consensus of action to be taken. If not, he or she would ask for further discussion and then ask the group to determine how to resolve the deadlock. The supervisor would not be part of the decision. After the decision was made, the supervisor would ask the group to detail the decision by *standardizing* the criteria. He or she would ask for a time line, specific activities each group member would take, resources needed by the group, and indications of success. If there was no clear consensus on details of standardizing the plan, the supervisor again would ask the group for further discussion.

Please note that the supervisor using nondirective behaviors is in the role of expediter of the group making its own decision. The supervisor is not a participant in the decision, does not offer his or her own ideas, and does not influence the choices. The supervisor's role is to keep the group focused on steps for making its own decision.

Issues with Nondirective Supervision

Based on numerous skill-training sessions that I have conducted with school leaders on employing nondirective behaviors, some common issues and practical questions have arisen:

1. Can a supervisor really remain nonjudgmental and not influence the teacher's or group's decision?
2. What happens if the teacher or group desires the supervisor's input?
3. What does a supervisor do with a teacher or group that is reluctant or not capable of generating solutions?

4. How exact or variable is the sequence of nondirective behaviors?

5. In what circumstances should nondirective behaviors be used?

Whether or not a supervisor can really remain nonjudgmental is a legitimate concern. Even when one is consciously avoiding praise, not interjecting one's own ideas, and not offering solutions in the guise of questions, some influencing probably will take place. Studies by Mears, Shannon, and Pepinsky (1979) analyzing the tapes of counseling sessions conducted by the most renowned expert on nondirectiveness, psychologist Carl Rogers, revealed a definite pattern to his interrupting the patient and to which statements he selected to paraphrase. It is apparent that any interaction between humans is bound to be influential. Frequency of eye contact, timing of questions, facial expressions, and ways of paraphrasing can always be interpreted by a teacher as approving or disapproving. There is no way to avoid influencing through unconscious supervisory responses. The best one can do is to minimize those behaviors that knowingly influence. One should not knowingly offer ideas, praise, or directions that will influence the teacher's decision.

What if the teacher or group asks for the supervisor's suggestions? The answer to this question revolves around timing. If the suggestions are asked for and given in the initial stages of a conference or meeting before the teacher or group have been required to think through the issue, then such feedback will structure the stream of subsequent thought and heavily influence the decision. If the suggestions are given after the teacher or group have already narrowed their own choices of actions, however, a supervisor's answer will not be as influential. Ideally, it is better to refrain completely from giving one's own ideas. If asked, the supervisor might respond: "I'm sorry, but I don't want to answer that. Instead, I want you to think through what can be done. Only you know your own situation. Therefore, what *I* think is not as important as what *you* think." If the teacher or group will not make a decision without knowing the supervisor's ideas, then he or she might as well give up being nondirective and move into a more collaborative mode, which will be explained in the next chapter.

Being nondirective with an individual or group that is reluctant or not capable of generating solutions is tricky. Reluctance and capability are not necessarily inversely related. If the teacher is reluctant but capable, the worst possible response would be for the supervisor to take over decision making for the teacher. Such a move might reinforce the teacher's reluctance to speak his or her own mind. Reluctance usually stems from a disbelief that one will be listened to or allowed to act on one's own initiative. The supervisor must be patient, give constant encouragement, and be persistent. Patience is shown by listening and waiting, encouragement by accepting what the teacher says, and persistence by not allowing the teacher to rest without making a decision. A supervisor can be persistent by asking questions, by taking breaks from the conference, and by giving the teacher time for further reflections.

Capability is a different matter. What if a teacher or group is incapable of making a decision? If they continually insist they do not know what the problem is or have no ideas about what could be done, and if every supervisory prompt is met by vacant stares and shrugs of shoulders, then patience, encouragement, and persistence on the part of the supervisor will create further frustration and perhaps antagonism. If they simply don't know, no matter how nondirective the supervisor is, no decisions will be forthcoming. Obviously, if lack of capability is the source of nonresponsiveness, then the nondirective approach is an unwise choice of supervisory behaviors.

Finally, there is the question of sequence of nondirective behaviors. How precise is the order? The description of nondirective behaviors presented a prototype of ten steps within the supervisory behavior continuum (Figure 7-1). The behaviors are : (1) listening-waiting, (2) reflecting-verbalizing, (3) clarifying-probing, (4) encouraging-willing, (5) reflecting-paraphrasing, (6) problem solving—asking for possible actions, (7) problem solving—asking for probable consequences, (8) presenting—asking for a commitment, (9) standardizing—asking for criteria, and (10) reflecting—restating the plan. One might visualize these steps as analogous to playing the left-hand side of a piano keyboard. The supervisor-pianist begins the musical score with the furthest left-hand note (listening-waiting) and will end the score at note 10 (reflecting-restating). During the score (conference or meeting) the adept player will strike the notes (behaviors) back and forth between one and ten, pounding on some notes, lightly touching on others, returning, and swelling the underlying tone of the teacher or group voice. The score ends on note 10—reflecting and restating the teacher's or group's decision. The behaviors are not a prescription of fixed steps but rather a directionality of movements with a definite beginning and end.

When to Use Nondirective Behaviors

When and with whom should nondirective behaviors be used? To satisfy the reader's curiosity, let us lay out some quick criteria for using nondirective behaviors. Chapter 11 will take an in-depth look at this question after detailing all three supervisory approaches. For now, a supervisor should consider using a nondirective approach:

1. When the teacher or group possess most of the knowledge and expertise about the issue and the supervisor's knowledge and expertise are minimal: "If you don't know anything about it and they do, let them solve it."

2. When the teacher or group have full responsibility for carrying out the decision and the supervisor has little involvement: "If they are going to be accountable for it and you aren't, let them solve it."

3. When the teacher or group care about solving the problem but the problem doesn't matter to the supervisor: "If they want to act and you couldn't care less, let them decide."

The criteria of (1) expertise, (2) responsibility, and (3) care appear to be straightforward. Chapter 11 will show the greater complexity of this criteria and the critical role of supervisor judgment.

Practicing Nondirective Behaviors

Up to now we have explored nondirective behaviors as an exercise in reading. To understand nondirective behaviors fully demands real-life practice. Even if you think you already are proficient in these skills, it would be valuable to try out the exercise in Appendix B2 (skill practice in nondirective behaviors) and intentionally practice being nondirective in some school situations.

Summary

Supervisors can use nondirective behaviors in helping teachers determine their own plans. Such supervisory behaviors consist of listening, reflecting, clarifying, encouraging, and problem solving. When individuals and groups of teachers possess greater expertise, commitment, and responsibility for a particular decision than the supervisor does, then a nondirective approach is appropriate. Important considerations for a supervisor when using nondirectiveness are attempting to be nonjudgmental, hesitating in response to teachers' wishes for more supervisor input, and adjusting one's behavior when teachers demonstrate reluctance to generate solutions. The purpose of nondirective supervision is to provide an active sounding board for thoughtful professionals.

EXERCISES

Academic

1. Write an imaginary dialogue between a supervisor and teacher during a conference in which the supervisor successfully uses a nondirective approach. Be sure to include examples of each of the ten nondirective behaviors discussed in Chapter 7.

2. The chapter explains a sequence of ten nondirective behaviors that take place during a nondirective conference. Think of a situation in which a successful nondirective conference would start with the first suggested behavior (listening-waiting) and end with the tenth (reflecting-restating the plan), but would have a *different sequence* of eight intermediate behaviors. Describe the situation and modified sequence of nondirective behaviors in writing. Include a rationale for the suggested sequence.

3. Write an imaginary dialogue between a supervisor and a teacher in which the supervisor implements nondirective procedures with mechanical precision but still fails to be truly nondirective.

4. Write a paper comparing the nondirective approach as described in this book with the version of nondirective assistance espoused by an author cited in the References.

5. Assume you have just listened to a talk by a school administrator in which he or she argued against the use of nondirective behaviors by educational supervisors with *any* teacher. The thrust of the administrator's argument was that such an approach is essentially laissez-faire and allows complete deference to a teacher's decision, even when such decisions are clearly in error and are likely to result in harm to the teacher's instructional performance or to the students. The administrator further argued that for a supervisor to withhold his or her observations, perceptions, and suggestions, unless they are requested by the teacher, is counterproductive to the supervisory process. You have been asked to prepare a reply to the administrator to be presented at an upcoming seminar. Write a paper in which you argue for the use of nondirective behavior with certain teachers. Address the administrator's objections in your paper.

Field

1. Use a nondirective approach by either using the activity found in Appendix B or conducting an actual postobservation con-

ference with a teacher. Prepare a written report in which you (a) evaluate your success in displaying nondirective behaviors, (b) summarize the problems discussed and decisions made during the conference, (c) give your perceptions of the "teacher's" responses to your nondirective efforts, and (d) judge the conference in terms of overall success.

2. Observe an educational supervisor or other leader whom you know to possess a nondirective orientation. Based on your observations and interview with the leader, write a paper describing both successes and failures that he or she has experienced while using nondirective behaviors. Include possible reasons for the nondirective leader's greater success in some situations than in others.

3. Observe three teachers or staff members who clearly respond positively to nondirective supervision. Prepare a report examining personal and social characteristics of these individuals that may account for their positive response to a nondirective approach.

4. Prepare a picture album entitled "Self-Direction for Instructional Improvement." Each picture should be accompanied by a written explanation of how that entry relates to the album theme.

5. Videotape or audiotape a conference or staff development activity in which the supervisor is using a nondirective approach. As you review the tape, compare the recorded activities with the sequence of behaviors that, according to the author, exemplifies the nondirective approach of a supervisor during a decision-making process. Prepare a report on your findings.

Developmental

1. Through interaction with various individuals in a variety of situations, begin to establish a set of personal guidelines that will indicate when the nondirective approach is most appropriate in carrying out present or anticipated leadership functions.

2. Begin an in-depth study of the writings of a prominent humanistic educator or psychologist. Relate that author's ideas to the concepts of nondirective supervision discussed in this chapter.

3. Record a simulated or actual supervisor-teacher conference in which you, as supervisor, attempt to display nondirective behaviors. Review the tape for analysis of your performance. Over the next four weeks, attempt to practice nondirective leadership whenever appropriate opportunities arise. Record another sim-

ulated or actual conference in four weeks. Review both tapes to discover any improvement in terms of successfully displaying nondirective behaviors.

REFERENCES

Carkhuff, R.R. 1969. *Helping and human relations: A primer for lay and professional helpers*, Vol. 2: *Practice and research.* New York: Holt, Rinehart and Winston.

Combs, A., Avila, D.L., and Purkey, W.H. 1979. *Helping relationships: Basic concepts for the helping professions*, 2nd ed. Boston: Allyn and Bacon.

Gazda, G.M., Asbury, R.R., Balzer, F.J., Childers, W.C., and Walters, R.P. 1977. *Human relations development: A manual for educators*, 2nd ed. Boston: Allyn and Bacon.

Mears, N.M., Shannon, J.W., and Pepinsky, H.B. 1979. Comparison of the stylistic complexity of the language of counselor and client across three theoretical orientations. *Journal of Counseling Psychology 26*(3):181–189.

Mosher, R.L., and Purpel, D.E. 1972. *Supervision: The reluctant profession.* Boston: Houghton Mifflin. (See Chapter 6.)

Rogers, C.R. 1951. *Client-centered therapy: Its current practice, implications, and theory.* Boston: Houghton Mifflin.

Chapter 8

Collaborative Behaviors

Teacher: I refuse to have Steve sent out of my class.

Supervisor: Don't you think being hit by him and being bruised is the last straw?

Teacher: No, I don't. It's my body and I don't think Steve meant it. He was angry and didn't know what he was doing.

Supervisor: Listen, he's been in fights with other students since the first day of school, and the latest episode of striking could have resulted in serious damage. He has to come out.

Teacher: I know that you're thinking about my own welfare, but that kid is making progress. He's beginning to do some assignments and has been behaving better. The hitting incident was an accident. He's not bothering the other students too much.

Supervisor: I think you're wrong. Let's put him into a special classroom.

Teacher: No, he stays with me.

Supervisor: You know that whatever is done, we will both agree to do. You don't want him to leave and I think, for his own good, he should be given special attention. Steve is dangerous to you and the other students.

Teacher: I don't have anything against special attention. It's just that we've come so far and I hate to see him cut off from me and the class. He has a better chance to make it in our class than to begin all over in another class.

Supervisor: Then you would be receptive to having him receive special attention as long as he stays in your class?

Teacher: Yeah, I think so. I have no problem with a qualified person working with him in my classroom or even for a small part of the day outside of the classroom.

Supervisor: That seems reasonable, I think that we are getting somewhere. . . .

Collaborative Behaviors with Individuals

The foregoing script, based on a real conference, highlights collaborative supervisory behaviors. The supervisor wishes to resolve a problem that is shared equally with the teacher. The supervisor encourages the teacher to present his or her own perceptions and ideas. Yet the supervisor also honestly gives his or her own views. The result is a frank exchange of ideas. Both participants know they will both have to agree on any course of action. In fact, when the disagreement becomes obvious, the supervisor restates the disagreement and reassures the teacher that they will have to find a mutual solution. Disagreement is encouraged, not suppressed. As the conversation continues, some openings for possible agreements become apparent, and the supervisor steers the conversation toward those ends. Finally, they will either agree to an action or wind up stalemated. A stalemate will mean further negotiating, rethinking, and even the possible use of a third-party mediator or arbitrator.

Figure 8-1 shows a prototype of collaborative behaviors according to the supervisory behavior continuum. A conference between supervisor and teacher begins with an understanding of each other's identification of the problem and concludes with mutual agreement on the final plan. Again, the reader should think of the supervisory behaviors as a piano keyboard, with the musician beginning by hitting the keys on the left, then playing the keys back and forth, and culminating by hitting the middle key—negotiating.

1. Clarifying: *Identifying the problem as seen by the teacher.* First, ask the teacher about the immediate problem or concern: "Please tell me what is bothering you," or "Explain to me what you see as the greatest concern."

2. Listening: *Understanding the teacher's perception.* You the supervisor want to have as much information about the problem as possible before thinking about action. Therefore, when the teacher narrates his or her perceptions, the full range of nondirective behaviors should be used (eye contact, paraphrasing, asking probing questions, and being willing to allow the teacher to continue talking): "Tell me more." "Uh huh, I'm following you." "Do you mean . . . ?"

3. Reflecting: *Verifying the teacher's perception.* When the teacher has completed his or her description of the problem, check for accuracy by summarizing the teacher's statements and asking if the summary is accurate: "I understand that you see the problem as . . . . Is this accurate?"

4. Presenting: *Providing supervisor's point of view.* Until this

Figure 8-1 The supervisory behavior continuum: collaborative behaviors

1	2	3	4	5	6	7	8	9	10
Listening	Clarifying	Encouraging	Reflecting	Presenting	Problem Solving	Negotiation	Directing	Standardizing	Reinforcing

T
s

1. Identifying
   the problem
   as seen by
   the teacher

2. Understanding
   the teacher's
   perception

3. Verifying
   teacher's
   perception

4. Providing
   supervisor's
   point of
   view

5. Seeking teacher's
   understanding of

S
t

supervisor's
perception of
problem

6. Exchanging
   suggestions
   of options

7. Accepting
   conflict

8. Finding an
   acceptable
   action

9. Agreeing on
   details of
   plan

10. Agreeing
    to a final
    plan

Key: *T* = Maximum teacher responsibility *S* = Maximum supervisor responsibility
     t = Minimum teacher responsibility *s* = Minimum supervisor responsibility

point, we have seen an abbreviated nondirective conference. Instead of asking the teacher to begin thinking of his or her own possible actions, however, you now move in and become part of the decision-making process. Give your own point of view about the current difficulty and fill in any information about the situation of which the teacher might be unaware: "I see the situation in this way," or "The problem, as I see it, is . . . ." (To minimize influencing the teacher's position, it is better for you to give your perceptions only after the teacher has given his or hers.)

5. Clarifying: *Seeking teacher's understanding of supervisor's perception of problem.* In the same way that you paraphrased the teacher's statement of the problem and asked for verification, you now ask the teacher to do likewise: "Could you repeat what you think I'm trying to say?" Once you feel confident that the teacher understands your views, problem solving can begin.

6. Problem solving: *Exchanging suggestions of options.* If you and the teacher are familiar with each other and have worked collaboratively before, you can simply ask for a list of suggestions: "Let's both think about what might be done to improve this situation." Then listen to each other's ideas. If the teacher is not familiar with you or with the collaborative process, however, he or she may feel apprehensive about suggesting an idea that is different from the supervisor's. It might be better to stop the conference for a few minutes and have both supervisor and teacher write down possible actions before speaking: "So that we don't influence each other on possible solutions, let's take the next few minutes and write down what actions might be taken and then read each other's list." Obviously, once actions are in writing, they will not change according to what the other person has written. You the supervisor, therefore, have promoted a spectrum of personal ideas that are ready to be shared and discussed.

7. Encouraging: *Accepting conflict.* To keep the conference from turning into a competitive struggle, you need to reassure the teacher that disagreement is acceptable and that there will be no winners or losers: "It appears that we have some different ideas on how to handle this situation. By disagreeing we will find the best solution. Remember our agreement—we both have to agree with the solution before it will take place." You must genuinely believe that conflict between two caring professionals is productive for finding the best solution.

8. Problem solving: *Finding an acceptable solution.* After sharing and discussing, ask if there are suggestions common to both— "Where do we agree?"—and if there are suggestions markedly different—"Where do we differ?" If you find agreement, then the conference proceeds. But if there is a vast difference in suggestions,

then you can take four sequential actions. First, check to see whether the differences are as vast as they appear by having both yourself and the teacher explain thoroughly what is meant by your respective suggestions. Second, if the disagreement is still real, then find out how convinced each of you is that your suggestion be chosen: "How important is it to you that we do it your way?" If the importance of one person's suggestion is far greater than that of the other person's suggestion, then the question becomes whether one can give up his or her idea and live with the other's. Third, if grounds for agreement are not reached, you can consider a compromise: "How about if I give up this part of my suggestion and if you give up . . . ." Or see if a totally new idea can be found: "Since we can't agree, let's drop our top choices for solutions and see if we can find another one." Fourth, if there is still no movement and a true stalemate remains, then you can either call for a period of time for both parties to reflect on the issue before meeting again— "Look, we're not getting anywhere. Let's sit on this matter and meet again tomorrow"—or ask for a third person to play the role of a mediator or arbitrator: "We can't agree; how about if we call someone that we both respect to help us resolve this?" or "Since we can't agree, how about calling someone we both have confidence in to solve this for us?" A mediator or arbitrator is an extreme option for most conferences between a supervisor and a teacher and should remain a last resort. However, the teacher must know that the procedures of collaboration ensure that he or she does not have to go along with a plan that he or she disagrees with. There are other options available.

9. Standardizing: *Agreeing on details of plan.* Once agreement on an acceptable action has been reached, the supervisor needs to attend to the details of time and place. When will the plan be implemented? Where will it take place? Who will help? What resources are needed? These details need to be discussed and agreed to so there will be a clarity and precision to the final plan.

10. Negotiating: *Agreeing to a final plan.* The supervisor concludes the conference by checking that both parties agree to the action and details. The supervisor might do this verbally—"Could you repeat what you understand the plan to be and then I'll repeat my understanding"—or in writing: "Let's write this down together so that we are clear on what we've agreed to do."

Collaborative Behaviors with Groups

After meeting for the fourth time in the past month, most of the members of the school science textbook adoption committee have reviewed all the new commercial textbook series and have made up their own minds about which they prefer. It is 5:30 on Wednesday afternoon, and the meeting is in its second hour. The science supervisor, Roger Loren, is uneasy; he believes that some people have not said what's on their minds. He asks, "Do we wish to discuss the science programs anymore before voting?" Ten of the eleven members shake their heads.

The supervisor, seeing that Phyllis Moonale has not joined with the others, asks, "Phyllis, do you think we need more time before deciding?" Phyllis says quietly: "Yes, I do. From what I've been hearing from the other members, they already made up their minds to keep the old science program before we even started. That old program is ridiculously out of date. Just because we might have to change our lesson plans, bulletin board displays, and exam questions—that's no reason to keep the same series. Let's think about the students! They're not learning anything at all about recent science issues such as test tube babies or acid rain. We can't ignore these real science topics for the convenience of keeping our old lesson plans intact!"

The supervisor, after listening carefully, believes that what Phyllis has said is right. The supervisor says: "I agree, we shouldn't keep the old textbook; there are at least three others that would be an improvement over what we have now. I'd go along with any of those three texts."

Fred Willopt, who has been an adamant spokesperson for the old textbook series, speaks: "Come on, let's get on with it! We agreed that this was going to be a group decision; if we couldn't agree unanimously then we would take a majority vote. It's not bad to keep an old program—we do right well by it! Phyllis, why don't you teach those other radical topics all you want, but don't keep us from doing what we want. You and Roger are in the minority. It's time to vote!"

The supervisor responds, "O.K., Fred, you're right—we did agree that this would be a group decision. I don't want that old series. Maybe others don't either. We'll vote on it." Roger calls for a vote: "How many want to keep the old series?" Ten hands go up. "How many want the new series?" Phyllis and Roger raise their hands. Roger looks at Phyllis and can't help feeling disappointed. He says, "All right, we keep the old series. I don't agree, but we'll go along with what the group has decided. The meeting is over."

The supervisor has tried to convince the group to adopt his preference. When it comes to the final decision, however, his vote has no more weight than that of any other member. Furthermore, the group knows that the procedures for making the decision, explained at the first meeting, have been adhered to and that the final decision will be upheld.

A supervisor using a collaborative cluster of behaviors leads the members to a group decision. In the meeting described here, the collaborative supervisor did not exercise a veto when the decision was not turning out the way he preferred. The supervisor's responsibility is to ensure that the full range of ideas and feelings are discussed, including his or her own, before making the final decision. The example given was of a group meeting where collaborative supervision resulted in a decision by majority vote. Obviously, when collaboration is used in an individual conference with a single teacher, the final decision must be made by consensus. Both supervisor and teacher have equal say; if they disagree, no decision can be made. Further discussion about a compromise or alternative solution would be necessary to find a decision satisfactory to both persons. In a group meeting the same principle for resolving lack of consensus can be used with a majority vote. Collaborative supervisory behaviors, whether with an individual teacher or with a group of teachers, result in a mutually shared decision whereby the one-person, one-vote rule holds regardless of the status, title, or power of any individual.

The sequence of collaborative behaviors a supervisor uses in reaching a group decision are similar to those used in meeting with an individual. The main difference is that more time is needed for each member of the group to identify the problem and discuss everyone's suggestions. The supervisor needs to be sensitive to whether the meeting drags—for example, if the same issues are being discussed and positions are not being changed. The supervisor is both an advocate of his or her own position and an expediter of group movement toward a final decision. Let's quickly review collaborative supervisory behaviors in a group meeting.

The supervisor calls the meeting to order and, before discussion, *clarifies* the task and procedures for making the decision. He or she states that they are meeting on a certain issue (selecting next year's textbook) and that the procedures will be collaborative (one vote for each person, with the final decision being made either by consensus or by majority vote). Initiating the discussion, the supervisor asks each group member to *clarify* what he or she sees as the current needs in looking for a textbook. After soliciting group members' opinions, the supervisor *reflects* his or her understanding of what they have been saying, and then *presents* his or her own opinion. The supervisor's position is then clarified by asking the group to paraphrase his or her statements. The supervisor asks for questions. The next step is *problem solving*—asking the group to suggest possible actions to solve the identified problem. This is handled by allowing each individual to present his or her own suggestions. The supervisor might write down all suggestions coming from the group. The supervisor, as an equal member, offers any suggestions he or she may have. All group members are *encouraged* to offer their ideas, no matter how improbable or different from others'. When no more suggestions are forthcoming, the supervisor calls for the group to narrow down the list of possibilities to the two or three best ideas. If consensus about the best ideas is not apparent, the supervisor can ask members to rank all ideas and keep the three ideas with the highest scores. The group further whittles down the list to a single choice as the supervisor asks members to discuss the merits and demerits of each idea. Again, the supervisor leads the discussion by probing for agreements and negotiating between conflicting positions to find a common path. If agreement on a course of action is not emerging, the supervisor looks for ways to synthesize or compromise disparate ideas. Finally, if the choices of group members remain distant and there is no consensus, a majority vote can be taken. The winning idea is *standardized* by the group according to time, place, and persons to be involved in carrying out the plan. The supervisor must then *renegotiate* the final plan by consensus or majority vote on the final standardized and detailed plan.

Issues in Collaborative Supervision

My work with collaboration has shown that it is a deceptively simple set of behaviors for supervisors to understand. The reason is that collaboration appears to be the democratic way of doing things. Most of us have been schooled in equality and democracy, and collaboration appears to be democracy in action. Therefore, it seems apparent that we should ask others for input and that decisions should be made by the majority. However, collaboration with an individual or a group involves more than democratic procedures. It is an attitude of acceptance and a practice of being equal. Therefore, it is not always the mechanical procedures of democracy that demonstrate whether or not collaboration is in use. What appears to be nondemocratic might indeed be collaborative, and what appears to be democratic might not be collaborative. For example, two people can agree as equals that one is better qualified to make a particular decision; the less qualified person might ask the more qualified person to decide for both of them. Here, one person making the decision for both persons appears undemocratic, but it is collaborative. On the other hand, two people can appear to make a collaborative decision, but if one person has discreetly let the other know of his or her power—for example, a personal acquaintanceship with the superintendent of schools—the less powerful person might profess agreement with the more powerful person even though inwardly he or she did not agree. On the surface, the agreement appears to be collaborative, but in reality one person has knuckled under to the power of the other. The purpose of collaboration is to solve problems through a meeting of minds of equals. True equality is the core of collaboration.

One difficulty in working collaboratively occurs when the teacher (or group) believes a supervisor is manipulating the decision when in fact he or she is not. The teacher appears to concur with the supervisor's ideas and suggestions not because of their merit but because the teacher believes the supervisor is really giving a directive. The underlying message the teacher perceives is: "This is my supervisor telling me what she thinks I should do. Even though she says we are making a joint decision, I know I had better do what she says." How does the supervisor know whether a teacher's agreement is sincere or mere compliance? The supervisor might confront the issue by asking the teacher whether he or she is agreeing or only pretending to agree with the supervisor's idea. Acknowledging that the supervisor suspects something is amiss brings the issue out into the open. A teacher who responds, "I don't believe you really are going to let me have equal say" can be dealt with more easily than is possible when a supervisor guesses at the teacher's hidden feelings.

Teachers who refuse to disclose their feelings probably have a history of being mistreated by supervisors. Until the supervisor can demonstrate consistently that he or she really means to be collaborative, no progress will be made. The teacher is not going to believe the supervisor is being collaborative until there is proof. True intent can be demonstrated by refusing to allow decisions to be made without teacher feedback. With nonresponsive and readily acquiescing teachers, a supervisor might say: "I don't know if you're agreeing with me because you like the idea or because of some power I hold over you. We won't carry out any action unless we both agree with that action. I want to be collaborative because I believe you have as much expertise on this matter as I do. Together we can make a better decision than separately. I'm uncertain why you are agreeing with me. Please tell me what you think." A supervisor cannot find out what a teacher thinks without asking. As they continue to meet, the supervisor should begin by encouraging teachers to offer their own thoughts about the problem and suggestions for action. The supervisor should try to withhold any ideas of her own. Once the teacher's ideas are forthcoming, the supervisor can offer his or her own. When negotiating a final decision, the supervisor should let teachers take the lead. If teachers continue to be unresponsive or overly compliant with the supervisor after he or she has confronted the issue of perception and encouraged teacher initiative, then, after several unsuccessful attempts, the supervisor might consider another approach.

The collaborative group process appears to be predicated on the use of consensus or majority vote. However, a supervisor can work collaboratively with a group by using other decision-making procedures such as averaging, frequency ranking, the nominal method, the Delphi technique, or even minority or expert decision. We will explain these procedures in Chapter 18 on group development.

Collaboration is defined as working jointly with others in an intellectual endeavor (*Webster's* 1973). The work is done jointly, but one person can participate more than another. The test of collaboration in supervision is whether the agreed-on decision to improve instruction was satisfactory to all participants. Therefore, although the degree of involvement may vary, the end results are equally determined. With such a definition, we are intentionally allowing for times when a supervisor, teacher, or individual member of a group might convince others of the value of his or her own ideas because of his or her persuasiveness, expertise, and creditability. If ideas are judged on the basis of their merits and not of the power of the individual, then collaboration is at work.

The issues of collaboration are complex. First a supervisor must differentiate democratic procedure from collaboration. Second, he or she must differentiate between acquiescence to power and agreement with ideas. When acquiescence is suspected, the supervisor should bring the issue out into the open. Third, the supervisor needs to keep in mind that some teachers have a history of mistrusting supervisors and must be shown over a period of time that the supervisor truly intends to be collaborative.

It would be nice to say we can lay these issues to rest, but we cannot. Unless the supervisor remains conscious of the complexity of collaboration, he or she can mistakenly allow collaborative behaviors to become something other than they appear. For practice in collaborative behaviors, you might wish to do the activity found in Appendix B3 (Skill Practice in Collaborative Behaviors).

When to Use Collaborative Behaviors

There are circumstances in which a supervisor definitely should use collaborative behaviors. We will leave more detailed instructions for Chapter 11, but, for now, collaboration should be used:

1. When the teacher(s) and supervisor have approximately the same degree of expertise on the issue. If the supervisor knows part of the problem and teachers know the other part, the collaborative approach should be used.

2. When the teacher(s) and supervisor will both be involved in carrying out the decision. If teacher(s) and supervisor will be held accountable for showing results to someone else (say, parents or the superintendent), then the collaborative approach should be used.

3. When the teacher(s) and supervisor both intensely care about the problem. If teachers want to be involved, and if leaving them out will lead to low morale and distrust, then the collaborative approach should be used.

Summary

Collaborative supervision is premised on participation by equals in making instructional decisions. Its outcome is a mutual plan of action. Collaborative behaviors consist of clarifying, listening, reflecting, presenting, problem solving, negotiating, and standardizing. Collaboration is appropriate when teachers and supervisors have similar levels of expertise, involvement, and concern with a problem. The key consideration for a supervisor is the fact that collaboration is both an attitude and a repertoire of behaviors. Unless teachers have the attitude that they are equal, collaborative behaviors can be used to undermine true equality.

EXERCISES

Academic

1. Write an imaginary dialogue between a supervisor and a teacher during a conference in which the supervisor successfully makes use of a collaborative approach. Be sure to include examples of each of the ten collaborative behaviors discussed in Chapter 8.

2. The chapter suggests that a sequence of ten collaborative behaviors takes place during a collaborative conference. Think of a situation in which a successful collaborative conference would start with the first suggested behavior (identifying the problem as seen by the teacher) and end with the tenth (agreeing to final

plan), but would have a *different sequence* of eight intermediate behaviors. Describe the situation and modified sequence of collaborative behaviors in writing. Include a rationale for the suggested sequence.

3. Write an imaginary dialogue between a supervisor and a teacher in which the supervisor implements apparently collaborative procedures with mechanical precision but fails to be collaborative in an effective sense.

4. Prepare a report comparing the collaborative approach as described in this book with the version of collaboration espoused by an author cited in the References.

5. Listening, clarifying, encouraging, reflecting, presenting, problem solving, and standardizing are categories of behavior the chapter uses when describing the nondirective as well as the collaborative approach to supervision. Write a paper explaining how each of these seven categories actually refers to different behaviors, depending on whether the nondirective or the collaborative approach is being used. For each of the seven behavior categories, give a specific behavior that might be displayed by a nondirective supervisor and a specific behavior that might be displayed by a collaborative supervisor.

Field

1. Assume the role of a supervisor using a collaborative approach by either using the simulation activity found in Appendix B3 or conducting an actual postobservation conference with a teacher. Prepare a written report in which you (a) evaluate your success in displaying collaborative behaviors, (b) summarize the problems discussed and decisions made during the conference, (c) give your perceptions of the "teacher's" responses to your collaborative efforts, and (d) judge the conference in terms of overall success.

2. Participate in a group conference that results in a collaborative contract, with some type of instructional improvement as the anticipated result of contract fulfillment. Prepare a report on how the meeting was conducted, any problems that arose, and how the group reached decisions.

3. Observe an educational supervisor or other leader whom you know to have a collaborative orientation in dealing with individuals and/or groups. On the basis of your observations and/or an interview with the leader, prepare a report describing both successes and failures the selected leader has experienced while

using collaborative behaviors. Include possible reasons that the collaborative leader was more successful in some situations than in others.

4. Prepare a photo album entitled "Collaboration for Instructional Improvement." Each photograph should be accompanied by a written explanation of how that entry relates to the album theme.

5. Videotape or audiotape a collaborative conference or staff development activity. As you review the tape, compare the recorded activities with the sequence of behaviors that, according to the chapter, exemplifies the nominal collaborative decision-making process. Prepare a written report on your findings.

Development

1. Through interaction with various individuals in a variety of situations, begin to establish a set of personal guidelines that will indicate when the collaborative approach is most appropriate for your own use in carrying out present or anticipated leadership functions.

2. Initiate an in-depth study of Japanese-style management. As you proceed with your study, compare and contrast this style of management with the collaborative approach to supervision discussed in this chapter.

3. Record a simulated or actual supervisor–teacher conference in which you, as supervisor, attempt to display collaborative behaviors. Review the tape for analysis of your performance. Over the next four weeks, attempt to practice collaborative leadership whenever appropriate opportunities arise. Record another simulated or actual supervisor–teacher conference, and determine what changes you have made.

REFERENCES

Blumberg, A. 1980. *Supervisors and teachers: A private cold war,* 2nd ed. Berkeley, Calif: McCutchan.

Cogan, M. 1973. *Clinical supervision.* Boston: Houghton Mifflin.

Gordon, T. 1977. *Leader Effectiveness Training, L.E.T.: The no-lose way to release the productive potential of people.* New York: Wyden Books.

Harris, T. 1967. *I'm OK—you're OK: Practical guide to transactional analysis.* New York: Harper & Row, Chapters 3 and 4.

Wagner, A. 1981. *Transactional manager: How to solve people problems with transactional analysis.* Englewood Cliffs, N.J.: Prentice-Hall.

Webster's New Collegiate Dictionary. 1973. Springfield, Mass: Merriam, p. 219.

Wiles, K. 1967. *Supervision for better schools,* 3rd ed. Englewood Cliffs, N.J.: Prentice-Hall.

Chapter 9

Directive Informational Behaviors

Supervisor: So, in conclusion, what I've observed is that seven of your twenty-six students had little involvement in the discussion or question and answer period.

Teacher: Well, those seven who you are referring to show no interest in class. At least, if they are quiet, they don't interfere with the learning of others. However, I am surprised that they had such little involvement. I guess if they are quiet, I've just learned to tune them out.

Supervisor: I believe that a goal might be to involve those seven students actively in your future classes.

Teacher: I'd agree. None of my other classes are like this. If I only knew how to do that! When I call on them, they don't respond. When I give the class a controversial topic in U.S. History, most students jump right in, but Sheila, Aliendra, and the rest of them go blank, giggle, and seem not to care.

Supervisor: Well, based on my own experiences as a teacher and what I've seen others do with seemingly apathetic students, let me give you a list of possible actions. Think about them, and determine which of these are worth trying. First, you might establish individual contracts with each of those seven students, that they will be expected to participate at least twice in each class and can earn extra homework points for their participation. Second, you might move to the back and corners of the room during question and answer sessions. This is where most of these nonparticipating kids sit. In your lesson plans, make notes to call on each of these students at least once. Your physical presence close to them might help. Third, when you know that a topic to be introduced can be controversial, you might prep the students by using a cooperative learning format. Break the class into groups of three—put each of the nonparticipants with two active participants and ask each group to formulate a group position, with each member being responsible for reporting the position. Monitor the groups while they are working. At discussion times, occasionally call the nonparticipants to speak for the group. What do you think of these possibilities?

Teacher: Individual contracts for students isn't practical—other students would think I'm playing favorites. Moving around to the back and corners of the room is obvious, I could become more aware of doing that. The last idea of cooperative groups is one that I hadn't thought of with this class. I do that with my honors classes but never thought of using small groups here. I guess I assumed that it would be too confusing.

Supervisor: Which of these activities would you like to try?

Teacher: Moving to the back of the room, for sure! The cooperative learning, I'd like to try on a small scale to see how it would work. What do I need to do to prepare the groups to work together and how do I introduce the topic and task?

Directive Informational Behaviors with Individuals

The scenario, transcribed from a tape of an actual conference, shows a supervisor acting as the information source for the goal and activities of the improvement plan. The supervisor, through her observations, has determined a clear classroom goal for the teacher and directs the teacher to those activities she believes to have a high degree of probability in achieving the goal. Notice that, through each step of the conference, the supervisor remains the information source but always asks and considers teacher feedback. Furthermore, the supervisor provides a range of alternatives from which the teacher is asked to choose. The scenario concludes with the teacher's committing himself to using several activities. The supervisor then will detail with the teacher the what, when, and how of implementing the activities, set criteria for improvement, and reinforce the understanding of what is to be done. As we look at a sequence of directive informational behaviors (see Figure 9-1), keep in mind that the supervisor is constantly framing the direction and choices for the teacher.

1. Presenting: *Identifying the goal.* Based on the observation and previous experience she has with the teacher, the supervisor begins by reviewing her summarized observations and concluding with an interpretation that seven students being nonparticipants throughout a class period is problematic. Therefore, she sees an important goal as "involving all students . . . ."

2. Clarifying: *Asking teacher for input into the goal.* The su-

pervisor is careful not to move too quickly into a planning phase until she checks to see what the teacher thinks of her interpretation and goal. The teacher is surprised, agrees, and explains why these seven students have been neglected.

3. Listening: *Understanding the teacher's point of view*. The supervisor listens to determine if the teacher accepts the goal as an important one or if she needs to provide further explanation.

4. Problem solving: *Mentally determining possible actions*. The supervisor has given thought to some alternative actions that might be considered by the teacher. When the teacher explains the reasons for students being uninvolved and what has been done, the supervisor mentally prepares to lay out the alternative actions or suggestions.

5. Directing: *Telling alternatives for teachers to consider*. The supervisor carefully words the alternative actions as possibilities, based on her experience and knowledge, for the teacher to judge, consider, and respond.

6. Listening: *Asking teacher for input into alternatives*. The supervisor asks the teacher to react to her suggestions. The teacher has the opportunity now to give the supervisor information to modify, eliminate, and revise before finalizing the choices.

7. Directing: *Framing the final choices*. In a straightforward manner, the supervisor lays out what the teacher could do: "So, in the final analysis, these are the actions you could take . . . ."

8. Clarifying: *Asking the teacher to choose*. The supervisor asks the teacher to decide and clarify which activities or combinations he will use.

9. Standardizing: *Detailing the actions to be taken*. At this juncture, the supervisor assists the teacher in developing the specifics of the activities (i.e., introduce cooperative learning, set up three-somes, identify one controversial topic, try for fifteen minutes next Tuesday, etc.) and the criteria for success (i.e., "Let's see, when I come in next Thursday, whether four of these seven students can be called upon and give prepared, on-target responses").

10. Reinforcing: *Reporting and following up on the plan*. The supervisor concludes the conference by restating the goal, the activities to be taken, the criteria for success, and the follow-up time for the next observation and/or conference.

Directive Informational Behaviors with Groups

The six grade-level chairpersons are meeting with the school's instructional lead teacher. The topic of discussion is a widespread concern with the placement of new students in classrooms during

Figure 9-1 The supervisory behavior continuum: directive informational behaviors

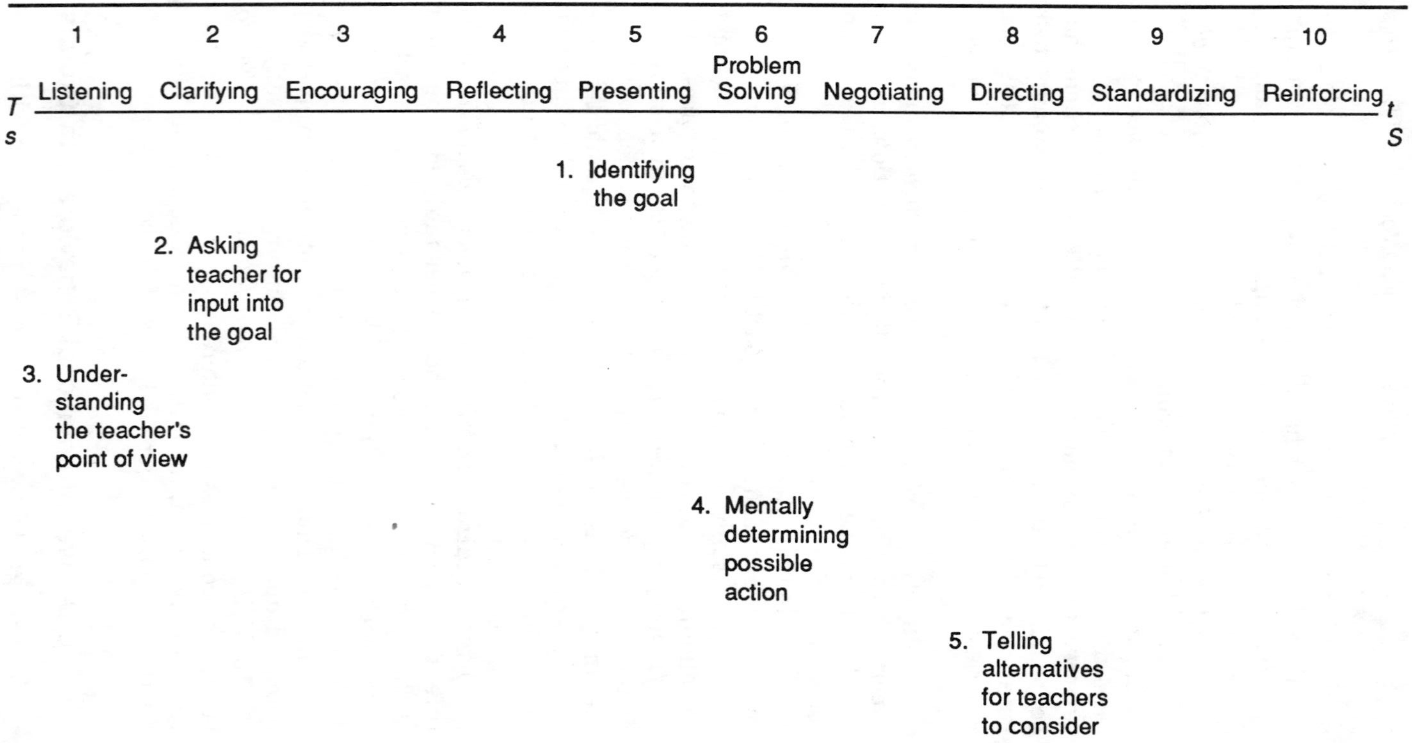

	1	2	3	4	5	6	7	8	9	10	
T	Listening	Clarifying	Encouraging	Reflecting	Presenting	Problem Solving	Negotiating	Directing	Standardizing	Reinforcing	t
s											s

1. Identifying the goal

2. Asking teacher for input into the goal

3. Under-standing the teacher's point of view

4. Mentally determining possible action

5. Telling alternatives for teachers to consider

154

6. Asking teacher for input into alternatives

7. Framing the final choices

8. Asking teacher to make choice

9. Determining the actions to be taken

10. Repeating and following up on plan

Key: *T* = Maximum teacher responsibility *S* = Maximum supervisor responsibility
t = Minimum teacher responsibility *s* = Minimum supervisor responsibility

the school year. As a result of previous discussions, it has become apparent that some teachers believe it unwise simply to place new students in the classrooms with the fewest number of students, without accounting for the particular needs of students and teachers. The premise is that some teachers are better equipped to teach students with special needs (bilingual, gifted, learning disabled, withdrawn, etc.). Prior to this meeting, the instructional lead teacher has spoken with the principal, the assistant superintendent for instruction, and the director of pupil personnel. The topic is a pressing one, as there are five transfer students who will begin classes next Monday, four short days from now.

Supervisor: The issue is clear. How should we place transfer students in classrooms? In the past, I've done it strictly according to class enrollment. It doesn't have to continue that way. School Board policy simply states that all classrooms are to be heterogeneously grouped.

Second-Grade Chairperson: Does this mean that as long as there isn't a disproportionate number of students with a particular level of ability in any one classroom, transfer students can be matched with the particular abilities of a teacher?

Supervisor: Yes and no. We have flexibility, but we can't make one classroom more of a place for all behavior-disordered students and another class for creative students.

Second-Grade Chairperson: I read you. We're on the same wave length. But we do have flexibility within reasonable heterogeneity.

Supervisor: Yes. As I see it, we do have several options. We need to make a quick decision, because tomorrow there are five new students to place. We could do the following. (A) Leave placement as is, let me continue to place new students according to classroom enrollment. (B) Let each grade chair determine the placement of each new student with the teachers in that grade. (C) Ask the individual teachers to identify the types of student that they can work well with and those that they don't work well with. That information could go either to me or to you, to make placements accordingly.

First-Grade Chair: I don't like that last idea. Some teachers would say that they don't work well with "rude" students. What's going to happen to them? Those teachers won't get any students who have records of misbehavior? Or if they do, they'll complain how someone went against their requests.

Third-Grade Chair: How about letting those grades who want to make their own placements do so, and for those who don't, you make them?

Supervisor: Nope, can't do that. I've talked with the principal and assistant superintendent. We need to be consistent in whatever we do. We can't have each grade level doing its own thing; we as a school must decide on a consistent procedure for placement of students. The choices, as I now see it, are (1) I do it according to numbers or (2) you do it according to your knowledge of individual teachers.

Third-Grade Chair: How about a combination of the two? You tentatively place according to classroom enrollment and then check with the grade-level chair to see if the receiving teacher is well equipped to work with the student. If not, between you and the grade level chair, another assignment can be made.

Supervisor: That's OK with me, just as long as all teachers are informed of the new procedures at tomorrow's meeting. We need to make sure that, if there is that disagreement that can't be resolved between me and the grade level chair, someone will have the final say.

Fifth-Grade Chair: No sense in involving anyone else. You have the final say. Let's try this procedure out for the remainder of the year and see how the new placement works.

Supervisor: Alright. Do we agree that beginning tomorrow, placement will be done in the following manner . . . . ?

The instructional lead teacher used a directive informational approach in having the group make a decision within a clearly articulated framework of supervisor alternatives. Each alternative initially proposed by the supervisor was acceptable to herself—she could live with any of them. After soliciting questions and discussions, she rejected some proposed alternatives as unacceptable, discarded one of her own as unacceptable to the group, and finalized the choices. At that point, she asked the group to choose from within the reconsidered and revised alternatives, and then detailed the specifics of the action (or combination of actions) to be implemented.

Issues in the Directive Informational Approach

Anyone who uses a directive informational approach needs to be aware of the degree of expertise that he or she has when delineating the choices available to others. Since the supervisor is placing himself or herself in the role of expert, the issues of confidence and credibility are crucial. The supervisor must be confident that he or she knows what practices will work in helping the teacher, because when the teacher chooses to use one or more of the supervisor's suggestions, the person ultimately responsible for the success or failure of the various practices will be the supervisor, not the teacher. After all, if I consider and select from your proposed actions, implement what you've suggested, and those actions don't work, I'm probably going to tell you the next time we meet, when we note that the goal is no closer to being achieved, "After all, I just did what you told me to do!"

The teacher is correct in holding the supervisor accountable for the results. Thus the issue of credibility hovers above the directive informational approach. Not only must the supervisor be confident that his or her own knowledge and experience are superior to and different from those of the teacher, but the teacher must also believe that the supervisor possesses a source of wisdom that he or she does not have. When confidence and credibility in the supervisor's knowledge are shared by both parties, and the teacher is either unaware, inexperienced, or stumped about what changes can be made, then the directive informational approach can be a most valuble set of behaviors to use. When we begin on a path where we have not ventured before, there is much to be learned from a person who has explored that trail successfully many times in the past. This might be the reason why directive informational approaches are seen as most helpful to teachers when they are inexperienced, confused, unaware, or simply at a loss for what to do about a particular classroom or school goal.

Finally, with a directive informational approach, it is imperative to remember that the teacher exercises some control in choosing which practice(s) to use. (This is not the case when we look at the fourth approach, directive control.) You might ask, "What if the teacher refuses to make a choice?" If so, the issue of confidence and credibility has not been resolved, and the supervisor must make a judgment whether to change in midstream to another approach (collaborative or directive control), table the conference, or continue discussion further to convince the teacher of his or her wisdom.

When to Use Directive Informational Behaviors

Directive informational behaviors revolve around expertise, confidence, credibility, and limiting choice (Greiner 1967). Therefore, they should be employed:

1. When teachers do not possess the knowledge about an issue that the supervisor clearly possesses.

2. When the teacher feels confused, inexperienced, or is at a loss for what to do, and the supervisor knows of successful practices.

3. When the supervisor is willing to take responsibility for what the teacher chooses to try.

4. When the teacher believes that the supervisor is credible—a person who has the background and wisdom to know whereof he or she speaks.

5. When the time is short, the constraints are clear, and quick, concrete actions need to be taken.

Further practice in using directive informational approaches can be found in Appendix B4.

Summary

Directive informational supervision is used to direct teacher(s) to consider and choose from clearly delineated alternative actions. The supervisor is the major source of information, goal articulation, and suggested practices. However, the supervisor is careful to solicit teacher input as he or she revises and refines the choices; ultimately, the teacher is asked to make a judgment as to which practices or combinations are feasible and realistic. Such an approach is useful when the expertise, confidence, and credibility of the supervisor clearly outweighs the teacher's own information, experience, and capabilities.

EXERCISES

Academic

1. Write an imaginary dialogue between a supervisor and a teacher, during a conference in which the supervisor successfully uses a directive informational approach. Be sure to include examples of each of the ten behaviors discussed in Chapter 9.

2. The last main section of the chapter delineates five examples in which it is appropriate to use the directive informational approach. Write a description of a situation for each example. Can you think of any other circumstances, other than the five given, for which the directive informational approach would be appropriate? If so, include such an example in your answer.

3. Write an imaginary dialogue between a supervisor and a teacher during a conference in which the supervisor implements directive informational procedures with mechanical precision but fails to be successful for one or a number of reasons.

4. Explain what you would do if you as a supervisor worked with a teacher who always wanted you to use the directive informational approach with him or her. This experienced teacher is quite comfortable in the classroom and when asked can clearly articulate concerns or problems he or she has for his or her students and the school. Yet, unlike his or her peers, who prefer the collaborative or nondirective approach, this teacher favors being given a choice from your suggestions. Do you feel you should continue using the directive informational approach with this teacher? Write a summary of your position and give reasons for your decision.

5. After reviewing a book on student discipline or management, compare the approach the author recommends using the directive informational approach. Why might these two approaches appear similar? Write a summary of your analysis.

Field

1. Assume the role of a supervisor using a directive informational approach, by either using the simulated activity in Appendix B4 or conducting an actual postobservation conference with a teacher. Prepare a written report in which you (a) evaluate your success in displaying directive informational behaviors, (b) summarize the problems discussed and decisions made during the conference, (c) give your perceptions of the teacher's responses to your directive efforts, and (d) judge the conference in terms of overall success.

2. Interview teachers who prefer the directive informational approach. Write a summary of your findings.

3. Record times you or a supervisor at your school has used the directive informational approach. Describe the situation being dealt with and the results. Overall, how successful have you or your supervisor been with this approach? Explain your answer.

4. Tape-record a faculty meeting during which the supervisor uses the directive informational approach. Analyze the tape to determine whether the meeting was successful. Make a chart with a space for each of the directive informational supervisory behaviors. As you listen to the tape, record each time a behavior is used and in what sequence. Does a correlation exist between

the overall success of the meeting and the frequency and sequence of the supervisory behaviors? Prepare a report of your findings.

5. Create a collage of pictures and/or words that shows when it is appropriate to use directive informational behaviors. Use the five examples given in this chapter to guide you.

Developmental

1. Tape-record a conference during which you, as the supervisor, attempt to use the directive informational approach. Review and analyze the tape. Note the sequence of behaviors. At a later date, record another conference during which you use the directive informational approach. Analyze the tape and note the sequence of behaviors. Was the sequence the same in both conferences? How did the sequences of behaviors affect the outcome?

2. Keep a log each time you use the directive informational approach. Record the problem discussed, the teacher(s) involved, and the decision made. After several months, study your log for any patterns. Do you use this approach with the same teachers? Are the problems similar? Consider the patterns, if any, to evaluate your behavior and effectiveness as a supervisor.

3. Begin a chart that delineates what you consider to be each teacher's expertise and experience level in your work situation. Ask four or five teachers to list those areas or topics about teaching in which they could use more information and specific suggestions. Do you find common areas where a directive informational group approach would be appropriate?

REFERENCE

Greiner, L.E. 1967. Patterns of organizational change. *Harvard Business Review* 45:119–130. See the "decisions from alternatives approach."

Chapter 10

Directive Control Behaviors

Supervisor: Have you been using the microcomputers yet? I haven't seen any students at the desks.

Teacher: Well, I really don't think computers are such an important topic for seventh-grade mathematics. The students need training in basic geometry, not in how to play games with a computer.

Supervisor: As you know, part of the geometry curriculum is on a computer disk. It's not just fun and games. They could be learning geometry as they become familiar with operating the computer.

Teacher: All this computer emphasis is ridiculous! It's another educational fad that's supposed to solve all our problems! I have enough trouble getting kids to learn what's in the book.

Supervisor: I understand your reservations about using the computer, but our school curriculum states that microcomputers are to be used in seventh-grade mathematics. We're committed to doing so, particularly after spending so much money on the equipment and software.

Teacher: I think it's ridiculous.

Supervisor: That's beside the point. I want to see your kids using them.

Teacher: I'd rather not. Couldn't they teach computers in science class? After all, computers are science.

Supervisor: We're probably going to see computer use in every subject before long, but for now it's to go on in mathematics. I'd like to see at least one-third of your class begin the software program on plotting graphs by next Friday.

Teacher: Who's going to show them how to operate the program? I don't know how to.

Supervisor: Mrs. Techno, you were a participant in the computer class last summer. You know how to do it.

Teacher: I didn't understand the foggiest bit of it. Professor Wallenwood was a terrible teacher. He just paid attention to all those teachers who already had a computer background.

Supervisor: Well, I wasn't aware that you were unsure of how to use the microcomputer in class. I'll call Fred Tirtial, director of media, to come into your class next week to demonstrate how to use the equipment. I'll see to it that he gets the program started in your class, and then you continue with it.

Teacher: Any help would be appreciated.

Supervisor: You keep me posted, and we'll shoot for at least one group of your students working on the graphing program by a week from Friday.

Directive Control Behaviors with Individuals

The foregoing scenario shows a supervisor using directive control behaviors to assist a teacher in improving instruction. The obvious question is that the teacher may respond to such directiveness with a firm refusal: "I am not going to meet with you or follow through with your plans." If the supervisor has a position of conferred authority over teachers, he or she can pull rank by restating the directive and telling the teacher to comply or suffer the consequences. If the supervisor does not have such authority—which, with the exception of school principals, is often the case—then he or she can direct only by convincing the teacher that the suggested plan is correct. Regardless of a line or staff relationship, the supervisor uses directive control behavior with teachers when there is an assumption that the supervisor has greater knowledge and expertise about the issue at hand. In other words, the belief behind directive control behaviors is that the supervisor knows better than the teacher what needs to be done to improve instruction.

It is evident in the scenario that the supervisor has taken over the teacher's problem. At first the supervisor identified the problem by gathering information from his own observations and discussing this information with the teacher. Next he told the teacher what to do and provided an explanation of why his suggestion would work. He concluded by reviewing the proposed action and reiterating his expectations for the teacher. The teacher was left with a concrete understanding of what she was expected to do. As we look at a typical sequence of behaviors along the supervisory behavior continuum (Figure 10-1), keep in mind that the sequence and fre-

Figure 10-1 The supervisory behavior continuum: directive control behaviors

T	1	2	3	4	5	6	7	8	9	10	t
s	Listening	Clarifying	Encouraging	Reflecting	Presenting	Problem Solving	Negotiating	Directing	Standardizing	Reinforcing	s

1. Identifying the problem

2. Asking teacher for input into the problem

3. Understanding the teacher's point of view

4. Mentally determining the best solution

5. Telling expectations for teacher

164

6. Asking teacher
   for input into
   the expectations

7. Detailing and
   modifying
   expectations

8. Repeating
   and following
   up on expecta-
   tions

Key: T = Maximum teacher responsibility S = Maximum supervisor responsibility
     t = Minimum teacher responsibility s = Minimum supervisor responsibility

165

quency of behaviors will vary, especially in the beginning of the conference, but the directive control approach will end with the supervisor making the final decisions for the teacher. This chapter will accentuate directive behaviors that control teacher actions.

1. Presenting: *Identifying the problem.* The supervisor begins with a general idea of what the needs and difficulties are. Having used observations and gathered information from other sources, the supervisor tells the teacher what seems to be the problem: "I understand that there is a problem with . . ."

2. Clarifying: *Asking teacher for input into the problem.* The supervisor wants to gather direct information from the teacher about the problem prior to the solution stage. This is done by using the teacher in an advisory capacity, asking the teacher such questions as, "How do you see the problem?" and "Why do you think these conditions exist?"

3. Listening: *Understanding the teacher's point of view.* To gather maximum information in the shortest amount of time, the supervisor must attend carefully to what the teacher says. He or she listens both to the surface messages—"Computers are a waste of time"—and to underlying messages—"I don't know how to use them"—in formulating a complete problem.

4. Problem solving: *Mentally determining the best solution.* The supervisor processes the information and thinks, "What can be done?" After considering various possibilities, he or she selects the needed actions. The supervisor should be confident of indeed having a good, manageable solution to the problem before conveying it to the teacher.

5. Directing: *Telling expectations to the teacher.* The supervisor tells the teacher in a matter-of-fact way what needs to be done: "I want to see you do the following . . ." The phrasing of the directive is important. Avoid timid, circular expectations: "Well, maybe you might consider doing . . ." or "Don't you think it would be a good idea to . . . ?" The supervisor is not asking or pleading with the teacher, but *telling.* On the other hand, directing does not mean being vindictive, overbearing, condescending, or insulting. Avoid personal slights or paternalistic references: "I don't know why you can't figure out what needs to be done." "Why can't you get it right in the first place?" "Now listen, honey, I'm going to help you by . . . ." A supervisor should state actions as *I* statements, not as what others think. Tell the teacher what *I* want to happen, not what parents, other teachers, or the superintendent would want to see. A statement such as, "If the superintendent saw this, he would tell you to do . . . ." is hiding behind someone else's authority. The

supervisor needs to make statements based on his or her own position, credibility, and authority.

6. Clarifying: *Asking teacher for input into the expectations.* Possible difficulties with the supervisor's directive should be known before the teacher leaves the conference. For example, if circumstances exist that make teacher compliance with the directive impossible, it is better to adjust to those circumstances during the conference than to find out two weeks later why the plan failed. Therefore, after telling the teacher what is expected—"I want one-third of your students using the computers"—the supervisor needs to ask such questions as, "What do you need to carry out this plan?" or "How can I help you carry out the plan?"

7. Standardizing: *Detailing and modifying expectations.* After considering the teacher's reactions to the directive, the supervisor solidifies the plan by building in the necessary assistance, resources, time lines, and criteria for expected success. The teacher is then told the revisions: "I can rearrange the visit time to . . . ," "I will find those materials for you," "I will arrange for you to attend . . . ," "I will change the time to three weeks."

8. Reinforcing: *Repeating and following up on expectations.* The supervisor reviews the entire plan and establishes times for checking on progress. The supervisor closes the meeting by making sure the teacher clearly understands the plan: "Do you understand what you're to do?" or "Tell me what it is you're now going to do."

Directive Control Behaviors with Groups

The seven Physical Education Department members meet with their supervisor. The supervisor addresses them.

Supervisor: I've been noticing that our physical education classes have not been starting on time. They are to begin at five minutes past the hour and end at fifteen minutes before the next hour. We're supposed to get in a full forty minutes of physical education. Some classes are being dismissed early, some late, and the other teachers in the school are complaining. They say our sloppiness is causing other problems—students loitering in the halls, looking into class windows, and straggling in late. We need to begin and end on time. Why is this happening?

Fred Soccerman: Those regular classroom teachers are fine ones to talk! They send the kids to us at all times of the day.

Supervisor: Is that true of all of you? [The other members all nod their heads in agreement.] Are there other problems, Shirley?

Shirley Dancercise: I don't intend to dismiss my students early or late, but I don't think the clocks in the lunchroom are synchronized with the classroom clocks.

Supervisor: I'll check on that. Are there other reasons?

Fred Soccerman: The students get a full period in my class; I don't think this is a real issue.

Supervisor: Maybe not, but I'm going to emphasize that we all begin class at five past and dismiss at quarter of. In the meantime, I'll check with the custodians about seeing that the clocks are synchronized, and at the faculty meeting I'll mention our concerns about other teachers sending their students to you at the wrong time. Does everyone understand what I expect of you? Walt?

Walt: I hope some of us are not intentionally letting the students out early. By gosh, we have enough to accomplish with the little time we have.

Supervisor: I'm not implying that we are shortening our instructional time. I'm simply stating that from now on we're going to have a full, consistent forty minutes of instruction for every teacher and every class. If need be, I'll be coming around to see that we are doing it.

Fred: Let's not make this such a big deal. We'll get it done. Now can we talk about the new aerobic exercise elective that we're supposed to be planning?

Although the issue of starting time at the supervisor's meeting might appear to be of relative unimportance to staff members, it was important to the supervisor. Instead of letting the issue pass and risking further complications with other teachers, she decided to meet the issue head on. In the supervisor's role of leader, expert, and possessor of a larger view, she judged that the staff needed to know of her concern and that they would be expected to comply with her directive. At the same time, she was willing to listen to their reactions and to use their information to remedy the situation. It was clear from the outset that the supervisor was making the decision and that the staff was being used in an advisory, not a decision-making, capacity.

In group meetings a supervisor uses directive control behaviors to give a clear message about what changes are expected. The supervisor states his or her understanding of the problem (*presenting*), asks group members if they have more to add (*clarifying*), listens to their input (*listening*), and then mentally reassesses the problem and possible solutions (*problem solving*). He or she proceeds to state what is to be done (*directing*), asks for input (*clarifying*), lays out the actual actions (*standardizing*), and monitors the expected performance (*reinforcing*).

Issues in Directive Control

Two of three major issues with using directive control behaviors have already been mentioned. One has to do with being forthright, the other with source of authority. The third issue is a consideration of time.

A supervisor who needs a teacher to do something has to tell the teacher exactly and honestly what it is. The precision and frankness of a message can be misconstrued or lost in a conference or meeting. Most of us find it difficult to look another person squarely in the eye and say, "I want you to do this." Instead, we often attempt to soften the message by equivocating. It is the difference between telling a person, "Maybe you could try to be more prompt in starting and ending your class" and telling him, "Starting tomorrow I want your class to begin at 8:05 A.M. and end at 8:45 A.M." "Be more prompt" is open to interpretation; "beginning tomorrow at 8:05" means just that. Being direct takes the ambiguity out of the expectations. I'll illustrate this with a personal example. An elementary supervisor I know would become angry at teachers for not doing what he expected of them, only to realize later that the teachers never understood what he meant. He learned a trick that helped him become clearer in giving such messages. He would write down word-for-word the critical statement he wanted to tell the teacher or group. He would keep the written statement in front of him during the conference or meeting. Thus there was no guesswork involved in giving the message. After a meeting he could look at the written statement and know whether he had delivered it or not.

To many of us, directive control connotes an adversary relationship. It conjures up an image of the pushy, authoritarian boss at work. This is a stereotyped connotation, however. Being directive basically involves letting the other person know (1) what the supervisor is convinced will improve the teacher's instruction *and* (2) that the supervisor is willing to assume complete responsibility for that decision. A teacher might welcome knowing the depth and clarity of the supervisor's expectations. It is better to be up front about the directive than to pretend that teachers have decision-making power over issues that in reality they do not control. Some supervisors avoid being directive controlling by going through the directive informational, collaborative, or nondirective behaviors of involving staff when they've already made the decision. One might be able to succeed with such manipulation temporarily, but once staff members become aware that their involvement was of no significance, they will be resistant to further involvement with the supervisor. With each issue, it is best to let teachers know the degree of their involvement, ranging from full involvement to none, rather than being nebulous. Anyone would prefer to work in a place where the game is *on,* not *under,* the table. Directive control should be viewed as being informative, decisive, and clear about what teachers have little control over. It also means listening and being willing to modify one's expectations according to reactions from teachers that point out the error of one's directives.

The other major issue raised by directive control behavior concerns power and authority. Unless a supervisor holds formal line authority over teachers, he or she cannot enforce directives: It is impossible to make the teacher do what he or she wants. Instead, a supervisor with a staff relationship can expect teachers to follow imposed plans only if they respect the supervisor and trust his or her judgment. The supervisor must demonstrate and convince the teachers of this superior expertise. If the supervisor has line authority over teachers, however, it is more difficult to separate teacher compliance due to respect for the supervisor from that due to a perceived threat to job security. The line supervisor might believe teachers are following orders because of his or her superior knowledge, but the teachers might actually believe the supervisor is an ignoramus. Because of such ambiguity, a line supervisor must be extremely careful when using directive control.

Directive control should be a measure of last resort when an immediate decision is needed. Other directive, nondirective, or collaborative approaches will normally ensure greater receptivity by teachers and greater likelihood of successful implementation of a decision, but decisions will take longer to make. Inevitably, when there are many people involved in a decision, discussion, conflict, and resolution will take more time than when only one person is deciding. However, not every instructional problem needs to be addressed at length; a supervisor using directiveness judiciously might actually save time for those decisions most important to staff. There are matters (such as scheduling or budgeting) in which teachers may not desire involvement. A supervisor who attempts to involve people in decisions they view as a waste of time is just as inept as one who does not involve people in decisions about which they care intensely. At times a supervisor with such authority does better by being directive and making the decision.

The issue of time includes the need for directive control in response to emergencies. When the flow of school life is interrupted by irate parents, student defiance, malfunctioning heaters, or media investigations, the supervisor may have to be unilaterally decisive. He or she will simply not have time to meet with teachers before responding. For example, a middle school principal was called at home by a newspaper reporter who sought her reaction to a fire marshal's report about unsafe cardboard partitions in a classroom of her school. The principal, totally unaware of the marshal's visit, refused comment and called the fire marshal to confirm the report. The marshal told her that all cardboard in classrooms was to be removed by the following morning. Deciding not to fight the fire marshal's orders and thus to avoid further newspaper attention, the principal told each teacher arriving at school the next morning of the fire marshal's report and told them to have their rooms cleared of all cardboard partitions before ten o'clock. She also informed them that they would meet later that afternoon to discuss the fire marshal's ruling and determine whether they wanted to appeal it. For the moment, she had used her own judgment. Later, when there was time to review the matter, she and the staff decided collaboratively to meet with the marshal about a proposal to reinstall cardboard partitions covered with fire-resistant plastic. This example shows that at a time of emergency a supervisor, whether ultimately right or wrong, must be directive.

When to Use Directive Control Behaviors

Since directive behaviors raise issues of power, respect, expertise, and line and staff relationships, the following guidelines are given with caution. Directive control behaviors should be employed:

1. When teachers do not have awareness, knowledge, or inclination to act on an issue that a supervisor, who has organizational authority, thinks to be of critical importance to the students, the teachers, or the community, then the directive control approach should most likely be used.

2. When the teachers will have no involvement and the supervisor will be involved in carrying out the decision. If the supervisor will be held totally accountable and the teachers will not, then the directive control approach should probably be used.

3. When the supervisor cares intensely about the issue and the teachers do not. When decisions do not concern teachers, and they prefer the supervisor to make the decision, the directive control approach should most likely be used.

4. In an emergency, when the supervisor does not have time to meet with teachers, the directive control approach should be used.

Summary

Directive control supervision is used to transmit supervisor expectations to teachers clearly. Supervisors in a line position *over* teachers can use directive controlling language and enforce via hierarchical control. Supervisors in a staff position can only hope for compliance based on trust and credibility with teachers. Directive control supervision consists of behaviors of presenting, clarifying, listening, problem solving, directing, standardizing, and reinforcing (with line authority). The direction of presenting, problem solving, and directing is mostly from supervisor to teacher. Directive control behaviors are useful in limited circumstances when teachers possess little expertise, involvement, or interest with respect to an instructional problem and time is short. In these circumstances, directive control is not an adversarial or capricious set of behaviors, but an honest approach with teachers to an emergency.

EXERCISES

Academic

1. Write an imaginary dialogue between a supervisor and a teacher during a conference in which the supervisor successfully uses a directive control approach. Be sure to include examples of each of the eight behaviors discussed in Chapter 10.

2. The chapter suggests that a sequence of eight directive control behaviors takes place during a directive conference. Think of a situation in which a successful directive control conference would start with the first suggested behavior (identifying the problem) and end with the eighth (repeating and following up on expectations), but have a different sequence of six intermediate behaviors. Describe the situation and modified sequence of directive behaviors in writing. Include a rationale for the suggested sequence.

3. Write an imaginary dialogue between a supervisor and a teacher in which the supervisor implements directive control procedures with mechanical precision but fails to be directive in an effective sense.

4. Write a paper comparing the directive control approach as described in this book with the version of directive informational behavior presented in the previous chapter.

5. Assume you have recently attended a seminar at which a university professor argued against educational supervisors using the directive control approach with any teacher. The professor proposed that the supervisor should play the role of a helper, not attempt to control a teacher's behavior. The speaker argued that successful change cannot be brought about unless the teacher perceives the need for change and has had a part in deciding how to bring about the needed change. He concluded that a directive control supervisory approach will only alienate teachers and make supervisors unwelcome in many classrooms. You have been asked to reply to the professor's arguments at an upcoming seminar. Write a paper in which you present an argument for using directive control behaviors with some teachers and under some circumstances.

Field

1. Assume the role of a supervisor using a directive control approach by conducting a simulated postobservation conference with a teacher. Assume that the teacher is in clear violation of a policy and has refused to change his or her practice. Prepare a written report in which you (a) evaluate your success in displaying control behaviors, (b) summarize the problems discussed and decisions made during the conference, (c) give your perceptions of the teacher's responses to your directive control efforts, and (d) judge the conference in terms of overall success.

2. Observe an educational supervisor or other leader whom you know to possess a directive control orientation in dealing with individuals and/or groups. On the basis of your observations and/or an interview with the leader, write a paper describing both successes and failures the selected leader has experienced while using directive control behaviors. Include possible reasons that the directive leader has been more successful in some situations than in others.

3. Observe three teachers or staff members who clearly respond positively to directive control supervision. Write a paper examining personal and social characteristics of these individuals that may account for their positive response to a directive control approach.

4. Prepare a photo album entitled "Supervisory Direction for Instructional Improvement." Each photograph should be accompanied by a written explanation of how it relates to the album theme.

5. Videotape or audiotape a conference or staff development activity led by a supervisor who typically uses a directive control approach. As you review the tape, compare the recorded activities with the sequence of behaviors that, according to the chapter, exemplify the directive process. Prepare a report on your findings.

Developmental

1. Through interaction with various individuals in a variety of situations, begin to establish a set of personal guidelines that will indicate when the directive control approach is most appropriate for your own use in carrying out present or anticipated leadership functions.

2. Begin an in-depth study of assertiveness training (see the References). As you progress through your study, note how training in assertiveness can be used by supervisors when they find themselves with teachers or in situations requiring a direct control approach.

3. Record a simulated or actual supervisor–teacher conference in which you, as supervisor, attempt to display directive control behaviors. Review the tape for analysis of your performance. Record another simulated or actual conference in four weeks. Review both tapes to discover any improvement in terms of successfully displaying behaviors the chapter describes as directive control.

REFERENCES

Alberti, R.E., and Emmons, M.L. 1974. *Your perfect right: A guide to assertive behavior.* San Luis Obispo, Calif.: Impact.

Lucio, W.H., and McNeil, J.D. 1979. *Supervision: A synthesis of thought and action,* 3rd ed. New York: McGraw-Hill.

Mager, R.F., and Pipe, P. 1970. *Analyzing performance problems or "You really oughta wanna."* Belmont, Calif.: Fearon.

Smith, M. 1975. *When I say no, I feel guilty.* New York: Dial Press.

Chapter 11

Applying Interpersonal Skills to Characteristics of Individuals and Groups

Now that we have explored the various supervisory behaviors and the four approaches (nondirective, collaborative, directive informational, and directive control), how do we determine which skills and approaches to use? The chapters explaining each approach provided some simple guidelines. Basically, when an individual teacher or group of teachers has expertise on an issue, has a strong commitment to its solution, and will be held accountable for the subsequent plan of action, then the supervisor might best work in a nondirective manner. On the other hand, when an individual or group of teachers has little expertise, little commitment, and no accountability, then the supervisor might best work in a directive informational manner. When the individual or group has some expertise, a moderate degree of commitment, and some accountability, then the supervisor might best work in a collaborative manner. Directive control is an approach of last resort where there is a critical issue needing to be resolved and the teacher or group is unknowing or unwilling. Furthermore, when an individual or group fluctuates from characteristic to characteristic—for example, has moderate expertise, low commitment, and high accountability—then a supervisor might best handle the situation with a collaborative approach.

As a rule of thumb, the collaborative approach should be the most successful with most individuals and groups of experienced teachers. Recent research bears this out. When a stratified sample of 210 K–12 teachers were asked for their preferred supervisory approach, 63 (30 percent) preferred a supervisor to work with them nondirectively; 141 (67 percent) preferred a supervisor to work with them collaboratively, and only 6 (3 percent) preferred a supervisor to work with them directively (Ginkel 1983). Blumberg also surveyed experienced teachers about supervisory behaviors they perceived to be most positive. As with the Ginkel study, experienced teachers split primarily into two groups. One group perceived collaborative supervisory behaviors—listening to the teacher as well as presenting the supervisor's own views—as most positive. The other group saw nondirective supervisory behaviors—primarily listening, reflecting, and asking the teacher—as most positive. Experienced teachers generally did not view forms of directive behaviors as positive (Blumberg and Weber 1968; Blumberg 1980).

Student or neophyte teachers prefer a different range of supervisory approaches. Various studies of preservice teachers have been conducted by Zonca (1973), Vudovich (1976), Copeland and Atkinson (1978), Copeland (1980), and Lorch (1981). The findings were consistent in that most preservice teachers preferred a directive informational supervisory approach. Most of them wanted a supervisor to tell them precisely what changes they could be expected to make to improve instruction. However, Humphrey (1983), in a study of entry-level teachers, found most of them to prefer a collaborative approach.

Three tentative conclusions can be drawn from these studies of experienced and preservice teachers:

1. Experienced teachers vary in their preference of supervisory behaviors between nondirective and collaborative. Between the two, collaborative supervisory behaviors are preferred by the majority of teachers.

2. Directive forms of supervisory behaviors are preferred by only a small minority of experienced teachers.

3. Neophyte teachers (student and beginning teachers) initially prefer a directive informational approach or collaborative approach by their supervisors.

There are explanations for these differences in supervisory preference among teachers with various levels of experience. Human development theory and teacher development theory might help the supervisor make judgments about which behaviors and approaches to use with certain individuals and groups. First, some important cautions: Rigorously controlled, experimental, and school-based studies on matching supervisory approaches to developmental characteristics of teachers have not been performed. Although we can make a substantial case for why certain supervisory approaches are more appropriate for certain teachers, we cannot prove it empirically. No one has taken a random sample of teachers, divided them into five groups, trained supervisors in each of the four approaches, applied a directive control approach to one group, a directive informational approach to another, a collaborative approach to another group, a nondirective approach to the fourth group, and no treatment to the fifth group, and then compared class performance changes across all five groups. Although studies have been completed that do show positive correlations between teachers' stages of development and supervisory approaches (Gordon 1989; Rossicone 1985; and Akinniyi 1987), it is unlikely that a fully controlled study within a school or school system will ever be done. The difficulty in conducting such research is that concerned administrators and supervisors will not knowingly allow an experiment to continue if it is improving the performance of one group of teachers over that of another group. This is an understandable ethical dilemma, typical of most education research that requires a treatment. In reading the remainder of the chapter, remember that the case for different approaches is built on theory, related research, logic, and common sense—not on proven, generalizable experiments.

The Need for Structure: More and Then Less

"As long as you have rules, you have a chance for freedom" (Suzuki 1970).

Let's again briefly review the research of Francis Fuller, described in Chapter 4 on teacher concerns. What a teacher is concerned about in the beginning of the first year is usually quite different from his or her concerns in the second, fifth, or tenth year. Fuller (1969; Fuller et al. 1974) conducted several studies with groups of teachers of various degrees of experience, from beginning teachers to teachers with many years of experience. She and her staff surveyed hundreds of these teachers with the question, "When you think about teaching, what are you concerned about?" She isolated a group of experienced and superior teachers (determined by administrator and peer ranking of teachers within each school). In these studies she found a consistent developmental pattern regarding beginning, experienced, and superior teachers. Beginning teachers were mostly concerned about their own adequacy or survival. They were worried about whether they could measure up as teachers. They wondered if their students would run away with the classroom, if the principal would judge them to be competent, and if other teachers in the school would accept them as real members of the staff. Beginning teachers were concerned with simply surviving from one day or week to the next. Experienced teachers were less concerned with their own survival and more concerned about their students'. They worried more about helping individual students and improving classroom instruction. They wanted to do more to help students learn. Once a teacher became confident of his or her own survival, concern shifted to the survival of the students. The quality of classroom life became paramount.

The third group of superior and experienced teachers also showed concern with their impact on students, but in addition they were concerned with helping other students, other classrooms, the school as a whole, and the teaching profession. Their concern went beyond their own classrooms to a desire to improve education for all participants. Fuller's studies of teacher concerns have been replicated in many geographic areas in diverse socioeconomic, rural, urban, and suburban communities, with largely the same results (Adams and Martray 1981).

Figure 11-1 is a generalized scheme for viewing teacher concerns as related to the developmental principles of moral reasoning as uncovered by Piaget (1965) and Kohlberg (1969). Stages of moral reasoning move from a preconventional, egocentric stage to a conventional, law-and-order stage to a postconventional, altruistic stage. There is a developmental pattern of stages of moral reasoning related to levels of teacher concerns. Teacher concerns with self-survival can be related to egocentric moral reasoning; teacher concerns with instructional impact on classroom students can be related to conventional law-and-order reasoning; and teacher concerns with students and teachers beyond the immediate classroom can be related to postconventional, altruistic reasoning. In Figure 11-1, note that levels of concern and stages of reasoning do not vanish when new levels and stages have been acquired. Instead, former levels and stages remain, but the new ones predominate.

Developmental theory is based on research that shows marked stages of thought, movement, language, and socialization that are structurally different from each other and loosely related to age. High stages of reasoning and concerns are acquired by relatively few persons, and usually those are older and more experienced teachers. There are exceptions to this rule, because the rate of passage through stages can vary from individual to individual. Therefore some first-year teachers might reason in ways characteristic of the highest stage. Some exceptional teachers might resolve their survival concerns with the first month of school and proceed rapidly to concerns with instructional impact and educational improvement by the end of the first year. On the other hand, there might be individual teachers in their fortieth year of teaching who remain in the self-survival stage, without thinking beyond the immediate needs of keeping their jobs. Stage theory characterizes movement of *groups* of beginning and experienced teachers, not

Figure 11-1 Relationship of teacher concerns to moral reasoning

	Beginning Teachers	Experienced Teachers	"Superior" Teachers
Concerns (Fuller 1969)	Self-survival ("Will I make it as a teacher?")	Impact on classroom students ("What can I do to make students learn?")	Impact beyond my own classroom ("What can I do to make education better for all?")
Moral Reasoning (Kohlberg 1969)	Preconventional egocentric ("Will I get caught?")	Conventional law and order ("What are the rules?")	Postconventional altruistic ("What is in the best interest of all people?")

individuals. Also keep in mind that few teachers reason in the highest or lowest stages and that reasoning and concerns can vary from one situation to another as well as regress to lower stages. A teacher might reason at the highest level in one school and, on being transferred to another school, reason at a lower stage. A teacher might have self-survival concerns with playground supervision but go beyond classroom concerns with teaching English literature. Human and situational variability must always be considered when thinking about development.

Maslow and Herzberg: Theories of Motivation

Stages of teacher concerns and moral reasoning can be seen in relation to human needs. Abraham Maslow developed a classical framework for understanding human motivation (Maslow 1954). Maslow's premise was that there exists a hierarchy of needs that motivate humans to act, in the following order.

Physiological Needs

The initial motivation for humans is to satisfy biological demands for food, oxygen, water, sleep, and exercise. Unless these needs are satisfied, a human is motivated by nothing else. For example, a woman who is starving is not interested in security, money, or companionship; she will exert all her energy to find food. The same is true of any unmet physiological need.

Safety

After physiological needs are satisfied, the individual is motivated to attend to the niceties of human life. He or she seeks a comfortable, regulated environment. Security, stability, dependency, and rules all eliminate anxiety and fear of the unknown. An individual is motivated to seek a shelter in a familiar location with a secure source of income.

Belonging and Love

After safety needs are satisfied and the individual has established a home in the broadest sense, he or she begins to seek involvement with others as a group member and as a partner. The person desires affectionate relationships with friends and acceptance as a member of a group—signified by affiliations in informal and formal clubs, associations, and teams. His or her identity becomes merged with other people in religious, social, civic, and/or informal groups.

Esteem

Once needs for belonging and love have been satisfied, the individual's motivation changes from gaining acceptance within a group to becoming a contributing and leading member of the group. It is no longer adequate to be one of the gang; the person wants to be an admired and visible member. The individual takes a role of initiating actions, assuming leadership and helping others so that they will see him or her as important. The attainment of status and prestige affirms his or her competence and value to the group.

Self-Actualization

The culminating human need comes after the acquisition of self-esteem and confidence in one's ability to be successful in the eyes of others. Motivation in the previous stage was based on being liked and admired by others. Now the motivation becomes to act and achieve according to one's own standards. The individual follows what he or she believes is best, regardless of what others might think. Being true to one's own inclinations becomes the mark of self-actualization or, as Maslow defined it, "What a man *can* be, he *must* be" (1954, p. 46). In strikingly similar terms, Belenky, Clinchy, Goldberger, and Tarule (1986, p. 137) defined woman's self-actualization as finding a voice of one's own.

Let's put the theory of human motivation into common language. An individual who is hungry does not care about shelter. A person who is no longer hungry begins to think about a roof to keep out the rain and four walls to ward off the cold. The person desires order and regulation in life. Once secure in his or her environment, the person cares about belonging and participating with others. After affiliating and becoming comfortable as a member of a group, he or she then desires to be regarded as an important member of the group. Finally, with confidence in the regard of others, the individual turns inward to what he or she wishes to become.

Human motivation is developmental. The needs of a lower stage must be satisfied before a person is motivated by needs of the next higher stage. The stages are hierarchical. Each person moves through them in the same sequence, from physiological needs to safety needs, to belonging and love needs, to esteem needs, to self-actualization needs. The rate of passage varies from individual to individual. Finally, retreat can occur when the individual's situation is dramatically altered. For example, a person might have acquired self-esteem in her present job; but when she is hired to fill a new position, she may suddenly be groping for safety, routine, and security in the work environment. Initially she is concerned with how to get a parking permit, how to fill out voucher forms, and where to apply for medical insurance. The furthest thought from her mind is leading the group or being self-actualized. All she wants to know is where her territory is, what the rules are, and what she is expected to do.

This retreat and recapitulation of needs is exactly what happens with teacher concerns and reasoning. It is not that a beginning teacher has been in an egocentric self-survival stage all of his or her life. Any person thrown into a new environment, regardless of his or her previous functioning, will go through a transition period of floundering and feeling insecure before feeling safe and ready to contribute to the world outside the self.

Herzberg's thirty years of research on human motivation supports Maslow's hierarchy of needs (Herzberg 1987). Herzberg, Mausner, and Snyderman (1959), in their study of engineers and accountants, were originally concerned with what business and service employees perceived as positive or "satisfiers" and negative or "dissatisfiers" about their jobs. To Herzberg's surprise, satisfiers and dissatisfiers were quite distinct from each other. Negative factors or dissatisfiers most often cited were:

- Organizational policy and administration
- Technical supervision
- Salary
- Working conditions
- Status
- Job security
- Effects on personal life
- Interpersonal relations

On the other hand, positive incidents most cited were:

- Work itself
- Achievement
- Possibility of growth
- Responsibility
- Advancement

Herzberg found that elimination of dissatisfiers did not improve an individual's performance. Dissatisfiers were maintenance or hygiene factors. In other words, if a person's major dissatisfaction with her job is poor working conditions (poor lighting or inadequate facilities), it will remain a source of irritation and might make her work less hard but, if corrected, will not make her work harder. If the lighting is fixed, she will no longer be dissatisfied, but it will not increase her productivity. Rather, she will accept the correction as the way it should have been in the first place.

The positive factors that Herzberg called satisfiers did motivate individuals to work harder. When an employee found the work itself exciting, when she had a sense of achievement, when she saw future growth in her career, when she was given responsibility or advancement—then she improved performance. If a teacher is given increased responsibility for making decisions about materials to use in his classroom and is encouraged to modify his teaching lessons to add more topics or projects that he believes to be exciting and valuable, then he will tend to put more time and energy into changing and improving his performance. In other words, if a teacher is given increased responsibility to make decisions, he will work harder to see that he succeeds. Herzberg, therefore, cited satisfiers as the key motivators to improving work performance. Since these original studies, there have been replications of Herzberg's research in other businesses (Herzberg 1966; King 1970; Hoy and Miskel 1982) and in education (Sergiovanni 1966; Schmidt 1976). Studies that have used Herzberg's research methodology have found the same distinctions between negative (or hygiene) and positive (or motivating) factors. For example, a study by Sergiovanni (1966) consisted of interviews of teachers. He found the same loadings of factors as Herzberg except that work itself and advancement were less often cited by teachers as motivators. This was probably attributable to the nature of the teaching career, which offered little change in the work itself and almost no possibility of advancement (Lortie 1975).

Cawelti (1976) and Drucker (1973) have pointed out the link between Maslow's theory of motivation and Herzberg's research on hygiene and motivators. We might view this relationship by placing Herzberg's factors side by side with Maslow's stages (Figure 11-2).

Without forcing a perfect one-to-one correspondence, it is apparent that Herzberg's hygiene factors, which maintain performance, correspond to Maslow's lower-level needs—physiological, safety, and love and belonging. This interaction between hygiene and lower-level needs characterizes the teacher's working to find

Figure 11-2 Interacting areas of Herzberg's factors with Maslow's stages

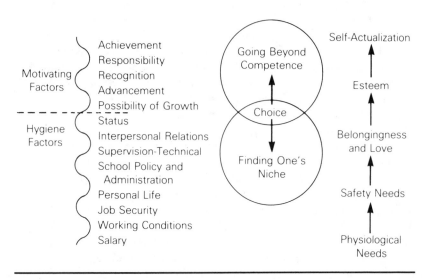

Sources: F. Herzberg, B. Mausner, and B. Snyderman, *The Motivation to Work* (New York: Wiley, 1959); and A.H. Maslow, *Motivation and Personality* (New York: Harper & Row, 1954).

his or her niche. The individual is learning to perform in an acceptable manner that is officially sanctioned by his or her peers, technical supervisors (evaluators), and the formal organization.

Herzberg's motivation factors likewise correspond with Maslow's higher stages. This interaction between motivation and higher-level needs defines an area in which the teacher is "going beyond competence." The individual knows performance is acceptable and now strives for excellence. Notice the small overlapping area in Figure 11-2 (between "finding one's niche" and "going beyond competence") called "choice." This is the critical area in which a teacher can choose either to remain minimally competent or to grow in new ways. The choice becomes available when hygiene factors and lower-stage needs have been met and when there is encouragement to go beyond competence by providing a sense of achievement, responsibility, recognition, and advancement so that teachers can choose to improve their instruction. The administrative function of a school should provide for the hygiene factors that enable teachers to reach the plateau from which supervision for improvement of instruction can proceed.

deCharms and Deci on Motivation

What does current research say about human motivation? Since 1973 there have been over seventy studies on the undermining effect of control versus individual choice (Morgan 1984). The research led by deCharms (1968, 1976) and Deci (1975, 1982) not only validates the work of Maslow and Herzberg but also adds to our understanding of why the interacting area of "choice" is the critical determinant in teacher improvement.

deCharms conducted studies whose findings contradicted motivation theories based on external stimulus. The most prevalent practices in industry and schools are based on the premise that individuals will change and increase their production if reinforced by rewards, bribes, or coercion (Ouchi 1981). Extrinsic-motivation theory posits that one motivates others by either positive means—praising, rewarding, and providing salary incentives—or negative means—threatening job security, withholding pay, or criticizing. Such motivation is based on behavioral, stimulus-response psychology identified with B.F. Skinner (1971) that humans are conditioned by external forces. Pure behaviorists consistently advocate positive reinforcement and believe that the use of negative reinforcement is ineffective. Yet practitioners of behavioral psychology in most organizations do not make such distinctions and readily mix rewards with punishments. deCharms's research upsets the behavioral applecart in finding that the most basic of behavioral propositions—positive rewarding of appropriate behavior—has undesirable after-effects. deCharms's experiments showed that groups of students and teachers who were not rewarded performed *better* on tasks than did groups who were positively rewarded (deCharms 1968, Chap. 10).

Deci (1975, 1982) has amplified deCharms's studies and has looked closely at the consequences of individual freedom of choice as contrasted with reinforcing an individual to act according to someone else's dictates. Deci and associates have conducted sets of controlled laboratory experiments wherein comparable groups of adults were placed in rooms with an assortment of puzzle activities. Members of one group were told to perform a certain activity and that they would be paid for completing that activity. The other group was told they could choose from any of the activities and could work as long as they pleased. No reinforcement was provided to the second group. The first study found that the rewarded subjects spent less time with the assigned activity and were less satisfied with doing the activity than were the subjects who had free choice. In the second study the same groups of subjects returned to the activity room and were told to work as they pleased. The previously rewarded group showed decreased attention and performance. The rewarded group avoided the activity they had been paid to do previously, whereas the free-choice group tended to return to the activity they had worked on before. The attitude and commitment of the previously unrewarded group was significantly higher than that of the rewarded group. Thus Deci, like deCharms before him, concluded that there are indirect and undesirable consequences of using external reinforcement to motivate humans.

The Issue of Choice

Deci, as a laboratory researcher, is convinced—and as a field-based educator I concur—that reinforcement or extrinsic motivation is not the way to promote professional and personal growth. External reinforcement is necessary in an organization as a way of satisfying Maslow's low-stage needs—physiological, safety, and the sense of belonging—and the hygiene factors of salary, work conditions and job security, to maintain minimal competence. Once the person is minimally competent, external reinforcements, even positive ones, are not growth-inducing.

Any type of organization must control employee behaviors within broad limits (a school cannot have teachers of moral education deal drugs any more than a crime syndicate can have drug peddlers who are moral educators). The nature of the organization limits the behaviors of its employees. Hence any organization must have control, which is an administrative function. Control means that some person representing the governance of the organization has the job of getting employees to comply with those limits (the ringleader of the drug syndicate must tell the moral educator among the drug peddlers to stop preaching or get out). With compliance inevitably comes some form of resistance. Although a person will do what he or she is told to do if the reward or sanction is great enough, the controller knows there will be an indirect consequence of resistance. If resistance were not inevitable, there would be no reason to control. The employee will perform but also might resent the controller, do the task grudgingly, or even do the opposite of what the controller wants when the controller is not present. A study by Brown (1975) found that teachers, when ordered by a supervisor to perform in a prescribed manner, often did the opposite of the orders. This type of resistance can be seen when teachers are told to use certain textbooks they do not like as part of school policy. They will bring out the books when the controller (principal or superintendent) is there. When the controller is not there, however, they will use the books halfheartedly (as a part of their lesson) or not at all (to keep the door open or for short students to sit on). An experienced school administrator or teacher is well aware that control leads to immediate compliance and subsequent resistance.

Many issues that arise with teachers in schools are issues of control. As part of the school organization, teachers simply must behave in certain ways. As the controls are articulated clearly, a teacher becomes familiar with the norms and minimum expectations of the organization. *But let's not confuse controlling behavior with improving instruction.* Ultimately the individual teacher always has a choice, even when the choice is "Do what I say or get out!" Yet the narrowing of choice is not motivating; rather, it is the expansion of choice or the opportunity to decide that motivates a teacher to go beyond competence.

Controlling versus Informational Environments

Deci distinguishes between working with people in controlling environments and informational environments. *Controlling* environments, as already mentioned, restrict individual choice, gain compliance, and create resistance. *Informational* environments expand individual choice, promote autonomy, and encourage commitment to improvement. An informational environment is one in which the individual considers alternative sources of feedback on his or her performance, thinks through consequences of his or her actions, and freely chooses according to his or her own interests and curiosity. The premise of an informational environment is that humans are innately curious and desire to follow their own inclinations. deCharms calls this drive to be powerful, independent, and active the quality of being an "origin." Persons who have been conditioned by a controlling environment to feel powerless, dependent, and passive he calls "pawns." When the professional environment matches the individual's need to be an initiator, then— and only then—does enduring improvement occur. Pajak and Seyfarth (1983) clarify the distinction between controlling and informational environments by referring to supervisory language. According to them, it is the difference between a supervisor working with a teacher in a "must" manner as opposed to working with a teacher in a "can" manner. Words such as *must, should, ought to,* and *need to* connote supervisor control and lack of teacher choice. Words such as *can, could, consider,* and *might* connote supervisor information and teacher choice. Anyone in a formal supervisory position might consider using the *must* context only when control is the paramount issue and using the *can* context when information and improvement are of greatest importance. A recent study has shown that teachers are extremely sensitive to the differences between controlling and informational language used by a supervisor (Pajak and Glickman 1984, 1989). Woe to the person who mistakenly uses *must* to mean *can,* or *consider* to mean *should.* We have trouble enough communicating our true intent to others without compounding the problem by unwittingly using control words when we mean to use informational ones or vice versa.

Finally, this discussion of human motivation in a supervisory context brings us back to the use of the delineated interpersonal approaches—directive control, directive informational, collaborative, and nondirective. For a supervisor working with individual teachers and group members, two environments must be considered when using various approaches. These two environments are depicted in Table 11-1.

In an informational environment, the supervisor allows the teacher to make his or her own choice. Yet the supervisor varies the source and amount of information depending on the teacher's expertise and competence in problem solving. The directive, informational approach (cell A), in which the supervisor tells the teacher what can be done to improve instruction ("I think student attention would be greater if you had smaller groups"), is predicated on the

Table 11-1   Supervisory environment and approach

Environments	Approaches		
	Directive	*Collaborative*	*Nondirective*
Informational	[A]Supervisor's information for teacher to consider	[B]Sharing information for both to consider	[C]Actively listening to teacher's information
Controlling	[D]Supervisor telling teacher what to do	[E]Guise of involvement: Make teacher believe he/she shared in decision	[F]Manipulating teacher to think he/she is making own decision

supervisor's knowledge of possibilities and the teacher's lack of such knowledge. The collaborative informational approach (cell B) is premised on both supervisor and teacher having helpful information ("This is what you think can be done . . . . This is what I think . . . .") The nondirective informational approach (cell C) is premised on the teacher's expertise and the supervisor's facilitation of teacher knowledge ("How do you see your classroom?") When we move into controlling environments, we are responding to beginning and/or insecure teachers' needs for safety, structure, and security. If the supervisor does possess formal authority, he or she can use the directive controlling approach (cell D) in emergency or survival situations ("You *must* stop using corporal punishment, it is against school policy"). The collaborative, controlling approach (cell E) and the nondirective, controlling approach (cell F) have no place in schools. To use collaborative skills to manipulate teachers to do what the supervisor had wanted all along or to use nondirective skills to subtly reinforce compliance with a supervisor's demand is dishonest and unethical. Besides the questionable ethics of such behavior, once the game is known the supervisor will reap the undesirable consequence of resistance from teachers.

A supervisor should use directive control in situations of potential harm to students and in case of apparent incompetence of a teacher. After all, directive control is really an evaluation approach for achieving compliance from an employee. The supervisor should use directive information, collaborative information, and nondirective information in his or her everyday work. The choice can be governed by the expertise and competence of the teacher or group. A supervisor can use criteria about an individual's or group's ability to solve problems as an indication of which approach to use first.

Teacher Problem Solving as Cueing Information for Deciding Supervisory Approach

Expertise refers to the body of knowledge, or know-how, an individual or a group possesses for improving instruction. *Competence* refers to the performance of an individual or group of teachers in achieving desired learning results with students. Therefore expertise is the knowledge (training and experience) that one brings to instructional problems; competence is one's on-the-feet performance with students. The process of problem solving is an integration of expertise and competence. One puts knowledge into action via decision making. This section will outline the rational decision-making method as providing cues to the supervisor in deciding which approach to use when working with a teacher. The rational decision-making method will be explained rather than a more intuitive method because teachers' rational decision making has been correlated with measures of teacher effectiveness (Clark and Joyce 1976; Hunt and Sullivan 1974; Porter and Brophy 1988; Riley 1980). Keep in mind that there are exceptions to the rules. Some teachers appear to be more intuitive and spontaneous, yet run exceptionally fine classrooms. Therefore, not all good rational planners are good teachers, nor are all poor rational planners poor teachers. More good teachers display rational problem-solving abilities than not, but the ultimate criterion must be whether teachers are achieving desired individual and collective goals of student learning.

Rational decision making can be viewed as an eight-step procedure with three major phases:

A. Goal identification phase
   1. Awareness of situations to be improved
   2. Identifying causes of situation
   3. Identifying the goal
B. Planning phase
   4. Generating alternative actions
   5. Exploring consequences
   6. Selecting actions to be taken
C. Implementation phase
   7. Testing selected actions
   8. Reviewing results

Steps 1, 2, and 3 identify the goal; steps 4, 5, and 6 plan the actions to reach the goal; and steps 7 and 8 monitor the actions to see if the goal is being achieved. Obviously, it is difficult to plan and achieve a goal that has not been identified correctly. One study has shown that when supervisors were given problem scenarios and asked to identify problems, over 80 percent of their responses were solutions (Clinton, Glickman, and Payne 1982). In other words, most supervisors tend to leap before they look. Rational decision-making skills are important for supervisors as well as for teachers. A supervisor might use the eight-step decision-making procedure when deciding which interpersonal approach is appropriate with which teachers. We first use our own expertise or knowledge about interpersonal skills and our own competence to perform the interpersonal skills. We then look at the teacher's decision-making abilities, gather information about teacher proficiency, generate alternative approaches toward working with the teacher, choose one, and try it out. Asking ourselves the following questions when assessing an individual teacher can help:

1. Is the teacher aware of improvements that can be made in the classroom? Can the teacher identify those needs?

2. Has the teacher considered possible causes of the instructional needs? Does the teacher gather information from multiple sources about the instructional needs?

3. Can the teacher generate several possible solutions? How carefully does the teacher weigh the merits of each solution? Does the teacher consider what he or she can do to reach the goal without looking unrealistically for outside help?

4. Can the teacher be decisive in choosing a course of action? Does the teacher commit himself or herself to an implementation procedure?

5. Does the teacher do what he or she says?

These are some questions to answer in determining the necessary degree of intervention with nondirective, collaborative, or directive approaches. A teacher who shows no inclination to improve and is considered less than competent by those with responsibilities for formal teacher evaluation is appropriately matched with a directive controlling approach. A teacher who desires to improve his or her performance but is at a loss for what to do is appropriately matched with a directive informational approach. A teacher who is aware, knowledgeable, and decisive about instructional improvement is appropriately matched with a nondirective approach. This application is obviously a bit simplistic, since each teacher will have variations of awareness, commitment, and thought depending on the particular topic or situation under consideration. Further amplification on appropriate matching with individuals will be found in Chapter 15 on direct teacher assistance.

Situational Leadership for Groups

Hersey and Blanchard's (1988) famous model of situational leadership of groups has been applied to education by Gates, Blanchard, and Hersey (1976) and Cawelti (1976). It is a generalized approach to leadership styles. They suggest that a leader consider the maturity level of a group before deciding on the type of leadership style to use. They define leadership in terms of relationship and task behaviors. Relationship behaviors are those that consider the feelings of group members (praise, encouragement, humor). Task behaviors are those that focus on accomplishing the task of the meeting (setting time limits, asking specific questions, proposing answers). Group readiness is determined by:

1. Ability of the group

2. Willingness on the part of the group to assume leadership

Figure 11-3 depicts the Hersey/Blanchard situational-leadership model. If the group is rated high on both characteristics (ability and willingness), they are considered a highly ready group—R4. If they score some combination of moderate to high of the two characteristics, they are considered a moderately high readiness group—R3. If they score low on one of the two characteristics, they are considered a moderately low readiness group—R2. If they score low on both, they are considered a low readiness group—R1. According to Hersey and Blanchard, an R1 group is best matched with a leadership of high task, low relationship, or a *telling* posture (S1). An R2 group is best matched with a leadership of high task and high relationship, a *selling* posture (S2). An R3 group is best matched with a leadership of high relationship and low task, a *participating* posture (S3). An R4 group is best matched with a leadership of low relationship and low task, a *delegating* posture (S4).

My own supervisory behavior continuum, alternative supervisory approaches, and matching with variables of individuals and groups of teachers have been influenced by Hersey and Blanchard's theory. Hersey and Blanchard have provided the framework for my own studies into the complexities of using supervisory behaviors and informational versus controlling environments. In Chapter 18 on group development, I will have more to say on the application of Hersey and Blanchard's theory to group situations.

Not Algorithms But Guideposts for Decisions

Life in the school world is ragged and complex. This chapter offers a great deal of information to ponder about available behaviors, human motivation, types of environments, and characteristics of individuals and groups. There are no algorithms to provide exactly correct responses to human behavior. Such formulas as "if individual exhibits characteristics A, B, and C, then supervisor Y should do D, F, and G" do not and should not exist. Such algorithms are useful only in mechanically and technically controlled systems (such as computer operations, assembly production, or chemical

Figure 11-3 The Hersey/Blanchard situational-leadership model (copy-righted material from Leadership Studies Inc.; all rights reserved)

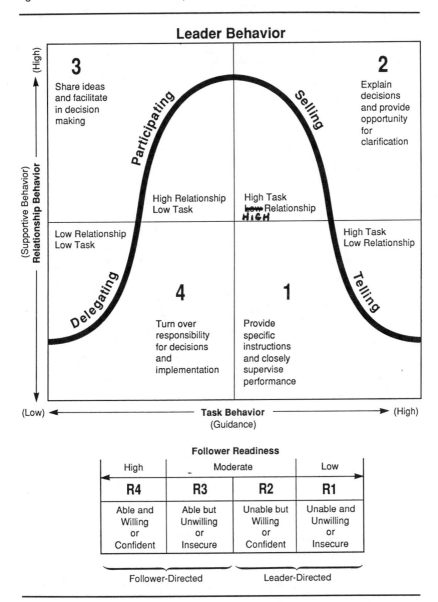

alterations). Algorithms work in technical but not human endeavors, and it would be misleading to suggest that such supervision formulas are available. Instead, what is available is information about ourselves and others than can serve as guideposts to suggest what *might* be of use. Such developmental guideposts can help reduce some of the infinite complexity of the school world so that supervision can be a purposeful and thoughtful function for improving instruction.

Summary

This chapter explored the application of interpersonal skills to characteristics of individuals and groups. I cited research showing that most entry-level teachers appear to prefer directive informational to collaborative approaches, whereas a large majority of experienced teachers prefer the collaborative and nondirective approaches. This preference was explained according to stage theory. Human motivation, according to Maslow, Herzberg, deCharms, and Deci, explains why information environments that provide choice for teachers are more likely to sustain instructional improvements than are control environments that limit choice. Steps in teachers' rational decision making can be clues used by supervisors for determining the degree of supervisory intervention. The supervisor needs to use his or her own decision-making abilities to identify, choose, and determine the most appropriate interpersonal approaches to use with his or her staff.

EXERCISES

Academic

1. Prepare written composite profiles of (a) a teacher who would benefit most from nondirective supervision, (b) a teacher who would benefit most from collaborative supervision, (c) a teacher who would benefit most from directive informational supervision, and (d) a teacher who would benefit most from directive control supervision.

2. Write an essay comparing Maslow's four highest human need categories to your own development within a work or social organization. Evaluate Maslow's theory of motivation in terms of whether it is relevant to your own needs, experiences, and

growth in progressing from a novice to an experienced member of the selected organization.

3. Create a written list of six motivating (intrinsic) factors and six hygiene (extrinsic) factors related to teaching within a public school setting. Categorize each of Herzberg's twelve related factors according to one of Maslow's stages by placing an *A* (self-actualization), *E* (esteem), *B* (belonging), *S* (safety), or *P* (physiological) after each factor. Give a brief rationale for each Herzberg- and Maslow-related classification you decide on.

4. Describe a situation in which a supervisor would be required to use directive control, and explain what specific behaviors you as a supervisor would exhibit in that situation. Describe a second set of circumstances in which directive information would be more appropriate, and explain specific behaviors you would display if you were the supervisor in that second situation.

5. Describe an instructional problem that is typically dealt with by a supervisor working with a group of teachers. Using that same problem for each of four descriptions, describe how a supervisor following the Hersey/Blanchard situational leadership model would interact with teacher groups, charged with solving the problem, that are of (a) low maturity, (b) moderately low maturity, (c) moderately high maturity, and (d) high maturity.

Field

1. Ask five teachers each to write a paragraph or two on the topic "What Motivates Me to Improve My Teaching." Write a paper comparing the teachers' responses with the research findings of deCharms and Deci.

2. Share a description of an actual classroom problem with a small group. (The teacher and/or students involved in the classroom problem should remain anonymous.) Simulate a problem-solving session in which the group (a) identifies causes of the problem, (b) proposes and considers alternative solutions to the problem, (c) chooses the most promising alternative, and (d) selects an appropriate method of testing the agreed-on solution. Write a report summarizing the problem-solving session and evaluating the quality of the problem-solving behaviors displayed by the group.

3. Observe an educational supervisor using what Hersey and Blanchard refer to as a "telling," "selling," "participating," or "delegating" leadership style with a group of teachers. Write a report in which you evaluate (a) the appropriateness of the leadership

style in relation to the maturity level of the group and (b) the effectiveness of the observed leadership style in terms of meeting instructional improvement objectives.

4. Examine developmental characteristics of an individual for whom you have supervisory responsibility. Use the supervisory approach (nondirective, collaborative, directive informational) that you perceive as the best match for the selected individual. Summarize and evaluate your matched supervision.

5. Evaluate the maturity level (as defined by Hersey and Blanchard) of a group for which you have leadership responsibility. Use the leadership style (high risk and low relationship, high task and high relationship, high relationship and low task, or low relationship and low task) that you perceive as the best match for the group in question. Summarize and evaluate your matched leadership.

Developmental

1. Begin an in-depth investigation of one of the following:
   a. Achievement motivation
   b. Organizational management
   c. Creative problem solving
   d. Job satisfaction
2. Continue to observe differing characteristics of beginning teachers, experienced teachers, and superior teachers. Hypothesize how supervision might be modified to accommodate such differences.
3. Begin to analyze ways in which your needs, concerns, and motivations change in relation to varying situations and changing circumstances.

REFERENCES

Adams, R.D., and Martray, C. 1981. Teacher development: A study of factors related to teacher concerns for pre, beginning and experienced teachers. Paper presented at the annual meeting of the American Educational Research Association, Los Angeles, April 13.

Akinniyi, G.O. 1987. Perceptions and preferences of principals' and teachers' supervisory behavior. Unpublished doctoral dissertation, University of Wisconsin.

Belenky, M.F., Clinchy, B.M., Goldberger, N.B., and Tarule, J.M. 1986. *Women's ways of knowing. The development of self, voice, and mind.* New York: Basic Books.

Blumberg, A. 1980. *Supervisors and teachers: A private cold war,* 2nd ed. Berkeley, Calif.: McCutchan.

Blumberg, A., and Weber, W.A. 1968. Teacher morale as a function of perceived supervisor behavioral style. *Journal of Educational Research 62*:109–113.

Brown, A.F. 1975. Teaching under stress. In B.M. Harris (Ed.), *Supervisory behavior in education,* 2nd ed. Englewood Cliffs, N.J.: Prentice-Hall, p. 218.

Cawelti, G. 1976. Selecting appropriate leadership styles for instructional improvement. Videotape. Alexandria, Va.: Association for Supervision and Curriculum Development.

Clark, C.M., and Joyce, B.R. 1976. Teacher decision making and teacher effectiveness. Paper presented at the annual meeting of the American Educational Research Association, San Francisco.

Clinton, B.C., Glickman, C.D., and Payne, D.A. 1982. Identifying supervision problems: A guide to better solutions. *Illinois School Research and Development 9* (1).

Copeland, W.D. 1980. Affective dispositions of teachers in training toward examples of supervisory behavior. *Journal of Educational Research 74*:37–42.

Copeland, W.D., and Atkinson, D.R. 1978. Student teachers' perceptions of directive and non-directive supervision. *Journal of Educational Research 71*:123–127.

deCharms, R. 1968. *Personal causation.* New York: Academic Press.

————. 1976. *Enhancing motivation: Change in the classroom.* New York: Irvington.

Deci, E.L. 1975. *Intrinsic motivation.* New York: Plenum.

————. 1982. Motivation. Paper presented to the annual meeting of the Midwest Association of Teachers of Educational Psychology, Dayton, Ohio, October 30.

Drucker, P. 1973. *Management.* New York: Harper and Row, pp. 232–245.

Fuller, F.F. 1969. Concerns of teachers: A developmental conceptualization. *American Educational Research Journal 6* (March):207–226.

Fuller, F.F., et al. 1974. *Concerns of teachers: Research and recon-*

ceptualization. ED 091 439. Austin, Tex.: Research and Developmental Center for Teacher Education, Texas University.

Gates, P.E., Blanchard, K.H., and Hersey, P. 1976. Diagnosing educational leadership problems. *Educational Leadership 33* (February):348–354.

Ginkel, K. 1983. Overview of study that investigated the relationship of teachers' conceptual levels and preferences for supervisory approach. Paper presented at the annual meeting of the American Educational Research Association, Montreal, April.

Gordon, S.P. 1989. Developmental supervision: Supervisor flexibility and the post-observation conference. Paper presented at the annual meeting of the American Educational Research Association, San Francisco, March.

Hersey, P., and Blanchard, K.H. 1988. *Management of organizational behavior*, 5th ed. Englewood Cliffs, N.J.: Prentice-Hall.

Herzberg, F. 1966. *Work and the nature of man*. New York: World, pp. 137–178.

————. 1987. One more time. How do you motivate employees? *Harvard Business Review 65*(5):109–120.

Herzberg, F., Mausner, B., and Snyderman, B. 1959. *The motivation to work*. New York: Wiley.

Hoy, W.K., and Miskel, C.G. 1982. *Educational administration theory, research and practice*, 2nd ed. New York: Random House.

Humphrey, G.L. 1983. The relationship between orientations to supervision and the developmental levels of commitment and abstract thinking of entry-year teachers. Doctoral dissertation, University of Tulsa. *Dissertation Abstracts International 44*:1644A.

Hunt, D.E., and Sullivan, E.V. 1974. *Between psychology and education*. Hinsdale, Ill.: Dryden Press.

King, N. 1970. Clarification and evaluation of the two-factor theory of job satisfaction. *Psychological Bulletin 74*:18–31.

Kohlberg, L. 1969. Stage and sequence: The cognitive developmental approach to socialization. In D. Goslin (Ed.), *Handbook of socialization theory and research*. Chicago: Rand McNally.

Lorch, N. 1981. Teaching assistant training: The effects of directive and non-directive supervision. Unpublished Ed.D. dissertation, University of California, Santa Barbara.

Lortie, D.C. 1975. *Schoolteacher: A sociological study*. Chicago: University of Chicago Press.

Maslow, A.H. 1954. *Motivation and personality.* New York: Harper and Row.

Morgan, M. 1984. Reward-induced decrements and increments in intrinsic motivation. *Review of Educational Research* 54(1):5–30.

Ouchi, W.G. 1981. *Theory Z: How American business can meet the Japanese challenge.* Reading, Mass.: Addison-Wesley.

Pajak, E.F., and Glickman, C.D. 1984. Teachers' perceptions of supervisory communication: Control versus information. Paper presented at the annual meeting of the American Educational Research Association, New Orleans, April.

———. 1989. Informational and controlling language in simulated supervisory conferences. *American Educational Research Journal 26*(1).

Pajak, E.F., and Seyfarth, J.J. 1983. Authentic supervision reconciles the irreconcilables. *Educational Leadership 40*(8):20–23.

Piaget, J. 1965. *The moral judgment of the child.* New York: Free Press-Macmillan.

Porter, A.C., and Brophy, J. 1988. Synthesis of research on good teaching? Insights from the work of the Institute for Research on Teaching. *Educational Leadership 45*(8):74–85.

Riley, J.F. 1980. Creative problem solving and cognitive monitoring as instructional variables for teaching training in classroom problem solving. Unpublished Ed.D. dissertation, University of Georgia.

Rossicone, G.N. 1985. The relationship of selected teacher background versus preferences for supervisory style and teacher perceptions of supervisory style of supervisors. Doctoral dissertation, St. John's University. *Dissertation Abstracts International 46*:321A.

Schmidt, G.L. 1976. Job satisfaction among secondary school administrators. *Educational Administration Quarterly 12*:68–85.

Sergiovanni, T. 1966. Factors which affect satisfaction and dissatisfaction of teachers. *Journal of Educational Administration 5*:66–82.

Skinner, B.F. 1971. *Beyond freedom and dignity.* New York: Knopf.

Suzuki, S. 1970. *Zen mind, beginner's mind.* New York: Weather Hill.

Vudovich, D. 1976. The effects of four specific supervision procedures on the development of self-evaluation skills in pre-service teachers. Paper presented at the annual meeting of the American Educational Research Association. ERIC Reproduction No. ED 146-224.

Zonca, P.H. 1973. A case study exploring the effects on an intern teacher of the condition of openness in a clinical supervisory relationship. Unpublished Ph.D. dissertation, University of Pittsburgh, 1973. *Dissertation Abstracts International 33*:658–659A.

PART III CONCLUSION

Critical vocabulary words in Part III included *supervisor behaviors; nondirective, collaborative, directive informational, and directive control approaches; skill practice;* issues of *control* versus *information; motivation* and *choice;* and *human variation, development,* and *complexity.* The purpose of Part III was to equip the supervisor with the interpersonal skills and behaviors needed to assist individuals and groups of teachers to develop their own thinking capacities. The question behind Part III was not how a supervisor motivates teachers to improve instruction, but rather how the supervisor provides choice to teachers to motivate themselves. The matching of interpersonal behaviors and approaches to teachers' developmental levels is one skill base for doing this. Having gained knowledge and interpersonal skills, you can now turn to the third dimension of supervision as a developmental function: the technical skill dimension.

Figure III-2 shows us where we've been and where we are going. We have concluded our discussion of the second dimension of interpersonal skills. One more prerequisite dimension remains before we apply the function of supervision to the five task areas.

Figure III-2 Supervision for successful schools

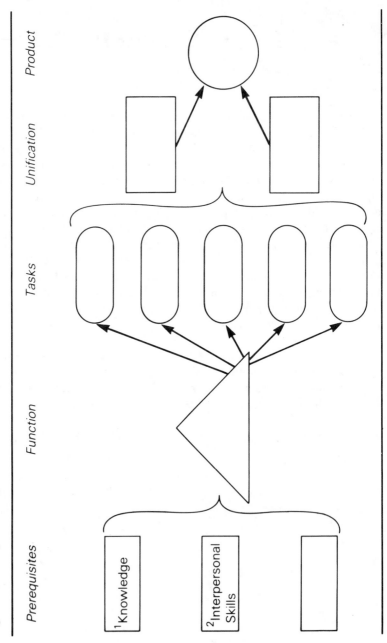

Prerequisites   *Function*   *Tasks*   *Unification*   *Product*

1Knowledge

2Interpersonal Skills

PART IV

TECHNICAL SKILLS

Introduction

The supervisor who knows about characteristics of successful schools, the norms that mediate against success, and the ways teacher development contrasts with optimal adult development can begin to formulate a supervisory belief system that becomes a reality when interpersonal and technical skills of supervision are applied in practice.

The previous section matched nondirective, collaborative, and directive interpersonal skills in working with developmental levels of individuals and groups of teachers. Part IV deals with the technical supervisory skills needed in working with teachers to assess, plan, observe, research, and evaluate the instructional program. Understanding schools and relating well to teachers are necessary components, but technical skills are equally important for accomplishing the tasks of supervision.

Chapter 12

Assessing and Planning Skills

A popular term used in the organizational literature is *envisioning* (Bennis, Benne, and Chin 1985). In discussing successful schools in the first two chapters of this book, I mentioned the importance of collective instructional goals that give power and purpose to individuals working in the same educational setting. The school engages in "the moral equivalent of war," teachers and administrators are involved in "a cause beyond oneself," and the function of supervision is to assist all educators in the school to make better instructional decisions about ways to improve student learning. Such thinking about the role of supervision and instructional leadership in bringing about a collective vision of what can be is a necessary first step. To create and implement that vision, those in supervision roles need technical skills of assessing and planning.

Assessing and planning skills are useful to a supervisor in setting goals and activities for himself or herself as well as for others. The chapter begins with personal organization of time—assessing one's current use of professional time and then planning and managing the use of future time. It goes on to focus on techniques for organizational planning for the improvement of instruction. Whether the changes to be made are in curriculum development, staff development, or direct assistance to teachers, a supervisor's forethought about the sequencing and organization of the program can increase the chances of successful implementation.

Assessing and planning are two sides of the same coin. *Assessing* involves determining where you and your staff have been and where you and your staff currently are. *Planning* includes deciding where you want to go and choosing the path you and your staff hope to traverse in order to reach that destination. Until you are certain of the origination and destination of your travel, a map is useless. Once you are certain, a route can be created.

Personal Plans

I recently returned from a consulting visit to a school system where I met with several first-year principals. The purpose of the consultation was for the new principals to talk to me privately about their beginning experiences and to discuss possible changes that might improve their situations.

One principal stated that she was averaging three hours a day observing and participating in classrooms. Her major concern was with the amount of waiting time students were experiencing. Most of her teachers had divided their heterogeneous classrooms into numerous small groups. The principal wondered whether, if certain classes were grouped homogeneously to begin with, there might be fewer groups and less waiting time. We discussed the possible consequences of such a major change and whether less radical changes within the existing instructional program might be better. She left the session with a plan to discuss with the faculty the issue of waiting time and student grouping at the next school meeting.

The second beginning principal I met with told me that his major problem was getting out of his office to visit teachers. He wanted to be with his staff but found that paperwork, phone calls, and student discipline referrals kept him trapped in the office. He could find barely an hour a day to talk with staff and visit classrooms. Furthermore, the one-hour time outside the office was often interrupted by the school secretary calling him back with urgent business. We proceeded to discuss why he was trapped in his office and what changes might be made.

After hearing about the second principal's situation, I realized that the second principal had no more constraints on his time than did the first principal, who was averaging three hours a day visiting classrooms. Both had schools of comparable size in the same neighborhood. They worked for the same superintendent and had identical job responsibilities. Yet one principal was functioning as a supervisor attending to instructional improvement, while the other one was functioning only minimally in the realm of supervision. It seemed that the real difference between the two principals was not their intentions to function as supervisors but their ability to assess and plan professional time to correspond with professional intentions. Let's look at the use of professional time.

Assessing Time

To organize future time, one must assess one's current use of time. This can be done by keeping a daily log for five to ten consecutive school days. Those supervisors who keep detailed appointment books might need only to return to their books at midday and at the end of the day to add notations on what actually transpired. Those who do not operate with such planned schedules can keep a daily log to be filled out at midday and at the end of the day. The log should be simple and should require only a few minutes to fill out. It might look like this:

Monday

8:00–8:50	Walked halls, visited teachers and custodians
8:50–9:20	Conference with parent
9:20–9:35	Phone call from textbook salesman
9:35–10:30	Emergency, covered for sick teacher
10:30–12:00	Worked on class schedules—made 3 phone calls, received 5 phone calls
12:00–12:30	Ate in cafeteria with teachers
12:30–12:35	Wrote morning log
12:35–12:55	Met with textbook salesman
12:55–1:30	Classroom visitation of Mr. Tadich
1:30–2:30	Meeting at superintendent's office
2:30–3:00	Helped supervise school dismissal
3:00–3:15	Talked with parents
3:15–4:00	Faculty meeting
4:00–4:15	Talked with teachers informally
4:15–4:50	Answered mail
4:50–5:00	Wrote afternoon log

After at least five days (preferably ten), the supervisor can analyze his or her current use of time by subsuming daily events in the log under large categories of time consumption. Figure 12-1 shows a sample categorical scheme.

Before transferring the daily log entries onto the time consumption chart, the supervisor should look at his or her job description and determine how his or her time *should* be spent according to job priorities. Which categories of supervisory involvement ought to receive the most attention? The supervisor can indicate approximate percentages according to this ideal use of time. After making a list of ideal time use, he or she can then write in actual time on the consumption charts, add up total time for each category, and then find the actual percentage of time being

Figure 12-1 Supervisor time consumption chart

	Monday	Tuesday	Wednesday	Thursday	Friday	Total	%
Paperwork							
Phone calls							
Private conference							
students							
parents & community							
faculty							
auxiliary personnel							
central office							
others							
Group meetings							
students							
parents & community							
faculty							
auxiliary personnel							
central office							
others							
Classroom visits							
School hall and ground visits							
Private time for thinking							
Miscellaneous: emergencies							

consumed for each category. He or she then has a comparison between preferred and actual consumption of time. The comparison might look like this:

Preferred Time	Actual Time
Paperwork—10%	25%
Phone calls—5%	6%
Private conferences—25%	25%
Students—5%	10%
Parents—3%	5%
Faculty—10%	5%
Auxiliary—3%	1%
Central office—1%	1%
Others—3%	3%
Group meetings—25%	28%
Students—2%	5%
Parents—5%	2%
Faculty—15%	7%
Auxiliary—1%	6%
Central office—1%	8%
Others—1%	0%
Classroom visits—25%	10%
School hall and ground visits—5%	2%
Private time for thinking—3%	1%
Miscellaneous visits—2%	3%

This comparison of time was that of the second principal, who complained about the inability to get out of his office. The comparison showed that he was indeed spending much more time in the office (10% perferred, 25% actual) and much less time on classroom visits (25% preferred, 10% actual). Further discrepancies were noted in considerably more time spent in private conferences with students (5% preferred, 10% actual) and group meetings with central office (1% preferred, 8% actual).

Changing Time Allocations: Planning

With this information on preferred and actual time use in front of the supervisor, he or she can decide what changes realistically can be made to attain the goal of increasing visitation time with teachers. The supervisor can consider a range of options to increase teacher visitation time. Some possibilities might be:

Paperwork: Delegate more clerical work to secretary, aides, or assistants. Schedule paperwork for uninterrupted hours after school.

Private conferences: Spend less time disciplining students by setting more stringent procedures for teacher referrals of students to office.

Group meetings: See if central office meetings could be shortened or scheduled after school hours.

Classroom visits: Increase classroom visits from one to two periods a day. Set up backup system with secretary to cover all but real emergencies when in the classroom. Schedule visits for a set time each day.

Naturally, this supervisor cannot hope to achieve exact congruence between preferred and actual time use, but he can come closer to his preference. Some time constraints, such as the time of central office meetings, probably are not under the principal's control. There are other factors over which he has direct control: when he will meet parents, accept phone calls, do paperwork, and accept student referrals. The key to future planning of time use is to accept the limitations that exist and work on those time periods that can be altered.

The first part of a plan to make actual use of time closer to preferred time use is to answer the question: "What is the objective?" A sample response might be, "To double classroom visitation time." The second part of the plan is to answer the question, "What actions need to be taken?" A sample response might be: "(a) Schedule set times each day for two classroom observations; (b) schedule uninterrupted paperwork in two two-hour blocks of time after school." The third part of the plan is to answer the question, "When will these activities be done?" Sample responses might be: "(a) Classroom visits from 9 to 11 A.M. Monday and Wednesday and 1:00 to 2:30 P.M. Tuesday and Thursday; (b) paperwork scheduled for Monday and Friday 3:00 to 5:00 P.M." The fourth part of the plan is to answer the question, "What resources will be needed to implement the activities"? Sample responses might be: "(a) Explain to secretary the need to protect uninterrupted times; (b) discuss with faculty the change and rationale behind my new schedule and arrange classroom visitation schedule." The fifth and final part of the plan is to answer the question, "How will the success of the goal be evaluated?" A sample response might be, "Check whether the new schedule was followed and, after two weeks, review daily log to see if time in classrooms has doubled."

A supervisor could engage in more elaborate planning techniques by developing a flow chart (see Figure 12-2). Although flow charts look impressive, they are not necessary for simple plans. When looking at more complex planning, however, keep flow charts in mind. As long as we can answer the five questions dealing with (1) objective, (2) activities, (3) time deadlines, (4) resources, and (5) evaluation, then implementation can proceed. If we cannot answer any of the five questions, the plan is incomplete. For example, if we know our objective but don't know what activities, resources, or evaluation to use, then we are still not sure of what to do. On

Figure 12-2 Flow chart for increasing classroom visits

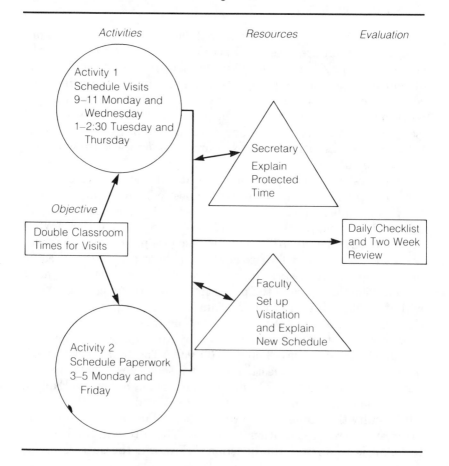

the other hand, if we know our objective, activities, and resources but don't know how to evaluate our success, we will be acting without any knowledge of results.

As we move from assessment and planning of personal change to assessment and planning of faculty improvement, the elements to be considered become more complex and planning becomes more detailed. Other techniques for planning may be necessary. Let's use a "wild" analogy. When a naturalist is tracking a single large elephant, she can basically track the beast by herself. But when the naturalist's task expands to tracking three herds of forty-five elephants each, then she needs other people, more equipment (radios, binoculars, cameras, jeeps, and helicopters), and an awareness of multiple potential obstacles (ill staff workers, malfunctioning equipment, rough terrain). This analogy can be extended only so far, as supervisors are not naturalists, nor are teaching faculties herds of elephants, but the point is that the larger the organizational effort, the more carefully one needs to account for the sequence and the relationships of activities, resources, and evaluation to overall objectives.

Assessing and Planning within the Organization

The five steps of assessing and planning are the same for both personal and organizational plans. Only the complexity and specificity differ. We might think of assessing and planning as a recipe (Bruce and Grimsley 1979). A plan for direct assistance, staff development, curriculum development, or group development has the same elements as a cooking recipe. *We decide our objective:* "to bake sweet potato soufflé" (thanks to Ms. Donna Bell for providing this culinary example). Knowing our family's previous history of food preferences, we are confident that if we cook the soufflé correctly, they will enjoy it and we will be held in positive regard for at least ten minutes. Next, *we determine the activities and when they will take place.*

Activity 1: Mash 6 cups of cooked sweet potatoes.

Activity 2: Beat into the mashed potatoes: 4 eggs, 1 cup butter, 2 cups sugar, 1 cup milk, 1 teaspoon vanilla.

Activity 3: Spread out in unbuttered pan.

Activity 4: Mix in a separate bowl: 1 cup brown sugar, 2/3 cup flour, 1 cup butter, 1 cup chopped pecans.

Activity 5: Spread this mix (Activity 4) evenly over the potatoes (Activity 3).

Activity 6: Bake at 350° for 1 hour.

With the activities and times determined, *we need to identify re-sources.* Equipment resources are an oven, measuring cups, measuring spoons, a large bowl, a pan, a mixing fork, and a spreading knife. Food resources are potatoes, eggs, butter, sugar, vanilla, brown sugar, flour, pecans, and milk.

Finally, *we will evaluate the success* of our cooking endeavor by the following criteria: Everyone in our family will eat the sweet potato soufflé (even Rachel). At least two of the three members (Sara, Jennifer, and Rachel) will ask for seconds. All of them will tell us we're wonderful cooks, and they will volunteer to wash the dishes.

If the supervisor tries acting as a gourmet of instructional cookery and planning recipes for success, all staff members will delight in the soufflé of instructional improvement. The food analogy has run its course (by now, you are probably heading for the refrigerator), and we can turn to assessing and planning within the school context. For purposes of illustration, let's take an example of an elementary reading supervisor who is responsible for developing revised curriculum guides in reading.

Ways of Assessing Need

The first question for the reading supervisor is, "What do we hope to accomplish with a new curriculum guide?" To answer this question, we need to collect information about the past and present state of reading instruction. The supervisor can use multiple ways of assessing need: (1) eyes and ears, (2) official records, (3) third-party review, (4) written open-ended survey, (5) check and ranking list surveys, and (6) the Delphi technique.

Eyes and Ears

Talk to teachers, administrators, aides, and anyone else who works directly with the task under consideration. In this case, the supervisor would want to ask teachers and aides individually and in small groups what they believe are the strengths and weaknesses of the curriculum guide. How is it being used? Is it helpful, and in what ways? Where does it break down? When is it not useful?

Official Records

Look at any documents that indicate the current use and effect of the task under consideration. In this case, what do reading achievement test scores show? How about diagnostic reading tests? Are students mastering reading skills, or are there certain areas (comprehension, fluency, vocabulary) that are consistently out of line with others? What about the curriculum guide itself? When was it last revised? What recent knowledge about writing curriculum guides, instructional approaches to readings, and reading topics are not reflected in the current curriculum?

Third-Party Review

Having a neutral outside person review the task area can be helpful. The supervisor might contact a university or central office consultant, a graduate doctoral student, or some other person with expertise to do an investigation and write a report. The third-party person should be given a clear description of the task (to look at the strengths and weaknesses of the reading curriculum guides), and care should be taken not to bias the third-party person's judgment. The report can then serve as an additional source of objective knowledge, not tied to any special interest in the forthcoming project.

Written Open-Ended Survey

To document and add to the information already received through eyes and ears and official records, a written survey can be administered. Send out a brief questionnaire that asks teachers, aides, administrators, and parents what they think about the current reading curriculum. Keep the survey brief, and word the questions simply, without education jargon. Again, an example of a survey is found in Figure 12-3.

Check and Ranking List

After gathering ideas of the strengths and weaknesses of the task at hand from many sources, the supervisor can ask staff to rank the ideas. The supervisor can then compile a group frequency and numerical priority for each idea previously mentioned. For example, if—through eyes and ears, official documents, and open-ended surveys—the supervisor has collected a list of ideas about perceived weakness of the current reading program, he or she then could disseminate the list back to teachers, aides, and others. The disseminated form might be as shown in Figure 12-4. The supervisor can meet with the staff and show the frequency of numbers assigned to each idea and the average score for each item. Those items receiving frequent low scores and/or with the lowest average scores

Figure 12-3   Survey of reading curriculum

Explanation: As you may know, this year we are determining changes to be made in our reading curriculum. Would you please take a few minutes to respond to the following questions. Please be frank! We will use the information to rewrite our curriculum guides.

Question 1.   What do you think about the current reading curriculum?

Question 2.   What are the strengths of the current reading curriculum?

Question 3.   What are the weaknesses of the current reading curriculum?

Question 4.   What changes do you believe would improve the reading curriculum?

Figure 12-4   Ranking ideas for improving reading curriculum

Directions: The following are the ideas for possible changes that you have suggested. Please prioritize this list by placing the number 1 next to the idea needing the greatest attention, number 2 next to the item needing the next most attention, and so on, until all items are ranked.

_____ Format of the guides.
_____ Readability of the guides.
_____ Activities to go with curriculum objectives.
_____ Objectives and units dealing with reading newspapers.
_____ Objectives and units dealing with reading in other subject areas.
_____ More phonic and word recognition objectives.
_____ Cross-reference units with materials in the classrooms.
_____ Cross-reference objects with fourth-grade competency-based reading test.

would be the first to focus on when discussing curriculum revisions. The ranking list can be further refined by having the participants do two separate rankings—first, to see how all the ideas rank, and then to rerank a shortened list of prioritized ideas.

Delphi Technique

Another written way to prioritize needs is the Delphi technique, developed by the Rand Corporation (Hostrop 1975; Weaver 1971). The technique, originally intended to forecast future trends, is often used for needs assessment. It is a combination of open-ended survey and ranking. The supervisor sends around a problem statement to staff: "We are looking at revisions in the reading curriculum. Write down what you believe needs to be done." The supervisor retrieves the written comments, reproduces everyone's comments, and returns all the comments to the participants. They read the comments and then individually write a synthesis of the various ideas. The supervisor then collects everyone's syntheses and makes a new list of all synthesized ideas. The new list goes back to the participants for ranking. The supervisor collects and computes average and frequency of ratings and then returns the tallies to participants to rerank. This procedure continues until clear priorities emerge.

Planning

After assessing needs and prioritizing ideas, planning proceeds. The steps of operationalizing include objectives, activities, time lines, resources, and evaluation. Techniques of planning include management by objectives (MBO), Gant charts, flow charting, program evaluation and review techniques (PERT), and program planning and budgeting systems (PPBS).

Management by Objectives (MBO)

Most teachers are familiar with classroom performance objectives used in lesson planning. Management by objectives basically involves setting performance objectives for organizational planning (Knezevich 1972). Management objectives make explicit how the goal is to be accomplished. The objective has four elements:

1. What will be performed?
2. When will it be performed?
3. Who will do it?
4. What will be the criteria of success?

Our example of reading curriculum revisions might contain an overall goal: "The reading faculty will update and revise curriculum guides to better meet the instructional needs of students." The goal provides general intent but does not offer the specifics of how it is to be accomplished. After conducting a needs assessment, the reading faculty might have decided on the following management objective: "By October 15, 1985, all reading teachers will be able to write daily lesson plans that incorporate objectives and activities of the new written curriculum guides."

Notice how the management objective has all four elements: what is to be done ("will be able to write in daily lesson plans that incorporate objectives and activities of the new curriculum guide"); when it will be performed ("by October 15, 1985"); who is to do it ("reading teachers"); what are to be the criteria of success ("*all* reading teachers"). To reach this management objective, management activities are specified, such as the following:

1. A representative teacher from each grade level will read the reading curriculum guides, write notations on changes to be made, and submit the changes to the curriculum council on October 1.

2. By December 1, the curriculum council will review five different formats for writing curriculum guides and approve a single format to be used for all grade levels.

3. The resource center director and staff will read the current guides and recommend a procedure for cross-referencing curriculum units with library and media materials to the council by February 1.

4. By April 1, the director of competency-based education and the council will decide on procedures of cross-referencing the sixth-grade competency reading exam with all lessons contained in the curriculum guides.

5. A reading consultant and four teachers will be selected by the council to do the actual rewriting and reformatting of the curriculum guides in order to have the final guides completed by August 1.

6. On August 28, the consultant, the four curriculum writing teachers, and the council will conduct a half-day in-service session for all reading teachers on the use of the new curriculum guides.

A comprehensive MBO system will have an identification of resources for each management activity. Figure 12-5 is an example of writing a complete management activity, including procedures and resources.

Figure 12-5   Revisions of curriculum guides

I. Management objective:
By October 15, 1985, all reading teachers will be able to show on their written daily lesson plans the use of the new curriculum guides.

Management activity
A. A representative teacher from each grade level will read their reading curriculum guides, write notations on changes to be made, and submit the changes to the curriculum council on October 1.

Procedures
1. _____ Explain task at first faculty meeting.
2. _____ Ask grade departments to elect representatives.
3. _____ Devise questions for representative teachers to use in their notations.
4. _____ Meet with representatives and review work to be done.
5. _____ Check on progress of individuals.
6. _____ Convene council meeting on October 1.

Resources: Meeting room, stipend of $50.00 for each teacher = $200.00 total, two copies of each curriculum guide, written questions mimeographed.

MBO provides a clear description of the system for implementing a goal. It demands that the supervisor think of the necessary steps and time lines for successful completion of the overall task. Time lines can be shown graphically by using a technique called a Gant chart.

Gant Charts

A Gant chart is simply a graph that portrays the beginning and completion dates of each activity involved in completing the overall task (Bishop 1976). As shown in Figure 12-6, the activities for revising the curriculum guides are placed on the left-hand side of the chart. The beginning and ending time for each activity is shown by a black solid line across the time line. The supervisor can refer to the chart at any time to check on the progress of the project and be reminded of what groups and what subtasks should be receiving his or her attention.

Program Evaluation and Review Technique (PERT)

PERT is another planning technique used for large projects that depend on the coordination of many individuals, groups, and subtasks. It shows the interrelationships of activities needed in a large project. It is usually found in conjunction with an MBO system and a Gant chart. The PERT flow chart was developed by the

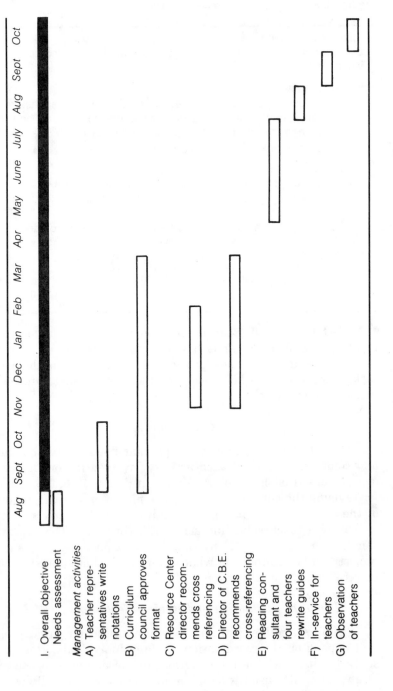

Figure 12-6 Gant chart task: Revising curriculum guides

218

organizers of the Polaris Fleet Ballistic Missile Program in 1958. It enabled federal managers to coordinate the work of hundreds of subcontractors in completing the construction of the ballistic missile program two years ahead of original expectations. Since then it has been adapted to planning in education settings (Case 1969; Cook 1966; Anderson 1975; Bishop 1976; Knezevich, 1984).

The supervisor thinks of all the events and activities needed to complete the task. Then he or she puts those events and activities into a sequence with durations of time. The sequence and duration of events and activities are then flow-charted (see Figure 12-7).

The circled numbers represent important points (meetings, selections and reports) on the way to completing the task. The critical path is the straight line. (1) → (3) → (7) → (9) → (10) → (11) → (12) → (13). The circles outside the critical path are activities at work simultaneously with other activities. They must also be carried out in order for the critical decision points to be completed. Circles stand for events such as reports submitted, decisions made, and documents produced. Arrows represent activities such as in-

Figure 12-7   PERT: Revising curriculum guides

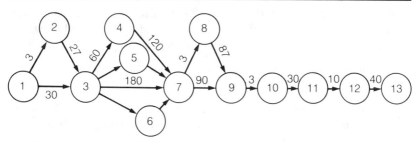

1. Need assessment of faculty, students, parents, and consultants.
2. Select grade-level representatives to write notations on current guides.
3. Curriculum council meeting to assign task of formating the guides.
4. Curriculum council proposes format.
5. Director of competency-based education proposes format.
6. Resource center director proposes format.
7. Curriculum council formalizes format.
8. Select four teachers with consultant to rewrite guides.
9. Curriculum council reviews and approves new guides.
10. Curriculum council plans inservice.
11. In-service held.
12. Council chooses, observes, and meets with teachers to explain rationale and logistics for observations.
13. Observation of teachers' lesson planning.

dividual and committee work in progress. The numbers above the arrows ($\underline{30}$) are the time (in days) needed to complete the activity. A PERT chart provides for close monitoring of a project and a clear description of how events and activities fit together. It also displays to persons involved with the project how their own work fits into the overall scheme.

Planning, Programming, Budgeting System (PPBS)

PPBS is a financial accounting system that supplements other planning systems such as MBO and PERT (Alioto and Jungher 1971). Originally a financial planning device used by the U.S. Department of Defense under Robert J. McNamara, PPBS has been adapted to education often under the name Education Resources Management System (ERMS) and Data Based Educational Planning Systems (DEPS). The basic concept is for managers and supervisors to request funds for programs in terms of program outcomes. Traditional requests for school programs have been based on general line items for textbooks, supplies, salaries, and consultants. PPBS is a planning system that shows the cost of a particular program and the expected results of the program in producing changes in student or teacher performance. For example, if a school desires to have 80 percent of all students reach a tenth-grade mathematics achievement level before graduation, a PPBS plan would respond to the following questions:

What changes in mathematics programs need to be made?

What would be the cost?

To reach the 80 percent objective, how much will a school system need to expend in terms of personnel, materials, facilities, and time?

What alternative plans and costs can be considered to reach the objective?

Eventually, the potential grantor of the program (superintendent, federal grant office, or school board) can consider alternative plans and costs and can make a financial decision based on the expected results.

Let's return to our example of revising curriculum guides. After a needs assessment, our objective is that "*all* reading teachers will be able to show on their written daily lesson plans the use of the curriculum guides." One plan has already been shown for achieving this objective (MBO, Gant chart, and PERT flow chart). Now, what will it cost to implement this plan? Let's say it will cost $3,000 in released time, $2,000 in materials and supplies, $500 for in-service, and $500 for a consultant—a total cost of $6,000. What are alternative plans? One plan might be to involve only one representative teacher instead of four, hire no consultants, and produce only half the needed curriculum guides (with the premise that two teachers would share a guide). Making these changes would reduce the cost by $3,500. Obviously, each plan has advantages and disadvantages that need to be explained. The $6,000 expenditure will involve more staff; the $2,500 expenditure will mean that the task will be done largely by central office staff. The degree of teacher acceptance might vary according to the plan chosen. The funding agent will make a decision about monies to be allocated based on an understanding of likely outcome. "Putting your money where your mouth is" is the cliché that best summarizes the PPBS approach.

Planning: To What Extent?

Keep in mind that a plan is intended to help you and your staff get where you want to go. It is a *means,* not an end in itself. Planning should not get in the way of doing. The extent of planning should depend on how much detail is needed. Frymier (1980) warns of the dangers of overplanning. Planning can be seductive; drawing circles and wording one's objectives can camouflage inactivity. Most supervisory tasks in schools do not need extensive management objectives, flow charts, graphs, or cost analysis. Providing immediate help only requires a supervisor to pause, think about what needs to be done, and then step out of the office and do it.

Extensive MBO and PERT charts are helpful when the proposed change will take place over a considerable amount of time (half a year or more) and will involve many individuals and groups. Extensive planning helps people remember the stages of a project. It is also helpful when many groups or individuals have overlapping or concurrent responsibilities; plans can help the supervisor know whom to contact, and when. Finally, extensive planning is essential when funding is contingent on such details. It is no coincidence that public school supervisors began writing plans with management objectives, time lines, and flow charts in the late 1960s, when federal funding became more available to schools. The federal government required such specifications as part of any proposal. Now most school superintendents, school boards, and state directors expect to see similar planning devices whenever a major instructional change is contemplated.

A final word about planning: Remember that plans are not

ironclad or unchangeable from beginning to end. As organizational theorists remind us, schools are not linear and rational places that move logically from one step to the next (Clark, Lotto, and Astuto 1984). Plans with nicely graphed charts, arrows, and circles are at most a guide to the much more complex world of real life. People become ill, snow days cancel critical meetings, and new initiatives and deadlines unexpectedly come tumbling down to interfere with anticipated plans. Plans provide a direction to success; when circumstances make a preplanned activity or event unnecessary or problematic, the supervisor and staff should be flexible enough to make substitutions and alterations. The final aim is to reach the goal, not to implement a predetermined plan.

Summary

This chapter has explained the complementary nature of assessment and planning for realizing a vision about instructional improvement. It began with examining ways to assess and plan supervisory time. The next topic was assessing and planning organizational change. Assessment techniques discussed were: eyes and ears, official records, third-party review, written open-ended surveys, check and ranking lists, and the Delphi method. Planning techniques discussed were: management by objectives (MBO), Gant charts, program evaluation and review techniques (PERT), and program planning and budgeting systems (PPBS). The last section discussed when to use extensive written and formalized plans.

Assessing and planning skills are generic; they help us to organize our own professional life as well as organize instructional improvement programs that involve many people. Assessing and planning enable us to take stock of present conditions, analyze consequences, and choose events, activities, and resources.

EXERCISES

Academic

1. Prepare a written summary of the major suggestions of one writer on time management. Discuss how the suggestions can be applied to educational supervision.

2. Describe and compare two program assessment processes suc-

cessfully used in a public school system and not discussed in this book.

3. Summarize and discuss a description, found in the educational literature, of the Delphi technique applied to an educational needs assessment.

4. Write a paper summarizing and discussing how the program evaluation and review technique (PERT) has been adapted to planning in educational settings.

5. Write a paper reviewing how the program planning and budgeting systems (PPBS) approach has been adapted for decision making in educational settings.

Field

1. After using the methods suggested in this chapter for assessing your work time (daily log, time consumption chart, comparison of preferred priorities to actual time spent), write out a personal plan for making actual use of time closer to preferred use. Be sure each of the five questions in a personal improvement plan is answered. Implement your plan over a period of two weeks. At the end of the implementation period, prepare a written evaluation of your plan.

2. Write out a personal work improvement objective. Prepare a flow chart as an aid for reaching your objective. Carry out the activities outlined in your flow chart; then evaluate whether your objective has been met. Write a report analyzing your improvement plan and its implementation. Include a discussion of the utility of the flow chart as part of your improvement effort.

3. Use at least one of the four ways of assessing need within an organization (eyes and ears, official records, third-party review, written open-ended survey) to determine needs within an educational program. Write a report on your assessment. Include a discussion of the assessment process and the needs that were discovered.

4. Participate in a group in which an educational improvement plan is created, using at least two of the following planning techniques: (a) management by objectives (MBO); (b) Gant charts; (c) flow charting; (d) program evaluation and review techniques (PERT); (e) program planning and budgeting systems (PPBS). Prepare a written report on the experience.

5. Interview a leader in business, industry, government, or the

military who has had extensive experience with one of the planning techniques listed in the previous exercise. Prepare a report on your interview, including a description of how the technique is used in the interviewee's field and a discussion of how it might be modified for use in an educational setting.

Developmental

1. Use a Gant chart to plan a long-range personal project. Carry the project through to completion.
2. Volunteer for participation in an educational planning process.
3. Begin an in-depth exploration of what prominent authors in educational supervision have to say about educational assessment and planning.

REFERENCES

Alioto, R.J., and Jungher, J.A. 1971. *Operational PPBS for education: A practical approach to effective decision making.* New York: Harper & Row.

Anderson, S. 1975. *Encyclopedia of educational evaluation.* San Francisco: Jossey-Bass, pp. 290–293.

Bennis, W.G., Benne, K.D., and Chin, P. 1985. *The planning of change.* New York: Holt, Rinehart and Winston.

Bishop, L.J. 1976. *Staff development and instructional development: Plans and procedures.* Boston: Allyn and Bacon.

Bruce, R.E., and Grimsley, E.E. 1979. Course supplementary reading—introduction to supervision. Unpublished manuscript, University of Georgia.

Case, C.M. 1969. The application of PERT to large-scale educational and evaluation studies. *Educational Technology* 9:79–83.

Clark, D., Lotto, L., and Astuto, T. 1984. Effective schools and school improvement: A comparative analysis of two lines of inquiry. *Educational Administration Quarterly* 20:41–68.

Cook, D.L. 1966. PERT: *Applications in education.* Cooperative Research Monograph No. 17. Washington, D.C.: U.S. Government Printing Office.

Frymier, J. 1980. Practical principles of educational leadership.

Annual Johnnye E. Cox lecture of the Georgia Association of Curriculum and Instructional Supervision, Athens, September.

Hostrop, R.W. 1975. *Managing education for results,* 2nd ed. Homewood, Calif.: ETC Publications.

Knezevich, S.J. 1972. MBO—Its meaning and application to educational administration. *Education 93*:12–21.

———. 1984. Administration of public education. New York: Harper and Row.

Weaver, W.T. 1971. The Delphi forecasting method. *Kappan 52*:267.

Chapter 13

Observing Skills

Observation seems simple. Anyone with normal vision appears to be observing every moment his or her eyes are open. Why, then, are there so many books, approaches, and debates about the types and uses of observation for instructional improvement (Acheson and Gall 1987; Beegle and Brandt 1973; Simon and Boyer 1967; Jones and Sherman 1980; Eisner 1985)? As *Webster's* defines it, observation is "(1) an act or the faculty of observing, (2) an act of recognizing and noting a fact or occurrence often involving measurement with instruments . . . , (3) a judgment and inference from what one has observed" (*Webster's* 1974, p. 792). Observation is thus the act of noting and then judging. The issue of observation in educational settings has focused on questions of instruments and the basis for inferences. These are some of the issues:

1. Is there a need for an externally structured instrument to measure what is happening in a classroom, or can a supervisor instead use subjective, anecdotal methods of observation?

2. What is the basis for inferring that observed instructional practices such as student behaviors or teacher actions are good or bad?

3. Does inference need to be derived from a numerical accounting of classroom events, or can a supervisor judge effective practices from a feel for the classroom?

These are complicated questions. The purpose of this chapter is to answer them by arriving at general agreement on observation procedures, describing the various methods of observation that can be used by supervisors, and then providing criteria for choosing appropriate observation forms.

Consider the classroom shown in Figure 13-1. If you were an observer of this classroom, what would you say is happening? Of course, one illustration is not enough basis for an observation, but pretend you are seeing this episode for an entire class period. Could you say that the students are behavior problems, discipline is lax,

Figure 13-1   Classroom picture

the teacher is not responding to the students' interests, or the teacher is lecturing too much?

If your observations are similar to those listed here, then you have fallen into the *interpretation trap,* which is the downfall of most attempts to help people improve their performance. How would you respond if your evaluator—say, the superintendent of schools— observed you conducting a faculty meeting and later told you that teachers lack respect for you? Your response probably would be a combination of defensiveness ("It isn't so"), confusion ("What do you mean?"), and quiet hostility ("Who are you to say that to me?"). The superintendent has inadvertently turned you against him or her, and compliance on your part will be grudging at best.

Observation is a two-part process—first *describing* what has been seen and then *interpreting* what it means. The mind almost simultaneously processes a visual image, integrates that image with previously stored images related to satisfactory and unsatisfactory experiences, and ascribes a value or meaning to that image. If we see a student yawn, our mind signals "boredom." If a teacher yells at students, our mind registers "losing control." A judgment derives from an image or a description of events. We must be aware of splitting that almost simultaneous process, of separating description from interpretation. When we lose the description of the event and retain only the interpretation, we create communication difficulties and obstacles to improvement.

Let's return to the superintendent's interpretation that "teachers lack respect." How much different would your response have been if the description behind the interpretation had been shared with you: "I saw that six of the fifteen teachers arrived late to your faculty meeting." You could agree that, indeed, six members did arrive late; however, you might disagree with the interpretation of lack of respect as arbitrary. You could not only accept that six members had been late, but also do something about it. You cannot do anything about lack of respect, because you don't know what needs to be changed. On the other hand, you can correct lateness and eventually improve the superintendent's interpretation of the teachers' respect. Sharing the description of events is the forerunner of professional improvement. Interpretation leads to resistance. When both parties can agree on what events occurred, they are more likely to agree on what needs to be changed.

Remember that if the goal of supervision is to enhance teachers' thought and commitment about improving classroom (and school) practice, observations should be used as a base of information to create an instructional dialogue between supervisor and teacher. Using description first when talking to a teacher about his or her classroom creates an instructional dialogue. Providing interpretations and evaluative statements first ushers in defensiveness, combativeness, or resentment in the teacher and stifles discussion (see Glickman and Jones 1986).

Differentiating description from interpretation in observation is so crucial for instructional improvement that we need to refer back to our original illustration of the classroom (Figure 13-1). Look at the picture again and tell what you now see going on. You might say that there are three students looking away from the teacher and talking to each other while the teacher stands in front of the room calling on a boy in the front row. Can we agree that this is happening? Probably so, and thus we can *later* judge the rightness or wrongness of the event in regard to student learning.

The teacher can more readily change the events of three students talking to each other and two others looking away than he or she can change being "a poor classroom manager." Now, we can move on to alternative ways of describing and interpreting.

Ways of Describing

In describing, the goal is to eliminate any confusion about what is happening. A good check is to use a person off the street as corroborator. One can feel confident about one's description of what is happening in a classroom if a sidewalk passerby could be pulled into the classroom and (no matter what his or her credentials) would in fact see what the observer is seeing. If the passerby would have to make any professional judgment—about, say, the rapidity of presentation, the responsiveness to learning style, or the permissiveness of discipline—then it would no longer be a description. If the passerby could describe such happenings as the frequency of teacher-student talk, interruptions, the arrangement of the room, the physical space used by the teacher, and what teacher and students are saying, then the person-off-the-street check has been passed, and you may remove the passerby from your mind. (Please do not physically pull people from the street into the classroom— the neighborhood school concept can be taken only so far.)

There are many ways to record descriptions. At the end of this chapter, there are multiple references to various observation methods and instruments. An observation instrument is a tool for organizing and recording different categories of classroom life. It can be as simple as a single category or as complex as a matrix of dozens of possible coded combinations. For example, an instrument can be used to count the displays on a classroom wall or to record the hundreds of students' and teachers' verbal and nonverbal interactions.

I have formed a strong bias from using observation instruments as a school principal and working with hundreds of administrators, supervisors, and teachers. Observation instruments developed for research purposes are usually too time-consuming and cumbersome to be used by practitioners. Most of us do not have the capability or inclination to record twelve categories of behaviors every three seconds and then transcribe the check marks into appropriate columns and ratios. I do not mean to attack instruments such as those developed by Bales (1951), Flanders (1970), or Medley and Mizel (1963). These instruments have contributed immensely to research on effective teaching and have directed practitioners toward instructional practices that need to be emphasized. However, the instruments have been used by trained (usually paid) data collectors and are not as easily used by a single supervisor with thirty or more faculty members to observe. I believe there are ways to adapt the more complicated instruments so that they can be used to provide valid descriptions for the nonresearch purpose of describing classroom events to a teacher. A listing and explanation of many adapted ways of observing will follow.

We will first look at quantitative observations, including categorical instruments, physical indicator instruments, visual diagramming, and space utilization. The second section will deal with qualitative observations, including detached open-ended narrative, participant observation, focused questionnaire observation, and educational criticism.

Quantitative Observations

Quantitative observations are ways of measuring classroom events, behaviors, and objects. Definitions and categories must be precise. Eventually the observations can be used for statistical operations.

Categorical Frequency Instrument

A categorical instrument is a form that defines certain events or behaviors that can be checked off at frequency intervals and then counted. There is nothing mysterious about it. Almost any aspect of classroom life can be isolated and counted. For example, teacher behaviors can be divided into verbal and nonverbal categories. Each category can then be subdivided into countable subcategories. Verbal behaviors could be information-giving, questioning, answering, praising, direction-giving, and scolding. An instrument might look like Figure 13-2.

The observer, after clearly defining each subcategory, would listen to each teacher verbalization and move down the sheet for each different statement made. One check exists for each horizontal line. Most instruments that record teacher verbal behavior also record student verbal behavior, so that verbal interactions between teacher and student and student and student can be analyzed.

Other classroom topics can be observed with categorical instruments. For example, one can focus on student academic behavior. Academic behavior can be divided into two categories: attentive and inattentive. Furthermore, attentive behavior can then be divided into subcategories: (1) watching instructor, (2) working

Figure 13-2 Teacher verbal behaviors

	Information Giving	Questioning	Answering	Praising	Direction Giving	Scolding
1.		X				
2.		X				
3.	X					
4.	X					
5.	X					
6.	X					
7.			X			
8.			X			
9.	X					
10.	X					
11.			X			
12.			X			
13.	X					
14.	X					
15.	X					
16.	X					

on assignments, and (3) talking to others about the learning task. Inattentive behavior can be broken into: (4) staring off into space, (5) not doing assignments, and (6) talking to others about non-academic matters. The instrument would then look like Figure 13-3.

The observer would pick ten students at random and follow them throughout the period for one-minute observations at random intervals. Each one-minute observation would result in a check for what each student was seen to be doing. Therefore each horizontal line would contain ten checks. A slightly different version of this instrument could be used to record student on-task behavior, broken into categories of attentive to task, inattentive but passive (non-disruptive), and inattentive-active (disruptive) (see Figure 13-4).

As long as the categories can be precisely defined so that supervisor and teacher know what is to be observed, the instrument serves its purpose of providing a description of events. Every ten

Figure 13-3   Student academic behavior

	Attentive			Inattentive		
	1) Watching	2)Doing	3) Talking	4) Not Watching	5) Not Doing	6) Talking
1.	XXXXX		X			XX
2.	XXX	XXXX		X		X
3.		XXXX	XX	XXX	X	
4.						
5.						
6.						
7.						
8.						
9.						
10.						

minutes, the observer could take a one-minute sample of the same ten students. From the foregoing sample, the observer could readily share with the teacher the changing pattern of on-task behavior and discuss the circumstances that might explain an increase in attentive behavior.

The preceding categorical frequency instruments are not suitable for research purposes unless they have been developed further for interrater reliability and validity. However, if supervisor and teacher find the information gathered useful for their purpose, they should use the instruments.

Figure 13-4   On-task behavior

	Attentive to Task	Inattentive/Passive	Inattentive/Active
11:00	XXXXXX	XXX	X
11:10	XXXX	XXXX	XXX
11:20	XXXXX	XXXX	X
11:35	XXXXXXXX	X	X
11:40	XXXXXXXXX	X	

Physical-Indicator Instruments

Physical-indicator instruments are usually of the yes/no type: Either the indicator does or does not exist. For example, an instrument focused on the physical classroom might be as shown in Figure 13-5.

A physical-indicator instrument of the classroom is simple to record. As a descriptor, it is relatively value- or interpretation-free. For example, if indicator 6 is checked no, it means there is litter on the classroom floor. In discussing this information with the teacher, the supervisor might find that litter on the floor is all right, since students are assigned to cleaning up after school. On the other hand, it may not be all right if the teacher was unaware of the litter and had not noticed that students were not keeping their desk areas clean at all times. The supervisor's check, whether yes or no, should not prejudge desirability but should allow for clarification, later judgment of desirability, and teacher action when appropriate.

Performance-Indicator Instrument

A performance-indicator instrument also calls for a yes/no response, but the items focus on teacher or student actions, either observed or not. Figure 13-6 is an example of a performance in-

Figure 13-5   Physical classroom

Classroom	Yes	No	Uncertain
1. Walls and floors clear of graffiti and blemishes.			
2. Student displayed materials.			
3. Teacher displayed materials.			
4. Student materials on display are less than four weeks old.			
5. Teacher materials on display are less than four weeks old.			
6. Floors clear of litter at conclusion of class.			
7. Student resource materials filed in storage area.			
8. Teacher resource materials filed in storage area.			
9. "In" and "Out" box for student papers clearly marked.			
10. Checkout system posted for classroom library.			

Figure 13-6 Illustration

Indicator communicates with individual learners about their needs and progress.

Item	*Response*

a. Classroom questioning is used to help learn-   Yes _____ No _____
   ers identify learning problems.
   Explanation: Many types of oral classroom
   questioning techniques may be used by a
   teacher. The teacher may question a student
   to find out whether the student understands
   or to determine areas of difficulty. Another
   method of questioning is often referred to as
   the Socratic approach.

> After adding 14 and 17 and getting a sum of
> 21, the child is asked how he proceeded with
> the problem.
> *Student:* First I added 7 and 4.
> *Teacher:* What is their sum?
> *Student:* 11.
> *Teacher:* How many 10s is that and many 1s?
> *Student:* It's one 10 and one 1.
> *Teacher:* What do you do with the one 10?
> *Student:* Oh, I see. I need to add it to the 10s.

Learning problems are difficulties encountered
during the unit of study.

b. Progress check results are used to help   Yes _____ No _____
   learners identify learners' problems.
   Explanation: Feedback on progress checks
   is given to students during the unit.

c. Learners are given feedback on summative   Yes _____ No _____
   test scores.
   Explanation: Learners receive feedback on
   their unit tests.

d. Conferences are conducted with individual   Yes _____ No _____
   students to discuss learning or motivational
   problems.
   Explanation: Teacher discusses individual
   problems in private conferences with the student. One-to-one discussions may occur in
   or out of the classroom.

---

dicator derived from an early teacher performance assessment instrument used to assess beginning teachers by the Georgia Department of Education (Capie et al. 1979).

The observer sits in on a classroom session, reviews student and teacher work, talks with students and teachers, and then checks whether the descriptors were evident or not. Did the teacher ask learners questions to help identify learning problems? Was there evidence that progress results were used by students to determine further study for future tests? Did learners receive oral or written feedback on their unit tests? Were individual conferences conducted? Descriptors such as these provide for the occurrence but not the frequency of the occurrence. For example, an observer would check yes if individual conferences were held, regardless of whether the teacher held two or thirty conferences. Frequencies or degrees of performance can be made by changing the response from yes or no to an amount (see Figure 13-7). The change from yes/no to amount provides further precision.

Remember that descriptors for observation purposes should not imply a prejudged standard. Whether a teacher holds conferences with 25 percent or 100 percent of students, it is neither good nor bad until supervisor and teacher discuss the circumstances surrounding the evidence.

Visual Diagramming

Visual diagramming is another way to portray what is occurring in a classroom. Videotaping a classroom captures the closest representative picture of actual occurrences. Without videotapes, however, there are other ways to portray observations such as ver-

Figure 13-7   Frequency of performance indicators

	Frequency			
Performance Indicators	10–25% of Students	25–50% of Students	50–75% of Students	50–100% of Students
Learners given feedback on summative test scores				
Conferences conducted with individual students to discuss learning or motivational performance				

bal interactions among teachers and students and how a teacher uses space. After diagramming the occurrence, the supervisor and the teacher can view the picture and then analyze the events.

Classroom verbal interactions can be charted by drawing arrows symbolizing verbal statements between members in a classroom (see Figure 13-8). The observer can use six separate sheets of this

Figure 13-8   Diagram of verbal interaction, 9:10–9:15

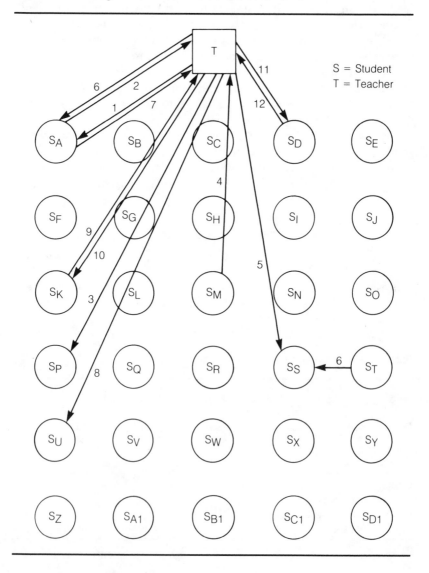

diagram and fill out one sheet for each time sample of five minutes spaced throughout the hour. Each arrow drawn on the diagram would indicate a full statement directed to another person. The arrows are numbered in the sequence of statements. After diagramming, the observer would then have information on the frequency of individual student interaction, the amount of interaction with different areas of the room, which students triggered interactions among others, and which students were excluded. For illustration purposes, if the diagram was a sample consistent with the other five samples of the classroom period, the observer would be able to state some of the following conclusions:

1. Interaction is mainly directed toward the left aisle and front row.

2. There is almost no attention to the last two rows in the back of the room or the two rows on the right.

3. Of fourteen interactions, twelve included the teacher, two were between students.

Such diagramming is easier to follow with small groups and when students are not moving around the classroom. Class activities such as teacher lecturing interspersed with questions and answers or classroom discussions would be instructional sessions appropriate for diagramming. Another type of diagramming is flow-charting teacher space utilization, which follows the teacher's movement throughout the classroom. A sketch of the physical classroom is done first; then the observer follows the teacher by using arrows on the sketch (see Figure 13-9).

Figure 13-9 illustrates a period of reading instruction. The arrow follows the teacher with each movement and is labeled with the time on the clock. After a class period, the observer and the teacher can see where the teacher has been and for how long. Such information might help make a teacher aware of the relationship of his or her space utilization to concerns of classroom management and instruction. For example, in Figure 13-9 there is much physical presence in the front and on the left side of the classroom, with no presence at the rear learning centers or the middle work area.

Quantitative and Qualitative Instruments

Structured forms used to record categorical frequencies, physical indicators, performance indicators, and visual diagrams all measure classroom occurrences. Categorical forms can measure the amount of verbal, nonverbal, on-task, or off-task behaviors of teach-

Figure 13-9   Teacher space utilization

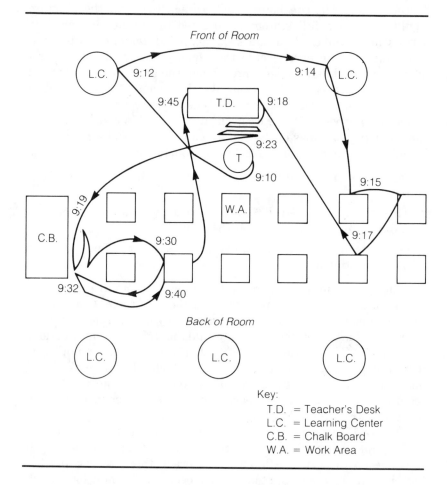

Front of Room

Key:
T.D. = Teacher's Desk
L.C. = Learning Center
C.B. = Chalk Board
W.A. = Work Area

ers and students. One can derive percentages, ratios, and means of total and type of behaviors (total teacher talk, ratio of teacher to student talk, breakdown of amount of teacher questions, directions, answers, and so on). The performance-indicator instruments are a measure of occurrence one time (yes/no) or frequency of time. For example, a performance indicator entitled "feedback on tests" can be measured by teacher-written comments. Therefore the observer looks for teacher-written comments on tests and possibly at the number of tests. Diagramming events in classrooms is another way to count occurrences, lengths of occurrences, and placement of occurrences. For example, the observer can record how much time a teacher spends in different areas of the classroom and the frequency with which the teacher repeats certain walking patterns. All these instruments are quantitative in that they isolate occurrences in the classroom, provide a measurement standard for compiling the amount of occurrences, and lend themselves to further statistical treatment. Structured instruments enable the observer to know precisely what he or she is looking for prior to entering the classroom.

There are alternative means of observing based on not knowing exactly what is to be recorded. These are called qualitative or descriptive forms of observation. The observer goes into the classroom with a general focus, or no focus at all, and records events as they occur. The events are not made to fit into a specific category, nor are they measured. Only after the recording of events does the observer rearrange his or her observations into themes. Such recording of observations defies the use of an instrument (an instrument is technically a measurement device). Instead, qualitative observations record the complexity of classroom life. Suppose two supervisors go into the same classroom. Supervisor A fills out a quantitative instrument on interaction; supervisor B qualitatively describes classroom life. They both observe the teacher asking: "Why did Britain go to war in Argentina? Doesn't anyone know? What a bunch of dummies." Supervisor A listens and places two check marks in the teacher question box and another check in the teacher statement box. Supervisor B writes: "Ms. Egghart smiles and asks if anyone knows why Britain went to war. With no response, she asks if anyone understands the question. She looks up, rolls her eyes, throws up her hands and says 'what a bunch of dummies.' The students smile and laugh. She laughs with them."

	Question	Statements	Directions
11	X		
12	X		
13		X	

The quantitative observation reveals the *amount* and ratios of teacher questions and statements; the qualitative instrument reveals the *nature* of teacher questions, statements, and relations. Both observations are correct. However, one observation reduces the amount of information into fixed categories; the other builds a range of description to be compiled later into common, emerging themes.

Qualitative Observations

There are several types of qualitative observations. We will look at detached open-ended narrative, participant observation, focused questionnaire observation, and educational criticism. These observations can be used by a supervisor to provide a broad and complex recording of classroom life.

Detached Open-Ended Narrative

Detached open-ended narrative occurs when the supervisor steps into a classroom and records every person, event, or material that attracts his or her attention. At the start the pages are empty, without questions, indicators, or categories. The heading might simply say:

Open-Ended Narrative

Observation Teacher:_____Time ____Observer_____

The recorder then has the task of writing, writing, writing . . . . A sample of such an observation might read:

> Students begin arriving at 10:13; the teacher is at his desk correcting papers. The bell rings at 10:15 to begin third period. Students keep arriving. Mr. X gets up from his desk to begin class at 10:25. In the meantime, students have put away their school bags and are awaiting instruction, except three girls in the back corner who are talking, combing their hair, and spreading the contents of their pocketbooks on their desks. Five minutes after Mr. X begins, he talks to them and they put away combs and pocketbooks. Mr. X describes the activities for the day but then cannot find his prepared handouts. After two minutes of looking, he finds the papers in his desk drawer.
>
> The intercom comes on at 10:30 with two announcements by the principal. Mr. X gives the assignments, and the class begins to read at 10:33. Two students are reprimanded for talking, and occasional student talk can be heard as Mr. X moves around and reviews yesterday's homework with students. He talks with twelve

students before asking for class attention at 10:45. He then lectures on the classification of insects. The overhead projection on the board is difficult for students in the back to read. One student asks if he can darken the lights. . . .

With practice the observer can write in shorthand to keep up with the flow of events. It is impossible to record all that could possibly be seen and heard in a classroom. The observer must constantly scan the entire classroom and decide what is significant.

Participant Open-Ended Observation

Participant open-ended observation occurs when the supervisor becomes a functioning part of the classroom (Spradley 1980). He or she assists in the instruction, helps students with questions, uses classroom materials, and talks with teacher and students. Being involved in the classroom gives the supervisor an inside-out view of the classroom different from that of the detached observer who tries to be invisible and keep away from students and teachers. Obviously, events cannot be written down as they occur if the supervisor is engaged in talking, moving, and assisting. Instead, he or she must write between pauses in the action. The observation form can be carried on a clipboard so that notes can be taken on the run.

The participant observer takes sketchy notes (catch phrases and words) during classroom time so that afterward he or she can write in greater detail. These quick notes serve to remind the observer of the situation that will be described more fully after the observation period is over. The following is an example of such short notes.

Teacher X directs students into study groups.

John B. does not understand the assignment. I work with him on organizing the theme of a play.

Sally T. and Ramona B. are wandering around. I ask them if they need help; they say no and leave the room (ask teacher about this).

Sondra and her group are ready to role play their theme. I listen as they read through their parts.

Steven's group is stuck; he doesn't know how to find materials on historic buildings. I suggest calling the town historic society.

Susan is not participating at all—looking at *Teen Magazine*. The rest of the group just leaves her alone. (I wonder why?)

The filmstrip shown has everyone's attention.

Teacher B dismisses the class. I overhear a student say, "This class goes so quickly, I wish other classes were as much fun."

These are some notes from a fifty-minute classroom period. Much more happened in the classroom than is noted, but the observer picks up insights from his or her involvement. The supervisor can later fill in details—the two girls leaving the classroom, the specifics of John's confusion about the theme, Susan's absorption in *Teen Magazine.*

Focused Questionnaire Observation

Qualitative observation can be done in a more focused manner by having general topics to use in recording events. An observer seeks information about specific questions.

Particular instructional models and learning goals can be used in a focused questionnaire. For example, if a teacher were attempting to use a teacher-centered, direct instruction model to teach short-term, specific skills or facts in a lesson, the following questions to focus the observer on recording relevant descriptions might be appropriate (Rosenshine 1986).

What does the teacher do to

1. Review the previous learnings that are prerequisites for the lesson?

2. Present new materials (statement of goals, examples, modeling, checking for understanding)?

3. Provide guided practice (questions, feedback, success rate, closure before independent practice)?

4. Feedback for correct answers and incorrect answers (clues, reteaching) and specific praise?

5. Provide independent practice (overview, initial steps, practice, automatic response, routines for slower students)?

6. Conduct weekly and monthly reviews?

If a teacher were attempting to use a student-centered approach aimed at increasing critical and creative thinking about a current world concern, the observer might be able to focus descriptions according to the following questions (Marzano, Brandt, Hughes, Jones, Presseisen, Rankin, and Suhor 1988).

What does the teacher do to assist students to acquire core thinking skills of

1. *Focusing:* Defining problems and setting goals?

2. *Information gathering:* Observing to obtain information and formulate questions to seek new information?
3. *Remembering:* Storing and retrieving information?
4. *Organizing:* Comparing, classifying, observing, and representing?
5. *Analyzing:* Identifying attributes and components, relationships and patterns, main ideas, and errors?
6. *Generating:* Inferring, predicting, and elaborating?
7. *Integrating:* Summarizing and restructuring?
8. *Evaluating:* Assessing the reasonableness and quality of ideas?

A focused questionnaire can revolve around a particular instructional model, such as direct instruction, cooperative learning, jurisprudence, advanced organizers, or indirect learning. It can be as narrow as looking at one or two questions within a particular model or be as extensive as to include numerous questions about a model, or be generic in posing questions that would cross different teaching practices.

In order to answer the questions, the observer writes pertinent evidence. For example, Harris (1975, pp. 364–376) has developed a detached observation questionnaire that has as its topics: (1) classroom, (2) teacher, (3) pupil, and (4) lesson. Figure 13-10 shows sample questions taken from each category.

Figure 13-10   Focused questionnaire

Topic 1:   Classroom
How is the classroom made attractive?

Topic 2:   Teacher
What shows that the teacher has a warm, friendly relationship with the pupils?

Topic 3:   Pupil
What indicates that pupils know what they are doing and why they are doing it?

Topic 4:   Lesson
How do classroom and homework assignments indicate that consideration is given to, and use made of, resources of the community and real-life situations of pupils?

An observer enters the classroom with questions in hand and looks for the answers. Some questions lend themselves to detached observations; others demand participant observations. For example, the question, "What shows that the teacher has a warm, friendly relationship with pupils?" could be answered by participant observation, such as: "Overheard three students saying how nice Ms. Y is. Noticed how Ms. Y put her hand on the shoulders of five different students when speaking to them." The question "How is the classroom made attractive?" could be answered by detached observation: "Classroom freshly painted, bulletin boards have recent work. Student art work is framed and evenly spaced." It is the task of the observer to respond to these questions with descriptions of the evidence.

Educational Criticism

Elliott Eisner (1985) has developed an approach to observation that merges detached and participant observation with description and interpretation. Observers are trained to look at the classroom as an art critic might look at a painting. Just as a person would have to accumulate the experience of viewing numerous paintings and become knowledgeable in the history and variations of particular art forms to be a critic, so must an educator become familiar with many types of classrooms and forms of instruction to be an education critic.

Eisner believes classroom observations can be done via the same procedures of criticism. He calls the needed educational expertise "connoisseurship." Just as a wine connoisseur can look at the color, viscosity, smell, and taste of a wine to form specific judgments about its overall quality, so can an educational connoisseur make judgments about the specifics of classroom events and the overall quality of classroom life.

Eisner argues that supervisors can develop educational connoisseurship by finding what the classroom *means* to the participants. The education critic attempts to take the perception of students and teachers in viewing the influence of the classroom environment, events, and interactions and then makes the hidden meaning of the classroom known to the participants to see whether they agree. Teachers and students may be so involved in the classroom that they are unaware of the meaning of what they do. The participant observer attempts to describe and interpret events through their eyes.

The following are excerpts from an observation that Eisner

made of William Bennett, former United States Secretary of Education, teaching a high school civics class (Eisner 1986, pp. 2–4).

"All right, let's get to work. I'm putting my name on the board so you can write me if I make mistakes."

Sarcastic? Hard to tell. Neither Bennett nor the students laugh. Perhaps he is serious. With preliminaries over, our champion takes off his suit coat, hangs it on the chair adjacent to the desk, rolls up his sleeves, and begins to pace back and forth in front of the room. "Why read *Federalist 10*?—Why bother? Why not watch the Georgia–Alabama game?" His voice, his slight crouch, his hand gestures—but most of all the intensity of his gaze—leave no doubt that this is a serious encounter. "Let's get to work," his opening phrase is apt. Today's lesson will be no "once over lightly", no open-ended superficial discussion of anything on anyone's mind, but a serious examination of the ideas which he seems to care about deeply. . . .

This material, for Bennett, is no stranger. It is obvious that he has taught it before, and often. How do we know? He repeats passages verbatim from Madison's *Federalist 10*. The book he uses he proudly tells the class is "properly dog-eared". And dog-eared it is, almost falling apart in his hands. In some ways its condition is reminiscent of the overly loved teddy bear that has grown into middle age. Madison and Bennett are old friends. "What is a faction?", he asks, "and why is it a problem in a society like ours? Why does liberty cause the problem of faction?"

Notice how language is expository, nontechnical, and elaborated; "sarcastic?", "intensity of his gaze," "overly loved teddy bear." The writing is intended to capture the tone or feel of the class so that the observation can be used to verify the particulars and the general aspects of classroom life. Education critics record their information by playing both roles of distant and participant observer—distant observer by being apart from the classroom and participant observer by listening to students and teachers talk with each other to uncover further insights into the participant's perceptions of the classroom.

At first glance, an education critic would seem to differ little from the observer mentioned in the beginning of this chapter. That observer failed to distinguish between interpretation and description and instead wrote what he or she liked or disliked ("the classroom is a mess"). However, the education critic knows the difference. The critic has carefully recorded descriptions intermingled with interpretations derived from the participants' perspective. The education critic has caught the atmosphere (which later would be given to the teacher to verify); the nondiscriminating evaluator is left with only his or her own judgments of events.

Types and Purposes of Observations

Figure 13-11 illustrates the types of observation available to a supervisor. The purpose of the observation should determine the type, method, and role of observation. The categorical-frequency observation is a quantitative method used by a detached observer for the purpose of counting, totaling, and statistically analyzing behaviors. The physical-indicator observation is quantitatively used by a detached observer for finding physical evidence. In the same manner, a performance-indicator observation is quantitatively used by a detached observer to record evidence of human behavior. Visual diagramming is a quantitative observation used by a detached observer for the purpose of depicting verbal interaction. Human space utilization observation is a quantitative measure used by a detached observer for the purpose of depicting the length and pattern of physical movement. The detached open-ended narrative is a qualitative observation used by a detached observer for recording events as they unfold. Participant open-ended observation is a qualitative technique used to record how people and events unfold to one involved in the classroom. The focused questionnaire is another qualitative method that can be used by a detached or participant observer for the purpose of gathering evidence according to general questions about classroom topics. Finally, educational criticism is a qualitative observation conducted by a combination of detached and participant observation for the purpose of capturing the meaning of classroom life from the teacher's and students' perspective.

Observation Instruments
Are Not Evaluation Instruments

An observation instrument used to describe what is occurring in a classroom (consistent with what teacher and supervisor agreed to focus on and later discuss) is a means for professional growth and instructional improvement. Therefore the use of an observation instrument is conditioned on prior agreement about what is most worthy of learning by that teacher in that classroom—whether the interest is derived from a desire to know more about himself or herself as a teacher, attempting a particular instructional model, experimenting with a new practice or strategy, or struggling with a problem or weakness. An evaluation instrument, on the other hand, is an externally imposed, uniformly applied measure, intended to judge all teachers on similar criteria to determine their worthiness, merit, and competence as employees within the same organization. Evaluation instruments are intended to summarize

Figure 13-11 Observation alternatives

Type	Method		Role of Observer		Purpose
	Quantitative	Qualitative	Detached	Participant	
Categorical frequency	X		X		Count Behaviors
Physical indicator	X		X		Evident or not
Performance indicator	X		X		Evident or not
Visual diagramming	X		X		Picture verbal interaction
Space utilization	X		X		Picture movement
Detached open-ended narrative		X	X		Attention to unfolding event
Participant open-ended observation		X		X	Inside-out view
Focused questionnaire		X	X or	X	Focus on particular events
Educational criticism		X	X or	X	Meaning to participants

and judge competence. Observation instruments are intended to provide information to teachers on what they and their supervisors have agreed to as important; competence is not the issue. Therefore evaluation instruments tend to be checklists, rating scales, or narratives of worth about the teacher's competence, whereas observation instruments are descriptive findings that move to interpretations for further goals and professional learning. Observation instruments are chosen for use between teacher and supervisor. Evaluation instruments are dictated to teacher and evaluator. Although evaluation instruments have their rightful place in schools, they should not be confused with observation instruments. These important distinctions will be discussed in the section on school and district procedures for direct assistance and formal evaluation, in Chapter 15.

Further Cautions When Using Observations

To reiterate, the purpose of observation should determine the type, method, and role used. No one type of observation is superior to all others; rather, some types of observations are better for serving certain purposes. If the goal of an observation is to determine the frequency of praise, then educational criticism or open-ended narrative would be inappropriate when categorical frequencies would accomplish the goal. If the purpose of an observation is to determine those activities with greatest student interest, then a categorical- or performance-indicator instrument would be of little value, and a focused questionnaire would be more useful. There is a tendency for educators to view a new method of observation as a panacea to use at every opportunity. This has been the case with categorical-frequency instruments. Training programs, workshops, and courses have prepared thousands of supervisors with skills in defining and checking off categories. Hordes of prepared supervisors have run back into classrooms ticking off behaviors. In some cases it was important for future instructional improvement to know the ratio of teacher statements, questions, and directions given. In other classrooms, interaction frequencies and ratios were never a concern to begin with, and the observation was meaningless. The new techniques of educational criticism should not be used indiscriminately by every supervisor in every classroom simply because they are new. Instead, they should be used only when the supervisor and teacher share a concern about the meaning of the classroom to participants. An instrument should not become a focus for all observation because of its availability or newness. It should be used only if it is a priority concern of teachers and supervisors.

Summary

There are many ways to observe classrooms. The choice of a particular type of observation depends on the purpose and focus of the observation. Observation enables a supervisor to put a mirror of the classroom up to the teacher, who can then attend to matters previously unknown. Several studies (Brophy and Good 1974, pp. 297–328) have shown that teachers often change instructional behaviors on their own after their classrooms have been described to them by an observer. The mirror can often be the stimulus for change. The observer must be careful in using interpretations, because such value judgments can actually cloud the mirror and prevent the teacher from seeing his or her own image. At all times, the observer needs to distinguish description from interpretation when recording and explaining events to the teacher.

EXERCISES

Academic

1. Review a system either developed by or adapted from Bales (1951), Flanders (1970), Medley and Mizel (1963), or Hyman (1975), designed to aid in the observation of classroom behavior. Write a paper describing the specific purpose(s) of the chosen system, procedures involved in its use, your perceptions of the utility of the system for direct assistance, and supervisory goals for which use of the system would be most appropriate.

2. Locate one example of each type of instrument listed here in outside literature on educational supervision. Describe each instrument, and discuss the specific purpose and procedures for the use of each.
   a. A categorical-frequency instrument.
   b. A physical-indicator instrument.
   c. A performance-indicator instrument.

3. Write a paper comparing and contrasting quantitative classroom observation with qualitative classroom observation. Cite rele-

vant works found in the references for Chapter 13 in your writing.

4. After reviewing relevant portions of Eisner's *The Educational Imagination* (1985), write a paper summarizing Eisner's ideas on educational connoisseurship.

5. Write an essay giving your position on each of the three issues presented at the beginning of this chapter. Support your position with citations from relevant readings listed in the references for Chapter 13.

Field

1. Use a categorical-frequency instrument. Arrange to observe a class and try out the instrument.

2. Use a performance-indicator instrument. Use the instrument during a classroom observation.

3. Write a detached open-ended narrative during a visit to a classroom.

4. Visit a classroom. Write a description of the classroom, learning activities, and teacher–student interactions from the teacher's perspective. Next, write the same three descriptions of the classroom, learning activities, and teacher–supervisor interactions from the students' perspective.

5. Review instruments used by supervisors in a selected school district during classroom observations. Prepare a written evaluation of the instruments. Include your opinion on whether the instrument fulfills its stated purpose as an observation rather than an evaluation of teaching.

Developmental

1. Continue to differentiate between *descriptions* and *interpretations* of observed events by listening to others discuss observations they have made and by reviewing your own comments regarding your observations.

2. Continue to review systems and instruments designed for use as tools for quantitative observations. Attempt to match different systems and instruments with different observation purposes and goals.

3. Through continued readings and practice in classroom observation, especially in listening to teachers and students, begin to develop the skills of Eisner's educational critic.

REFERENCES

Acheson, K.A., and Gall, M.D. 1987. *Techniques in the clinical supervision of teachers. Preservice and inservice applications,* 2nd ed. White Plains, N.Y.: Longman.

Bales, R. 1951. *Interaction process analysis.* Reading, Mass.: Addison-Wesley.

Beegle, C., and Brandt, R.M. (Eds.). 1973. *Observational methods in the classroom.* Washington, D.C.: Association for Supervision and Curriculum Development.

Brophy, J.E., and Good, T.L. 1974. *Teacher-student relationships: Causes and consequences.* New York: Holt, Rinehart and Winston.

Capie, W., Johnson, C.E., Anderson, S. J., Ellet, C.D., and Okey, J.R. 1979. *Teacher performance assessment project.* Atlanta: Georgia Department of Education.

Eisner, E.W. 1985. *The educational imagination: On the design and evaluation of school programs,* 2nd ed. New York: Macmillan.

————. 1986. A secretary in the classroom. Paper presented to the American Educational Research Association, San Francisco, April.

Flanders, N.A. 1970. *Analyzing teacher behavior.* Reading, Mass.: Addison-Wesley.

Glickman, C.D., and Jones, J.W. 1986. Research in supervision: Creating the dialogue. *Educational Leadership* 44(3):83.

Harris, B.M. 1975. *Supervisory behavior in education,* 2nd ed. Englewood Cliffs, N.J.: Prentice-Hall.

Hyman, R.T. 1975. *School administrator's handbook of teacher supervision and evaluation methods.* Englewood Cliffs, N.J.: Prentice-Hall.

Jones, K., and Sherman, A. 1980. Two approaches to evaluation. *Educational Leadership* 37:553–557.

Marzano, R.J., Brandt, R.S., Hughes, C.S., Jones, B.F., Presseisen, B.Z., Rankin, S.C., and Suhor, C. 1988. *Dimensions of thinking: A framework for curriculum and instruction.* Alexandria, Va.: Association for Supervision and Curriculum Development.

Medley, D.M., and Mizel, H.E. 1963. Measuring classroom behavior by systematic observation. In N.L. Gage (Ed.), *Handbook of research on teaching.* Skokie, Ill.: Rand McNally.

Rosenshine, B.V. 1986. Synthesis of research on explicit teaching. *Educational Leadership* 43(7):60–69.

Simon, A., and Boyer, E.C. 1967. *Mirrors of behavior: An anthology of classroom observation instruments.* 6 vols. Philadelphia: Research for Better Schools.

Spradley, J.P. 1980. *Participant observation.* New York: Holt, Rinehart and Winston.

Webster's new collegiate dictionary. 1974. Springfield, Mass.: Merriam.

Chapter 14

Research and Evaluation Skills

Perhaps no area in education has gone through such a dramatic expansion in knowledge, techniques, and attention than the field of educational research and evaluation. What once seemed the province of experts, consultants, and "university types" doing laboratory experiments has now become a part of day-to-day operations in schools. The national accountability and testing movement has certainly been a contributing cause. More important has been the role of the literature on effective and successful schools, which has made clear that decisions about instructional changes should be made from a base of comprehensive and credible data about students and that those affected most directly by instructional change (i.e., teachers) should be involved in defining, implementing, and interpreting the research and evaluation agenda.

For example, in a study of fifteen exemplary elementary and middle schools in three school districts that had improved instruction in reading and mathematics over a three-year period, a common characteristic of these schools was found to be the deliberate collection of information about student progress and the use of that information to decide upon school-wide actions for changing curriculum, lesson planning, staff development, and individual assistance to teachers. The schools continuously collected and used data about student achievement to determine whether positive changes had resulted and what further revisions in practice needed to be implemented.

> What was notable in all schools and central offices in the three systems was a constant dialogue about instruction. There was time built into the normal work days and there were people who saw their responsibility as engaging teachers in talk about . . . their students' progress. Teachers were involved in planning and implementing actions [Glickman and Pajak 1987, p. 48].

Similarly, Gottfriedson (1986) found that two features prominently mentioned in connection with effective schools were

- A system for monitoring performance and achievement, and use of data to assess progress.
- Collaborative planning and collegial relations, a bias for action [Gottfriedson 1986, p. 11].

In schools and districts that do improve instruction, evaluation and research are not perfunctory paper assignments done by a particular person or division to fulfill district or state requirements. Rather, evaluation and research are seen as the basis for determining professional actions as to the what and the how of improving learning for students. Knowledgeable decision making about instruction comes from intense and critical study of the consequences of the common work of teachers: teaching. Including teachers in determining the criteria, procedures, and use of evaluative data in schools was not simply a nice thing to do; *it was essential to do*. If teachers were to extend their own thinking and commitment about collective instruction, they had to be part of the research and evaluation process. Without their involvement, policy makers would have denied teachers the intellectual engagement of viewing teaching as a collective activity—"a cause beyond oneself."

Such engagement, in itself, enhances thinking and decisions about individual practice. In a high school in the Southeast, during the year when teachers and administrators in the school began to collect data on profiles of high school dropouts, the dropout rate decreased by more than 12 percent (Glickman 1989). This was *before* the school had determined what interventions to make. One teacher said, "It simply never occurred to me, until we researched and evaluated our school, that we had a problem with dropouts. I and most of my peers have certainly changed our attitudes towards overage students. The dropout rate is coming down right now because of our awareness. I can't wait until next year when we implement new programs!"

Judgments

How do we know our instructional programs are successful? Should we continue with the same curriculum, instructional methods, scheduling, and grouping practices, or should changes be made? Evaluating is the act of making such a judgment. How do we decide whether something is good or bad? Frequently, we make judgments with statements such as, "What a great reading program," "What a lousy classroom," or "What wonderful students." How do we really know if something is great, lousy, or wonderful? Wolfe (1969) offers a tongue-in-cheek classification of five typical methods by which we make such judgments:

Cosmetic Method: You examine the program, and if it looks good it is good. Does everybody look busy? The key is attractive and full bulletin boards covered with projects emanating from the project.

Cardiac Method: No matter what the data say, you know in your heart that the program was a success. This is similar to the use in medical research of subclinical findings.

Colloquial Method: After a brief meeting, preferably at a local watering hole, a group of project staff members conclude that success was achieved. No one can refute a group decision.

Curricular Method: A successful program is one that can be installed with the least disruption of the ongoing school program. Programs that are truly different are to be eschewed at all costs.

Computational Method: If you have to have data, analyze it to death. Whatever the nature of the statistics, use the most sophisticated multivariate regression discontinuity procedures known to humans.

Wolfe's methods aside, let's look at reasonable, valid ways of evaluating. In the turbulence of instructional change, it is useful to know whether the new practice is going to be any better than the old. If not, then we may be investing large amounts of energy without a justifiable increase in instructional benefits to students. As discussed in Chapter 12 (assessing and planning), if we are to make a commitment to instructional change, we must also make a commitment to evaluating that instructional change. If not, then we truly do not know what we are doing.

How does one make a judgment of worth? In education, there are at least three components of a comprehensive evaluation:

1. Determine whether the instructional program took place as planned. Did teachers and administrators carry out the intended program? This is called *fidelity* or *implementation evaluation.*

2. Determine whether the instructional program achieved its instructional objectives for students. Did the program accomplish what it set out to do? This is called *product* or *outcome evaluation.*

3. Determine whether unforeseen consequences to students and teachers resulted from the program. Were there any benefits or drawbacks for students as by-products of the program? This is called *serendipitous evaluation.*

These three components of evaluation, when done thoroughly, provide the people who have program decision responsibilities (school committees, curriculum councils, superintendent, school boards, state and federal agencies) with a comprehensive report on the results of the instructional program.

This chapter will deal with topics of evidence of instructional progress, research designs, procedures, and models of evaluation.

Evidence

What constitutes evidence of the success of a project, grade level, department, school, or district? The criteria and guidelines for the Joint Dissemination Review Panel (1986) of the United States Department of Education, which is commissioned to examine evidence from schools that claim to be effective in attaining goals, describes several models of evidence:

Model One: Achievement/Changes in Knowledge and Skills of Students

Types of evidence

- Tests of all types (norm-referenced, criterion-referenced, locally developed)
- Direct ratings of performance/products of performance (e.g., holistic or analytical ratings of writing samples)
- Structured observations of skill demonstrations
- Content analyses of students' projects or products

Model Two: Improvements in Teachers' Attitudes and Behaviors

Types of evidence

- Assessment of attitudes in the form of rating scales, surveys, and interviews
- Structured observations of changes in teaching behaviors
- Records of teachers' use of instructional time (e.g., planning books, logs)
- Self-reports of instructional time use and instructional methods
- Case studies of changes in teaching behaviors/classroom climate

Model Three: Improvements in Students' Attitudes and Behaviors

Types of evidence

- School records review (e.g., attendance, courses, grades, promotion and retention, vandalism)

- Health records review
- Attitude assessments
- Case studies of individual students, classes, or schools
- Structured interviews with teachers, parents, and students
- Structured interviews with community service agencies, police, etc.
- Records of disciplinary action
- Postgraduate follow-up to next school level, college, or career choice
- Participant and/or expert testimonials

Selected evidence from the above models can be used to research and evaluate a particular instructional project with a selected population within a school (i.e., computer literacy for special education students in elementary school, or a new approach to teaching humanities to bilingual students in middle school) or can be used to research and evaluate grade-level, departmental, school, or district instruction.

Epstein (1988) counsels that evidence and design for research and evaluation needs to be conducted in a realistic manner, within the limited scope, financial resources, and human time of a school. She urges that schools first look to existing data, such as student progress reports, achievement scores, exhibits, and attendance, before looking for additional data. Likewise, Gable, in reviewing guiding principles for program evaluation, states:

> Data collection for evaluation will, to the extent possible, make primary use of existing data sources. The history of local school district practices in effectively using existing information for evaluation is poor [Gable 1986, p. 5].

Epstein concludes by reminding us of the purpose of evaluation.

> Research and evaluation are not magical processes. Good evaluations make intuitive sense—they ask meaningful questions and answer them in logical ways. What questions do you ask yourselves when you wonder how well your program is doing? Those are the questions you should be answering [Epstein 1988, p. 12].

Multiple Sources of Data

The answer to most of our questions about the effectiveness of instructional programs will most likely include multiple sources of evidence. Do we have a good science program? The answer should include an assessment of student achievement scores, attitude surveys, grades, exhibits, awards, extracurricular science activities, interviews of selected students, and surveys and/or interviews of teachers and parents. Furthermore, we would probably desire a fidelity check to determine whether the science curriculum is being used as intended, through teacher self-reports, observations of science classrooms, reports on material utilization, and surveys (see Hall and Hord 1987). After collecting data from these multiple sources and breaking it down (by comparing grade levels, boys versus girls, racial minority versus majority, and low versus middle socioeconomic status), we could then make an evaluation as to how well the present science curriculum is doing for all of our students.

In the same manner, when we are to assess the overall success of an entire school, we would wish to use multiple sources of data. Besides the usual criterion-referenced and norm-referenced achievement test scores, grades, promotion and retention rates, attendance, enrollment, and discipline referrals, we might desire to assess the school climate and attitudes, perceptions, and behaviors of teachers and students in a school by means of a learning and attitude inventory such as *The Effective School Battery* (Gottfriedson 1985), the Organizational Climate Description Inventory (Hoy and Clover 1986) or the National Study of School Evaluation (1987). Many schools are looking at student achievement through a wider lens than standardized competencies tests by collecting portfolios of students' works, exhibits, and projects (Wolf 1988) and measuring the problem solving and creative and critical thinking of students (Shepard 1989; Shipman 1983; Watson and Glaser 1980; Torrance 1974). In some school districts, teachers and supervisors develop their own achievement tests to measure what they believe important for their students to learn (Rose 1987). This practice is quite common in other countries, such as Australia, where panels of teachers make up yearly subject-area examinations and there is virtually no reliance on nationally normed or criterion-referenced, standardized tests (MacCrostie and Hough 1987).

Methods and Derivatives of Research Applied to School Evaluation

When a determination is made to evaluate a program or an entire school, it must be decided what data to collect and what research method and analysis to use. There are the same distinctions between qualitative and quantitative methods of research as between qualitative and quantitative methods of observation (see Chapter 13).

Quantitative research collects and analyzes data that is numerical. Variables and hypotheses are clearly defined prior to the study. Methods used are correlational, experimental, or quasi-experimental. Variables are measurable on ordinal, nominal, or continuous numerical scales. Hypotheses are analyzed and tested statistically. Qualitative research uses the methodologies of ethnography, case studies, participant observations, focused or open-ended observations, interviews and surveys. Data is recorded, transcribed, and analyzed to find emerging categories, themes, and questions. A quantitative study of student success in an "outward bound" physical education course might collect "before and after" numerical data on skills, knowledge, and attitudes. A hypothesis would be established: For example, students in the course, when contrasted to comparable students not in the course, will show a greater gain on pre- and post-measures. A quasi-experimental design is used. A statistical analysis, with a predetermined significance level, would then be conducted. On the other hand, a qualitative study of the same program might consist of a participant observant methodology, whereby the researcher participates, talks, and observes students and teachers throughout the whole semester, keeping field notes, taping and transcribing interviews, and relaying analyzed categories of success and failure and questions back to the participants for their reactions throughout the year. At the end, the study would report on what had happened during the semester through the thoughts and experiences of the students and teachers.

Qualitative studies, used to understand and form explanations about what is transpiring in schools, have become an increasingly useful methodology for researchers and evaluators. This movement has been likened to "the silent, scientific, revolution in education" (Fetterman 1987). The texts on qualitative approaches to educational evaluation are now numerous (see Fetterman and Pitman 1986; Goetze and LeCompte 1984; Eisner 1987).

Even so, quantitative research, particularly the use of correlation studies, continues to be a predominate mode of research conducted in education. Collecting available information and then seeing how one measure relates to another can be done with little disruption to the school. On the other hand, pure experimental studies, once the vanguard of educational research, have become increasingly difficult to conduct. In most cases it is impossible to split students and teachers randomly into experimental and control groups and withhold a potentially beneficial treatment from one group. Ethical and political considerations often limit the feasibility of pure experiments. To counter such difficulties, Campbell and

Stanley (1963) derived a form of study known as *quasi-experimental*—an adaptation of experimental design to the realities of schools. It has become a widely used and accepted research methodology for evaluators.

Quasi-experimental researchers accept that randomly assigned groups of teachers and students within identically controlled environments are an unrealistic goal. Instead, quasi-experimental research uses volunteers or preselected groups who are already involved in a particular program. For example, one would not randomly assign students to a remedial reading program or randomly assign teachers to a particular workshop. More often, the researcher has to work with a preestablished group as the experimental group. Quasi-experimental design treats the preselected or volunteer group as the experimental group. Then the researcher chooses a *comparable* group, who will not receive the same treatment. The comparable group functions as the control group. The researcher must establish that the two groups are comparable. Remedial reading students could be matched with other students in the same school who would have qualified for the remedial program, or students participating in a new reading program could be compared to students in another school in the same system who have equivalent socioeconomic backgrounds and similar reading test scores from previous years. Therefore, the gains in reading of students in the school receiving the new reading program can be analyzed against those of the students in the adjacent school using the traditional reading program. A further example of a quasi-experimental design would be to compare the effects of in-service training on a group of volunteer teachers with the effect on nonvolunteers who are comparable in age, experience, and academic background. Teacher B, who does not volunteer, is matched with Teacher A, who does volunteer, because they are of the same age, have the same amount of experience, and have completed the same level of graduate work. Another use of quasi-experimental design involves comparing a group's performance to its own past performance. For example, students in a new junior high school math program perhaps have averaged a gain of 0.7 year in past years. Their gain over the current year in the new program could be compared to past gains.

Every research design has flaws. Pure experimental design, with random groups and controlled conditions, provides results that are generalizable and conclusive, but it is very difficult to perform. Quasi-experimental design, with comparable groups and less controlled conditions, provides results that are less conclusive, but it is easier to carry out. Correlational studies are relatively easy to conduct, but measures must be isolated *a priori*. Also, causes and effects are difficult to determine. (For example, more people die in hospitals than anywhere else. Should we therefore avoid hospitals?) Qualitative studies do not intrude markedly into the normal operations of school, but they are labor-intensive to conduct. In designing a study, the researcher must always balance feasibility against definitiveness.

This brings us to another educational derivative that attempts to balance the limitations of various research designs: the *multimodel approach* (see Patton 1980).

> Through the use of such designs, evaluators and researchers can observe and study the basic program operation, as well as the personal interactions and relationships embedded in the program [Bower, Anderson, and Thompson 1987].

We can use qualitative, correlational, and quasi-experimental research as part of evaluation. We can use a particular research methodology or combine several methodologies. Evaluation that uses descriptive study can be combined with a correlational or quasi-experimental study. For example, if we evaluated an in-service program by using a quasi-experimental study, we also might conduct interviews, case studies, and participant observations to try to determine what other changes were occurring in the classrooms and in the minds of students and teachers involved in the experiment. Such description might account for the *fidelity* (degree of implementation) and *serendipity* (side effects of the in-service program), whereas the experimental study would account for the *outcome*. Combining different approaches can provide a deeper and more comprehensive evaluation of instruction than reliance on a single method.

Overall Instructional Program Evaluation

Evaluating the overall instructional program is different from evaluating special projects. In such an overall evaluation, decision makers can choose to refine existing practices or to launch special projects. This section will mention two such overall program evaluations: the cybernetic model of William Cooley and the self-study model of the National Study of School Evaluation. The supervisor would not necessarily be the data collector or analyzer of such comprehensive evaluation models but would more likely see him or herself in the role of organizer and coordinator.

William Cooley, past president of the American Educational Research Association and director of program evaluation for the

Pittsburgh, Pennsylvania, public schools, discusses his cybernetic model, used for evaluating both individual schools and an entire school system:

> It involves developing and monitoring a variety of performance indicators. Then whenever an indicator moves into an unacceptable range, an attempt is made to determine just where that condition is most severe. Focused corrective action is then taken which I call tailoring practice [Cooley 1983, p. 7].

It is interesting that Cooley combines process and product measures into performance indicators of school or school system rather than focusing evaluation on an individual program. He believes that a school or school system should first evaluate what it is currently doing in total via the use of indicators and should attempt through staff development programs and direct assistance to fine-tune the existing system before launching and evaluating new programs.

Cooley classifies performance indicators according to three constructs: (1) efficacy of the system, (2) quality of present experience, and (3) equality of educational opportunity. The first construct, *efficacy,* consists of indicators that measure students' abilities, interests, progress in school, and achievement. The second construct, *quality* of school life, consists of indicators that focus on the richness of the school experience, such as teacher attitudes, the physical and aesthetic work environment, and the organizational climate of classrooms and schools as perceived by students and faculty. The third construct, *equality* of educational opportunity, consists of indicators that measure the fairness of the educational system, such as the progress, attendance, achievement, attitudes, and opportunities of minority students compared with those of the majority population of students (that is, do racial-minority students succeed academically in the same ratio as racial-majority students from year to year?). Cooley believes that evaluation based on these three constructs should measure multiple levels of performance at the classroom, grade, department, school, and district levels.

Let's examine briefly how a cybernetic evaluation system might work with a hypothetical example. (Cooley and his associates have been using this evaluation model since 1978 with the Pittsburgh schools.) Suppose that in our school system we have determined (via a needs assessment and planning process as outlined in Chapter 12) that an acceptable range of the efficacy of the school system would be that 90 percent of students pass to the next grade; an acceptable range of quality of school life would be that 80 percent of students perceive the school environment as enjoyable and supportive; and an acceptable range for equality of educational opportunity would be that students of minority populations are represented proportionally in accelerated classes. We then use multiple measures to determine if the indicators fall in the acceptable ranges. After collecting our data, we find they are acceptable except for the quality of school life. After analyzing the classroom climate surveys and student interviews, we find that only 70 percent of students perceive the environment as an enjoyable and supportive one. By aggregating the information at the classroom, grade, department, and school levels, we find that fewer than 50 percent of freshman students see the school as supportive, as opposed to 85 percent of upperclassmen and women. We then can target our improvement on the freshman class and, with freshman students, teachers, parents, and guidance counselors, plan ways to improve the quality of school life.

It is crucial that the tests, surveys, and observation forms used are actual indicators of the constructs. Obviously, if a school system wants to evaluate but uses inaccurate measures, the results will be worthless. For example, if one indicator for quality of school life were the number of classroom discipline referrals sent to the principal, an unacceptable range could be corrected by simply having the principal refuse to accept teacher referrals. The indicator would show an acceptable range without the quality of school life being improved. Students might still be creating discipline problems, but those problems would not show up in the number of discipline referrals. Therefore multiple indicators should be used and revised if they do not appear to be measuring the construct.

The Self-Study Model

The self-study model of program evaluation was developed by two complementary organizations, the National Study of School Evaluation for Elementary Schools (NSSEES) (1973) and the National Study of Secondary School Evaluation (NSSSE) (1969). The National Study of School Evaluation originated in 1933 with the aim of developing effective instruments and procedures for schoolwide evaluation. Its workbooks and manuals form the basis of the school accreditation process used by the New England Association of Schools and Colleges, the Middle States Association of Colleges and Secondary Schools, the Southern Association of Colleges and Schools, the North Central Association of Colleges and Secondary Schools, the Northwest Association of Secondary and Higher Schools, and the Western Association of Schools and Colleges.

The model is based on the premise that "Self-study is to improve the quality of the school's program through the means of self-evaluation, introspection, and comprehensive examination of what is happening to children in the school environment." (National Study of School Evaluation 1973, p. 4). Furthermore, the study consists of four parts (National Study of School Evaluation 1973, p. 8):

1. Self-analysis of the school's program and services.
2. Objective reaction to the school's analysis by a visiting committee.
3. Oral and written reports to the school by the chair of the visiting committee.
4. A resultant program of continuous improvement by the school itself.

A self-study steering committee of between five and seven members is appointed. They in turn appoint subcommittees of faculty to prepare various sections of the self-study. The sections are *school and community demographics, philosophy and objectives, curriculum learning areas, curriculum overview, individual faculty data, school staff and administration, student activities program, learning media services, student personnel services, school plant,* and *plans and priorities.* For each section, the manual provides a format for the subcommittee to check on whether the school philosophy and objectives are relevant and being accomplished. Data is collected by means of teacher-designed tests, criterion-referenced tests, observations, checklists, and surveys. The various National Study of School Evaluation manuals contain validated instruments that a subcommittee can choose to use. Each subcommittee completes its report by showing the degree to which the school is achieving its objective, and makes recommendations for correcting weaknesses. The subcommittee's report goes to the entire faculty for reactions and approval (National Study of School Evaluation 1983).

In the next stage of the evaluation process, the steering committee selects a visiting team of outside educators with expertise in the various sections of the self-study. A chairperson of the visiting team is also selected. Visiting committees usually consist of between four and fifteen members, depending on the size of the school. The committee visits the schools and has free access to observe, interview, and survey students, teachers, administrators, and parents. The visiting committee's task is to determine the accuracy of the school's self-study and to measure school accomplishment against the school's own objectives. The committee then writes a report of fact-finding, strengths, weaknesses, and recommendations for each section of the study, as well as an overall evaluation with prioritized recommendations for the school as a whole. If the visiting team is being used for regional accreditation purposes, they will make a recommendation with respect to accreditation. At the conclusion of the visit, the report is summarized orally to the faculty, and the chairperson of the visiting committee compiles and edits a comprehensive written report that is given to the school's steering committee.

The school's steering committee reads the written report and then develops a plan for acting on the recommendations. The self-study takes approximately six to nine months to complete, the visiting committee spends three to four days visiting, and the completed written report is delivered within three weeks after the visit. The improvement plan developed by the steering committee usually is implemented over several years.

Other Considerations for Evaluation

Certain considerations arise for a supervisor regardless of the type of evaluation to be employed.

Statistical versus Educational Significance

The discussion of quantitative research of special school projects should include the distinction between statistical significance and educational significance. An uninformed consumer of educational research can be impressed by statistics and lose sight of educational significance. *Statistical significance* is the mathematical analysis of scores that gives a confidence level about the truth of the results. *Educational significance* includes the overall benefits of using a particular treatment program. For example, if we study the results of an in-service program for social studies teachers and find that student attitude gains from the experimental teachers were significant at the .01 level over student attitude gains from the control group, does this mean that all social studies teachers should undergo the in-service? Maybe, but maybe not. Besides the obvious need to see whether there were other student gains—in achievement, attendance, or work completed—we also need to consider the *magnitude* of the gain against its *cost*. If we had tested attitudes of 100 students in both experimental and control groups and found that on a nine-point scale the experimental students increased from a pretest average score of 5.0 to a posttest score of 6.5, and the control students increased from a pretest average of 5 to a posttest score of 6.1, the 0.4 difference might be statistically significant at the .01 level. The instructional supervisor would have to consider whether a 0.4 difference on a nine-point attitudinal scale is worth the in-service cost, including teacher time, expense for consultants, administrative work, and so on. Decisions about educational significance can be aided greatly by knowledge of statistical significance, but human judgment must be used to weigh the overall benefits.

What about the Use of Achievement Tests?

The use of achievement tests as a single indicator of academic achievement of program or school effort is misleading and can give schools inaccurate results, leading to inaccurate evaluation. Educators can improve test scores without making real changes in curriculum and instruction, by such ploys as withholding the test from students expected to perform poorly, relabeling students at a lower grade level on test-taking days, teaching test items, and guiding students to the correct answers (see Prell and Prell 1986). As a result of such manipulations, test scores can be high and totally invalid. Furthermore, even without manipulations, gains or losses in achievement scores can be erroneously interpreted. For example, schools evaluate the success of their basic-skills programs by comparing the previous year's standardized test scores with the current year's scores. Unfortunately, only a comparison of alternative forms of the same test will yield valid results. Likewise, schools might use the same publisher's test in early fall and late spring and find large but inaccurate gains because the scores in late spring were normed to the fall population of test takers. Another common error in using achievement tests for evaluation is the lack of pre- and posttest scores for *each* student. Often the average pretest scores of a group of students will be compared to the average posttest scores of the same group, even though the group at the end of the year is seldom the same group as at the beginning. Some students will have moved away, been suspended, or been reassigned; new students will have replaced them. Only the scores of those students who participated in the project both at the beginning and at the end can be used for program evaluation.

A further problem with achievement tests is using the score on the selection test for a program as the pretest and then using an alternative form of the same test as the posttest. This is a common problem with federally funded and state-funded compensatory programs in schools. If a remedial reading program or a gifted education program uses an alternative form of the original screening test as a posttest, the results will be hopelessly skewed because of what is called *regression toward the mean*. If we test all students on an achievement test and then retest the lowest and highest scorers on the following day, the low scorers will test significantly higher and the high scorers will test significantly lower. This is true because of the test, not the students. Therefore, using a form of the test used to screen high or low students as a posttest for program evaluation will show gains or losses that have nothing to do with the program. The easiest way to prevent this problem is to use a different test, not from the screening test, for pre- and posttest evaluation. (A supervisor who plans to use achievement tests for program evaluation should read the excellent and inexpensive federal publication entitled *A Practical Guide to Measuring Project Impact on Student Achievement*, No. 1, U.S. Office of Education, Washington, D.C.)

Many of the aforementioned problems with achievement tests are eliminated by using criterion-referenced tests instead of nationally normed tests. A *nationally normed test* gives grade equivalence scores in comparison to students all across the country. A *criterion-referenced test* gives the percentage of correct responses. Therefore pre- and posttest scores of criterion-referenced tests more accurately demonstrate what a student has learned.

A wall chart comparing states on student achievement was introduced by United States Secretary of Education Terrell Bell in 1984 and further promoted by his successor William Bennett. The chart has manifested itself at the school and district level. It is now common to see in the local newspaper a display of comparisons of schools on test achievement performance. The largest educational testing companies in the world, Educational Testing Service (ETS) and the College Board, have argued against the use of such comparisons of test scores as single indicators or barometers of success. According to Stewart (1988), they are inaccurate; the comparisons of diverse student populations with differing backgrounds, resources, and education expectations are not valid; and more importantly, tests are not synonymous with what is educationally valued. George Hanford, past president of the College Board (which is the developer of the Scholastic Achievement Test), wrote

> What if, along with rising SAT scores, dropout rates are declining, enrollments in honors courses are increasing, reading scores are improving and college admissions are going up? That is a picture that reflects a positive evaluation. If the trends are reversed, the picture would be negative. If the trends are mixed, so is the picture. The point is that if all the other measures were improving, even declining SAT scores would not necessarily call for a negative evaluation. Nor, if they were all going down, would rising SAT scores necessarily offset the bad news [Hanford 1986, p. 7].

Hanford goes on to state that the scores produced by tests exude "an aura of precision out of proportion to their significance, which in turn fosters an unsuitable reliance on them, to the exclusion or neglect of other indicators that are equally important and useful" (Hanford 1986, p. 9).

Achievement scores, if used appropriately, can provide a measure for evaluating a program, project, or school. Yet, as Arthur Wise (1988) warns, "Many schools no longer teach reading, they teach reading skills; no longer do they teach important reading skills but instead, they teach only reading skills measured on the achievement test."

Donald Stewart, current President of the College Board, sums up the issue of achievement test scores and evaluation: " . . . we must realize that only people can make decisions, and well-considered decisions require information from many sources" (Stewart 1988, p. 8).

Who Should Evaluate?

Only professors of educational evaluation from the University of Georgia should be hired as program evaluators. (This is a paid advertisement by my colleagues from the Center for Educational Research and Evaluation at the University of Georgia.) If only the answer were so simple! Whether the supervisor, a team of faculty members, central office personnel, and private consultants should have major control over evaluation depends on the particular school's resources and the purpose of the evaluation. However, it is critical that teachers be involved in evaluation of instructional programs and the overall instructional effectiveness of their schools and district. All stakeholders (those affected by the decisions from the evaluation) should be not only subjects of study but co-investigators of the study as well. As Greene has noted, there exists a "consensus on the need for stakeholder participation" (1986, p. 1), and such participation is defined as "shared decision making, rather than just advising or providing input" (1986, p. 9).

Most school systems have scarce financial resources. If they are concerned with formative evaluation, they might proceed by using exclusively their own personnel. The teachers and coordinators of school programs could form an evaluation committee and conduct their own data collection and analysis. Since the purpose of the evaluation is to improve the program, there is no reason that participants and supporters (perhaps with the assistance of someone with specialized skills) should not be the predominate evaluators.

On the other hand, if the evaluation is for summative purposes—to determine if a particular project is to continue or not—then it is best to have persons external to the projects conduct a major portion of the evaluation, so that there is no perception of undue bias or conflict of interest. Most state and federally funded school projects require such unattached persons as evaluators.

When looking for evaluators, the supervisor might check with other school systems and acquire a list of prospects. He or she should check on references. The standards for evaluators presented in *Standards for Evaluations of Educational Programs, Projects, and Materials* (Stufflebeam 1981) would serve as a guide to hiring ethical and competent persons. As in any profession, those who call themselves evaluators span the entire spectrum. The majority are persons of fine character, but there are a few charlatans. An evaluator should be interviewed to determine his or her view of evaluation, how she or he would proceed, and whether or not he or she will be the type of person in whom others would confide.

How Should an Evaluation Be Reported?

After collecting the results of tests, observations, surveys, interviews, and testimonials, how should the evaluation be reported? The answer is largely determined by the audience. Most school board members and superintendents will not read a 200-page technical report on the raw data, statistical treatments, and evaluation methodologies. They are interested in the results and conclusions. The technical report should be available to decision makers as a reference to the summarized paper. Any reader of the condensed paper who is confused or desires more information about certain parts of the paper can check the complete technical report. On the other hand, if the audience for the evaluation report consists of people with sophisticated evaluation skills, a complete technical report would be in order. In a study of violations of evaluation standards (Newman and Brown 1987, p. 9), among the most frequent violations were "those concerning the evaluator's lack of knowledge of the audience."

What Is the Supervisor's Role in Evaluation?

A supervisor cannot be personally involved in every evaluation but should be responsible for seeing that evaluation of special projects and of the overall instructional programs is ongoing. The supervisor, whether school principal, department head, lead or master teacher, district director, or assistant superintendent, should constantly remind himself or herself of the standards for evaluation of educational programs (Stufflebeam 1981).

1. *Utility:* Ensure that an evaluation will serve the practical information needs of the audiences.
2. *Feasibility:* Ensure that an evaluation will be realistic, prudent, diplomatic, and frugal.
3. *Propriety:* Ensure that an evaluation will be conducted legally, ethically, and with due regard for the welfare of those involved in the evaluation, as well as those affected by its results.
4. *Accuracy:* Ensure the conveyance of technically adequate information.

With those standards in mind, there are two questions that serve as the core to a purposeful school (Hamilton 1980).

1. Is what we are doing working?
2. How does it work?

Answers to those questions can be gathered through informal means such as surveys, interviews, and group discussions, or through the more formal means of observations, questionnaires, and tests. Only as we remind ourselves of these questions and seek answers can actions be taken that improve instruction. Chapter 19 will show how such asking and answering can be an integral supervisory task of everyday school life.

Summary

Educational evaluation has been influenced heavily by educational research design. The attention to school performance has stimulated multiple data sources, research designs, and compositions of evaluators. A consensus on the need for involving stakeholders in evaluation has occurred. We must be cautious in selecting instruments that measure what we truly wish to find out about a program. Various types of educational evaluations are used for special projects and for the overall instructional program. It is not sufficient to know intuitively that a program is good or bad. Rather, decisions about revising, improving, or discarding need to be made with multiple sources of information. Finally, the school as a collective enterprise must center its work on questions of educational value and use answers to those questions as guidance for instructional change.

EXERCISES

Academic

1. Locate one qualitative study, one correlational study, and one quasi-experimental study in educational research. Write a summary of each study. Include in each summary a description of the study's purpose, participants, methodology, results, and conclusions.

2. Choose a topic of educational study of significance to supervision. Write a paper outlining ideas for a descriptive study, a correlational study, and an experimental study related to the chosen topic.

3. Compare and contrast experimental with quasi-experimental research. Refer to at least four outside sources in the paper.

4. Compare and contrast quantitative research with qualitative research. Refer to at least four outside sources in the paper.

5. Write a paper entitled "Criteria for Effective Evaluation of a School's Instructional Program." Refer to at least four outside sources in your paper.

Field

1. Interview the individual in a school district who is ultimately responsible for instructional program and special project evaluation about procedures for carrying out such evaluations. Write a report summarizing the interview and evaluating the school district's instructional program and special project evaluation methods.

2. Interview a person who has served on a self-study team as part of a school evaluation. Include questions on the interviewee's role and function as a team member, self-study methods used by the team, team conclusions and recommendations, changes ultimately made as a result of the self-study, and the interviewee's reactions to his or her participation. Prepare a report on the interview.

3. Develop a written plan for evaluating a specific area of an instructional program with which you are familiar (for example, a K–6 math program, a senior high school Spanish program, or a remedial reading program).

4. Interview a supervisor to determine his or her views on the three universal concerns about evaluation addressed in the chap-

ter: Who should evaluate? How should an evaluation be reported? What is the supervisor's role in evaluation? Prepare a written or verbal report on the interview.

5. Visit a school or system that is currently attempting to follow one of the evaluation models discussed in Chapter 14 or cited in the chapter references. Discuss problems the school or system is experiencing in attempting to follow the selected model; note deletions, additions, and modifications the school or system has made in its use of the model. Prepare a report on your investigation.

Developmental

1. Begin to analyze judgments made by educational leaders and others regarding instructional programs to determine which decisions are based on comprehensive evaluation and which are based on cosmetic, cardiac, colloquial, curricular, or computational methods.
2. Begin an in-depth investigation of alternative models for instructional program evaluation.
3. If the opportunity presents itself, volunteer for membership on a school self-study team or a visiting school evaluation team.

REFERENCES

Bower, J.C., Anderson, B.N., and Thompson, B. 1987. Increasing the utility of research via the application of multiple model designs. Paper presented to the annual meeting of the American Educational Research Association, Washington, D.C., April.

Campbell, D.T., and Stanley, J.C. 1963. Experimental and quasi-experimental designs for research of teaching. In N.L. Gage (Ed.), *Handbook of research on teaching.* Chicago: Rand McNally.

Cooley, W.W. 1983. Improving the performance of an educational system. *Educational Researcher 12*(6):4–12.

Eisner, E.W. 1983. Anastasia might still be alive, but the monarchy is dead. *Educational Researcher 12*(5):23–24.

———. 1987. *The educational imagination: On the design and evaluation of school programs.* New York: Macmillan.

Epstein, A.S. 1988. A no frills approach to program evaluation. *High Scope Resources* 7(1):1–12.

Fetterman, D.N. 1987. Qualitative approaches to evaluating education. Paper presented to the annual meeting of the American Educational Research Association, Washington, D.C., April.

Fetterman, D.N., and Pitman, M.A. (Eds.). 1986. *Educational evaluation: Ethnography in theory, practice, and politics.* Beverly Hills, Calif.: Sage.

Gable, R.K. 1986. State and local collaborative efforts toward participatory evaluation: Connecticut's priority school district program. Paper presented at the annual meeting of the American Educational Research Association, San Francisco, April.

Glickman, C.D. 1989. *The story of Ogelthorpe County High School: Five years of shared decision making.* Athens, Ga.: Monographs in Education.

Glickman, C.D., and Pajak, E.F. 1987. Concepts of change in school systems improving criterion referenced test scores. Presentation to the American Educational Research Association, Washington, D.C., April.

Goetze, J.P., and LeCompte, N.D. 1984. *Ethnography and qualitative design in educational research.* New York: Academic Press.

Gottfriedson, G.D. 1985. *The Effective School Battery: User's manual.* Odessa, Fla.: Psychological Assessment Resources.

————. 1986. Using the *Effective School Battery* in school improvement and effective schools programs. Presentation to the annual meeting of the American Educational Research Association, San Francisco, April.

Greene, J.C. 1986. Participatory evaluation and the evaluation of social programs: Lessons learned from the field. Paper presented to the annual meeting of the American Educational Research Association, San Francisco, April.

Hall, G.E., and Hord, S.M. 1987. *Change in schools: Facilitating the process.* Albany, N.Y.: State University of New York Press.

Hamilton, S.F. 1980. Evaluating your own program. *Educational Leadership* 37(6):545–551.

Hanford, G.H. 1986. The SAT and statewide assessment: Sorting the uses and caveats. In *Commentaries on Testing.* Princeton, N.J.: College Entrance Examination Board.

Hoy, W.K., and Clover, S.I. 1986. Elementary school climate. *Educational Administration Quarterly* 22(1):93–110.

Joint Dissemination Review Panel. 1986. *Criteria and guidelines for the JDRP*. Washington, D.C.: United States Department of Education.

MacCrostie, J., and Hough, M. 1987. Personal conversations with Australian educators, November.

National Study of School Evaluation. 1969. *Evaluative criteria for the evaluation of secondary schools*. Washington, D.C.: Author.

————. 1973. *Elementary school evaluative criteria: A guide for school improvement*. Arlington, Va.: Author.

————. 1983. *K–12 school evaluative criteria: A guide for school improvement*. Falls Church, Va.: Author.

————. 1987. *School evaluation stimulation*. Falls Church, Va.: Author.

Newman, D.C., and Brown, R.D. 1987. Violations of evaluation standards: Frequency and seriousness of occurrence. Paper presented at the annual meeting of the American Educational Research Association, Washington, D.C., April.

Patton, N.O. 1980. *Qualitative evaluation methods*. Beverly Hills, Calif.: Sage.

Popham, W.J. 1975. *Educational evaluation*. Englewood Cliffs, N.J.: Prentice-Hall.

A practical guide to measuring project impact on student achievement. Number 1 in a series of monographs on evaluation in education. Under contract OEC-0 = 73-6662, U.S. Office of Education, Washington, D.C.

Prell, J.M., and Prell, P.A. 1986. Improving test scores—teaching test-wiseness: A review of the literature, *Research Bulletin*, CEDR, Phi Delta Kappa No. 5., November.

Rose, J.S. 1987. Better curriculum, instruction, and evaluation. Paper presented at the annual meeting of the American Educational Research Association, Washington, D.C., April.

Shepard, L.A. 1989. Why we need better assessments. *Educational Leadership* 46(9):4–9.

Shipman, V. 1983. *New Jersey Test of Reasoning Skills*. Upper Montclair, N.J.: IAPC Test Division, Montclair State College.

Stewart, D.M. 1988. *The ethics of assessment commentaries on testing*. Princeton, N.J.: College Entrance Examination Board.

Stufflebeam, D. 1981. *Standards for evaluations of educational programs, projects, and materials*. New York: McGraw-Hill.

Torrance, E.P. 1974. *Torrance tests of creative thinking: Directions manual and scoring guide.* Lexington, Mass.: Ginn.

Watson, G., and Glaser, E.M. 1980. *Watson–Glaser critical thinking appraisal.* San Antonio, Tex.: Psychological Corp.

Wise, A., 1988. Restructuring schools. Presentation to the Annual Georgia Leadership Institute, Athens, Ga., June.

Wolf, D.P. 1988. Opening up assessment. *Educational Leadership* 45(4):24–29.

Wolfe, R. 1969. A model for curriculum evaluation. *Psychology in the Schools* 6:107–108.

PART IV CONCLUSION

Part IV was devoted to the technical skills the supervisor needs in assessing, planning, observing, researching, and evaluating the instructional program. Let's highlight some of these skills. Chapter 12 on assessing and planning looked at organizing personal plans; managing time; flow-charting; conducting needs assessments; management by objectives; Gant charts; program evaluation and review techniques; and planning, programming, and budgeting systems. Chapter 13 on observing dealt with description and interpretation; quantitative uses of categorical frequencies, performance indicators, and visual diagramming; and qualitative uses of narrative, participant involvement, focused questionnaires, and educational criticism. Chapter 14 discussed research and evaluation skills, including types of evaluation; sources of data; qualitative and quantitative study; and applied school research, the cybernetic model, and the self-study model.

The technical skills of Part IV have concluded the prerequisites needed by a supervisor in implementing the supervision function (see Figure IV-1). With knowledge about schools, teachers, and self; with interpersonal skills matched to developmental characteristics of teachers; and with technical skills in assessing, planning, observing, researching, and evaluating, the supervisor can function knowingly and skillfully in the realm of instructional improvement and can carry out the five developmental tasks of supervision.

Figure IV-1 Supervision for successful schools

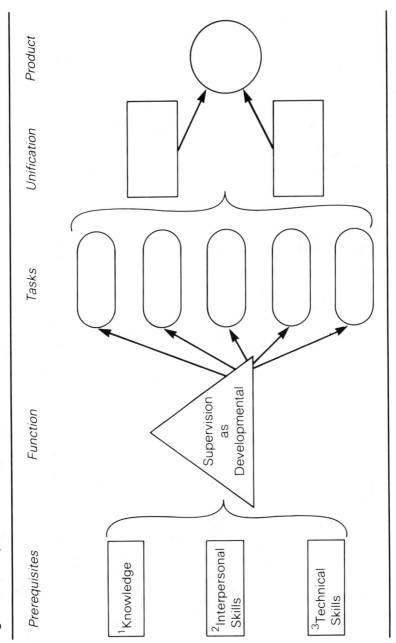

Prerequisites · Function · Tasks · Unification · Product

¹Knowledge

²Interpersonal Skills

³Technical Skills

Supervision as Developmental

PART V

TASKS OF SUPERVISION

Introduction

If one has responsibility for the improvement of instruction, what does one do? We've accounted for what the supervisor needs to possess in terms of knowledge, interpersonal skills, and technical skills. What are the tasks of supervision that can bring about improved instruction? They are direct assistance to teachers, staff development, curriculum development, group development, and action research. How does instruction improve?

Direct assistance: The supervisor can provide one-to-one feedback with teachers to improve instruction.

Staff development: The supervisor can provide learning opportunities with teachers to improve instruction.

Curriculum development: The supervisor can provide for changes in teaching content and instructional materials to improve instruction.

Group development: The supervisor can provide for instructional problem-solving meetings among teachers to improve instruction.

Action research: The supervisor can provide teachers with ways to evaluate their own teaching to improve instruction.

Each of these tasks is directly related to improved instruction. A supervisor needs to take responsibility for these tasks if a school is to become increasingly effective. Part V will detail how these tasks can be performed so that teachers take individual and collective responsibility for instructional improvement.

Chapter 15

Direct Assistance to Teachers

Direct human assistance to help teachers improve instruction can come from different sources. This book has contended that someone needs to take responsibility for the supervisory function of direct assistance to ensure that teachers receive feedback, are not left alone, and are involved as part of a collective staff. Research by Dornbush and Scott (1975) and Natriello (1982) has shown that teachers who receive the most classroom feedback are also most satisfied with teaching. Other research studies have shown that teachers in need of assistance tend to seek out first fellow teachers and second supervisory or administrative personnel (Lortie 1975, pp. 75–77). Direct assistance to teachers is one of the crucial elements of a successful school (Little 1982; Rosenholtz, 1985). Keeping the frequency and source of direct assistance in mind, we will look at an established structure for assisting teachers and then at some alternative ways of implementing the structure.

Clinical Procedures for Using Observations

Although there are multiple ways of observing, the structure or steps for conducting observations with teachers is relatively standard and accepted, and has a respectable research base (Sullivan 1980; Adams and Glickman 1984; Pavan 1985). In fact, over 90 percent of school administrators in a southern and a midwestern state have cited their knowledge of the use of this structure with teachers (Bruce and Hoehn 1980). The structure, commonly referred to as *clinical supervision,* is derived from the pioneering work of Morris Cogan with supervisors of intern teachers at Harvard University. Cogan's *Clinical Supervision* (1973) and Robert Goldhammer's book, also entitled *Clinical Supervision* (1969), are publications resulting from this pioneer work. Since then numerous refinements and alterations of clinical supervision have been made (Goldhammer, Anderson, and Krajewski 1980; Acheson and Gall 1987; Costa and Garmston 1985). Those desiring an in-depth study of the research and development of clinical supervision can find references at the end of this chapter. The structure of clinical supervision can be simplified into five sequential steps:

1. Preconference with teacher
2. Observation of classroom
3. Analyzing and interpreting observation and determining conference approach
4. Postconference with teacher
5. Critique of previous four steps

Step 1

At the *preconference*, the supervisor sits with the teacher and determines (1) the reason and purpose for the observation, (2) the focus of the observation, (3) the method and form of observation to be used, (4) the time of observation, and (5) the time for postconference. These determinations are made before the actual observation, so that both supervisor and teacher are clear about what will transpire. The purpose of the observation, as mentioned in Chapter 13, should provide the criteria for making the remaining decisions on focus, method, and time of observation.

Step 2

The next step, *observation*, is the time to follow through with the understandings of the preconference. The observer might use any one observation or combinations of observations. Methods include categorical frequencies, physical indicators, performance indicators, visual diagramming, space utilization, detached open-ended narratives, participant observation, focused questionnaire, and educational criticism. The observer should keep in mind the difference between *descriptions* of events and *interpretations*. Interpretation should follow description.

Step 3

The *analysis* and *interpretations* of the observation and determination of approach are now possible. The supervisor leaves the classroom with his or her observations and seeks solitude in an office or corner. He or she lays out the recorded pages of observations and studies the information. The task might be counting up frequencies, looking for recurring patterns, isolating a major occurrence, or discovering which performance indicators were present and which were not. Regardless of the instrument, questionnaire, or open-ended form used, the supervisor must make sense out of a large mass of information. Then the supervisor can make interpretations *based* on the analysis of the description. Figure 15-1 is a form that can be used to organize this task.

A case study might help to clarify this worksheet. Supervisor A has completed a verbal interaction instrument for students and teacher. She reviews the ten sheets, tallies the columns, and writes in the worksheet under analysis:

1. The teacher asked 27 questions and received 42 answers.

2. Out of 276 total verbal moves, 6 were student to student; the other 270 were teacher to student or student to teacher.

3. . . .

The supervisor, knowing that the purpose of the lesson was to encourage student involvement, now makes interpretations on the worksheet *corresponding* to the analysis:

1. The teacher encouraged students to answer questions.

2. There was little interaction among students.

3. . . .

Note the relationship between analysis 1 and interpretation 1. There is clear documentation of evidence leading to the supervisor's judgment.

Let's examine one more case, this time of supervisor B doing

Figure 15-1

Worksheet for Analysis and Interpretation of Data
A. Analysis: Write the major findings of your observation. Write down
              only what has been taken directly from your observation.
  1.
  2.
  3.
  4.
  5.
B. Interpretations:Write below what you believe is desirable or not
              desirable about the major findings.
  1.
  2.
  3.
  4.
  5.

---

a participant observation. The supervisor reads through his brief classroom notes, picks out the most significant events, and writes under "analysis":

1. James, Tyrone, Felix, and Sondra asked me about the assignment they were supposed to be doing.
2. Kirk and Felipe were talking with each other about sports the three times I overheard them.
3. ...

From this analysis the supervisor makes the following interpretation:

1. The teacher was not clearly communicating the directions to some students.
2. At least a couple of students were not interested in the classwork.
3. ...

Although one could argue with the supervisor's interpretation, it is readily apparent how it was logically derived from the recorded descriptions.

The last determination for the supervisor to make in step 3 of the clinical structure is to choose what interpersonal approach to use with the teacher in the postconference. The nondirective, collaborative, directive informational, and directive control orientations to supervision were explained in Chapters 7, 8, 9, and 10, respectively. Should the supervisor be directive informational by presenting his or her observations and interpretations, asking for input, setting a goal, and providing the teacher with alternative actions to choose? Should the supervisor be collaborative by sharing the observation, allowing the teacher to present his or her own interpretations, and negotiating a mutual contract for future improvement? Should the supervisor be nondirective by explaining his or her observations and encouraging the teacher to analyze, interpret, and make his or her own plan? The supervisor must consider the individual teacher's level of abstraction and level of commitment in deciding the approach, as explained in Chapter 11.

Step 4

With the completed observation form, completed analysis, and interpretation form, and with the chosen interpersonal approach, the supervisor is ready to meet with the teacher in a *postconference*. The postconference is held to discuss the analysis of the observation and, finally, to produce a plan for instructional improvement.

The first order of business is to let the teacher in on the observation—to reflect back to the teacher what was seen. Then the supervisor can follow the chosen approach—directive informational, collaborative, or nondirective. The responsibility for developing a future plan may reside with the supervisor, be equally shared, or belong to the teacher. The conference ends with a plan for further improvement. Figure 15-2 can be used to develop such a plan.

The *objective* is a statement of what the teacher will attain for the next observation: "I will improve student-to-student interaction by 50 percent in group discussions." *Activities* are listed preparation points to accomplish the activity: "(1) Practice pausing at least three seconds before answering a student response. (2) Practice using open-ended questions. (3) Set up ongoing mini-debates." *Resources* are the materials and/or people needed to do the activities: "(1)

Figure 15-2   Plan for instructional improvement

Postconference Date _____ Observed Teacher _____
Time _____   Peer Supervisor _____
Objective to be worked on:

Activities to be undertaken to achieve objectives:

Resources needed:

Time and date for next preconference:

Read book on *Leading Discussion Groups*. (2) Attend workshop on 'Involving Students.' (3) Observe Mr. Filler when he holds a science discussion." *Date* and *time* specify when the teacher will be ready to display his or her improvement. Such a plan—whether teacher-, supervisor-, or jointly designed—should be clearly understood by both parties before they leave the postconference.

Step 5

The *critique* of the previous four steps is a time for reviewing whether the format and procedures from preconference through postconference were satisfactory and whether revisions might be needed before repeating the sequence. The critique might be held at the end of the postconference or in a separate conference after a few days. It need not be a formal session but can be a brief discussion, consisting of questions such as: "What was valuable in what we have been doing?" "What was of little value?" "What changes could be suggested?" The critique has both symbolic and functional value. It indicates that the supervisor is involved in an improvement effort in the same way as the supervisee. Furthermore, the feedback from the teacher gives the supervisor a chance to decide on what practices to continue, revise, or change when working with the teacher in the future.

The five steps are now complete, and a tangible plan of future action is in the hands of the teacher. The supervisor is prepared to review the plan in the next preconference and reestablish focus and method of observation.

Peer Use of Clinical Supervision: Coaching

The number of teachers that a supervisor has will influence the frequency of clinical observations conducted by the supervisor. An English department head who teaches five periods a day and has fifteen staff members will have a difficult time conducting full clinical cycles with every teacher during the school year. A principal of a large school, without assistants to take on administrative and disciplinary responsibilities, will find it an overwhelming task to meet and observe each teacher frequently. From experience, we know the frustration of starting a preconference only to be interrupted by an irate parent, a breakdown of the plumbing system, or two misbehaving students. A supervisor cannot provide direct assistance to teachers unless he or she establishes priority, energy, and time for doing so. Other nonsupervisory matters will have to be ignored, delegated to others, or simply put off. Most often, direct assistance to teachers receives the lowest priority. This sad state of affairs is shown by the evidence that the overwhelming majority of school teachers receive little or no direct assistance (Natriello 1982, Ellett and Garland 1986). Most teachers state that supervisors do not visit them for the purpose of providing help. In most cases, when a supervisor or administrator is in the classroom, he or she is there to pass on school information or to pick up attendance records.

If a supervisor is convinced of the critical need to provide direct assistance to teachers and cannot do it alone, the question is, "Who else can do it?" This is where the technical skill of planning becomes important. The supervisor has to determine the amount of time available for direct assistance, how many teachers can be seen in that time, and which teachers should be given special attention. In a pilot study of principals providing an intensive two cycles of direct supervision to teachers, it was found that the upper limit was nine to eleven teachers. Beyond that number administrative and other instructional services began to suffer (Gwinnett County Pilot Teacher Evaluation Framework 1987). Then the supervisor needs to determine how else assistance for all teachers can be provided on a regular basis. Authorities on clinical supervision believe the cycle should be conducted a minimum of twice a year with each teacher (see Snyder, Johnson, and MacPhail-Wilcox 1982).

Since teachers naturally turn to each other for help more often than to a supervisor, and since supervision is concerned primarily with improving instruction rather than with summative evaluation (renewal of contracts), teachers helping teachers has become a formalized and well-received way of assuring direct assistance to every staff member. With the advent of extended responsibilities for career-ladder teachers, mentor teachers, master teachers, grade-level chairpersons, team leaders, and department heads, the time and resources for peer assistance have increased (see the theme issues of *Educational Leadership* 1987a; 1987b; and *Journal of Staff Development* 1987). If teachers become proficient in observation skills and the format of clinical supervision, the supervisor can take on the role of clarifier, trainer, scheduler, and troubleshooter—clarifier by determining the purpose; trainer by preparing the teachers for the task; scheduler by forming teams or trios of teachers who take responsibility for preconferencing, observing, and postconferencing with each other; and troubleshooter by consulting with teams of teachers who are experiencing difficulties and with individual teachers who need more specialized attention. The use of teachers helping teachers through clinical supervision has been labeled *peer supervision* or *colleagueship* (Alfonso and Goldsberry 1982). Joyce and Showers (1982) introduced the term *coaching* to characterize practice and feedback following staff development sessions. The terms peer supervision and peer coaching have now become indistinguishable in the literature. Research by Roper, Deal, and Dornbush (1976), Goldsberry (1980), Mohlman (1982), Coe (1985), and Sparkes and Bruder (1987) has shown positive results with peer assistance. The research has shown mostly gains in teachers' attitudes and perceptions; more studies focusing on changes in teacher decision making and behaviors and student outcomes are necessary to determine whether peer supervision works as well as clinical supervision by a supervisor. However, the reality of tight budgets and large teacher/supervisor ratios remains. If direct assistance is a worthy task for instructional improvement but a supervisor cannot provide it on a regular basis, the choice is either to have teachers provide help to each other or simply not to offer the help.

Obviously, the way to begin such a program is not to call a staff meeting and announce: "Since I can't see each of you as much as I would like, why don't you start to visit each other? Go to it!" Without planning and resources, disaster is inevitable. To be successful, peer supervision needs components addressing purpose, training, scheduling, and troubleshooting. Let's take each in turn.

Purpose

Before beginning a peer supervision or coaching program, clarity of purpose and goal is necessary (Garmston 1987). First, is it really a question of peer assistance (reciprocal interactions of equals) or is it a matter of hierarchical, one-way assistance (a better trained or more experienced teacher helping less well-trained or less experienced teachers)? Mentoring programs to help novices are fine, and master teacher programs to help struggling teachers are worthy, but they are not peer programs. Second, in a peer program, who is to be the recipient of assistance? Should a teacher who is the observer take from the observation some ideas to use, or should the teacher who is the observed take from the observation some actions to use? Third, will the observations and feedback focus on common instructional skills that each teacher is attempting to learn and implement, or will the observations and feedback focus on the teacher's own idiosyncratic concern with his or her teaching? Fourth, should the observations and feedback focus on the teacher's teaching or on individual students' behaviors? Fifth, is the goal of coaching to be greater awareness and more reflective decision making, or is it to implement particular teaching skills? Ultimately, how does the coaching goal fit into the larger school goal of improving instruction for students?

These are not idle questions. A peer program void of articulated definition and purpose has no rudder for steering and selecting the training, scheduling, and troubleshooting essential for success. Instead, it becomes another fad, exciting in that it's on the "cutting edge" of school change, but lacking substance in terms of what is to be accomplished. If there is a lack of direction in peer assistance programs, well-intentioned teachers will have a vague sense of having done something pleasant but little sense of accomplishment (see Little, Galagaran, and O'Neal 1984). Therefore, the first step is to meet with teachers to discuss how a proposed peer supervision program would fit into a school's or district's instructional goals and then to decide on the specific purposes of the program. For example, if the purpose is simply to acquaint teachers with each other's rooms, less training is needed than if the purpose is to provide teachers with feedback on their teaching and assisting them in developing action plans for further follow-through. The next subsection provides some training guidelines for proceeding with a peer assistance program that is focused on the purpose of reflective decision making.

Training

Before implementation, training of teachers would include (1) understanding the purpose and procedures of peer supervision, (2) conducting a preconference for determining the focus of observations, (3) conducting and analyzing an observation to distinguish between observing and interpreting classroom events, and (4) conducting two postconferences with different approaches for developing action plans—one using a nondirective approach, the other using a collaborative approach.

A standard form for writing instructional improvement plans in the postconference should be reviewed. The form should be simple and easy to fill out. Each peer member should understand that a completed plan is the object of the first four clinical steps and the basis for beginning the next round of supervision. For purposes of training, you may use the forms found in this chapter and in Chapter 13.

Training sessions of about six hours should provide the minimum knowledge and skills to begin peer supervision. Chapter 16 (staff development) will provide more detail on the sequencing of training to ensure some degree of transference from the training to initial implementation. After peers have gained some familiarity with the process through demonstrations, modeling, and practice in the workshop setting, they will be anxious but ready to begin a cycle. For the initial attempts, perfection is not expected, of course. After the first cycle of implementation, a follow-up meeting should be held to discuss what has occurred and what revisions need to be made before beginning the second cycle. It is often convenient to review the past cycle and conduct the preconference for the next cycle during the same meeting. This gives participants a sense of sharing and learning from each other, enables the trainer to answer questions, allows for observation schedules to be arranged, and eliminates the need to meet another time to hold the preconference. From this point on, follow-up meetings concluding and beginning further cycles can be held every two to three weeks until the agreed-upon number of peer cycles have been finished. For the first year it is recommended that at least four cycles be conducted—two times being the coach and twice being coached.

Toward the end of the year, a culminating meeting should be held to summarize the advantages and disadvantages of using peer supervision and to make a recommendation on whether to continue the program for the following year.

Let's emphasize that the program should be based on *agreement* and *voluntarism*. If an entire staff is willing to be involved, that's fine, but if only three teachers are willing, it is still a beginning and a previously unavailable source of help for those three teachers.

Scheduling

A teacher will have a more difficult time becoming enthusiastic about a project if it means increasing the amount of personal time and energy expended beyond an already full day. Because peer supervision will require additional time, the program should be voluntary, at least in the beginning. Greater participation of teachers is likely if the supervisor can schedule time for peer supervision during the school day. For example, placing teachers together in teams that share the same planning or lunch periods would allow for pre- and postconferences during the school day. Hiring a few substitutes for two days, twice a year, would allow teachers to be relieved of class duties so that they can observe their peers. One substitute could relieve six classroom teachers for one period at a time. Relief could also be found by having the titled supervisor (we mean you!) occasionally substitute for a teacher for one class period. This would enable the teacher to observe and would also give the supervisor a glimpse into the operating world of the classroom. Another way of freeing time for peer observations is for teachers to release each other by periodically scheduling a film, lecture, or some other large-group instruction so that two classes can be taught by one teacher. Whatever the actual schedule used to release teachers for peer supervision, preplanning by supervisor and teachers is needed to ensure that teachers can participate without extreme personal sacrifice. Research on lasting classroom change has shown that having scheduling time for teachers during the school day is critical (Humphries 1981).

Another issue is arranging teams of teachers. As in most issues in education, there are no hard and fast rules. Generally, teachers should be grouped with each other so that they are comfortable together but not necessarily at identical levels of experience and/or competence. It may be useful to put experienced teachers with new ones, superior teachers with adequate ones, or adequate teachers with struggling ones.

Cognitive psychologists have demonstrated that an individual's thinking becomes more abstract and varied when he or she interacts with persons at higher levels of mental organization (Kohlberg 1969). Such matching enables a person to consider ideas he or she would not have thought of; the novelty of the ideas spurs the person to rethink problems. If the groupings are too disparate—a concrete thinker with a highly abstract thinker, or a struggling teacher with a self-assured teacher—then little of such sparking of ideas will occur. There must be some degree of understanding and comfort to begin with. Hence it is undesirable to match people who think alike but also undesirable to match those who think too differently. The goal is to match people who are different but still can respect and communicate easily with each other.

Cognitive matching will work if there are enthusiastic participants who are willing to be matched. A supervisor working with staff who are skeptical about using peer supervision in the first place might be better served by forgetting cognitive matching and instead allowing self-selection of teams. Each teacher could present anonymously a list of teachers he or she would like to work with. The supervisor could then match up preferences. The choice is between an ideal way to match people based on cognitive growth and a practical way to match them based on people's need for security with a new program. The practical match might be best when starting the program; after peer supervision becomes a familiar ongoing activity, the supervisor could rearrange teams toward greater cognitive matching.

Troubleshooting

The third component of establishing a peer supervision program is the close monitoring of peer progress. The supervisor should be available to peer teams as a resource person. For example, what happens when the preconference concludes with an agreement to observe a teacher's verbal interaction in the classroom, and the peer supervisor is at a loss about where to find such an observation instrument? The training program should answer such questions, but orientation meetings cannot cover all possible needs. The supervisor must therefore monitor the needs of peer teams and be able to step in to help.

An elaborate monitoring device is not necessary. The supervisor might simply wander around the halls and check with peer supervisors every few weeks. At periodic faculty meetings, he or she might ask peer supervisors to write a note on their team progress. The supervisor should be sure that books, films, tapes, instruments on clinical supervision, and methods/instruments for observations are catalogued and available to teachers in the professional library.

Now that the supervisor can attend to *purpose, training, scheduling,* and *troubleshooting,* a peer supervision program can be implemented. The initial implementation of such a program undoubtedly will create more work for the supervisor. However, the initial work is less than would be necessary for providing clinical supervision to every teacher two or three times a year. If it is important enough to supervisor and staff, the time spent at the start in preparing for the program will pay off with ongoing instructional improvement of teachers.

Other Means of Direct Human Assistance

It is 10:30 A.M., and Ms. Golan, the reading supervisor, is on her way to present the recommended reading budget for next year to the principal. Principal Malone told her last week that the recommendations were to be in today by 11 A.M. if he was to have them for his luncheon meeting with the superintendent. Ms. Golan has worked on the budget day and night for the last three days and finally has it finished. She needs to explain some of the budget items to Principal Malone personally. Suddenly, someone catches her by the arm and gently spins her around. It's Phillip Arostook, the remedial reading teacher, who says: "Boy, am I glad you're here. I have a meeting with Mr. and Mrs. Cougar at noon. They want my head. They claim I've been neglecting their son William, and that he's not learning anything. They want him out of my class. How do I handle this? I need your help!"

This incident is typical of the numerous unplanned occasions on which one is called to provide direct human assistance. Clinical supervision is focused on long-term, carefully planned instructional improvement. There is still the matter of immediate needs, however. It is just as important for teachers to have someone to confer with in handling the short-term issues that arise each day. What would you do (or what have you done) in Ms. Golan's place? Ms. Golan could handle the situation by (1) telling Phillip she'll be back to see him in a half an hour; (2) telling Phillip she is pressed for time and can speak to him only for a few minutes on her way to the principal's office; (3) telling Phillip she's sorry but she has no time and he'll have to handle it on his own; or (4) sending the budget with a note to the principal via a student, forgetting about explaining the budget, and then calmly sitting down with Phillip. Ms. Golan (and Phillip) would have been better off if there were an established procedure for handling frequent needs for human assistance. The procedure should be premised on *accessibility, arranged time,* and *delegation.*

Human help must be physically available and *accessible.* On a daily basis, the supervisor should visit in the lounge or in classrooms with teachers before school, during breaks, and after school. Of course, the supervisor cannot hold lengthy conversations with every teacher daily and also have time for much of anything else. Therefore the supervisor might consider brief check-ins with teachers—taking the time to pause and speak with a certain number of teachers each day to ensure that by the end of the week every teacher has had the opportunity to bring up classroom concerns. Often such a brief exchange will alert the supervisor to a teacher's concern that should be followed up with a scheduled conference.

The supervisor's schedule should also have *arranged weekly times* set aside for such conferences. The supervisor might plan a particular afternoon every week to follow up on teacher concerns. Teachers know that the supervisor will be in the lounge or office every Thursday afternoon to listen and help. Finally, the supervisor should consider *delegation.* The supervisor can use these Thursday afternoon times to provide personal help, can refer the concern to a specialist such as the school counselor or reading teacher, or can use the time for teachers to share instructional concerns and help each other. For example, some schools set aside every other Thursday for voluntary after-school meetings, in which teachers share discipline problems and plan concrete ways to help each other (see Glickman and Esposito 1979). More about specific procedures and structures for efficient meetings can be found in Chapter 18 on group development.

Let's return to the case of Ms. Golan and Phillip Arostook. If Ms. Golan had planned for accessibility, scheduled time, and delegation, the crisis situation could have been prevented, with both the budget report and Phillip's need for counseling being satisfied. She would have known from checking in with Phillip that he was having difficulties with William. With a scheduled time for conferences, they could have reviewed the matter and scheduled a meeting with the parents.

The hectic life of schools—even when accessibility, arranged time, and delegation are planned—will still create unusual dilemmas for the supervisor (as anyone involved in education well knows). Planning for direct human assistance will reduce the number of such dilemmas if teachers know they will be able to speak to their supervisors weekly to discuss serious problems and find resources to meet their needs. Such supervisory attention to ongoing concerns creates a climate of confidence and purpose rather than one of confusion and frantic reaction to unexpected crises.

Differences between Direct Assistance and Formal Evaluation

Formal evaluation is quite different from the direct assistance being discussed here. *Formal evaluation* is performed to determine whether or not a teacher measures up to a standard of acceptable work—that is, to sum up the value of the teacher. *Direct assistance* is concerned with helping a teacher assess and work on his or her own classroom needs—that is, to form a focus for future improvement. Therefore, observation of teachers for purposes of direct assistance should be distinct from observation for decisions about renewal or nonrenewal of contracts. Direct assistance involves helping the teacher in continuous reassessment and change. When the task is one of getting a teacher to meet a prescribed level of performance—whether established by school administrators, central office, school board, or principal—the procedures used for working with teachers are less supervisory and collegial and more administrative and directive.

Ideally, it is best to keep these tasks separate. Supervision as a function concerns itself with improvement of classroom instruction. Administration as a function concerns itself with the overall maintenance of school operations, including the contractual aspects of teacher performance, which might include dress, attendance, punctuality, record keeping, and extra school assignments. Supervision focuses on direct assistance for improving classroom instruction. Administration focuses on satisfactory performance in all contractual matters. To delineate these differences further, let's look at two examples of conferences: one for purposes of formal evaluation and the other for purposes of direct assistance.

Example A

Mrs. Readell, the supervisor, sits down with Mr. Hopewell, the teacher, and reports her evaluation: "Mr. Hopewell, you have performed well in almost all aspects of the teacher evaluation. I have rated you as satisfactory on all categories under instruction, discipline, dress, school relationships, and extra school duties. The one area I have marked unsatisfactory is in the paperwork category. Your quarterly attendance records have been late for the last two quarters. Although I have recommended strongly that you be rehired, I do want you to get those attendance records in on time. Without them, we are delayed in receiving our state attendance allotments."

Example B

Mr. Sonjan, another supervisor, sits down with Mr. Hopewell and begins: "Well, Mr. Hopewell, as we agreed, I observed those three boys in the back of the classroom. These are the frequency charts, and the results are that they spend over 80 percent of their time off task, talking and passing notes to each other. Notice how for the first ten minutes they were fairly attentive, but in the last twenty minutes you had to stop and speak to them seven times. What do you suppose is happening?" Mr. Hopewell responds, "I was aware that they lose attention, but not that dramatically! I think I need to give them shorter but more frequent activities." Mr. Sonjan: "Maybe if you had them sit up closer where you could check their work more often, they would be more attentive."

These examples should highlight the differences between formal evaluation and direct assistance. In teacher evaluation the concern is with adequate performance, as shown in example A. The teacher is either doing well or not, according to a single, prescribed standard for all teachers. If the teacher has met the standards, no further attention is needed. In direct assistance the concern is exclusively instruction-related and focuses on the teacher's own professional needs, as shown in example B. Instruments and forms used can vary from teacher to teacher. Observation times and methods are agreed on, and improvement is ongoing *regardless of* the competence level of the teacher. Instructional improvement is relative; there are always changes that might make the classroom better. Therefore, instructional improvement is continuous, whereas teacher evaluation is periodic. Other writers have noted these differences, calling direct assistance *formative evaluation* and formal evaluation *summative evaluation* (see McGreal 1982). Many writers of supervision texts (Harris 1975; Oliva 1976) believe a supervisor should have a staff relationship with teachers in order to be responsible totally for direct assistance (that is, helping teachers to help themselves), whereas administrators such as school principals should have line relationships *over* teachers so as to be totally responsible for formal evaluation. The rationale for these distinctions is understandable. A teacher is more prone to allow an observer to see the real classroom, warts and all, if the observer is present solely to help. A teacher is more prone to confide in a staff person. When the observer is in the role of evaluator, the teacher is more likely to hide the real classroom and, instead, give a rehearsed and stilted performance to meet the standards of the evaluation form. The teacher will be reluctant to discuss what is wrong or inadequate in his or her own teaching if the supervisor might use the information to document unacceptable teaching standards. Simply put, individuals speak more easily about their real selves to a friend than to a boss. Since help with real classroom problems can be provided only if a supervisor can see the real classroom, a staff relationship with teachers is helpful.

Most school organizations reflect this separation through job descriptions. Any combination of distinct roles might do—principals as evaluators and assistant principals, department heads, lead and master teachers, or peer teachers as direct assistors; or central office personnel as evaluators and principals as direct assistors. This book, however, treats supervision as a function, not as a particular position or role. The main concern is that direct assistance be provided. Which persons or positions provide the help can vary from system to system, depending on school resources. However, if a school is to become more successful with instruction, the task of direct assistance *must* be performed.

In many school systems, one or more persons are expected to do both formal evaluation and direct assistance. Can such dual responsibilities be done well? Can a person do a credible job if he or she is responsible for both improving and judging a teacher? The answer might surprise the reader: It is *yes* (Glickman and Pajak 1986; Lunsford 1988). It can be done, but with difficulty and only by an individual who can maintain a relationship of trust and credibility with teachers. Ask yourself: Is there someone you would trust to evaluate you for contract renewal purposes as well as to assist you with your own professional improvement? Could you let your hair down with this person? There probably is someone, but it must be a very special person. Only if you believed that the person is *primarily* concerned with helping you would you be comfortable, receptive, and willing to reveal your areas of greatest need. The point is that to do both jobs well is an extraordinary accomplishment. In a school system that has supervisors whom teachers thoroughly trust and respect, dual responsibilities are possible. More often, teachers have a natural wariness toward those higher up in the organization. Therefore, separating the roles is often advisable.

School and District Procedures for Direct Assistance and Formal Evaluation

A study by Blankenship and Irvine (1985) found that 50 percent of experienced teachers in one state had never in their careers been observed, given feedback, or had a conference focused on instructional improvement. The only time anyone had entered their classrooms to observe was for the purpose of a formal evaluation, to rate their competence. Even more remarkable, 80 percent of experienced teachers had never observed a peer in the same school. If this study is representative of other states, as it probably is (see Darling-Hammond, Wise, and Pease 1986; Ellett and Garland 1986), most teachers in the United States and Canada have never had the experience of being observed and given feedback as helpful sources of information, nor have they been engaged in postconferences that stimulate their thinking and planning for future instructional improvement. Even with the establishment of new programs in peer coaching, mentoring, and supervision, many teachers have difficulty accepting that a person can come into a classroom, observe, and offer help without being judgmental or using the observation for formal evaluation (Bird and Little 1984). The reasons for such mistrust are quite understandable. For the most part, teachers have known classroom observations only for the purpose of evaluations. Unless the procedures for direct assistance (supervision, and professional growth) are made clearly distinct and separate from evaluation (formal contract renewal and judgment of competence), one can talk until one is blue in the face about supervision as a helping and formative process, but teachers will not believe it.

What remains to be resolved is the age-old dilemma of how a school or district is to ensure that teachers are both held responsible for satisfactory performance and at the same time engaged in professional growth and classroom-based assistance that allows them to open their hearts, souls, and minds to another, thinking critically and actively planning improvements to their teaching. It is not an easy dilemma to resolve! Two noted education theorists and researchers at the same institution (U.C.L.A.), James Popham

(1988) and Madeline Hunter (1988), come down on totally opposite sides of this issue. Popham argues that supervision must be divorced from evaluation, and Hunter argues that they must be wedded together!

Most school districts spend their time evaluating performance, judging, and rating teachers. The other dimension of supervision— true intellectual engagement around the core issue of the work of teaching—is left to chance. As a result, the overwhelming majority of teachers do not mind being evaluated, but they also remark that the process does little to improve their teaching. Furthermore, those who do the evaluation see themselves entrapped in a required process that in most cases has become a meaningless ritual (McCarty, Kaufman, and Stafford 1986). The truth is that most teachers are satisfactory and their evaluators know that they are competent. Therefore both parties, in the past, have used a tremendous amount of time to verify what each knew before the year began. Supervisory time that could have been used in an intellectual, nonevaluative growth process has been usurped. Of course, it is necessary to have evaluation that "weeds out" or "shapes up" the few teachers who border on incompetence. So how does a district measure competence as well as focus on professional growth beyond competence?

In the past few years, teams of teachers and administrators in various school districts have been attempting to resolve the dilemma of evaluation and supervision in creative ways. National studies indicate that teachers want to be observed *more,* they want *more* feedback, and they want to talk *more* with other professionals about improving learning for their students (Glickman and Rogers 1988; Rogers 1986; Glickman and Jones 1986). Teams of teachers and administrators in diverse places (Gwinnett County, Georgia; Swift Current, Saskatchewan; Upper Perkiomen Valley, Pennsylvania; and Brattleboro and South Burlington, Vermont) have concluded that if classroom assistance for professional growth is desired, it is necessary to establish operational procedures for doing so while recognizing the need for periodic evaluation of employees. The following are various procedures that some of the above districts have used both to supervise and to evaluate (Glickman 1987).

1. *Annually, separate competent from marginal teachers through evaluation by late fall.* The evaluator uses a standard, uniform evaluation instrument to make an initial judgment, after one full cycle of observations, as to which teachers are competent and which are questionable. The questionable teachers are placed on a "needs improvement" plan that details what changes need to take place for them to reach satisfactory performance on the next evaluation cycle. Teachers who are judged as competent after the first cycle

are asked to establish their own instructional classroom goals and professional growth plans. Further cycles of observations and conferences are no longer tied to evaluation but rather to feedback about their growth plans.

2. *Establish a two-track, three-year program* of two cycles of observations and conferences per year with each teacher. In track 1, teachers are observed by an evaluator in accordance with a standard evaluation form, used throughout the school system for contract-renewal purposes. Teachers judged satisfactory after the first cycle of observation move into track 2, which focuses on supervision and instructional improvement. Observations for the remainder of the three years are focused on enhancing competence. Track 2 involves three phases—preobservation, observation, and postobservation—leading to the development of an instructional professional development plan. In track 2, no rating scales are kept, nor are formal records kept or reported to any other party. Teachers who do not pass the first cycle of track 1 remain in track 1 until they satisfy the required evaluation, or they are removed from employment.

3. *Divide the process so that the evaluation procedures and the direct-assistance supervision procedures can occur simultaneously but are viewed as discrete from each other.* One way of doing this is to develop an instructional improvement sequence in which each teacher chooses an instructional improvement goal and selects the sources of assistance he or she believes most helpful in achieving it (see Glatthorn 1984). Possible sources of assistance include a school administrator, a teacher from the same school, a central office supervisor, a teacher from another school, or some other suitable professional. The teacher discusses the year's direct-assistance plan with a designated coordinator (school principal, department head, or team leader) and arranges visiting schedules. The normal contract evaluation process conducted by the designated evaluator continues throughout the year, separate from the instructional improvement process.

4. *Establish separate roles for evaluators and supervisors.* In some school districts, central office supervisors conduct all formal evaluations, and the principals provide instructional improvement assistance. More often, it is the other way around: Principals conduct evaluations and central office or school-based personnel (master teachers, lead teachers, department heads, assistant principals, or peers) provide assistance. In either case, one position is clearly delineated as a staff position, concerned with assisting teachers, and another is designated as a line position, concerned with evaluating teachers.

5. *Integrate direct assistance with school-based in-service conducted by peers and trainers.* The focus for in-service education developed by the staff can become the focus for direct assistance. Meanwhile, the regular evaluation process remains intact. For example, a school decides to study and employ a new instructional model (cooperative learning, mastery learning, or cognitive monitoring). As part of teachers' professional growth, they individually set goals on what each plans to do to implement the model; then each teacher receives a minimum of two cycles of observations and conferences from peers or trainers to refine or expand his or her skills. Such communication is kept confidential between teachers and assistors. The district evaluation to judge overall teacher competence continues to be conducted by the official school evaluator.

6. *Redefine evaluation between evaluators and teachers.* Many states and districts require an annual evaluation and summarized report on each teacher, done by an officially designated, school-based evaluator. Yet some states or districts do not define the content or purpose of the evaluation. In such cases a district committee, a school council, or an individual evaluator and teacher can define at the outset the types of evaluation to be done. Will it be a summative evaluation to determine competence or a formative evaluation to promote professional growth? Any of the five previously listed procedures, or a combination thereof, might be utilized, with the terminology of formative and summative evaluations, to conform with mandated requirements for annual evaluation of all employees.

Developmental Considerations in Direct Assistance and Formal Evaluation

Of course, rigorous, well-documented, formal, summative contract-renewal evaluation is not meant to be treated as unimportant. As a profession, we would be doing ourselves a disservice by allowing teachers who are incompetent, uncaring, and harmful to continue working with students. Summative evaluation is clearly a need of schools and districts. Several sources (McGreal 1983; *Educational Leadership* 1987c; Duke and Stiggins 1986; Stanley and Popham 1988) provide information on ways to develop evaluation systems that attempt to save marginal teachers and are legally defensible. The point is, however, that most teachers in most schools are not incompetent; if we are to provide meaningful stimulation for continuous renewal, we need another process that ensures time, focus, and structure for people to get close to each other to plan better teaching that is goal-directed rather than problem- and deficiency-directed.

When thinking about ways to improve direct assistance to staff, it is once again critical to involve people who are affected by the decision in making the decision. A study group composed of teachers, building administrators, and central office staff (with a majority of teachers) is one approach to deal with the issue of direct assistance. Teachers' union representatives should be active members of the study group, because proposed changes will often involve issues subject to collective bargaining. Proposed changes should usually be piloted first with a few schools, grades, or departments and evaluated and revised before full-scale implementation.

The same factors must be considered if particular direct-assistance interventions are to be tried in an individual school. Perhaps a school study group can be established; maybe a few teachers are willing to try peer coaching, or a high school department head wants to try his or her skills in working with a few teachers. The idea is to try, pilot, revise, and expand.

The word *development* implies that school units will be in different stages of readiness, commitment, and abstraction with regard to improving direct assistance to teachers. In one school it may be the principal and two teachers who are willing to spend observation time in direct assistance and formative feedback, to see if this new way (as distinct from summative evaluation) is worth pursuing. In another school a majority of teachers might want to arrange for informal conferences about teaching on the first Thursday of each month.

A few years ago I explained to a district study group the need to move slowly in implementing a full-scale direct-assistance supervision program. The fifteen school representatives asked me why. They were excited, ready to go, and didn't want to lose momentum. They were ready to move, and who was I to say no? The point is a simple one. Educators ask themselves the question, "How can we improve direct assistance to teachers in our school?" Remember that organizations as well as individuals are at different levels of development. The answer to the question may be to begin on a small or a large scale, but the important thing is to answer the question rather than avoiding it. We cannot ignore demonstrated benefits of implementing direct-assistance supervision programs in public schools. Such programs have resulted in improved teacher reflection and higher-order thought, more collegiality, openness, and communication, greater teacher retention, less anxiety and burnout, greater teacher autonomy and efficacy, improved attitudes, improved teaching behaviors, and better student achievement and attitudes (Glickman and Bey 1990). We must think seriously about whether we can afford to dismiss direct assistance to teachers and continue to use summative evaluation as the prime reason for observing and talking with teachers.

Summary

Regardless of how or where the responsibilities reside, no school or school system can hope to improve instruction if direct assistance is not provided to teachers. To leave classroom teachers alone and unobserved in their classrooms, without professional consultation and without school resources tailored to their unique needs, is a statement (intended or not) that teaching is unimportant. The message to teachers is that what is important is keeping your class quiet, your doors shut, and your problems to yourself. Assuredly, this is not the message we want to give.

A different message can be given by arranging for observation, feedback, and discussion of classroom improvement. Clinical supervision is a recognizable structure for assistance that peers can use to help each other. Furthermore, supervisors can be accessible, arrange contact times, and refer specialists to teachers. Direct assistance separated from formal evaluation will help teachers confide, improve, and move with each other toward collective action.

EXERCISES

Academic

1. Locate three research studies on clinical supervision. Write a summary of each study, including purpose, participants, methodology, results, and conclusions.

2. Write a paper (a) giving advantages and disadvantages of having supervision done by a formally designated supervisor, and (b) giving advantages and disadvantages of having supervision performed by other teachers (peer supervision). Refer to at least three outside sources in your paper.

3. Locate three research studies on peer supervision. Write a summary of each study, including purpose, participants, methodology, results, and conclusions.

4. Assume you are a supervisor who has been asked by the superintendent to begin a program of clinical supervision by peers

in one of the district's medium-sized schools. Prepare a written plan for introducing clinical supervision to all the school's teachers, training a volunteer group of teachers in the clinical process, selecting teams (matching teachers), scheduling an initial round of clinical cycles, and monitoring the peer supervision program.

5. A traditional question debated in supervision is whether a single supervisor should be involved in both direct assistance and summative evaluation of teachers, or whether these two functions should be performed by different supervisors. Find one author (other than the author of this book) on each side of this issue. Write a paper summarizing the arguments of each author.

Field

1. Interview a supervisor who follows the clinical model in supervision of teachers on the practical advantages and disadvantages of clinical supervision. Prepare a report on your interview.

2. Arrange to supervise a teacher using the clinical model (preconference, observation, analysis and interpretation, postconference, critique). Record the preconference, postconference, and critique on audiotape, and write a summary of the clinical cycle.

3. Conduct a group interview with a team of teachers involved in peer supervision on the specifics of the peer supervision program, problems encountered, and perceived value of peer supervision for instructional improvement. Prepare a report on the interview.

4. Prepare a survey instrument to be completed by teachers that (a) defines direct assistance, (b) asks teachers to list the types of direct human assistance they desire from supervisors, and (c) asks teachers to list the types of direct human assistance they desire from other teachers. Distribute the survey to at least ten teachers, and request that they respond anonymously, in writing, to the two survey questions. Collect the surveys and process and analyze response data. Prepare a report on which types of direct human assistance the respondents desire from supervisors and from fellow teachers.

5. Interview a school administrator who has primary responsibility for providing direct human assistance to teachers *and* summative evaluation of teachers. Ascertain whether the administrator attempts to separate these two functions, and if so, how he or she attempts to maintain such separation. Question the admin-

istrator on the advantages and disadvantages of such dual responsibility. Prepare a report on your interview.

Developmental

1. Begin an in-depth study of the development of clinical supervision by comparing three major works in clinical supervision, such as Goldhammer (1969); Cogan (1973); and Goldhammer, Anderson, and Krajewski (1980).
2. Begin an in-depth study of peer supervision, beginning with Alfonso and Goldsberry (1982).
3. As you continue your readings on the tasks of supervision, note the interrelationship of direct assistance with the other tasks of supervision and how previously discussed knowledge and skills of supervisors are common prerequisites for each task.

REFERENCES

Acheson, A.A., and Gall, M.D. 1987. *Techniques in the clinical supervision of teachers,* 2nd ed. New York: Longman.

Adams, A., and Glickman, C.D. 1984. Does clinical supervision work? A review of research. *Tennessee Educational Leadership* *11*(11):38–40.

Alfonso, R.J., and Goldsberry, L.F. 1982. Colleagueship in supervising. In T.J. Sergiovanni (Ed.), *Supervision.* Alexandria, Va.: Association for Supervision and Curriculum Development.

Bird, T., and Little, J.W. 1984. Supervision and evaluation in the school context. Paper presented at the annual meeting of the American Educational Research Association, New Orleans, April.

Blankenship, G., Jr., and Irvine, J.J. 1985. Georgia teachers' perceptions of prescriptive and descriptive observations of teaching by instructional supervisors. *Georgia Educational Leadership* *1*(1):7–10.

Bruce, R.E., and Hoehn, L. 1980. Supervisory practice in Georgia and Ohio. Paper presented at the annual meeting of the Council of Professors of Instructional Supervision, Hollywood, Fla., December.

Coe, E.E. 1985. Towards collegial inquiry: A case study in clinical supervision. (ERIC Document Reproduction Service No. ED 281 847.)

Cogan, M. 1973. *Clinical supervision.* Boston: Houghton Mifflin.

Costa, A.L., and Garmston, R. 1985. Supervision for intelligent teaching. *Educational Leadership 42*(5):70–80.

Darling-Hammond, L., Wise, A., and Pease, S. 1986. Teacher evaluation in the organizational context: A review of the literature. *Review of Educational Research 53*(3):285–328.

Dornbush, S.M., and Scott, W.R. 1975. *Evaluation and the exercise of authority.* San Francisco: Jossey-Bass.

Duke, D.L., and Stiggins, R.J. 1986. *Teacher evaluation: Five keys to growth.* Washington, D.C.: (joint publication) AASA, NAESP, NASSP, NEA.

Educational Leadership. 1987a. Theme issue: Staff Development through Coaching. *44*(5).

Educational Leadership. 1987b. Theme issue: Collegial Learning. *45*(3).

Educational Leadership. 1987c. Theme issue: Progress in Evaluating Teaching. *44*(7).

Ellett, C.D., and Garland, J.S. 1986. Examining teacher evaluation practices and policies: Results from a national survey of the 100 largest school districts. Paper presented at the annual meeting of the American Educational Research Association, San Francisco, April.

Garmston, R.J. 1987. How administrators support peer coaching. *Educational Leadership 44*(5):71–78.

Glatthorn, A. 1984. *Differentiated supervision.* Alexandria, Va.: Association for Supervision and Curriculum Development.

Glickman, C.D. 1987. Instructional improvement and the K–8 principal. *NAESP Streamlined Seminar 5*(4).

Glickman, C.D., and Bey, T.M. 1990. Research on supervision in teacher education. In R. Houston (Ed.), *Handbook of Research on Teacher Education.* New York: Macmillan.

Glickman, C.D., and Esposito, J.P. 1979. *Leadership guide for elementary school improvement.* Boston: Allyn and Bacon, pp. 233–250.

Glickman, C.D., and Jones, J.W. 1986. Research in supervision: Creating the dialogue. *Educational Leadership 44*(3):83.

Glickman, C.D., and Pajak, E.F. 1986. The supervisor as evaluator or helper: Research on a controversial issue. *Canadian School Executive* 6(3):3–5.

Glickman, C.D., and Rogers, M.G. 1988. Supervision: State of direct supervisory services. *Educational Leadership* 46(1):84.

Goldhammer, R. 1969. *Clinical supervision: Special methods for the supervision of teachers.* New York: Holt, Rinehart and Winston.

Goldhammer, R., Anderson, R.H., and Krajewski, R.J. 1980. *Clinical supervision: Special methods for the supervision of teachers,* 2nd ed. New York: Holt, Rinehart and Winston.

Goldsberry, L.F. 1980. Colleague consultation: Teacher collaboration using a clinical supervision model. Unpublished Ed.D. dissertation, University of Illinois, Urbana-Champaign.

Gwinnett County pilot teacher evaluation framework. 1987. Unpublished manuscript, Lawrenceville, Ga.

Harris, B.M., 1975. *Supervisory behavior in education,* 2nd ed. Englewood Cliffs, N.J.: Prentice-Hall.

Humphries, J.D. 1981. Factors affecting the impact of curriculum innovations on classroom practice: Project complexity, characteristics of local leadership and supervisory strategies. Unpublished Ed.D. dissertation, University of Georgia.

Hunter, M. 1988. Effective reconciliation between supervision and evaluation. A reply to Popham. *Journal of Personnel Evaluation in Education 1:*275–279.

Journal of Staff Development. 1987. Theme issue: Peer Coaching. 8(1).

Joyce, B., and Showers, B. 1982. The coaching of teaching. *Educational Leadership* 40(1):4–10.

Kohlberg, L. 1969. Stage and sequence: The cognitive-development approach to socialization. In D. Goslin (Ed.), *Handbook of socialization theory and research.* Chicago: Rand-McNally.

Little, J.W. 1982. Norms of collegiality and experimentation: Work place conditions of school success. *American Educational Research Journal* 19(3):325–340.

Little, J.W., Galagaran, P., and O'Neal, R. 1984. Professional development roles and relationships: Principles and skills of "advising." (Contract 400-83-003.) San Francisco: Far West Laboratory for Educational Research and Development.

Lortie, D.C. 1975. *School teacher: A sociological study.* Chicago: University of Chicago Press, pp. 75–77.

Lunsford, B.F. 1988. Perceptions of relationships between teachers and supervisors during the implementation of a new teacher evaluation model. Doctoral dissertation, University of Georgia.

McCarty, D.J., Kaufman, J.W., and Stafford, J.C. 1986. Supervision and evaluation: Two irreconcilable processes. *Clearing House 59* (April):351–353.

McGreal, T.L. 1982. Effective teacher evaluation systems. *Educational Leadership 39*(4):303–305.

————. 1983. *Successful teacher evaluation.* Alexandria, Va.: Association for Supervision and Curriculum Development.

Mohlman, G.G. 1982. Assessing the impact of three inservice teacher training models. Paper presented at the annual meeting of the American Educational Research Association, New York, March.

Natriello, G. 1982. The impact of the evaluation of teaching on teacher effect and effectiveness. Paper presented at the annual meeting of the American Educational Research Association, New York, March.

Oliva, P.F. 1976. *Supervision for today's schools.* New York: Harper & Row.

Pavan, B.N. 1985. Clinical supervision: Research in schools utilizing comparative measures. Paper presented at the annual meeting of the American Educational Research Association, Chicago, April.

Popham, W.J. 1988. The dysfunctional marriage of formative and summative teacher evaluation. *Journal of Personnel Evaluation in Education 1:*269–273.

Rogers, M.G. 1986. Teacher satisfaction with direct supervisor services. Unpublished doctoral dissertation, University of Georgia. *Dissertation Abstracts International 47:*4260A.

Roper, S.S., Deal, T.E., and Dornbush, S. 1976. Collegial evaluation of classroom teaching: Does it work? *Educational Research Quarterly* (Spring):56–66.

Rosenholtz, S.J. 1985. Effective schools: Interpreting the evidence. *American Journal of Education 93:*352–388.

Snyder, K.J., Johnson, W.L., and MacPhail-Wilcox, B. 1982. The implementation of clinical supervision. Paper presented at the annual meeting of the Southwest Educational Research Association, Austin, Tex., February.

Sparkes, G.M., and Bruder, S. 1987. How school-based peer coaching improves collegiality and experimentation. Paper presented at the annual meeting of the American Educational Research Association, Washington, D.C., April.

Stanley, S.J., and Popham, W.S. (Eds.). 1988. *Teacher evaluation: Six prescriptions for success.* Alexandria, Va.: Association for Supervision and Curriculum Development.

Sullivan, C.G. 1980. *Clinical supervision: A state of the art review.* Alexandria, Va.: Association for Supervison and Curriculum Development.

Chapter 16

Staff Development

Bob Jeffries, director of staff development, calls six school principals into his office to plan for the upcoming in-service day. He begins by explaining that the in-service program will start with a morning session, attended by the entire school system faculty, in the high school auditorium. The afternoon will consist of individual school activities, with the principal being responsible for whatever transpires. He asks the principals: "What might we do for the morning session?" One principal suggests that at this time of year teachers could use an emotional lift, and that an inspirational speaker would be good. Another principal adds that she had heard a Dr. Zweibach give a great talk entitled "The Thrill of Teaching" at a national principals' conference last summer. She thinks he would be a terrific speaker. Bob Jeffries likes these suggestions and tells the principals he will call Dr. Zweibach and make arrangements for his appearance.

On the in-service day 238 teachers file into the auditorium and fill all but the first eight rows of seats. Mr. Jeffries makes a few introductory remarks about how fortunate "we" are to have Dr. Zweibach with "us" and then turns the session over to Dr. Zweibach. A rumpled, middle-aged university professor walks to the microphone and launches into his talk on the thrill of teaching. Within ten minutes, signs of restlessness, boredom, and bitterness are evident throughout the audience. Twelve of the teachers are sitting through a talk they had heard Dr. Zweibach deliver verbatim two years earlier at a teacher convention. Fifteen others are thinking about the classroom work they could be doing to prepare for next semester and wondering, "Why in the world are we sitting through this talk?" Another twenty-two teachers have become impatient with Dr. Zweibach's continual reference to the academic high school settings where he found teaching thrills. Their own work settings are vocational, special education, and elementary; they can't relate what he is saying about high schools to their world. Eventually some teachers begin to correct papers, read, or knit; a few appear to fall asleep. On the other hand, nearly half the members of the audience remain attentive and give Dr. Zweibach a rousing ovation when he concludes. The other half appear relieved that the talk is finally over and they can return to their own schools. Upon leaving the auditorium one can overhear such remarks as "What a great talk!" and "Why do we have to put up with all this staff development crap?"

This depiction of an in-service day is typical of many school systems. Some teachers find it valuable, but many do not. Staff development has been referred to as "the slum of American education, neglected and of little effect" (Wood and Thompson 1980). In-service is often viewed by supervisors, administrators, and teachers as a number of days contracted for in the school calendar that simply need to be endured. Four crucial questions will shape this chapter. (1) Why is in-service and staff development needed? (2) How should it be planned and conducted? (3) What is the relationship between in-service and staff development? (4) Are teachers to be the objects or the agents of staff development? A supervisor with responsibility for in-service and staff development cannot hope to make every activity interesting and valuable to every teacher, but he or she can expect staff development to be, overall, of value and interest to most if not all staff members. The ultimate outcome should be improved instruction for students.

Why the Need for Staff Development?

Over 85 percent of a total school budget is used to pay employee salaries. Education is a human enterprise. The essence of successful instruction and good schools comes from the thoughts and actions of the professionals in the schools. So, if one is to look for a place to improve the quality of education in a school, a sensible place to look is the continuous education of educators—that is, staff development. Some of the options that school districts can provide for staff development are contracted in-service days, optional in-service sessions for recertification credits, early-morning or after-school times for workshop minisessions, college courses, faculty meetings, teacher centers, visits to other schools, attendance at local, state, and national conferences, travel for cultural enrichment, and readings and video- and audiocassettes (Speak and Hirsh 1988). Virtually any experience that enlarges a teacher's knowledge, appreciation, skills, and understandings of his or her work falls under the domain of staff development.

When I gave a presentation to a Michigan school board to explain the need to allocate more money for staff development, I used an analogy to the automobiles made in Detroit. When a customer purchases a new car costing upwards of $20,000, he or she brings it in every 5,000 miles for preventive maintenance and fine-tuning. The customer continues to put additional money into the car to prolong its life and performance. Simply to run the car into the ground would be a dumb way to protect such an investment! In education, the school board is the customer, who purchases more than a new car with its $20,000 initial investment—it purchases a living and breathing professional! Without resources for maintaining, fine-tuning, and reinvigorating the investment, the district will run teachers into the ground. This is far more consequential than a neglected car. The district will lose teachers, physically and/or mentally. The real losers will be the students of these teachers.

Staff development has gathered increased attention in both research and resource allocation across the nation. States have dramatically increased their expenditures for staff development in local districts and schools since the series of national reports issued in the mid-1980s. The National Staff Development Council has become the fastest-growing educational organization in the United States. Until 1957 only about fifty studies had been conducted on staff development in schools (Showers, Joyce, and Bennett 1987). Now more than three times that number of studies are being conducted every year.

The terms *staff development* and *in-service* are used interchangeably in most of the literature, but there is a distinction that is important to remember in applying them to supervision of instruction. Staff development is the total of learning experiences available to a professional that are both directly and indirectly related to his or her work. In-service comprises the specific learning experiences, sanctioned and supported by the school and district, directly related to the instructional goals of the school and district (Orlich 1989). In-service is a subcomponent of staff development. A summer trip to the Aztec ruins by a history teacher as part of her vacation could be a staff development activity, whereas a series of workshops on improving the school's or district's teaching of critical thinking to students would be an in-service activity. Staff development is a smorgasbord of learning experiences for professional renewal; in-service is the restricted menu offered by the schools. Both staff development and in-service activities are necessary. If there is only a smorgasbord of staff development activities, teachers may be happy and excited, but the school has little collective direction. If there is only in-service, the school may be well focused, but there is a lack of individual experimentation and expansion. Too often teachers receive little of substance of either activity (Guskey 1986). In a study of the attitudes and beliefs of 150 highly competent teachers, Karst (1987) found that "they found their avenues of growth outside of the normal in-service and professional development routines" (p. 26) and that these teachers continued to grow despite the lack of meaningful school-derived learning experiences. "It was amazing how silently resistant most of them felt about . . . [school and district] philosophy that included no serious organizational plans for dealing with their professional aspirations and development" (p. 28). For teachers who are not so resilient, self-directed, and efficacious, "These are the conditions that create teachers who quit teaching . . . become dead souls, without vision, without ideals, without hope that things will get better" (p. 28).

Since in-service education of staff should be a responsibility of those who supervise, the research and application discussed here will focus on the use of successful in-service education to improve instruction. According to a study of teachers and administrators in New York state (Tetenbaum and Mulkeen 1987, p. 11), the primary criticisms of in-service programs are that the activities are "one-shot deals" and that there is "no integration with a comprehensive plan to achieve school goals." Let's see how these criticisms can be avoided.

Research on In-Service Programs

Considerable research exists on successful in-service programs. Let's focus on some of these findings, with a particular look at the works of Berman and McLaughlin (1978), Lawrence (1974), Mohlman, Kierstead, and Gundlach (1982), and Showers, Joyce, and Bennett (1987).

The Rand Corporation was contracted by the federal government to conduct a four-year study of educational projects (Berman and McLaughlin 1978). The researchers surveyed 852 administrators and 689 teachers and conducted on-site observations of projects. Two years later they resurveyed 100 projects and revisited 18 sites where the innovative projects had continued beyond their funded period. The researchers found that successful projects had common characteristics of in-service (see McLaughlin and Marsh 1978; ERIC 1980). The findings were that:

1. Training was concrete, continual, and tied to the world of the teacher.
2. Local resource personnel provided direct follow-up assistance to teachers after in-service activities.
3. Peer observation and peer discussion provided teachers with reinforcement and encouragement.
4. The school leader participated in the in-service activities.
5. Regular project meetings were held with teachers for problem solving and adapting techniques and skills of the innovation that were not working as expected.
6. Released time was used for teachers instead of monetary payment for after-school work.
7. In-service was planned with teachers prior to and during the project.

Humphries's study on curriculum innovation of thirty-six schools in Georgia from 1980 to 1981 affirmed the findings of Berman and McLaughlin. Humphries found that collaborative planning of in-service was a particularly powerful explanatory variable related to program success (Humphries 1981).

Lawrence (1974) reviewed ninety-seven studies of in-service programs and separated effective programs from less effective ones. The findings of effective programs are similar to those of the Rand study but contain some additional information. The findings were:

1. Individualized in-service activities are more effective than large-group activities.
2. Programs that incorporate demonstrations, trials, and feedback of ideas are more effective than lecturing and reading of ideas.
3. In-service programs are more successful when teachers are active planners and help each other.

Joyce and Showers have shown that in-service programs that use presentation, demonstration, and practice as well as classroom feedback and coaching are more successful than programs that do not use feedback and coaching. In other words, teachers acquire and use in-service skills more readily when there is follow-up into their own classrooms. Stallings (1980) has shown that small-group problem-solving workshops in which six to seven teachers share and experiment show greater results than workshops with large groups.

Finally, Mohlman has compared three different in-service models (Mohlman 1982; Mohlman-Sparks 1986). The first contained presentation, demonstration, practice, and feedback; the second contained presentation, demonstration, practice, and feedback followed by peer observation; and the third contained presentation, demonstration, practice, feedback, and trainer coaching. She found that participants acquired more classroom skills with the second model of peer observation. The trainer-coaching model ranked second in skill acquisition, and the model that did not have peer observation or coaching ranked last.

The Mohlman, Kierstead, and Gundlach model (1982), used with the California Department of Education, incorporates various elements of effective in-service. It includes:

1. Small-group workshops spaced three weeks apart
2. Peer observations
3. Postobservation analysis and conferencing focused on skills introduced in workshops
4. Classroom experimentation and modification of implemented skills

The major findings can be summarized in a planning checklist (see Table 16-1). When reviewing or developing a plan for in-service, the supervisor can check to see if the established components are provided.

Individual Teacher-Based In-Service

There are many ways to determine topic priorities for in-service programs. Chapter 12 detailed the techniques of eyes and ears, official records, third-party review, written open-ended surveys, check and ranking lists, and the Delphi technique. Any of these techniques would give a planning committee an idea of in-service topics desired by participants. For example, the director of staff development might survey the teaching personnel of the school system for individual priorities and might find that *discipline* appears as the top-priority topic for both elementary and secondary teachers. This does not mean, however, that the planning committee can be assured that if they find an expert on discipline to work with staff throughout the school year, they will have a successful in-service program. When teachers check off a topic such as discipline as their top priority, *those individual checks mean different things to different people.* An eleventh-grade teacher who checks discipline thinks, "I want to learn how to handle those big, tough,

Table 16-1   Checklist for planning in-service

Participants involved in planning	_____
Planning, long-term	_____
Released time for participants	_____
Training, concrete and specific	_____
Small-group workshops	_____
Peer observations and feedback	_____
Demonstration, trial, and feedback in workshops	_____
Feedback and coaching in classrooms after workshops	_____
Regular participant meetings for problem solving, experimentation and alterations	_____
Instructional and school leaders participating in activities	_____

obnoxious students who keep making me back down." Another eleventh-grade teacher checks the discipline box thinking, "I want to learn how to conduct class discussions so students will listen more attentively to each other." A seventh-grade teacher checks the discipline box thinking, "I want to encourage self-discipline and have students take on more responsibility for their homework, studying for tests, and asking for help." An in-service program on discipline that does not account for what individual teachers mean will be a hit-or-miss affair. The content of a general session on discipline will, by chance, fit the needs of some and miss those of others. A consultant who is an expert on teaching assertive behavior will be of real benefit to the eleventh-grade teacher who is being intimidated by students; the same consultant would be of some benefit to the eleventh-grade teacher who wants to conduct classroom discussions but of little benefit to the seventh-grade teacher who desires students to develop self-discipline. To be relevant, in-service needs to be planned not only according to prioritized topics but also according to the individual meanings ascribed to the topics.

Gene Hall and his associates at the Research and Development Center for Teacher Education have made substantial contributions to the planning of in-service programs based on individual meaning to participants (Hall and Hord 1987). They found that teachers have different levels of interest, commitment, and needs when it comes to instructional changes. As in our example on discipline, they found that an innovation such as individualized instruction, mastery learning, or team teaching has different meanings to individuals and that teachers are concerned with different aspects of the proposed topics.

How does one find out what a teacher means by his or her priority for in-service? As Hall and associates found, the best way to find out is simply to ask. If discipline emerges as a school system's number-one priority for in-service, a follow-up form might be sent to teachers. A simple open-ended form has been developed by Newlove and Hall (1976):

WHEN YOU THINK ABOUT DISCIPLINE, WHAT ARE YOU CONCERNED ABOUT? Do not say what you think others are concerned about, but only what concerns you *now*. Please write in complete sentences, and please be frank.

From reading the responses, the in-service planning committee can group the concerns into different categories. Some may be concerned with assertiveness, some with leading discussion groups, some with giving students more self-responsibility, and some with schoolwide rules. Common concerns could be handled through large-group instruction; more individualized concerns could be handled by various choices of small-group workshops. An additional way of using concerns as a guide to planning in-service is for a school or school system to propose a program innovation. Hall, Wallace, and Dossett (1973) found that teacher concerns about a particular program innovation could be grouped into stages that would provide information about the focus of in-service. These stages of concern are found in Figure 16-1.

If a school system or individual school had decided to implement a new program such as mastery learning in mathematics, the concern survey could be administered to find whether staff were largely in the awareness, informational, personal, management, consequence, collaboration, or refocusing stage. Hall, Loucks, Rutherford, and Newlove (1975) have proposed matching stages of concerns with level of utilization to decide on the focus of in-service. Teachers with concerns at the awareness, information, or personal stage, and whose current level of utilization of an innovation is low, should have in-service that focuses on orienting, providing information, discussing the rationale for the innovation, and demonstrating the personal benefits of the change. Teachers with management and consequence concerns, who also have begun to use the innovations in their classrooms, should have in-service that focuses on the mechanics, routine, and refinement of the skills through workshop practice and classroom application. Those who have collaboration or refocusing concerns as well as proficiency in utilizing the innovation should have in-service based on integration of individual skills with those of other colleagues and should be encouraged to reevaluate and modify the innovation.

The work of Hall and his associates has added individual concern and utilization of innovations as factors to be considered when planning in-service. The knowledge that teachers want help in

Figure 16-1 Stages of concern about the innovation

---

0 AWARENESS: Little concern about or involvement with the innovation is indicated.

1 INFORMATIONAL: A general awareness of the innovation and interest in learning more detail about it is indicated. The person seems to be unworried about himself/herself in relation to the innovation. She/he is interested in substantive aspects of the innovation in a selfless manner such as general characteristics, effects, and requirements for use.

2 PERSONAL: Individual is uncertain about the demands of the innovation, his/her inadequacy to meet those demands, and his/her role with the innovation. This includes analysis of his/her role in relation to the reward structure of the organization, decision making and consideration of potential conflicts with existing structures or personal commitment. Financial or status implications of the program for self and colleagues may also be reflected.

3 MANAGEMENT: Attention is focused on the processes and tasks of using innovation and the best use of information and resources. Issues related to efficiency, organizing, managing, scheduling, and time demands are utmost.

4 CONSEQUENCE: Attention focuses on impact of the innovation on students in his/her immediate sphere of influence. The focus is on relevance of the innovation for students; evaluation of student outcomes, including performance and competencies; and changes needed to increase student outcomes.

5 COLLABORATION: The focus is on coordination and cooperation with others regarding use of the innovation.

6 REFOCUSING: The focus is on exploration of more universal benefits from the innovation, including the possibility of major changes or replacement with a more powerful alternative. Individual has definite ideas about alternatives to the proposed or existing form of the innovation.

Source: Reprinted from Richard M. Bents and Kenneth R. Howey, "Staff Development—A Change in the Individual." In *Staff Development/Organization Development: ASCD 1981 Yearbook,* © 1981. Reprinted by permission of the Association for Supervision and Curriculum Development, Alexandria, Va. Original concept from G.E. Hall, R.C. Wallace, Jr., and W.A. Dossett, *A Developmental Conceptualization of the Adoption Process within Educational Institutions,* © 1973. Adapted by permission of the Research and Development Center for Teacher Education, University of Texas, Austin.

discipline (or any other topic or program) is simply not enough information for planning effective programs. As will soon become clear, other information about teachers can also be used for planning in-service.

Conceptual and Psychological States

McKibbin and Joyce refer to David Hunt's principle of "optimal mismatch." Training environments should be oriented just above the level at which someone functions most comfortably. If the optimal mismatch is achieved, the teacher can function adequately but is pulled toward greater development (McKibbin and Joyce 1980, p. 254). Increasingly, in-service programs are planned to incorporate optimal mismatch of activities with conceptual and psychological levels of teachers (Thies-Sprinthall 1981; Oja 1981; McCarthy 1982; Wilsey and Killion 1982).

Chapter 4 discussed how conceptual thinking of individuals moves from concrete and restrictive to abstract and multiperspective. Individuals with particular thought structures are able to process and respond to certain modes of training. For example, a concrete thinker is better able to respond to demonstrations of specific, isolated skills; an abstract thinker is better able to respond to discussion and making independent decisions on how to apply new skills. Let's reiterate the levels of abstract thinking discussed in Chapter 4 (see Table 16-2).

Putting teacher abstraction aside momentarily, let's think of Hall's work on major stages of concern. The major stages of teacher concerns are *orientation* concerns ("What is this skill, project, or

Table 16-2   Levels of abstract thinking

Low	Moderate	High
Confusion about situation	Can define situation by focusing on one dimension	Can define situation by drawing on relationships between several sources of information
Doesn't know what can be done	Can think of several responses	Can relate the information to changes in classroom practice
Asks to be shown	Has difficulty in thinking of consequences of changing the situation	Can generate many alternative responses
Have habitual responses to varying situations		Can evaluate the consequences of each response and choose the one most likely to succeed

topic? What will it do for me?"); *integrating* concerns ("How can I make this skill better in my classroom? How can I rearrange my instruction to make this skill, project or topic more effective?"); and *refinement* concerns ("How can I share and work with others to make this practice part of our team?").

The amount of emphasis to place on particular activities in an in-service program can be shown by displaying a graph with teacher concerns on the vertical line and teacher abstraction on the horizontal line (see Figure 16-2).

Teachers who have a low level of abstraction and whose concerns are with orientation would benefit from in-service training that demonstrates the benefits of the new practice, skill, or program. Since they are hesitant, unaware, and inexperienced in applying the necessary skills, in-service with such individuals or groups must focus on giving information and providing specific demonstration and practice. Finally, the workshops should focus on teachers' understanding of the personal advantages of the proposed changes. It would be foolish to move in-service into the integration phase until teachers have the willingness, confidence, and ability to implement the new skills.

Teachers at moderate levels of abstraction and concerns with integration would benefit from in-service that focuses on classroom practice with several cycles of observation, feedback, and coaching given by peers and supervisors. Obviously, the beginning activities of explanation and demonstrations are necessary in any in-service program, but the major focus for this group should be the application of skills into their classroom settings.

The third group of teachers displayed on the graph are those with high levels of abstraction and refinement concerns. In-service for such persons should be focused on experimentation, modification, brainstorming, and group problem solving to improve on skills and practices already implemented. Since these teachers are already well informed and able to apply the new skills, the first two in-service phases, demonstration and application, can be dismissed quickly.

The Experience Impact of In-Service Activities

As we acquire information on faculty members' varying thinking, needs, and utilization of new practices, and as we match those individual characteristics with a particular focus for in-service programs, we also need to think about the order of activities most suitable for a particular focus. Ben Harris (1980) has listed the

Figure 16-2 Level of abstraction and concern as focus for in-service

	Abstraction		
	Low	Moderate	High
Orientation	*Demonstration of skill* ⁘ INFORMATION EXPLANATION, *DEMONSTRATION* AND WORKSHOP PRACTICE— SHOW PERSONAL BENEFITS	*Demonstration of skills* Information explanation, *Demonstration* and workshop practice— show personal benefits	*Demonstration of skills* Information explanation, *Demonstration* and workshop practice— show personal benefits
Integration	Classroom practice and observation, Direct assistance and peer supervision Application of skills	CLASSROOM PRACTICE ⁘ AND OBSERVATION, DIRECT ASSISTANCE AND PEER SUPERVISION APPLICATION OF SKILLS	Classroom practice and observation Direct assistance and peer supervision Application of skills
Refinement	*Improving skills* modification of classroom practice through teams. Brainstorm and group problem solving	*Improving skills* modification of classroom practice through teams. Brainstorm and group problem solving	*IMPROVING SKILLS* ⁘ MODIFICATION OF CLASSROOM PRACTICE THROUGH TEAMS, BRAINSTORM AND GROUP PROBLEM SOLVING
Concern			

⁘ = emphasis for inservice

array of in-service activities with a description of each activity according to sensory involvement, group size, experience, and type of objective. The supervisor and in-service committee can consider the chart shown in Table 16-3 in choosing the order of various activities. Harris defines sensory involvement, group size, and objective as follows:

> Sensory involvement refers to the physiological senses utilized by the participant. Only those clearly used in the activity are included. Each of the senses is listed in order of importance for learning. For instance, "(19) Panel Presenting—Audio, Visual" indicates listening is most important, while visual involvement with the several panelists is less important for participant learning.
>
> Group size indicates the group that probably represents optimum use of the activity. For many activities, both larger and small groups are feasible, but effectiveness may be sacrificed or special arrangements may be required.
>
> Type of objective refers to the outcomes that are most probably and clearly possible under normal conditions of use of the activity. Other objectives are always potentially possible, of course. For instance, a lecture could be so dramatically presented as to have affective outcomes. Testing could be employed under special circumstances to produce affective outcomes. The interview could relate to problem solving in ways that model and hence produce problem-solving skills [Harris 1980, pp. 77, 81]

Experience impact is the degree to which the individual participant will be totally involved on each dimension of senses, interactions, experience control, focus, activeness, originality, and reality. The experience impact score was derived by totaling the scores on each dimension (1 = low, 3 = high) for each dimension of the activity. The total score is an estimate of the impact on the individual. Although Harris's experience impact scale is theoretically derived and not empirically tested, it has much common-sense appeal when deciding on activities.

Let's look at how we can use this experience impact of activity for planning in-service with three hypothetical situations involving various groups of teachers concerned with discipline.

Situation 1

Group 1 consists mostly of teachers who readily use corporal punishment for most student infractions. They are unaware of and reluctant to use other approaches to discipline. Their concern is with how to get students to "shape up." Behavior problems are

Table 16-3 Basic activities for in-service education session design

Activity	Sensory Involvement	Group Size	Experience Impact	Type of Objective
1. Analyzing and calculating	Visual, kinesthetic	Ind.	16	Cognitive
2. Brainstorming	Audio, visual, oral	Med.	13	Cognitive
3. Buzz session	Audio, oral	Sml.	14	Cognitive, affective
4. Demonstrating	Visual, audio	Med.	12	Cognitive
5. Discussing, leaderless	Audio, oral, visual	Sml.	10	Cognitive
6. Discussing, leader-facilitated	Audio, oral, visual	Ind.	11	Cognitive, affective
7. Film, television, filmstrip viewing	Visual, audio	Med.	10	Cognitive affective
8. Firsthand experience	Audio, oral, visual, kinesthetic	Ind.	21	Skill, cognitive, affective
9. Group therapy	Audio, oral, visual	Sml.	16	Affective
10. Guided practice	Kinesthetic, visual, audio	Ind.	19	Skill, cognitive
11. Interviewing, informative	Audio, oral	Ind.	9	Cognitive
12. Interviewing, problem-solving	Audio, visual, oral, kinesthetic	Ind.	15	Cognitive
13. Interviewing, therapeutic	Audio, oral, visual	Ind.	17	Affective
14. Lecturing	Audio	Lrg.	7	Cognitive
15. Material, equipment viewing	Visual, kinesthetic	Med.	12	Cognitive
16. Meditating	Kinesthetic	Ind.	12	Affective, cognitive
17. Microteaching	Audio, visual, oral	Sml.	18	Skill, affective
18. Observing systematically in classroom	Visual, audio	Sml.	13	Cognitive, affective
19. Panel presenting	Audio, visual	Lrg.	8	Cognitive
20. Reading	Visual	Ind.	14	Cognitive, affective
21. Role playing, spontaneous	Audio, visual, oral	Sml.	16	Affective
22. Role playing, structured	Audio, visual, oral	Sml.	18	Cognitive, skill
23. Social interaction	Audio, visual, oral	Sml.-Med.	13	Affective, cognitive
24. Tape, radio, record listening	Audio	Lrg.	7	Cognitive, affective
25. Testing	Audio, kinesthetic	Med.	16	Cognitive
26. Videotaping or photographing	Visual, kinesthetic	Ind.	16	Cognitive
27. Visualizing	Visual	Lrg.	9	Cognitive
28. Writing or drawing	Visual, kinesthetic	Ind.	12	Cognitive

Source: B.M. Harris, *Improving Staff Performance through In-Service Education.* Reprinted by permission of Allyn and Bacon. Adapted from Ben M. Harris, *Supervisory Behavior in Education*, 2nd Ed., © 1975, p. 73. Adapted by permission of Prentice-Hall, Inc., Englewood Cliffs, N.J.

viewed as student problems, not problems for which the teacher might share responsibility.

Assessment of Situation 1. We can identify this group as in the *orientation stage* of concern with a *low or concrete level of abstraction*. They appear to need in-service that will focus both on demonstration of new approaches and on discussion of the personal benefits of using new approaches.

Selection of Activities. The criteria for choosing activities are that they should provide specific, demonstrated skills but be nonthreatening and of low experience impact.

Planners of in-service consider the list of experience impact activities (Table 16-3). They might choose to begin with these five activities:

1. *Panel presenting.* A group of representative teachers will discuss their current difficulties with discipline, what they have tried, and what they would like to do in the future. This is a low-impact, cognitive, large-group activity that involves the visual and audio senses.

2. *Discussing, leader-facilitated.* The next activity will have small groups of teachers discuss their own attitudes, problems, and thinking about new approaches to discipline. This small-group activity is of modest experience impact; involves audio, visual, and oral senses; and will provide a chance for teachers to assess their own beliefs.

3. *Lecturing.* An expert on discipline will present discipline approaches that have been found to be efficient in reducing teacher time for handling troublesome students. This low-experience, audio, cognitive, and large-group activity provides a concrete understanding for the teachers of the benefits and use of specific skills.

4. *Demonstration.* An activity in which an expert shows the teachers how to use the skills explained in the previous lecture. The expert might actually work with a group of students in front of the teachers, or show a videotape of such work, or use teachers to play the roles of students. This activity is of low experience impact, involves the visual and auditory senses, is a cognitive activity, and can be done with a medium-sized group.

5. *Role-playing, structured.* Teachers will now be asked to try out the demonstrated skills in a nonthreatening, gamelike situation. Teachers are assigned roles and asked to use the new skills. This activity uses all the senses, helps a teacher gain confidence in being able to use the practiced skills later in a real classroom

setting, is best done in small groups, and provides for cognitive learning.

Situation 2

Group 2 comprises mostly teachers who have been dissatisfied with their current classroom discipline practices and have been attempting in a random fashion to do things differently. They read articles on discipline in popular teacher magazines and are aware of some of the new practices. They are experiencing difficulties in selecting and integrating new practices (a time-out area, new classroom rules, a reinforcement system) into their instruction. Many of the new practices have been started haltingly but stopped when unforeseen problems arose. This is indicative of the integration stage. The teachers want to improve discipline, are willing to continue to work on improvement, but desire help in organizing and streamlining their actions.

Assessment of Situation 2.   We can identify this group as being concerned with management and consequences, with a willing attitude toward new practices. Yet their level of abstraction about such practices is moderate. They can define their discipline problems, have a sense of changes that might be made, but are uncertain about making these changes on their own.

Selection of Activities.   Activities should provide classroom practice, direct observation, coaching by an expert, peer observation, and peer supervision. The focus of in-service would be on applying skills in the ongoing classroom. The experience impact should be relatively high, using all senses, and should involve each teacher with practice in his or her own classroom. The sequence of activities might be as follows:

1. *Demonstrating.* This relatively low experience impact activity, conducted by an expert or by teachers themselves, serves as a review of the various discipline practices that might be used. Discipline practices that have been used by teachers in the group could be demonstrated to the entire group. Thus the in-service begins on a cognitive, informational basis.

2. *Role playing.* This higher-impact activity will consist of individual teachers selecting one or two of the previously demonstrated skills and practicing those skills in a workshop setting. An example might be a role-playing triad. One teacher might be a disruptive student in class, a second teacher would practice a skill

of dealing with the disruptive student, and a third teacher would be an observer giving feedback to the teacher after the scenario was concluded. The actors would then switch roles until each teacher had a chance to practice and receive feedback.

3. *First-hand experience.* The teachers will then try out the new skill over a period of time in their classrooms and keep a report of their progress. This real experience then serves as the basis for future guided practice and observation.

4. *Guided practice.* This activity will incorporate the use of another person (perhaps a supervisor) in reviewing the teachers' first-hand progress with the skill and reviewing what the teacher will attempt to practice during a short classroom observation. The teacher will demonstrate the skill prior to the session, and the supervisor will suggest corrections. The teacher will then demonstrate the same skills during the classroom observation. This activity is of high impact, involves all the senses, and is real.

5. *Discussion, leader-facilitated.* The teachers will step away from the classroom with an activity that provides a chance to discuss in small groups the future work needed to consolidate their new practices into the ongoing classroom routine. They might explain their needs, receive suggestions from other teachers, and arrange to observe each other. The activity leader helps each individual teacher to organize classroom practice and arranges for peer classroom visits.

6. *Systematic observation in classroom.* This technical, moderate-impact activity will prepare teachers to observe each other. They will learn how to focus on the specific classroom practices they have learned as a result of in-service. They will be given observation forms and use these forms on trial tapes. This activity is of moderate experience impact, is both cognitive and affective in nature, and is best done in small groups.

7. *Guided practice.* This highly involving activity will repeat itself. This time teachers will guide and observe each other's practice rather than having the formal supervisor do so. Teachers will have the opportunity to learn how others are using the in-service skills and be able to provide feedback to each other. This activity is of high experience impact, involving all the senses.

At this point, implementation of new practice should be well established, and a new focus for in-service will emerge.

Situation 3

Group 3 consists of teachers who are highly proficient with respect to discipline. They are confident in their ability to handle classroom disruption but believe that discipline could be even more productive if teachers used complementary discipline approaches from classroom to classroom. They realize that from time to time even the best teacher will confront a situation with an individual student or small group of students that will strain his or her tolerance. They are concerned with ways to help each other when stressful discipline situations occur, and they are concerned with adopting mutual practices to improve discipline throughout the school.

Assessment of Situation 3.   This is a group of teachers with refinement concerns: collaboration and refocusing. They view discipline in highly abstract ways by considering multiple options for dealing with disruptive students. They have a history of being decisive and thorough in implementing new procedures.

Selection of Activities.   The activities chosen should be ones that help teachers reflect on current individual practice and think about ways to complement each other. The first activities might be cognitive, collaborative, and of low experience impact. The next phase might be implementation activities, which are of high experience impact. Implementation might be followed by collaborative activities to revise and refine team practices. Let's follow a sample sequence of activities on discipline that should build individual discipline skills into consistent team skills.

1. *Analyzing and calculating.* Teachers will individually express how teaming efforts could help their own classrooms. Teachers will fill out a form and then read what they have written to the entire group. This activity, of moderate experience impact, allows for each person's thoughts to be considered by the entire group before they discuss the merits and drawbacks of ideas.

2. *Discussion, leaderless.* Teachers will work in small groups to discuss common ways to support each other in the area of discipline. They might be grouped according to grade level, department, or adjoining classrooms. Some solutions a small group could decide on might include a system of signals to call on other teachers to leave their classrooms to help when a particular teacher finds himself or herself facing an emergency, or a reinforcement system for certain students that would be consistent from classroom to classroom. This cognitive, low-impact activity serves as preparation for the implementation phase.

3. *Role-playing, structured.* The team will practice among themselves the new practices to be used. For example, a consistent reinforcement system might be practiced by having teachers role play,

responding to different disruptive behaviors and then determining whether teachers have applied consistent rewards and sanctions. This activity is close to reality. It is of higher experience impact than the previous two activities and is basically cognitive.

4. *First-hand experience.* This activity will usher in the experimentation phase, and teachers will keep notes on the progress of the plan. They are now individually responsible for their own parts in the team plan. The activity is of the highest experience impact, involving all senses, with both cognitive and affective involvement.

5. *Buzz session.* The individuals will return to an activity that enables them to reflect on the first-hand experience and discuss their progress reports. They reveal happenings, actions, and feelings about the plan. This low-impact activity allows teachers to be empathetic and reflective about each other's progress and involvement. This session is a time for generating feelings and thoughts without judging individual progress.

6. *Discussion, leaderless.* This activity kicks off the cycle of refining and changing team practices. Team members have learned from the first-hand experience and have shared in the buzz session what they perceive to be happening. In this activity, they agree as a team on changes to be made before going on to the next phase of role playing and first-hand experience.

Sequence of Activities and Variations in Plans

The sequencing of in-service activities appropriate to groups of teachers has been described as one way of selecting activities. Other activities could have been chosen according to teachers' needs. In-service will have a greater chance of positive reception and will be more likely to promote enduring teacher change if teachers' individual and group characteristics are considered. As a rule of thumb, experience impact of activities should proceed from low to high. For teachers with concerns of orientation and personal benefits, activities should be of relatively low experience impact. Teachers cannot be expected to implement new skills without having a chance to understand and accept the benefits of such skills. Teachers will not be committed to change until they themselves see the need for change. For teachers concerned with management and consequences of new skills in the classroom (integration concerns), activities should move from moderate to high experience impact. These teachers want practical applications, lectures and discussions. Finally, teachers who have refinement concerns—working as teams with others beyond their own classroom walls—desire in-service programs on collaborative planning; implementation activities should be of high experience impact.

These explanations have depicted groups of teachers as largely homogeneous. In the three situations the teachers were of similar levels of concern and abstraction. Teacher concern and degree of abstraction are not always closely related, however. For example, a teacher could have a low-level, orientation concern about an in-service topic but might be a highly abstract thinker. He or she might be able to process new information quickly and be ready for immediate application of new practices. Therefore in-service that is planned only according to teacher concerns and not in relation to degree of abstraction could run into trouble, causing participants impatience and boredom. Pacing of activities is therefore an important consideration. For teachers of moderate and high levels of abstract thinking, quick pacing of activities is needed. For teachers of low abstract ability, slower, more repetitive activities are more appropriate.

Most school faculties, departments, and grade levels are not composed of teachers with identical stages of concern and/or abstraction. A more realistic solution would be to develop an in-service plan that meets the needs of the majority of teachers and provides individual options for those with different needs. In-service aimed at promoting discussion about instructional matters among knowledgeable professionals can help achieve a school-wide commitment to "a cause beyond oneself," which is a key characteristic of successful schools.

Cautions on In-Service Research

Showers, Joyce, and Bennett (1987), in a meta-analysis of nearly 200 research studies, cautioned that most studies of in-service have dealt with relatively simple teaching skills and behaviors and have not attended to the cognitive aspects of teaching. It is simpler to train people to learn a behavioral skill than to educate people in the more intellectually demanding process of deciding whether and when to use that skill. It is the latter domain, thinking about what to do, that is more important to successful teaching; there is a need for more studies on programs that equip teachers to be better decision makers.

A teacher does not need to believe positively in a particular instructional practice in order to learn to use it. However, once mastery of a skill is at hand, its further use is conditioned by judgment of importance and cost by the teacher in achieving his or her learning goals for students. The development of increased cognitive competence needs to be studied. To hazard a guess, critical components of self-analysis, collegial and open-ended coaching, and reflective group discussion will probably be found to be more important than the already established components of in-service needed to learn behavioral skills.

A further caution is that an in-service session does not always need to have a pragmatic purpose. In-service need not aim at all times to increase useful teaching knowledge and skills. There is nothing wrong with an inspirational speech, a humorous workshop, or an aerobic session! There are times when an in-service that is not solely instruction-driven might produce benefits that would be just as valuable to the ultimate recipients—students. For example, I once conducted a two-day workshop for teachers and administrators in western Canada. Afterward, I inquired of the staff development director who was driving me to the airport, "What do you think the participants learned? What will they use?" She replied, "Oh, I'm sure they learned something, but that's really not important. What's important is that everyone had a wonderful time during the two-day retreat!" My serious belief in my self importance as a consultant was shaken. "What do you mean, it's not important?" I groaned. "I came 1,500 miles to teach applications to school improvement!" Her response was serene. "You don't understand. Every year, we have this two-day event. We hold it in the woods, where everyone can let their hair down. We find a consultant who is entertaining, who tells good jokes, and perhaps has a message or two for us to think about. The food is great, the evening skits are hilarious, and the party goes on until late. The real purpose of staff development for these days is to show teachers and administrators in this district that they are the most important people in the world! What they learn to use in the schools is not as important as simply having a good time." I listened to her, remembered an article about the importance of symbolic functions in schools, and smiled (slowly, sheepishly, and not very profoundly).

The Nuts and Bolts

This chapter has covered a great deal of information for planning in-service, but the best planning is useless if the supervisor forgets the nuts and bolts of in-service. What value is an excellent speaker who lectures in a room where the acoustics garble every word? What good is a fast-paced microteaching demonstration if it conflicts with other teacher meetings so that few can attend? What good is an exciting role-playing activity whose participants have had no chance to eat, unwind, or use the restroom during the previous two hours? If one is going to the trouble to plan in-service, then one should go the extra step to ensure an environment that enables participants to be responsive and comfortable. Here are six important considerations:

1. *Prepare speakers by telling them exactly what they are expected to do.* If a speaker is invited to conduct an activity, make sure he or she understands the assignment. Speakers will do whatever they normally do unless someone tells them otherwise. Most speakers have their own topics, their own rehearsed presentations, and their own formats. If a speaker is expected to demonstrate a particular skill (for example, asking higher-order questions) or to include role playing (scripts of classroom discussions), *tell him or her so.* Speaker and participants are both in an embarrassing situation when the speaker, through no fault of either party, is not doing what the participants have been led to expect.

2. *Check the facility beforehand for seating arrangements, media, and acoustics.* Make sure the facility is appropriate to the activity. For example, small-group discussions in an auditorium give teachers stiff necks and a stiffer attitude toward the next in-service. See that all equipment is operating correctly. Check microphones, cassettes, and overheads. Move around the room to see if displays on screen or walls can be viewed clearly by everyone. Have at hand spare bulbs and replacement equipment in case of an equipment failure.

3. *Provide refreshments and transition time at the beginning.* Tell participants where the restrooms are. Provide drinks and snacks. Informally greet the participants at the door and tell them when the session will begin. When formally beginning, inform participants when other breaks are scheduled.

4. *Check the comfort of the room.* Beforehand, check whether the room will maintain a comfortable temperature. Find out if the heating or cooling system is turned off at the time of the meeting and, if so, arrange to have the system operating. Estimate the temperature of the room when it is full. A room that feels comfortable when only a few people are present can become oppressively hot when full to capacity.

5. *Have materials run off and a plan for easy dissemination to participants.* Prior to the session, check with the leader of the activity to make sure all desired materials will be prepared. Also before the session, figure out a distribution system for materials.

Often it is sufficient to place a table next to the entrance with collected materials and make one person responsible for telling entrants to pick up the materials.

6. *Have evaluation forms for participants to fill out after the session.* Asking participants to evaluate the session allows existing problems to be corrected before the next session. A simple form to be filled out anonymously by participants can be seen in Figure 16-3.

Teachers as Objects or Agents in Staff Development

A superintendent remarked that he had been at a national conference and attended a presentation on "elements of effective instruction." He decided that this was exactly what the teachers needed. As a result, the district was off and running with a three-year commitment to training all principals and teachers in "elements." Highly paid national consultants were brought in; personnel were identified for advanced training and traveled during the summer to faraway sites; and virtually all contracted in-service time and school supervision was devoted to "elements." It was not long before a new evaluation instrument was established to check that every teacher was using the training in effective instruction in the same prescribed manner. Over the three years, expenditures by the school district exceeded $300,000, not including the cost of human time. What have been the results? No appreciable gain in student achievement, considerable grumbling by a core of "malcontent" teachers, enthusiasm by the chosen core of teachers who received special training and compensation, and a firm claim by the superintendent that "we now have focused, long-term staff development on scientifically derived principles, and our teaching is more effective." In the past few years education has been bombarded by packaged programs on "effective teaching," "effective schools," "effective supervision," and "effective discipline." All claim to be derived from research and to have documented success, and all use the components and sequence of transfer of training that have been sorely lacking in traditional in-service programs. The programs provide for explanation, demonstration, modeling, role playing, practice, and coaching. They are not one-shot; they are focused; and they are classroom based. The only problem is that the people who think these programs are worth the cost and effort are the same people who have a personal investment and commitment to use them (see Garman and Hazley 1988; DiBernardo and Stiles 1988). If the programs are not as successful as predicted, the de-

Figure 16-3 In-service evaluation

We would like your feedback to plan future in-service sessions. Please circle the number closest to your feelings and provide comments in the space provided on the form. If you need more space, feel free to use the back of the sheet. As you leave, please drop this form in the box on the back table.

In-Service Topic _____

Date _____

	Poor	Satisfactory	Good	Excellent
1. The session today was	1	2	3	4

Comments _____

_____

_____

2. The organization of the session was	1	2	3	4

Comments _____

_____

_____

3. The meeting room was	1	2	3	4

Comments _____

_____

_____

4. The materials were	1	2	3	4

Comments _____

_____

_____

Suggestions for future meetings: _____

_____

_____

cision makers do not blame the program but rather the lack of enough training to ensure that teachers "do it right" (Lambert 1988). Schools, districts, and states that have committed themselves to such programs come to the ludicrous conclusion that they need more training, more money, and greater enforcement to see that all teachers will finally learn to teach as prescribed more frequently and correctly. This is an incredible rationalization by policy makers that their initial decision was right, regardless of the effect that the program is having on teachers. This rationale underscores the point that was made about adult development and motivation in the first part of the book. Motivation is premised on two dimensions: One is choice, and the other is responsibility to make knowledgeable decisions about one's work. That's why the superintendent wants so badly to see this program in "effective elements" work. The superintendent had the choice and took responsibility for making the decision. The selected core of teachers also want to see this program work, because they were given choice and responsibility in making decisions on how to train others. Yet most teachers and principals were not given any choice or responsibility in these decisions about the needs of their students and themselves. Instead, they were treated as objects rather than as agents of staff development, without due regard for their capacity to make wise decisions in the interest of students and teaching. Without choice or responsibility to make knowledgeable decisions about their work, they have little motivation or commitment to somebody else's program.

To use knowledge about sequencing in-service for transfer of training, without an awareness of the need truly to involve teachers as decision makers in staff development, will leave us where we currently are. We will be more sophisticated in teaching teachers how to follow someone else's program, but we will find little commitment on the part of teachers or little stimulation to increase teachers' own collective and critical capacities to make lasting changes.

Summary

For staff development to be meaningful to teachers and to lead to teacher renewal and instructional improvement, it must operate at two levels. First, teachers as individuals should have a smorgasbord of learning opportunities to support their pursuit of their own personal and professional career goals. Second, teachers as part of a school and district organization should together define, learn, and implement skills, knowledge, and programs that achieve common goals of the organization. Staff development encompasses both levels of individual and collective operation, while in-service programs focus on the collective actions of a school and district.

In-service must be geared to the stages of teachers' concerns and thoughts. Research on successful in-service programs has shown an emphasis on involvement, long-term planning, problem-solving meetings, released time, concrete training, small-group workshops, peer feedback, demonstration and trials, coaching, and leader participation in activities. Consideration for individual and group characteristics can help make in-service more relevant to the participants. Research on stages of concern has shown that teachers differ according to awareness, informational, personal, management, consequence, collaboration, and refocusing needs. Teachers also vary from concrete to abstract in their thinking about particular in-service topics. The experience impact of in-service activities also can be used to choose activities with particular groups. Nuts-and-bolts considerations—informing speakers, checking facilities, and providing refreshments, materials, and evaluation—can increase the comfort and attentiveness of teachers. It's time to change the perception that in-service education is a waste of teachers' time to the perception of in-service as time well spent. Viewing teachers as the agents rather than the objects of staff development will be the impetus for such change.

EXERCISES

Academic

1. Write a paper defining and discussing the concept of *the coaching of teaching*. Include descriptions of successful in-service coaching techniques found in the professional literature.

2. A small group of senior high teachers has requested an in-service program on making better use of open-ended questions during class discussions. The teachers are at a moderate level of abstraction, and their concern is at the integration stage. Outline a plan for an in-service program for these teachers on the requested topic.

3. A small group of elementary teachers from the same school has requested an in-service program on strategies for more effective team teaching. All these teachers have had considerable expe-

rience in team teaching, but they wish to improve their skills in this area. The teachers are at a high level of abstraction, and their concern is at the refinement stage. Outline a plan for an in-service program on team teaching for these teachers.

4. A general needs assesssment, administered districtwide, has revealed that the number-one perceived need of teachers in the district is for increased communication skills. Prepare a plan for assessing *specific* needs of various groups of teachers within this general topic, and include teachers in planning an in-service program that will meet their group and individual needs.

5. Write a paper summarizing three recent research studies on in-service education not discussed in this chapter. Include the purpose, participants, methodology, results, and conclusions of each study. Analyze the findings in terms of whether they are congruent with research findings cited in this chapter.

Field

1. Evaluate the needs assessment process a school district employs in planning in-service programs. As part of your evaluation, interview teachers to determine whether decisions on in-service activities reflect actual teacher needs. Include recommendations for improvement of the needs assessment process in your report.

2. Attend an in-service session for teachers. Evaluate the in-service session in terms of (a) the extent to which the session reflects the major research findings on effective in-service programs, (b) whether varying levels of abstraction and stages of concern are taken into consideration, (c) organization, (d) facilities, and (e) materials. Note informal reactions of teachers attending the session. Include suggestions for improving future in-service sessions.

3. Interview five teachers concerning a program innovation that is being proposed or introduced in their school. On the basis of the interviews, attempt to classify each teacher according to his or her stage of concern about the innovation.

4. Interview an individual who has considerable experience at planning in-service sessions on the practical aspects of preparing for such sessions. Ask him or her to relate past experiences that illustrate potential problems to avoid, eventualities to consider, and areas in which special preparation is necessary. Prepare a report on your interview.

5. Interview the individual in charge of staff development on a

school system's long-range staff development program. (Be sure the school system *has* a long-range staff development program before arranging the interview!) Prepare a report describing and evaluating the program.

Developmental

1. As you attend in-service activities over a period of time, observe the experience impact of different activities on various groups of teachers (the effects of high- and low-impact activities on teachers of various levels of abstraction and concern).
2. Develop a file of ideas for in-service activities. Research on successful in-service programs can serve as a planning source. Activities can be developed for individuals and groups at various stages of concern and abstraction. Experience impact can be considered when designing activities for teachers of different concern and thinking levels.
3. Volunteer to help plan and implement in-service activities in your school or school system. Try to incorporate the research on effective in-service into the plans.

REFERENCES

Berman, P., and McLaughlin, M.W. 1978. *Federal programs supporting educational change,* Vol. 8. *Implementing and sustaining innovations.* ED 159 289. Santa Monica, Calif.: Rand Corp.

DiBernardo, G., and Stiles, D. 1988. The Madeline Hunter and Lee Canter teacher improvement packages: What every school needs? *Democratic Schools 3*(2):1–9.

ERIC. 1980. ERIC Research Action Brief—Clearinghouse on Educational Management, No. 10. EA 021 256. Eugene, Ore.: University of Oregon.

Garman, N.B., and Hazley, H.M. 1988. Teachers ask: Is there life after Madeline Hunter? *Kappan 69*(9):669–672.

Guskey, T. 1986. Staff development and the process of teacher change. *Educational Research 15*(5):5–12.

Hall, G.H., and Hord, S.M. 1987. *Change in Schools: Facilitating the Process.* Albany, N.Y.: State University of New York Press.

Hall, G.E., Loucks, S.F., Rutherford, W.S., and Newlove, B.W. 1975.

Levels of use of the innovation: A framework for analyzing innovation adoption. *Journal of Teacher Education* 26(1):52–56.

Hall, G.E., Wallace, R.C., Jr., and Dossett, W.A. 1973. *A developmental conceptualization of the adoption process within educational institutions.* Austin, Tex.: Research and Development Center for Teacher Education, University of Texas.

Harris, B.M. 1975. *Supervisory behavior in education,* 2nd ed. Englewood Cliffs, N.J.: Prentice-Hall.

————. 1980. *Improving staff performance through in-service education.* Boston: Allyn and Bacon.

————. 1989. *In-service education for staff development.* Boston: Allyn and Bacon.

Humphries, J.D. 1981. Factors affecting the impact of curriculum innovations on classroom practice: Project complexity, characteristics of local leadership, and supervisory strategies. Unpublished Ed.D. dissertation, University of Georgia.

Joyce, B.R., and Showers, B. 1980. Improving in-service training: The message of research. *Educational Leadership* 37:379–385.

————. 1983. *Power in staff development through research on training.* Alexandria, Va.: Association for Supervision and Curriculum Development.

Karst, R.R. 1987. New policy implications for in-service and professional development programs for the public schools. Presentation to the annual meeting of the American Educational Research Association, Washington, D.C., April.

Lambert, L. 1988. Staff development redesigned. *Kappan* 69(9): 665–668.

Lawrence, G. 1974. *Patterns of effective in-service education: A state of the art summary of research on materials and procedures for changing teacher behaviors in in-service education.* ED 176 424. Tallahassee, Fla.: Florida State Department of Education.

McCarthy, B. 1982. Improving staff development through CBAM and 4 MatTM. *Educational Leadership* 40(1):20–25.

McKibbin, M., and Joyce, B. 1980. Psychological states and staff development. *Theory into practice* 19(4):248–255.

McLaughlin, M.W., and Marsh, D.D. 1978. Staff development and school change. *Teachers College Record* 80(1):69–94.

Mohlman, G.G. 1982. Assessing the impact of three in-service teacher training models. Paper presented at the annual meeting of the American Educational Research Association, New York.

Mohlman-Sparks, G. 1986. The effectiveness of alternative training activities in changing teaching practices. *American Educational Research Journal 23*(2):217–225.

Mohlman, G.G., Kierstead, J., and Gundlach, M. 1982. A research-based in-service model for secondary teachers. *Educational Leadership 40*(1):16–19.

Newlove, B.W., and Hall, G.E. 1976. *A manual for assessing open-ended statements of concern about an innovation.* Austin, Tex.: Research and Development Center for Teacher Education, University of Texas.

Oja, S.N. 1981. Adapting research findings in psychological education: A case study. Presentation at the annual meeting of the American Association of Colleges for Teacher Education, Detroit, February.

Orlich, D.C. 1989. *Staff development: Enhancing human potential.* Boston: Allyn and Bacon.

Rubin, L. (Ed.). 1978. *The in-service education of teachers.* Boston: Allyn and Bacon.

Showers, B., Joyce, B., and Bennett, B. 1987. Synthesis of research on staff development: A framework for future study and a state of the art analysis. *Educational Leadership 45*(7):77–87.

Speak, L., and Hirsh, S. 1988. A rationale for released-time staff development in the Richardson Independent School District. *The Developer* (March):1–4.

Stallings, J. 1980. Allocated academic learning time revisited or Beyond time on task. *Educational Researcher 9*(11):11–16.

Tetenbaum, T.J., and Mulkeen, T.A. 1987. Prelude to school improvement: Understanding perceptions of staff development. Presentation to the annual meeting of the American Educational Research Association, Washington, D.C., April.

Thies-Sprinthall, L. 1981. Promoting the conceptual and principled thinking level of the supervising teacher. Unpublished research funded by St. Cloud State University, 1978 and 1979. Reported in Educating for teacher growth: A cognitive developmental perspective. Paper presented at the annual meeting of the American Educational Research Association, Los Angeles, April.

Wilsey, C., and Killion, J. 1982. Making staff development programs work. *Educational Leadership 40*(1):36–38, 43.

Wood, F.W., and Thompson, S.R. 1980. Guidelines for better staff development. *Educational Leadership 37*(5):374–378.

Chapter 17

Curriculum Development

"Teaching is a moral activity that implies thoughts about ends, means, and their consequences" (Zeuli and Buchmann 1987). Moral activity is explicitly expressed in a school's curriculum. To be an effective school is of little matter unless the personnel within an organization first have defined what is meant by a good school—what should students learn in order to be well educated? The institutional job then becomes one of effectively achieving that definition of goodness. As Sergiovanni remarked (1987), "it's not important to do things right, unless we are doing the right things!" Curriculum is the moral deliberation on what is "right" for students to be taught.

Hirsch, in *Cultural Literacy: What Every American Needs to Know* (1987), attacks American education as abandoning the essential literature, ideas, and facts of the national culture. Bloom, in *The Closing of the American Mind* (1987), likewise indicts schools for abandoning the core programs of traditional liberal arts education. In *What Do Our 17-Year-Olds Know?* (1987), educators Ravitch and Finn (1987) write that a large proportion of high school students don't know such basic facts as in what half-century the Civil War took place. Hirsch, Bloom, Ravitch, and Finn believe it is both necessary and right to reduce the school curriculum to a focus on predetermined, essential knowledge.

Yet the National Assessment of Educational Progress (NAEP), in its report card on high school students' knowledge of literature and U.S. history, suggests that students' inadequate knowledge may be because

> The typical course relies heavily on a textbook ... students regularly are expected to memorize important information, and are tested frequently ... class time is spent listening to the teacher lecture... [Applebee, Langer, and Mullis 1987].

Indeed, what is taught and how it is taught according to the NAEP study of literature and history is no different from what Goodlad found in his national study of schooling. Goodlad (1984) found that nearly 90 percent of teaching across all subjects and grade levels is up-front teaching—lecturing, with students passively listening except for an occasional opportunity to answer questions. On one side, academic essentialists argue that the problem with curriculum is that too much stress is placed on process skills (problem solving, inquiry, and critical thinking) to the detriment of straight, old-fashioned teaching of content and basic skills. Social activists and experimentalists such as Goodlad reply that such teaching is what already exists and is to blame for inadequate student comprehension. Their argument is that there should be less facts and memorization and more active problem solving and conceptual understanding.

A study of the elementary mathematics curriculum by Porter (1987) brings out related curriculum issues of coverage and balance.

> We found that 70 to 75% of mathematics instruction was spent teaching skills, essentially how to add, subtract, multiply, and divide, and occasionally how to read a graph... [p. 7].
>
> Our findings of heavy emphasis on skill development and slight attention to concepts and applications is consistent with the United States' relatively poor standing among other nations on mathematics problem solving. In some ways the U.S. curriculum is even more out of balance than the above suggests [pp. 9–10].
>
> ... as troublesome as the lack of emphasis given to problem solving and conceptual understanding, a very large percentage of the topics taught receive only brief, perhaps cursory coverage [p. 11].

Sizer (1984) reasons that schools are too concerned with teaching all subjects superficially. Instead, schools should teach fewer subjects, topics, and skills more thoroughly—"teach less, better" rather than "teach more, quicker." Others argue that curriculum should expose students to a vast array of educational experiences. Howard Gardner, a noted cognitive psychologist, says (in Brandt 1988b) that his research on human intelligence indicates that elementary and middle schools should not be concerned with subjects; instead, curriculum should focus on long-term core projects that integrate rather than separate learning of language, mathematics, science, reading, art, and physical education.

How does one make sense of these topsy-turvy controversies about curriculum? How can so many esteemed experts have so many contradictory ideas? It comes down to a matter of educational philosophy (as discussed in Chapter 5). Curriculum experts are humans too! They possess the same ideological, philosophical, and political biases as the rest of us. They may argue more eloquently and have better support for their claims than we do, but at the bottom of their discourse are philosophical premises and assumptions about education no different from ours. Ultimately, decisions about a good school, appropriate curriculum, and needs of students should be made by those closest to students. After considering the available experts, research, readings, and articulated conflicts, people in the schools, districts, and local communities should ultimately decide what is worthy to teach. However, by default, pressure, and abdication, curriculum decisions have generally been made by those farthest from the classroom action.

Teacher-Proof Curriculum

Imagine we have just heard about a phenomenal new chemistry curriculum that has been field-tested in twenty-seven school systems throughout the United States and has resulted in a 100 percent student success rate. The curriculum has been created by some of the most distinguished chemists and educators in the country. All students in grades ten, eleven, and twelve who have been taught by the new curriculum have scored in the upper 10 percent of a nationally normed chemistry achievement test. Furthermore, their attitudes toward chemistry are far superior to those of comparable high school students who have been taught by other chemistry curricula.

To verify this success story, we travel to some of the school sites, review the curriculum materials, and look over test results. We find that it's true, and we decide that the curriculum should be used immediately in our schools. We will need to purchase the materials and hire a consultant to show teachers how to use the curriculum. We believe we will have immediate success.

The truth is that if we proceed as planned, we will probably not achieve much success with this curriculum. Teachers will use it half-heartedly and keep returning to their old lecture notes and traditional instructional activities. Within a few years most of the new materials will be lost or abandoned. Ten years from now, stacks of the new curriculum materials might be gathering dust in the school attic.

From the late 1950s to the early 1970s, the National Science Foundation allocated millions of dollars for the development of such new curricula. University scholars were hired to develop materials to improve instruction in elementary and secondary science and mathematics. The U.S. Office of Education similarly spent large sums of money to hire subject specialists to develop curricula in

English and social studies. The curricula were carefully constructed, field-tested, revised, and tested again—only to be resisted, misused, and abandoned when implemented in public schools.

Some of the best curricula developed, such as "Man: A Course of Study" (MACOS) and the Physical Science Study Committee's physics course (PSSC) showed overwhelming student success during the pilot phase, yet they are hardly used now. A series of reports on the results of twenty years of federally supported curriculum development concluded that nearly all such curricula have been bypassed by schools (see Ponder 1979; Yager and Stodghill 1979; Gibney and Karns 1979). Why is this so? Doll (1989) explains: "It seems likely that an important reason many of the massive curriculum projects . . . proved so disappointing is that they did not take into account the differing situations in which the projects were expected to take root."

One lesson to be learned by supervisors is that it makes no difference how good a curriculum is if teachers will not use it. To think of any curriculum as being teacher-proof—the label used for those federally supported curricula—was a mistake. *Teacher-proof* implies that the curriculum is so complete and detailed that it is immune to teacher practice and belief. Since then we've learned a multimillion-dollar lesson: Curricula cannot be teacher-proof as long as schools are loosely coupled organizations (Weick 1976).

A *loosely coupled* organization is one in which there is an absence of continual monitoring of the work force. A tightly coupled organization, on the other hand, is characterized by managers closely monitoring the work force. Schools are loosely coupled because teachers are surrounded by four walls; only infrequently does anyone with managerial control see what they do. Educators know among themselves (but keep the fact from the public) that *basically teachers do whatever they want to do*. Therefore, in a loosely coupled organization, unless a teacher really desires to implement a curriculum, he or she won't. No one is going to stand over a teacher six hours a day, 180 days a year to see that the curriculum is being implemented. On those rare occasions when a person in authority does stand over a teacher, the teacher can usually give the person what he or she is expecting and then return to the usual method once the authority is gone. Therefore, any notion of a curriculum being teacher-proof simply flies in the face of reality. For a curriculum to be implemented by teachers, they have to be involved in choosing, adapting, and developing it. It must serve the needs of teachers, and they must want to use it.

Sir Alex Clegg wrote disparagingly of such so-called teacher-proof materials:

I have no time whatever for any system which recruits high-powered thinkers to contour and foist a curriculum on the schools. This cannot work unless we believe that the teacher of the future is to be a low-grade technician working under someone else's instructions rather than a professional making his own diagnoses and prescribing his own treatments [cited in Tanner and Tanner 1980, p. 629].

Denver Superintendent Jesse H. Newlon knew about curriculum and loosely coupled organizations as far back as 1922, when he originated the Denver plan, which gave curriculum development and implementation to committees of teachers. Tanner and Tanner wrote of Newlon as a person of

... deep and abiding faith in the teacher as a professional. Because of this confidence and because he believed that the study of curriculum problems was the best possible kind of inservice training, Newlon put teachers at the heart of the curriculum-making process ... [Tanner and Tanner 1980, p. 341].

The eight-year study completed in 1942 confirmed Newlon's idea of the teacher at the heart of curriculum. In this historic study, thirty private and public secondary schools were selected on the basis of having a nontraditional, non-college-preparatory curriculum. Instead, the curriculum was unique to each high school and was developed by the high school faculty. The students who graduated from these thirty schools were matched with students who graduated from high schools having a traditional, college preparatory curriculum with little faculty involvement in curriculum development.

Both groups of students were followed through college. It was concluded from the study that graduates of the innovative, teacher-involved schools had higher grade point averages, received more academic honors, and were found to be more precise, systematic, objective, and intellectually curious than were those who graduated from the traditional, non-teacher-involved schools (Aiken 1942). It was clear that schools operating with teacher involvement in curriculum development provided a better education than did schools operating without such involvement.

Thirty-three years later, the Rand Corporation found that lasting and successful curriculum implementation projects were characterized by "mutual adaptation." The Rand researchers found that when teachers were involved in selecting, revising, and changing an externally prescribed curriculum, the curriculum took hold and lasted (Berman and McLaughlin 1978).

It is clear that in order for schools to be successful, teachers need to be involved in curriculum development. The issues that remain for the supervisor are: (1) In what *ways* can curriculum be developed? (2) To what *degree* should teachers be involved?

In What Ways Can Curriculum Be Developed?

Curriculum, for purposes of this book, is the *what* of instruction: what is intentionally taught to students in a district, school, or classroom; the guides, books, and materials that teachers use in teaching students. The elements of curriculum are sequence and continuity, scope, and balance (Doll 1989). *Sequence* is the ordering of learning experiences, and *continuity* is the length or duration of such experiences. *Scope* is the range of learning experiences to be offered. *Balance* is the degree and amount of topics, subjects, and learning experiences that adequately prepare students. A curriculum is developed by deciding: (1) What should students learn? (2) What is the order of content for the student to follow? (3) How is the learning to be evaluated? (See Firth and Newfield 1984; Glatthorn 1987; Brandt 1988a.)

Decisions about curriculum are influenced by priorities of state and federal governments, values of professional educators and local community, knowledge of student development, current economics, and future societal conditions. Ultimately, what goes into a curriculum is derived from a philosophical decision about the purpose of schools (see Eisner and Vallance 1974). For example, an essentialist philosophy is reflected by a curriculum that emphasizes rote learning, memorization of facts, and academic achievement. An experimentalist philosophy is reflected by a curriculum that emphasizes social activism, trial-and-error learning, and cooperation. An existentialist philosophy is reflected by a curriculum that emphasizes individual awareness, creativity, and self-exploration.

Philosophical emphasis can be detected further by the format used in writing curriculum. This section will describe behavioral-objective, webbing, conceptual-mapping, and results-only formats. Curricula that follow a behavioral-objective format are reflections of essentialism. Curricula that follow a webbing or conceptual-mapping format are reflections of experimentalism. Curricula that follow a results-only format are reflections of existentialism.

Behavioral-Objective Format

Predetermined knowledge, facts, and skills are written in curriculum guides in a linear cause-and-effect format. The curriculum developers determine what is to be learned, state the learning as a behavioral objective, specify the teaching/learning activities, and conclude with a posttest to see if the objective has been achieved. The progression is

Objective   Activity   Evaluation

Figure 17-1 is an example of a behavioral objective guide written for a fifth-grade social studies class. Curriculum developers break their unit into the most important facts or skills that cover the subject. They write behavioral objectives for each fact or skill. Each behavioral objective involves a sequence of activities and evaluation. The teacher who uses such a curriculum guide is expected to follow the sequence of activities and administer the evaluation. Recycling activities might be included in the guide for those students who do not pass the evaluation. Each behavioral-objective plan is tightly sequenced so that one objective is mastered before a student moves to the next (for example, after identifying and spelling the original thirteen American colonies, the next objective might be identifying and spelling those states that came into the Union from 1776 to 1810).

Most school curricula that have been written in the last decade follow a behavioral-objective format. It is particularly easy to use in subjects such as mathematics and physical sciences, where skills are obvious and facts are clear. (2 plus 2 is always 4, for example, but is war always justifiable?) So prevalent has been the behavioral-objective format in curriculum writing in the last few years that many educators know of no other way to write curricula. Before

Figure 17-1   Behavioral-objective format

Behavioral objective: At the end of the week, students will recall and spell the original thirteen colonies at a 100 percent level of mastery.

Activities:

1.   Lecture on thirteen colonies.

2.   Students fill in map of thirteen colonies.

3.   Students read pp. 113–118 of text and do assignments on p. 119 as homework.

4.   Call on students at random to spell the various colonies.

Evaluation: Ask students to recall the names and spell correctly each of the thirteen original colonies on a sheet of paper.

---

this current period, behavioral objectives were virtually unknown, and curriculum formatting was largely of the webbing variety.

Webbing and Conceptual Mapping

Curriculum can be written in a format that shows relationships of activities around a central theme. William Kilpatrick popularized this type of curriculum in writing about the work unit (Kilpatrick 1925). Instead of predetermining the knowledge or skills, the curriculum developer determines the major theme, related themes, and then possible student activities.

The webbing format can be conceived of in this way:

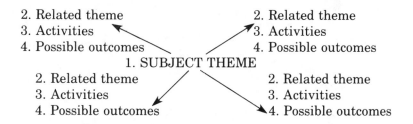

2. Related theme   2. Related theme
3. Activities   3. Activities
4. Possible outcomes   4. Possible outcomes
1. SUBJECT THEME
2. Related theme   2. Related theme
3. Activities   3. Activities
4. Possible outcomes   4. Possible outcomes

After the activities have been written, the curriculum developers write possible learning outcomes: "Students will be able to identify four major environmental issues." "Students will be able to argue and give evidence for both the pro and con sides of both issues." "Students will take a personal stance on each issue." In planning activities, developers consider multimodes of learning via reading, writing, listening, and constructing, and then integrate many fields of knowledge around a central theme. Notice how the theme of environmental issues integrates activities in sociology, mathematics, economics, history, journalism, physics, and biology. Included in the guide are the resources needed to conduct the activities. In our example, resources might include tape recorders, newspapers, books, and community volunteers.

A webbing curriculum guide would contain a blueprint of the web followed by sections for each related theme with activities, possible outcomes, and resources needed (see Figure 17-2.) Notice that the web curriculum includes possible outcomes and allows for the possibility of others. In a behavioral-objective curriculum, activities are controlled toward predetermined ends. In a webbed curriculum, activities lead to possible and unanticipated learning.

A webbed curriculum is useful in subjects that emphasize affect, attitude, and social learning, and where answers to problems are

Figure 17-2   Webbing format

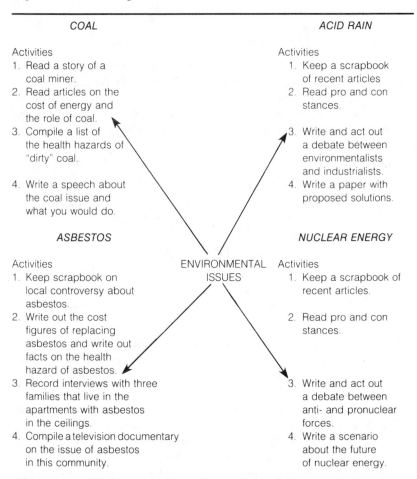

COAL	ACID RAIN
Activities 1. Read a story of a coal miner. 2. Read articles on the cost of energy and the role of coal. 3. Compile a list of the health hazards of "dirty" coal. 4. Write a speech about the coal issue and what you would do.	Activities 1. Keep a scrapbook of recent articles 2. Read pro and con stances. 3. Write and act out a debate between environmentalists and industrialists. 4. Write a paper with proposed solutions.

ENVIRONMENTAL ISSUES

ASBESTOS	NUCLEAR ENERGY
Activities 1. Keep scrapbook on local controversy about asbestos. 2. Write out the cost figures of replacing asbestos and write out facts on the health hazard of asbestos. 3. Record interviews with three families that live in the apartments with asbestos in the ceilings. 4. Compile a television documentary on the issue of asbestos in this community.	Activities 1. Keep a scrapbook of recent articles. 2. Read pro and con stances. 3. Write and act out a debate between anti- and pronuclear forces. 4. Write a scenario about the future of nuclear energy.

not clear-cut. Courses such as art, music, social science, and language are prime subjects for such an approach.

Conceptual Mapping Format

Posner and Rudnitsky (1982) have developed a curriculum format, called *conceptual mapping,* which is an interesting integration of webbing and behavioral objectives. It includes the following:

1. Rationale for the course including the overall educational goals.

2. List of intended learning outcomes for the course, categorized according to type of learning.

3. Conceptual maps depicting the relationship among the important ideas to be learned in the course.

4. Instructional plan describing a) what each unit is about, b) what learning outcomes each unit is intended to accomplish and c) what general teaching strategies could be used in each unit to accomplish the intended learning outcomes.

5. Evaluation plan describing behavioral indicators for each high-priority intended learning outcome (main effects), together with a list of some unintended, undesirable learning outcomes (side effects) to be on the lookout for [Posner and Rudnitsky 1982, p. 8].

Conceptual mapping uses both webbing and behavioral-objective curricula. It provides the teacher with specific directions for accomplishing predetermined skills, as well as general strategies for teaching concepts.

Results-Only Format

A results-only format for curriculum provides teachers with the widest latitude for using materials, activities, and methods. Such a curriculum specifies the goals and general learning about a subject, theme unit, or course. The guide might include ways to evaluate the learning. For example, a results-only guide in elementary reading might specify the following skills to be learned:

Comprehension

1. Develops powers of observation
2. Classifies by name, color, shape, size, position use
3. Anticipates endings to stories
4. Discriminates between fact and fantasy
5. Understands who, what, when, where, how, and why phrases
6. Recalls a story sequence
7. Reads to find the main ideas of a story
8. Reads to draw a conclusion
9. Compares and contrasts stories

It is then left to the teacher to determine when and how to teach these skills. The teacher is held accountable only for the results, not for the procedures used.

Bloom's Taxonomy as a Guide for Choosing Formats

Benjamin Bloom's taxonomy of learning might serve as a guide for determining the specificity and structure of curriculum formats (see Table 17-1). His lower-level learnings—(1) memory and (2) translation—are based on students recalling and demonstrating

Table 17-1   Bloom's taxonomy

Category Name	Description
1. Memory	Student recalls or recognizes information.
2. Translation	Student changes information into a different symbolic form or language.
3. Interpretation	Student discovers relationships among facts, generalizations, definitions, values, and skills.
4. Application	Student solves a life problem that requires the identification of the issue and the selection and use of appropriate generalizations and skills.
5. Analysis	Student solves a problem in the light of conscious knowledge of the parts and forms of thinking.
6. Synthesis	Student solves a problem that requires original creative thinking.
7. Evaluation	Student makes a judgment of good or bad, right or wrong, according to standards designated by students.

Source: G. Manson and A.A. Clegg, Jr., "Classroom Questions: Keys to Children's Thinking?" *Peabody Journal of Education 47*, No. 5 (March 1970): 304–305. Reprinted by permission of Peabody Journal of Education.

known answers. His intermediate levels of learning—(3) interpretation, (4) application, and (5) analysis—are based on students using logic to find sequential, verifiable knowledge. His higher levels of learning—(6) synthesis and (7) evaluation—are based on combining various knowledge, facts, skills, and logic to make unique personal judgments. Therefore, *behavioral objective* formatting might be more appropriate for lower-level learning, *webbing* and *conceptual mapping* might be more appropriate for intermediate levels of learning, and a *results-only* format might be more appropriate for higher levels of learning. A use of all formats in the same curriculum would provide balance to all levels of learning.

Curriculum Format as Reflective of Choice Given to Teachers

Previously noted was the rough approximation of curriculum formats with educational philosophy: behavioral objectives and essentialism, webbing and experimentalism, results-only and existentialism. The less specificity and detail a curriculum has, the greater the choice given to teachers to vary instruction according

Figure 17-3   Curriculum format as a reflection of teacher choice: The curriculum cone

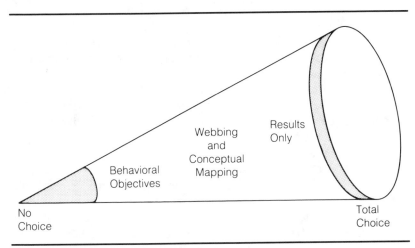

Webbing
and
Conceptual
Mapping

Results
Only

Behavioral
Objectives

No
Choice

Total
Choice

to the situation. Figure 17-3 illustrates the enlargement of teacher choice by curriculum.

Picture being in a curriculum cone where, at the behavioral-objective bottom, a teacher can barely budge. As the teacher moves toward the webbing and conceptual-mapping area, he or she finds room to move hands, feet, elbows, and knees. At the results-only end of the cone, the teacher can extend fully. If the teacher is allowed to step out of the curriculum cone, there are no limits on where and how he or she can move. Behavioral-objective formats predetermine the *what* and *how* of teaching as much as possible in a loosely coupled organization. Webbing and conceptual-mapping formats focus on themes and relationships of possible activities for teachers but give them a choice of actual activities, duration of activities, and evaluation methods. A results-only format focuses on generalized learning and gives teachers the latitude to proceed as they wish.

It would appear relatively easy to match teacher's stages of development to curriculum formats. It is not so easy, however; further examination of type and degree of involvement in curriculum development is necessary.

How Curriculum Is Developed and Used

If a school has decided to use a behavioral-objective format, that does not necessarily mean that classroom teachers have little choice about how to teach. Perhaps the teachers have chosen to use that format; perhaps they wrote the curriculum themselves. Also, an elaborately detailed behavioral objective curriculum could be presented to teachers as a reference guide to use as they wish. Simply knowing the format of the curriculum would not tell us how much choice was given to teachers. Although behavioral curricula usually are used as prescriptive teaching and can be equated with limiting choice, this is not always so. Therefore, before completing the picture of curriculum and teacher choice, it is necessary to consider how curricula are developed, interpreted, and implemented.

Curricula can be developed at many levels—by outside specialists, school district specialists, school curriculum teams, and teachers alone. At the national level, commercial materials such as textbooks, learning kits, and audiovisual materials are developed mainly by outside specialists. The common practice of textbook publishers is to hire subject-matter experts from universities or private agencies to write their materials. There might be a public school representative on the advisory or consulting board for a curriculum textbook, and occasionally teachers are used to field-test the materials before they are mass-produced. Curriculum is supported at the federal level, but for the most part this is true only in legislated areas such as education for the handicapped, bilingual education, and vocational education. At the state level, departments of education have become increasingly active in curriculum development. Many states have legislated statewide competency tests for student promotion and graduation and have developed curriculum guides for local schools to ensure the teaching of those competencies. (For example, in the state of Georgia, there now exist mandated and state-developed minimum curricula in every subject area for grades K–12.) At the local level, some school systems have written their own curriculum guides for coordinating instruction across grade levels. This is done either by having curriculum specialists at the district level write the guides themselves or by having such specialists work with representative teams of teachers (perhaps with community and student representation). Rarely do local schools turn curriculum development over entirely to teachers and provide them with support services such as a curriculum specialist.

We can think about levels of curriculum development according to Figure 17-4 (see Oliva 1984). Most curricula are developed at the state, federal, and commercial levels. Commercial companies are by far the greatest producers of curricula. In other words, most curricula are produced far away from the local teacher and the local schools.

Jessie H. Newlon noted in the early 1920s: "No program of

Figure 17-4   Illustration of levels of curriculum development

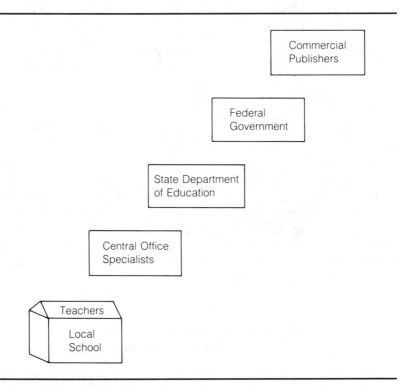

study will operate that has not evolved to some extent out of the thinking of teachers who are to apply it" (Saylor et al. 1981, p. 16). The fact that curriculum development is largely done far away from local schools might help explain why so many schools are floundering and ineffective. On the other hand, local involvement in curriculum development might explain the success of those schools that are effective (Goodlad 1984, pp. 235–238).

It cannot be said that all externally developed curricula are bad and all internally developed curricula are good. Consideration must be given not only to the formatting and development but also to the implementation of curricula before making a judgment of worth. Commercial textbooks will not disappear from the educational horizon. Greater school effectiveness will not be found by simply removing external curricula and having teachers create their own. After all, the fact that external curricula, particularly textbook curricula, have survived so long means that they must be serving a useful purpose.

Jackson (1969, p. 130) wrote of the purpose of that textbook:

It is portable, compact, and enduring. It can be read for a few minutes at a time or for many hours at a stretch. It can be studied or skimmed quickly, read once, or reread often. All students can be given the same reading assignment or each can be given a different one. They can move through the material at the same pace or at very different speeds. The reader can move from the beginning of the book to the end or he can jump erratically from one section to another. . . . He can use his book in class, at home or in the library.

Textbooks can be a valuable aid to a teacher. It is not necessary for teachers to recreate the wisdom of subject specialists and scholars in developing new curricula. Instead, they might fit together what is already available into a total curriculum. Let's remember that, in considering degree of teacher involvement in curriculum, we need to look at the format of the curriculum, the development of the curriculum, and the implementation of the curriculum. We can allow for teacher judgment and choice even with tightly written and externally developed curricula if teachers are given responsibility to alter, expand, or change them.

Levels of Teacher Involvement in Curriculum Development

Tanner and Tanner (1980) wrote of teachers and local schools functioning in curriculum development at one of three levels: (1) imitative-maintenance, (2) mediative, and (3) generative. Teachers at level 1 are concerned with maintaining and following the existing curriculum. Teachers at level 2 look at development as refining the existing curriculum. Teachers at level 3 are concerned with improving and changing the curriculum according to the most current knowledge about learning and societal conditions. Tanner and Tanner explain these three levels according to Table 17-2.

Level I: Imitative-Maintenance

Teachers operating at Level I rely on textbooks, workbooks, and routine activities, subject by subject. Skills are treated as dead ends rather than as means of generating further learning. Ready-made materials are used without critical evaluation, resulting in a multiplicity of isolated skill-development activities. (The already segmental curriculum is further fragmented.) The imagination of the teacher does not go beyond maintaining the status quo. This teacher would like to think that he or she has less freedom than he or she may actually have for curriculum improvement. In the

Table 17-2 Levels of teacher involvement in curriculum development

Level	Locus	Tasks and Activities	Principal Resources
Level I: Imitative-maintenance	Microcurriculum Established conditions Segmental treatment	Rudimentary Routine Adoptive Maintenance of established practice	Textbook, workbook, syllabi (subject by subject), segmental adoption of curriculum packages, popular educational literature School principal
Level II: Mediative	Microcurriculum Established conditions Segmental treatment Awareness of emergent conditions aggregate treatment macrocurriculum	Interpretive Adaptive Refinement of established practice	Textbook, courses of study (subject by subject with occasional correlation of subjects), multimedia, adaptation of segmental curriculum packages, professional literature on approved practice Pupils, teacher colleagues, helping teacher, supervisor, curriculum coordinator, parents, community resources, school principal, in-service courses
Level III: Generative-creative	Macrocurriculum Emergent conditions Aggregate treatment	Interpretive Adaptive Evaluative problem-diagnosis problem-solving Improvement of established practice Search for improved practice	Textbook, courses of study (across subjects and grade levels), alternative modes of curriculum design, professional literature on research and approved practice, multimedia, projects Pupils, teacher colleagues, helping teacher, supervisor, curriculum coordinator, parents, community resources, school principal, in-service courses, outside consultants, experimental programs, professional conferences and workshops

Source: Daniel Tanner and Laurel N. Tanner, *Curriculum Development: Theory into Practice*, 2nd ed., p. 637. Copyright © 1980 by Macmillan Publishing Co., Inc., New York. Reprinted by permission.

secondary school, concern for curriculum development is largely confined to each departmental domain.

When change is made, it is made on the adoption level, without adaptation to local needs. As shown in [Table 17-2], curriculum development at this level is plugging in the package to the existing situation without attention to the resulting interactions. Teachers at this level tend to be left alone to struggle with innovations that are handed to them from above. Schools are turned inward, with the principal as the sole resource for classroom assistance.

Level II: Mediative

Teachers at Level II are aware of the need to integrate curriculum content and deal with emergent conditions. (Societal problems such as the energy crisis and children's questions about things that interest and concern them are examples of emergent conditions.) Although teachers at this level may have an aggregate conception of curriculum, implementation does not go beyond the occasional correlation of certain subjects. The focus of curriculum remains segmental; theory remains divorced from practice; curriculum improvement remains at the level of refining existing practice.

Yet teachers at the second level of curriculum development do not blindly plug in an innovation or curriculum package to the existing situation. The necessary adaptations, accommodations, and adjustments are made [see Table 17-2]. Teachers are aware of and capitalize on a range of resources for curriculum improvement, including pupils, parents, and peers; and they utilize resources beyond the local school. Teachers are consumers of professional literature on approved practices and tap the resources of the university through in-service courses. The mediative level is a level of awareness and accommodation. Teachers are attracted to, and can articulate, new ideas but their efforts to improve the curriculum fall short of the necessary reconstruction for substantive problem solving.

Level III: Creative-Generative

As shown in [Table 17-2], teachers at Level III take an aggregate approach to curriculum development. Ideally, the curriculum is examined in its entirety by the teacher and the whole school staff, and questions of priority and relationship are asked. While individual teachers can and should be at the generative-creative level, a macrocurricular approach requires cooperative planning for vertical and horizontal articulation.

Granted that teachers as individuals usually cannot create new schoolwide curricula, an individual teacher can establish continuities and relationships in his or her own teaching and with other teachers. Teachers at Level III use generalizations and problems as centers of curriculum organization. They stress the broad concepts that specialized subjects share in common, and they use and develop courses of study that cross subject fields. These are aggregate treatments.

Teachers at the third level of curriculum development think about what they are doing and try to find more effective ways of working. They are able to diagnose their problems and formulate hypotheses for solutions. They experiment in their classrooms and communicate their insights to other teachers.

Teachers at this level are consumers of research and seek greater responsibility for curriculum decisions at the school and classroom levels. They exercise independent judgment in selecting curriculum materials and adapt them to local needs. They regard themselves as professionals and, as such, are continually involved in the problems of making decisions regarding learning experiences. To this end, their antennae are turned outward to a wide range of resources [Daniel Tanner and Laurel N. Tanner, *Curriculum Development: Theory into Practice*, 2nd ed., pp. 636, 638–639. Copyright © 1980 by Macmillan Publishing Co., Inc., New York. Reprinted by permission.]

Integrating Curriculum Format
with Developers and Levels of Development

To integrate what has been said about curriculum format, developers, and development, refer to Figure 17-5. When the developers are either outside the school system or from the district level and the curriculum is in a tightly prescribed format, development will be primarily *imitative,* characterized by teachers following the course of study. When the developers are intermediate teams of teachers led by district specialists and the curriculum is written with objectives and suggested activities, development will be primarily *mediative,* characterized by teachers revising and adapting the course of study to their immediate situation. When curriculum developers are teams of teachers using specialists as resource persons or individual teachers with a results-only curriculum format that identifies what students should learn and leaves activities to the teacher, then development is *generative,* characterized by ongoing creativity.

Of course, there are other variations of these combinations. For example, the developers might be an inside team of teachers assisted by a central office curriculum specialist, and they might develop a tightly presented curriculum. Therefore the development would be at a generative level, with the implementation at an

Figure 17-5 Integrating curriculum format with developers and levels of development

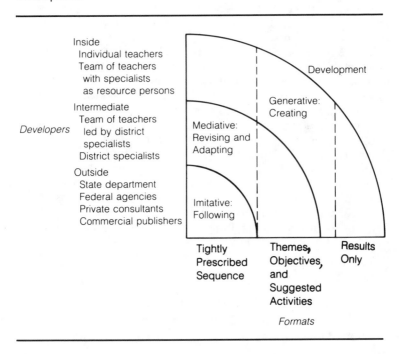

imitative level. Figure 17-5 shows the integration between format, developers, and development.

Matching Curriculum Development with Teacher Development

A progression of curriculum development matched with teacher development might look like Figure 17-6. The supervisor might think of his or her staff in terms of the commitment, abstraction, and expertise they currently bring to curriculum and then determine whether the current curriculum is appropriately matched with teachers' level of curriculum functioning. If the present curriculum is inappropriate to teachers' development, readjustments to the curriculum would be in order.

A staff that has a low level of curriculum functioning—as displayed by little commitment to change, little ability to suggest possible changes, and little curriculum expertise—would be appropriately matched with an outside-developed, behavioral-objective, and imitative curriculum. They should be allowed to make minor

Figure 17-6   Progression of curriculum matched with characteristics of staff

Staff Characteristics	Low	Moderate	High
Commitment to curriculum change	Low commitment to change	Would like to make change	Eager to make change
Abstraction in thinking about curriculum	Low ability to think about possible changes	Can think of some possible changes	Has many suggestions
Expertise in curriculum procedures	Low expertise in how to proceed	Does not know how to write curriculum	Knows how to proceed

Curriculum Characteristics

Developers	Outside developers	Outside developed but substantially revised by team of teachers led by specialists	Internally developed by team of teachers with specialists as resource
Format	Behavioral-objective, highly structured	Eclectic format using behavior objectives, webbing, and/or conceptual map	Results-only, with suggested activities
Development	Imitative, with allowance for minor revisions	To be mutually adapted	To be discussed and changed continually

revisions in adapting the curriculum to their classrooms. On the other hand, a staff that has a moderate level of curriculum functioning (as displayed by a desire to change, ability to think of possible changes, but a lack of expertise in writing curriculum) would be appropriately matched with a curriculum originally developed by outside experts but substantially revised by an internal team of teachers led by a curriculum specialist. The format of the curriculum might be eclectic in its use of behavioral objectives, webbing, and conceptual maps. Throughout the development and implementation, teachers should have problem-solving meetings for purposes of curriculum adaptation. Finally, a staff that is at a high level of curriculum functioning (as displayed by initiating and suggesting ways to change and knowing how to proceed in creating curriculum) would be appropriately matched with an internally developed curriculum. The format should emphasize results only and suggested activities, and should be continuously open to revision.

The supervisor should keep in mind the question: "How does one increase teacher control over curriculum making?" If a staff has been appropriately matched—for example, low-functioning staff with an imitative curriculum—and successful implementation is occurring, then the supervisor should plan for the next cycle of curriculum development to give teachers additional responsibilities by serving on decision-making teams under the leadership of a curriculum specialist. This would lead to more mutually adaptive curriculum and at the same time continue to stimulate and increase teacher commitment, abstraction, and expertise.

The supervisor also might think about using curriculum matching when working with individual teachers for improving classroom instruction. Some teachers with low levels of abstraction, expertise, and/or commitment would benefit, at least initially, from a highly prescriptive curriculum. Others teachers with moderate or mixed levels of abstraction, expertise, and commitment would benefit from the use of an eclectic curriculum that offered choices of two or more texts or guides. The highly abstract, committed, and expert teacher would benefit from having the freedom to pick, choose, and create his or her own plans.

Curriculum Development as a Vehicle for Enhancing Collective Thinking about Instruction

It is a shame that most educators view curriculum as something given, which they must follow. Books about curriculum development are widely neglected. Course work in educational leadership programs give curriculum short attention (at best, one required course). The criteria for assessing school leaders' performance largely ignores curriculum work as an important aspect of leadership responsibilities. Instead, assessment criteria emphasize "the monitoring of teachers using the district curriculum."

Why is it that curriculum is no longer a province for school inquiry and action, but rather a matter of complying with external mandates? The reason is that in the era of legislated learning, teachers and school leaders are seen as incapable of knowing what their students should be taught.

A standardized test would set the educational objectives for the teacher. Curriculum alignment would insure that the teacher would cover the material to be tested. The teacher would prepare plans and write reports to inform supervisors in the bureaucracy that the material was being covered. Evaluators would observe and inspect to make sure that teachers were using the proper methods. And, finally, the external test would demonstrate whether the teacher had properly executed his or her duties [Wise 1988, p. 330].

What a pathetic—though realistic—depiction of the lack of trust in local educators. It is the familiar "tail wags dog" story.

In the past decade, we have seen statewide standardized achievement tests shape the curriculum. Wise (1988, p. 330) wrote

> By mandating educational outcomes through standardized tests, content through curriculum alignment, and teaching methods, states set in motion a chain of events that alter educational ends and means.

What Kirst and Walker wrote in 1971 is even truer now than it was then. Test developers and textbook publishers shape school curricula, rather than local schools shaping and adapting external materials to their curriculum.

> The bald fact is that most teaching in our schools is and must be from a textbook or other commercial package. We do not trust teachers to write their own materials, we do not give them the time or money, and we insist on standardization. So long as this is true, the suppliers of teaching materials will have a potentially powerful effect on the curriculum [Kirst and Walker, p. 49].

The tragedy in this view of curriculum and teachers is the loss of a powerful vehicle for creating an instructional dialogue in a school or district, to enhance teachers' individual and collective thinking about instruction and consequently improve system-wide and school-wide instruction. Most teachers—when trusted, when given time and money, and when given the assistance, choice, and responsibility to develop curricula—will make extraordinarily sound decisions about what students should be taught. Often their decisions will be far superior to those made in central offices, state departments, or commercial publishing firms (McEvoy 1986; McNeil 1988).

Teachers who are involved in making decisions about school curriculum go through changes in their own thinking about teaching. To discuss, debate, fight, and finally come to an agreement with peers about what is important for students to know is an intellectually challenging experience. Curriculum development is a less intimidating task for a group than the other supervision tasks (direct assistance, staff development, group development, and action research). After all, the question here is not *how* we teach but *what* we should teach (what the goals, objectives, themes, and materials for our students should be). It is an easier task to use when intervening in a school to begin a dialogue about the core of professional work—instruction. *The Fifteen Thousand Hours* (Rutter et al. 1979, p. 136) noted, "It was striking, however, that in the less successful schools teachers were often left completely alone, with . . . little coordination with other teachers to ensure a coherent course from year to year."

What happens when a school sees curriculum development as their creation rather than as a given? In Columbus, Ohio, the Reading Recovery Program uses a teacher-developed, nonstandardized curriculum and has shown an 80 percent rate of success in bringing students back on grade level within sixteen weeks (Pinnell 1989). The Annehurst school (Cornbleth 1981), which developed its own curriculum classification scheme, has been cited as one of the most successful schools over a five-year period of time. Such schools as Huron High School and Lawton Elementary School in Michigan and Franklin Middle School in New Jersey provided excellent examples of teachers involved in the mediative and generative levels of curriculum development in mathematics, with superior student results (Driscoll 1988). The "City as Schools" program in New York City and the Public School of Choice in Connecticut are other validated cases of generative curriculum development across high school subject areas (National Diffusion Network 1987). There are not too many other examples in this era of legislated learning. However, in the next era of reform, we will see very different and better schools, programs, and curricula, once teachers and local educators are viewed as worthy rather than untrustworthy.

Summary

Teachers will implement curriculum successfully if they have been involved in its development and can adapt it to their specific classroom and school situation. The failure of the teacher-proof curriculum movement should remind us that imposing curriculum from outside is useless. Instead, the questions for supervisors to consider have to do with type and degree of curriculum development. The supervisor can pick from three arenas. One arena consists of format, which includes behavioral objectives, webbing, conceptual mapping, and results-only. The second arena consists of sources of development, ranging from teachers to district-level personnel, state and federal experts, and commercial writers. The third arena consists of types of involvement, which include imitative, mediative, and generative. Based on teachers' prior experiences and knowledge of curriculum, the supervisor should choose format, sources, and types of curriculum development that will increase teachers' choice and commitment to curriculum implementation. Curriculum, when treated as a task for school action, is a powerful, relatively nonthreatening intervention for enhancing collective thought and action about instruction.

EXERCISES

Academic

1. Review one of the reports on the results of federally supported curriculum development referred to in Chapter 17. Prepare a written summary and discussion of the highlights of the chosen report.
2. Prepare a written summary and discussion of one of the following:
   a. The Denver plan
   b. The eight-year study
   c. The Rand Corporation study
3. Summarize the recommendations of two curriculum textbook authors providing each of the following in a school curriculum.
   a. Sequence and continuity
   b. Scope
   c. Balance
4. Create one or two sample pages of curriculum guides that reflect each of the following formats for curriculum development:
   a. Behavioral-objective format
   b. Webbing format
   c. Results-only format
5. Summarize, analyze, and evaluate conceptual mapping curriculum as described by Posner and Rudnitsky (1982).

Field

1. Examine the curriculum guide of a school with which you are *not* familiar. What philosophy of education is reflected by the curriculum guide? What national, regional, and local priorities are reflected? What examples of knowledge of student development, current economics, and predicted future societal con-

ditions can be derived from the guide? What format was used in developing the curriculum? What categories from Bloom's taxonomy are evident in the curriculum objectives? What parental, central office, teacher, and student influences are recognizable? What commercial publishing influences can be discerned? Does the guide reflect an imitative-maintenance, mediative, or generative level of curriculum development? Was the guide most likely developed by outside developers with minimal revision, by outside developers with substantial revision, by a team of teachers led by a specialist, or internally by a team of teachers with specialists as resource people?

Write a paper answering each question and provide examples from the guide to support your answers.

2. Examine the living curriculum of a school (what is actually taught) to determine how the development of that curriculum has been significantly affected by one of the following:

   a. The federal government
   b. The state department of education
   c. The local community
   d. Parents of students attending the school
   e. Central office personnel
   f. Teachers
   g. Students

   Write a paper discussing the effects of the chosen entity on the development of the school's living curriculum.

3. Examine a so-called canned curriculum, including the teacher's guide, teacher-proof texts and/or materials, programmed methods of measuring student progress, and all other major components of the program. Prepare a report describing and evaluating the selected curriculum. If your report is a verbal one, display and discuss physical components of the curriculum as part of your presentation.

4. Interview a teacher to determine to what extent the schools' curriculum guide determines what he or she teaches. Probe for other influences on what is taught (for example, what the teacher was taught when he or she was a student, the text being used, other teachers, administrators, nationally normed achievement tests, and so on). Prepare a report summarizing and analyzing the interview.

5. Observe a working meeting of a curriculum development or curriculum review committee. What is the prevailing educational philosophy of the group? What influences (government, com-

munity, parental, administrative, commercial publishers) are influencing the group's decision making? What are some characteristics of individual members of the group (levels of commitment, abstraction, expertise)? Is the curriculum development taking place at an imitative, mediative, or generative level? What curriculum development format (behavioral-objective, webbing and conceptual mapping, or results-only) is in evidence? Prepare a report on your observation, including answers to each of these questions. Support your answers with descriptions of behaviors or artifacts observed at the meeting.

Developmental

1. Volunteer for membership on a curriculum development or review committee.
2. Examine the writings of authors on educational supervision to compare their positions on the role and function of the supervisor in curriculum development.
3. Over a period of time, compare a school's written curriculum with its living curriculum (what is actually taught from day to day). How much congruence is there between the formal curriculum and what is actually taught?

REFERENCES

Aiken, W.M. 1942. *The story of the eight-year study.* New York: Harper.

Applebee, A.N., Langer, S.A., and Mullis, V.S. 1987. *Literature and U.S. History: The instructional experience and factual knowledge of high school juniors. The nation's report card.* Princeton, N.J.: Educational Testing Service.

Berman, P., and McLaughlin, M.W. 1978. *Federal programs supporting educational change,* Vol. 8. *Implementing and sustaining innovations.* Ed 159 289. Santa Monica, Calif.: Rand Corp.

Bloom, A. 1987. *The closing of the American mind.* New York: Simon and Schuster.

Brandt, R.S. 1988a. Content of the curriculum, 1988. In *ASCD Yearbook.* Alexandria, Va.: Association for Supervision and Curriculum Development.

————. 1988b. On assessment in the arts: A conversation with Howard Gardner. *Educational Leadership* 45(4):30–34.

Brubaker, D.L. 1982. *Curriculum planning: The dynamics of theory and practice.* Glenview, Ill.: Scott, Foresman.

Cornbleth, C. 1981. Curriculum materials can make a difference. *Educational Leadership* 38(7):567–568.

Cremin, L.A. 1976. *Public education.* New York: Basic Books.

Doll, R.C. 1989. *Curriculum improvement: Decision making and process,* 6th ed. Boston: Allyn and Bacon.

Driscoll, M. 1988. Transforming the "under achieving" math curriculum. *ASCD Curriculum Update* (January), p. 6.

Eisner, E.W., and Vallance, E. 1974. *Conflicting conceptions of curriculum.* Series on Contemporary Educational Issues. Berkeley, Calif.: McCutchan.

Firth, G.R., and Newfield, J.W. 1984. Curriculum development and selection. In J.M. Cooper (Ed.), *Developing skills for instructional supervision.* New York: Longman.

Gibney, T., and Karns, E. 1979. Mathematics education, 1955–1975: A summary of the NSF findings. *Educational Leadership* 36(5):356–359.

Glatthorn, A.A. 1987. *Curriculum renewal.* Alexandria, Va.: Association for Supervision and Curriculum Development.

Goodlad, J. 1984. *A place called school.* New York: McGraw-Hill, Chapter 4.

Hirsch, E.D., Jr. 1987. *Cultural literacy: What every American needs to know.* Boston: Houghton Mifflin.

Jackson, P.W. 1969. Technology and the teacher. In Committee for Economic Development, *The school and the challenge of innovation.* New York: McGraw-Hill.

Kilpatrick, W.H. 1925. *Foundations of method.* New York: Macmillan.

Kirst, M., and Walker, D. 1971. An analysis of curriculum policymaking. *Review of Educational Research* 41(5):479–509.

McEvoy, B. 1986. "Against our better judgments." Three teachers' enactment of mandated curriculum. Paper presented at the annual meeting of the American Educational Research Association, San Francisco.

McNeil, L.N. 1988. Contradictions of control, Part 2. Teachers, students and curriculum. *Kappan* 69(6):432–438.

Oliva, P.F. 1984. *Developing the curriculum,* 2nd ed. New York: Longman.

Pinnell, G.S. 1989. A systemic approach to reducing the risk of reading failure. In J. Allen and J. Mason (Eds.), *Risk makers, risk takers, risk breakers: Reducing the risks for young literacy learners.* Portsmouth, N.H.: Heinemann.

Ponder, G. 1979. The more things change . . . the status of social studies. *Educational Leadership 36*(7):515–518.

Porter, A. 1987. A curriculum out of balance: The case of elementary school mathematics. Paper presented to the annual meeting of the American Education Research Association, Washington, D.C., April.

Posner, G.J., and Rudnitsky, A.N. 1982. *Course design: A guide to curriculum development for teachers,* 2nd ed. New York: Longman.

Ravitch, D., and Finn, L.E., Jr. 1987. *What do our 17-year-olds know? A report of the First National Assessment of History and Literature.* New York: Harper and Row.

Rutter, M., Maughan, B., Mortimore, P., Ouston, J., and Smith, A. 1979. *Fifteen thousand hours: Secondary schools and their effects on children.* Cambridge, Mass.: Harvard University Press.

Saylor, J.G., Alexander, W.M., and Lewis, A. 1981. *Curriculum planning for better teaching and learning,* 4th ed. New York: Holt, Rinehart and Winston.

Sergiovanni, T. 1987. Introduction to the Breckinridge Conference on Restructuring Schools, San Antonio, Tex., August.

Sizer, T.R. 1984. *Horace's compromise: The dilemma of the American high school.* Boston: Houghton Mifflin.

Tanner, D., and Tanner, L.W. 1980. *Curriculum development: Theory into practice,* 2nd ed. New York: Macmillan.

Weick, K.E. 1976. Educational organizations as loosely coupled systems. *Administrative Science Quarterly 21*:1–19.

Wise, A. 1988. Legislated learning revisited. *Kappan 69*(5):328–333.

Yager, R.E., and Stodghill, R. 1979. School sciences in an age of science. *Educational Leadership 36*(6):439–445.

Zeuli, J.S., and Buchmann, M. 1987. Implementation of teacher thinking research as curriculum deliberation. Presentation to the annual meeting of the American Educational Research Association, Washington, D.C., April.

Chapter 18

Group Development

Learning the skills of working with groups to solve instructional problems is a critical task of supervision. Just as cooperative learning with students has been found to produce significant gains in academic and social outcomes (Slavin 1987), so have collegial adult groups been shown to produce higher adult achievement and performance than individualistic or competitive learning (Johnson and Johnson 1987b). This chapter covers knowledge, skills, and procedures for developing productive instructional improvement groups: using group observations, changing group leadership styles, dealing with dysfunctional members, resolving conflict, preparing for meetings, and facilitating large-group involvement.

Professional people who are brought together to deal with pressing mutual problems have the right to expect results. Meetings that drag on, with seemingly endless and unfocused discussion, are morale breakers. Participants become reluctant, apathetic, and sometimes hostile toward future meetings. They might even suspect that the group leader is deliberately leading them astray, so that the group's inability to decide can be used as an excuse for the leader to do whatever he or she wishes. Regardless of whether the leader is actually trying to create confusion or truly desires a group decision, the lack of clear results erodes unity and common purpose. We already know how important unity, common purpose, and involvement are in developing a cause beyond oneself related to school success.

Groups that work productively, efficiently, and harmoniously generally have a skillful leader. Unfortunately, since being part of a group is such an everyday occurrence in professional, personal, and social life, we seldom stop to think about what makes some groups work well and others fail. It is unrealistic for the leader of a new group to expect the group to proceed naturally in a professional manner. A leader needs to be conscious of the elements of a successful group, select clear procedures for group decision making, be able to deal with dysfunctional behavior, use conflict to generate helpful information, and determine appropriate leadership style.

Dimensions of an Effective Group

There are two dimensions of an effective professional group (Bales 1953): the task dimension and the person dimension. The *task* dimension represents the content and purpose of the group meeting. The task is what is to be accomplished by the end of the meetings. Typical tasks of professional groups might be deciding on a new textbook, writing a new instructional schedule, coordinating a particular curriculum, or preparing an in-service plan. An effective group, obviously, accomplishes what it sets out to do. The *person* dimension of an effective group comprises the interpersonal process and the satisfaction participants derive from working with each other. Concern and sensitivity to participants' feelings create a climate of desiring to meet with each other from week to week to accomplish and implement the group task.

Let's explain these two dimensions in a different way. Specific task behaviors are clarifying the group's purpose, keeping discussions focused, setting time limits, and appraising group progress toward the goal. A leader who says, "We're getting off the track; let's get back to discussing textbooks," is exhibiting a task behavior. Specific person behaviors seen in a group include recognizing people for their contributions, smiling, injecting humor, and listening attentively. A leader who says, "Fred, I'm following what you've been saying; it's a point worth considering," would be demonstrating a person behavior. Imagine a group that exhibits only task behaviors. The meeting would be formal, cold, and tense. People would not receive feedback, would not be encouraged, and probably would swallow hard before addressing the unsmiling, staring faces. Such a group would accomplish its task quickly, with little mutual support. The decision would be quick because participants would wish to remove themselves from the tense environment as soon as possible. The formality of the sessions would prevent in-depth discussions of feelings, attitudes, and differences of opinion. Decisions would be made on the basis of incomplete information and commitment from group members. The implementation of the decision would be problematic at best.

Next imagine a group that exhibits only person behaviors. There would be much personal chatter, humorous story telling, and frequent back slapping and touching. People would be smiling and laughing. The image of a raucous cocktail party might characterize a group with all person behaviors and no task behaviors, and the morning-after hangover is also analogous to the sense of accomplishment after a meeting devoid of task behaviors. People would enjoy each other's company for its own sake; everyone would have a wonderful time, but little would be done.

Little's study of six urban, desegregated schools (three elementary and three secondary schools) provides evidence that the two schools identified as "high success" on teacher involvement in schoolwide projects held meetings that encompassed both personal and task behaviors. Little (1982, p. 331) described the successful schools in this way:

> Teachers engage in frequent, continuous, and increasingly concrete and precise talk about teaching practice. . . . By such talk, teachers build up a shared language adequate to the complexity of teaching, capable of distinguishing one practice and its virtues from another, and capable of integrating large bodies of practice into distinct and sensible perspectives on the business of teaching.

As Little has shown, successful schools have collegial, industrious meetings. Teachers involve themselves with each other in professional dialogue to accomplish better schoolwide instruction. In summary, productive groups have meetings that emphasize both task and person dimensions. It falls to the group leader to ensure that both dimensions are present.

Group Member Roles

First the leader needs to determine what behaviors are indicative of roles already in existence. Are some members displaying task roles and/or person roles? What roles are ongoing? Are certain roles lacking? Remember that both task and person roles are functional to group performance. Another set of roles and behaviors, called *dysfunctional,* distract a group from task and person relations. Dysfunctional roles, unlike functional roles, are a concern when present. After listing and briefly describing the most common functional member roles, we will examine dysfunctional roles.

Task Roles

The following descriptions are adapted from those listed by Benne and Sheats (1948).

Initiator-contributor: Proposes original ideas or changed ways of regarding group problem of goal or procedure. Launches discussion, moves group into new areas of discussion.

Information seeker: Asks for clarification in terms of factual adequacy. Seeks expert information and relevant facts.

Opinion seeker: Asks for clarification of values pertinent to the group undertaking or to propose suggestions. Checks on other's attitudes and feelings toward particular issues.

Information giver: Provides factual, authoritative information or gives own experience relevant to the issue.

Opinion giver: Verbalizes his or her own values and opinions on the group problem; emphasizes what the group should do.

Elaborator: Picks up on other's suggestions and amplifies with examples, pertinent facts, and probable consequences.

Coordinator: Shows the link between ideas and suggestions, attempts to pull diverse proposals together.

Orienter: Clarifies the group's position, gives a state-of-the-scene review. Summarizes what has been discussed, points out where discussion has departed from the goal, and reminds the group of their ultimate goal.

Evaluator-critic: Evaluates the proposals of the group against a criteria of effectiveness. Assesses whether proposals are "reasonable," "manageable," "based on facts," and derived through fair procedures.

Energizer: Focuses the group to move toward decisions. Challenges and prods group into further action.

Procedural technician: Facilitates group discussion by taking care of logistics. Sees that the group has the necessary materials for the task (paper, pencils, chalk, and so on).

Recorder: Writes down the group's suggestions and decisions. Keeps an ongoing record of what transpires in the group.

A group needs these member roles to keep moving toward accomplishing its task. A leader can use these descriptions to figure out what roles are missing. Additional roles might need to be assigned to group members or incorporated by the leader. For example, if a group has many opinion givers but no information givers, then decisions would be made on the basis of feelings, without regard to actual experience or knowledge. A leader would need to consider ways to add more information giving. Perhaps he or she could assign people to gather more knowledge or ask outside experts for assistance. Likewise, if a group has many opinion givers and information givers but lacks orienters and coordinators, the members may be talking past each other. There would be a lack of direction and a lack of synthesis of the relationships among members' ideas. The leader would need to plan ways to coordinate discussions. As a final example, a group might contain most of the task roles except for a procedural technician or recorder. Such a group probably would converse easily but would bog down on re-calling what has been said. The leader who knows what roles are needed can ask for a volunteer to be a recorder and summarizer. Knowledge of task roles and behaviors enables a leader to assess what roles are evident and what further roles need to be assigned. The leader might take on some of the missing roles, assign them to others, or add particular persons to a group.

Person Roles

Similarly, the knowledge of person roles and behaviors provides a guide to the group leader.

Encourager: Affirms, supports, and accepts the contribution of other members. Shows warmth and a positive attitude toward others.

Harmonizer: Conciliates differences between individuals. Looks for ways to reduce tension between members through nonthreat-ening explanations and humor.

Compromiser: Offers to change his or her proposals for the good of the group. Willing to yield position or to acknowledge own errors by meeting other opposing ideas halfway.

Gatekeeper or expediter: Regulates flow of communication by see-ing that all members have a chance to talk. Encourages quiet persons to speak and puts limits on those who dominate the conversation. Proposes new regulations for discussions when participation becomes unbalanced.

Standard setter, ego ideal: Appeals to group's pride by not letting group members give up when trouble occurs. Exudes confidence that the group is a good one and can make sound decisions.

Observer and commentator: Monitors the working of the group. Records who speaks to whom, where and when most roadblocks occur, and the frequency and length of individual members' participation. Provides feedback when the group wishes to eval-uate its procedures and processes.

Follower: Is willing to accept the decisions of the group and follow them even though he or she has not been active or influential in those decisions. Serves as a listener to group discussion.

The seven person roles provide human satisfaction and group cohesiveness. People feel positive about meeting and talking with each other and comfortable enough to express their ideas. As a result, meetings are seen as pleasant times to continue the group's work. When person roles are missing, a group may face severe difficulties in making acceptable and committed decisions. Without person behaviors and roles, only the strongest, most assured, and vocal members will speak. Decisions might be made that more timid persons strongly reject but the group may not know that such strong disapproval exists. Again, it is the group leader's responsibility to see if people roles are evident. If roles are missing, then he or she can confront the group with their absence, pick up the role(s) himself or herself, quietly suggest particular roles to existing members, or add to the group other individuals who more naturally play such roles. *Both task and person roles, when not already in existence, need to be added.*

Dysfunctional Roles

Dysfunctional roles and behaviors are those that are conspicuous in their presence. Such roles and behaviors disrupt the progress towards a group goal and weaken group cohesiveness.

Aggressor: Personally attacks the worth of other members. Belittles and deflates the status, wisdom, and motivation of others. Examples of such verbal attacks are, "That's the most ridiculous thing I've ever heard," "You must be crazy to suggest. . . ."

Blocker: Sees all opinions and suggestions by group members as negative. Opposes any decision being made and stubbornly refuses to propose alternatives. Examples of such blocking statements are: "That's a terrible idea," "I don't want to do that," "It's futile to do anything."

Recognition-seeker: Uses the group setting to receive personal attention. Examples of such behaviors are dropping books, scattering papers, coughing incessantly, pretending to be asleep, raising hand and then forgetting what one would have said.

Self-confessor: Uses the group to ventilate personal feelings not related to the group's tasks. Talks about personal problems or feelings of inadequacy whenever he or she can see ways to slip such confessions into the group discussion. Examples of self-confessing statements are, "This discussion reminds me of when I was a little child and the weight problem I had," or when the group is talking about differences of opinion, "You should hear my son and me fight; I don't know what to do about him."

Playboy or playgirl: Displays lack of interest and involvement by using the group setting to have a merry time. Distracts other members from the group's purpose. Tells private jokes, passes notes, makes faces at others, plays cards, and so on.

Dominator: Asserts superiority in controlling group discussion and dictates what certain members should do. Claims to know more about the issue under discussion and have better solutions than anyone else. Has elaborate answers to almost every question and monopolizes the discussion.

Help-seeker: Tries to gain group's sympathy by expressing feelings of inadequacy or personal confusion. Uses such self-derogation as reason for not contributing: "This is all too confusing for me," "I can't make a decision on my own," "Why ask me? I can't help."

Special-interest pleader: Has no opinion or suggestions of his or her own but instead speaks for what others would say or do. Cloaks own bias by using an outside group: "We couldn't do that. Do you know what the school board would think?" "If those parents down in the local restaurant ever heard that we were going to change . . . ."

Dysfunctional roles are fairly self-evident in a group. The leader's responsibility is to reduce or eliminate such dysfunctional roles before they severely harm the morale and efficiency of the group. He or she might try to understand the dysfunctional member's reason for acting as an aggressor, playboy, special interest pleader, etc., and then might either confront the person privately or provide changes within the group to satisfy the unmet needs that are leading to the dysfunctional behavior. Methods for dealing with dysfunctional behaviors will be discussed shortly, but first let's focus on leadership styles matched with maturity levels of groups.

Changing Group Leadership Style

If a group lacks either task or person behaviors, the leader can choose a style that will fill the void. A group that exhibits much initiative, information, and competitiveness (high task) as well as hostility, aggression, and bitterness (low person) could benefit from a leadership style that is encouraging, praising, harmonizing, and humorous (high person). A group that exhibits much positive camaraderie (high person) but is being uninterested, apathetic, or uninformed (low task) could benefit from a leadership style that presses for information, sets goals, and enforces procedures (high task).

The work of Hersey and Blanchard (1969, 1988) on what they call the "life-cycle theory of leadership," also known as *situational leadership,* is a comprehensive theory of leadership style in response to group characteristics. Hersey and Blanchard identified four styles of leadership based on the relative emphasis on task and relationship (person) behavior:

Style 1 (S1): High task, low relationship. This is an autocratic style, whereby the leader tells the group members what is to be done, when, and by whom. The leader makes decisions for the group. This style is similar to directive control, discussed in Chapter 9. One word that describes this style is *telling.* The leader determines both the process and the content of decision making.

Style 2 (S2): High task, high relationship. This is a democratic style, whereby the leader actively participates with the group both as a facilitator of the decision-making process and an equal member contributing his or her own ideas, opinions, and information. This style is similar to collaborative supervision, explained in Chapter 8. One word that describes this influencing style is *selling.* The leader attempts to influence both the processes and the content of decision making by being a persuasive equal.

Style 3 (S3): High relationship, low task. This is an encouraging and socializing style whereby the leader promotes cohesion, open expression, and positive feelings among the members but does not influence or interfere with the actual decision. (The leader's role is one of clarification, encouragement, and reflection.) The style is similar to nondirective supervision, described in Chapter 7. Note that the leader participates by helping members express their ideas, opinions, and needs but does not participate in the sense of offering his or her own ideas, opinions, and needs. The leader participates in the process but not in the content of decision making.

Style 4 (S4): Low relationship, low task. This is a hands-off or laissez-faire style whereby the leader turns the task over to the group and does not participate in any manner. The leader tells the group what the task is and then physically or mentally removes himself or herself from any further involvement. One word that describes this style is *delegating.* The leader is involved in neither the process nor the content of decision making.

Hersey and Blanchard (1988) believe effective leadership is based on matching leadership style to the readiness of the group. The readiness of a group depends on the particular task; the same group could be of high readiness for one task and low readiness for another. Readiness can be assessed according to the characteristics of ability and willingness.

Ability is the knowledge, skills, and experience to achieve without the need for outside assistance.

Willingness is the degree of motivation, confidence, and interest in accomplishing certain tasks.

The leader can assess the readiness of individuals and a group according to these levels (Hersey and Blanchard 1988, pp. 176–177).

- Readiness Level One (R1)
  Unable and unwilling
  Unable and insecure
- Readiness Level Two (R2)
  Unable but willing
  Unable but confident
- Readiness Level Three (R3)
  Able but unwilling
  Able but insecure
- Readiness Level Four (R4)
  Able and willing
  Able and confident

Situational leadership matches leadership style to the readiness level of the group (see Figure 18-1 on matching and directionality of a developing group). An R1 group is best matched with a *telling* autocratic style (S1). An R2 group is best matched with a *selling,* democratic style (S2). An R3 group is best matched with a *partic-ipating,* encouraging style (S3). An R4 group is best matched with a *delegating,* laissez-faire style (S4).

Hersey and Blanchard's theory was originally called life-cycle leadership but is now more commonly referred to as situational leadership. This is an unfortunate change in terminology, because *life cycle* connotes development or growth in both leader and group behaviors, an implication that is missing from the term *situational.* Groups are complex human entities that respond to the gradual shifting of a group leader's external control in the same manner that an individual teacher will respond to gradual shifting of su-

Figure 18-1 Matching and directionality of a developing group

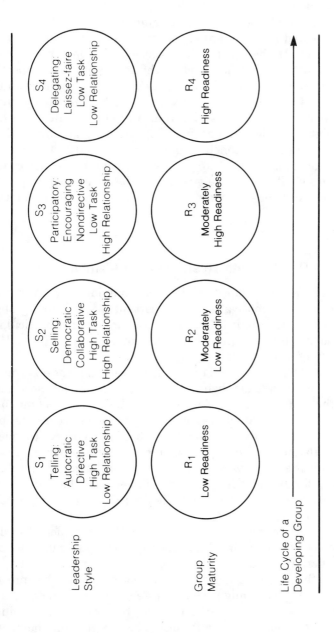

Leadership Style

S_1 Telling: Autocratic Directive High Task Low Relationship	S_2 Selling: Democratic Collaborative High Task High Relationship	S_3 Participatory: Encouraging Nondirective Low Task High Relationship	S_4 Delegating: Laissez-faire Low Task Low Relationship

Group Maturity

R_1 Low Readiness	R_2 Moderately Low Readiness	R_3 Moderately High Readiness	R_4 High Readiness

Life Cycle of a Developing Group

pervisory control. In other words, an R1 (low-readiness) group with an S1 (telling and autocratic) leadership style will not develop until the leader gradually allows them to gain greater internal control. An unmotivated group might work most efficiently with S1 leadership at first. As the group gains experience, as members become acquainted with each other, and as the group acquires expertise, the leader should be alert to those signals of increasing readiness and provide for greater group involvement by shifting to an S2 leadership style. It is conceivable that a group working on a long project might complete the entire life cycle by beginning with S1 (telling) leadership and concluding with S4 (delegating) leadership. A group leader might work toward eliminating his or her control over the group. The ultimate goal should be for a group to provide its own task and person behaviors and not be dependent on formal leadership.

Dealing with Dysfunctional Members

The fact that a group is made up of individuals with varying temperaments and motivations is important when thinking about ways to work with groups. Dealing with individuals, particularly those who display dysfunctional behaviors, is an additional responsibility of a group leader.

If the leader has observed the group at work and has determined that his or her own leader behaviors are appropriate for most members of the group, yet there continue to be a few dysfunctional members, then individual treatment might be in order. The procedure for treating a dysfunctional member is (1) observe the member, (2) try to understand why the member is acting unproductively, (3) communicate with the member about the behavior, (4) establish some rules for future behavior, and (5) redirect the unfavorable behavior (Corey and Corey 1982; Kemp 1970). Each step of this procedure will be amplified.

1. *Observe the member:* When and with whom does the dysfunctional behavior occur? What does the group member do, and how do others respond? For example, a dominator might start monopolizing the conversation as soon as he or she walks into the meeting. Other people might be interested in the dominator's talks for the first few minutes of the meeting but become increasingly annoyed as the dominator continues. They might roll their eyes, yawn, fidget, or make comments to each other.

2. *Try to understand the member:* Why does the member persist

with dysfunctional behavior? Does he or she know the behavior is unproductive? Is the behavior being used to mask some underlying emotion? For example, a playboy might be insecure about his own worth and pretend not to care rather than exposing inner thoughts to the scrutiny of the group.

3. *Communicate with the member:* What can you communicate about the group member's behavior and the situation? Describe the situation and the behavior to the member without denigration. Instead of saying, "You're being an aggressive son of a gun" say: "I've noticed that you speak loudly and angrily to Sara. At the last meeting you told her to keep her mouth shut." Tell the dysfunctional member the effect of the behavior on you as group leader: "When you tell Sara to shut up and tell Bob that he's stupid, it starts an argument that takes time away from the meeting. I can't complete the agenda on time when those arguments take place" (see Gordon 1980).

4. *Establish some rules for future behaviors:* Either ask the member to suggest some rules that he or she can abide by in the future, or tell the member your future rules, or establish them jointly. Regardless of which tactic is chosen, the leader should think of rules that would minimize further disruptions to the group. For example, the leader might say to a self-confessor, "The next time you have a personal problem, come speak to me privately about it," or to a dominator, "I'm going to enforce a two-minute limit on every member's participation," or to a blocker, "If you don't think we're on the right course, tell us your objection once and only once."

5. *Redirect the unfavorable behavior:* Pick up on the group member's dysfunctional behavior, and try to make it functional. A dominator can be assigned the role of recorder, summarizer, or time keeper. A playboy can be given an opening time for sharing a funny story to relax the group before starting official business. An aggressor can be asked to play devil's advocate and argue the position of an adversary.

The five steps outlined here will help the meeting leader understand and deal with individual dysfunctional behavior. The steps are predicated on the leader confronting the dysfunctional member in private. Dysfunctional behaviors that occur infrequently and in isolated situations might simply be ignored. The leader can respond to infrequent misbehaviors or make light of them: "Sara, I guess you really got wound up today; perhaps we might hear from someone else now." Only incessant behaviors that distract the entire group need to be dealt with via direct confrontation. Confrontation is not easy but is necessary at times for the sake of the group.

Resolving Conflict

The key to a productive group is the way ongoing conflict is resolved. Conflicts are particular disagreements that occur between two or more members at a particular time. *Conflict is not necessarily dysfunctional.* In fact, research has shown that successful groups exhibit much conflict (Johnson and Johnson 1987a). As Roger Johnson stated, "A critical moment of truth in a . . . group is when two teachers disagree strongly with each other and argue . . . " (Brandt 1987). A group can make wise decisions only when there is a wealth of information and ideas to consider. Information and ideas are generated through conflict. To suppress conflict is to limit the group's decision-making capacity. Therefore, the leader should encourage conflict, not stifle it. Of course, conflict, if not handled correctly, can degenerate into adversarial and harmful relations. It is not conflict that is bad; it is the way the leader deals with it that determines its value.

Conflict occurs when there is a disagreement over ideas. The leader should keep the disagreement focused on the ideas rather than on the personalities of the members. The following procedure for handling conflict serves as a ready reference for the group leader:

1. Ask each member to state his or her conflicting position.

2. Ask each member to restate the other's position.

3. Ask each member if conflict still exists.

4. Ask for underlying value position: Why do they still stick to their positions?

5. Ask other members of the group if there is a third position that synthesizes, compromises, or transcends the conflict. If not, reclarify the various positions. Acknowledge that there exists no apparent reconciliation, and move the discussion to other matters.

The following is an application of conflict resolution procedures to a high school meeting:

> The supervisor from the central office has called a meeting of the English high school department heads to discuss possible changes in the tenth-grade English curriculum. The topic of composition writing comes up, and two department heads begin to argue. Mrs. Strick of Toofarback High School says: "We need to require three formal compositions each semester from each tenth grader. Each composition should be graded according to spelling, punctuation, and format. I'm sick and tired of seeing kids coming into the eleventh grade without being able to put a sentence together!"

Mr. Ease of Space High School objects: "Are you serious? Six technical compositions a year should just about kill any remaining interest that tenth graders have in writing. That is a ridiculous idea!"

The language supervisor, Mr. Cool, is now aware of a conflict and wants to capitalize on these varying points of view in providing information to the group. At the same time, he is aware of emotional intensity in this conflict (words such as "sick and tired" and "ridiculous") and wishes to soften the emotion and promote the ideas. So he uses step 1 and asks the two members to state their conflicting positions.

"Mrs. Strick and Mr. Ease, you both have definite ideas about the requirements of technical compositions. We are interested in fully understanding what you think. Would you each take a few minutes and further explain your positions?"

After Mrs. Strick and Mr. Ease have stated their positions, the supervisor moves to step 2 by asking each member to restate the other's position.

"Now that you have stated your position, I want to make sure that you fully understand each other. Mrs. Strick, would you please paraphrase Mr. Ease's position, and Mr. Ease, would you repeat Mrs. Strick's position." Mrs. Strick says: "Mr. Ease thinks that technical writing assignments are a waste of time and students lose interest." Mr. Ease replies: "No, I didn't say they are a waste of time; but if such assignments are frequent, students learn to hate English class." Mr. Ease then restates Mrs. Strick's position: "You're saying that tenth graders need skills in the basics of writing. Technical required compositions would ensure proper spelling, grammar, and format." Mrs. Strick replies, "Yes, that's what I'm saying."

Now that both positions have been made and paraphrased, Supervisor Cool goes to step 3 and asks if conflict still exists.

He asks Mrs. Strick and Mr. Ease: "Are you both still far apart about composition requirements for tenth-grade English?" Mrs. Strick nods, but Mr. Ease says: "Well, not as far apart as at the beginning. I'm not against some technical writing requirements. It's the number, three for each semester, that hangs me up. I could accept one per semester." Mrs. Strick replies: "Well, I can't. If they are going to write correctly, they must do it frequently. Three compositions a semester is just the minimum!"

Mr. Cool, knowing that Mrs. Strick is adamant about her position, goes to step 4, asking for the underlying value:

Mr. Cool asks Mrs. Strick: "Could you explain why technical composition writing is important to you?" Mrs. Strick says: "Kids today
don't get any basics in writing. Everything is creativity, expression, write it like you speak it in the streets! I was taught standards of good manners and proper English. If these kids are to
succeed in later life, they have to know how to write according to
accepted business and professional standards. I'm not being hard-
nosed for my own sake. It's them I'm concerned about!" Mr. Cool
turns to Mr. Ease and says: "What about you? Why do you disagree?" Mr. Ease replies: "I don't completely disagree, but I'm
against making tenth-grade English class a technical writing drill.
Writing should be a vehicle for expression and students should
love, not dread, it. They should be able to write personal thoughts,
juggle words and formats, and not worry about every comma and
dotted *i*. Let them play with words before pushing standards at
them. I don't write letters with one-and-a-half-inch margins to my
friends or in my diary—why should kids have to? Sure, there is
a need for them to learn to write formally, but not at the expense
of hating to write!"

Mr. Cool restates the conflict to the group: "We have an obvious disagreement between Mrs. Strick and Mr. Ease. Mrs. Strick
believes there should be at least three technical compositions per
semester in the tenth grade. Mr. Ease believes there should be
less emphasis on technical writing and more on expressive
writing."

Supervisor Cool goes to step 5, *Asking other members of the group
if there is a third position that can be taken.* Some members might
side with one over the other, suggest a compromise (one technical
composition in the first semester, two in the second semester), or
offer a new alternative (let's require a three-week minicourse of
technical writing and let each school decide the type of work and
assignments). If the conflict between Mrs. Strick and Mr. Ease does
not resolve itself, the supervisor acknowledges that the conflict
remains: "We understand the difference of opinion that you both
have, and we can't find a ready solution." Then he moves to other
matters: "Eventually the committee will have to decide or vote on
what to do about required assignments. For now, we'll leave this
particular issue and discuss the tenth-grade testing program."

Conflict cannot and should not be avoided. Conflict, if encouraged and supported, will enable a group to make better decisions.
It is the group leader's handling of conflict that makes the difference. The group should have the feeling that it is all right to
disagree and that anyone who does disagree will be able to make
his or her full position known.

Preparing for Group Meetings

A group can proceed more easily with its task if the leader has made certain preparations. Preparation includes setting an agenda, writing guided discussion questions, and determining procedures for large group involvement.

Agendas

A group has to be clear on its task and purpose. Why are they meeting? What are they to accomplish? Is there to be a product? An agenda distributed several days before the actual meeting will inform members of the reasons for the meeting and what will be accomplished. The agenda need not be elaborate. See Figure 18-2 as a sample agenda. Notice how the agenda includes a brief explanation and a breakdown of items. Time limits for each item provide members with a sense of priorities as well as the assurance that the leader plans to end on time. Keeping to starting and ending times displays respect for group members' personal schedules.

Figure 18-2   Sample agenda

To: All physical education teachers
From: Morris Bailey, athletic director
Subject: Agenda for the meeting of February 23 in Room 253, 3:30–5:00

Next Thursday will be the last meeting before voting on the revisions of our student progress forms. Remember, bring any progress forms you have collected from other school systems. Sally and Bruce are to report on the forms provided by the state Department. At the conclusion of the meeting, we are to make specific recommendations of changes.

Agenda

I.	Review purpose of meeting	3:30–3:40
II.	Report from Sally and Bruce on state Department forms	3:40–4:00
III.	Report on other school system forms	4:00–4:20
IV.	Discussion of possible revision	4:20–4:40
V.	Recommendations	4:40–5:00

See you Thursday. Please be on time!

Guided Discussion

When meeting with a small group to discuss an issue, it is helpful to have in mind the type of questions to ask. Typically, questions to be asked will shift during a meeting. At the beginning of the meeting, the leader usually spends time clarifying the topic for discussion. During the meeting, the leader uses open-ended questions that allow for seeking, elaborating, and coordinating of ideas, opinions, and information. At the conclusion of the meeting, the leader asks questions that summarize what has been accomplished and what remains to be done.

Some discussion questions that might help as a reference are presented in Figure 18-3. Prior to a meeting, the leader might

Figure 18-3   Questions for use in leadership discussion

Questions Designed to Open Up Discussion

1. What do you think about the problem as stated?

2. What has been your experience in dealing with this problem?

3. Would anyone care to offer suggestions on facts we need to better our understanding of the problem?

Questions Designed to Broaden Participation

1. Now that we have heard from a number of our members, would others who have not spoken like to add their ideas?

2. How do the ideas presented so far sound to those of you who have been thinking about them?

3. What other phases of the problem should be explored?

Questions Designed to Limit Participation

1. To the overactive participant: We appreciate your contributions. However, it might be well to hear from some of the others. Would some of you who have not spoken care to add your ideas to those already expressed?

2. You have made several good statements, and I am wondering if someone else might like to make some remarks?

3. Since all our group members have not yet had an opportunity to speak, I wonder if you would hold your comments until a little later?

Questions Designed to Focus Discussion

1. Where are we now in relation to our goal for this discussion?

continued

Figure 18-3 *(continued)*

2. Would you like to have me review my understanding of the things we have said and the progress we have made in this direction?

3. Your comment is interesting, but I wonder if it is germane to the chief problem that is before us.

Questions Designed to Help the Group Move Along

1. I wonder if we have spent enough time on this phase of the problem. Should we not move to another aspect of it?

2. Have we gone into this part of the problem far enough so that we might now shift our attention and consider this additional area?

3. In view of the time we have set for ourselves, would it not be well to look at the next question before us?

Questions Designed to Help the Group Evaluate Itself

1. I wonder if any of you have a feeling that we are blocked on this particular question? Why are we tending to slow down?

2. Should we take a look at our original objective for this discussion and see where we are in relation to it?

3. Now that we are nearing the conclusion of our meeting, would anyone like to offer suggestions on how we might improve our next meeting?

Questions Designed to Help the Group Reach a Decision

1. Am I right in sensing agreement at these points? (Leader then gives brief summary.)

2. Since we seem to be tending to move in the direction of a decision, should we not consider what it will mean for our group if we decide the matter this way?

3. What have we accomplished in our discussion up to this point?

Questions Designed to Lend Continuity to the Discussion

1. Since we had time for partial consideration of the problem at the last meeting, would someone care to review what we covered then?

2. Since we cannot reach a decision at this meeting, what are some of the points we should take up at the next one?

3. Would someone care to suggest points on which we need further preparation before we convene again?

Source: Produced in group development course at the University of Georgia.

review the questions in Figure 18-3 and write down specific questions concerning the topic to have in front of him or her. When the discussion stalls, the leader can look at his or her notes and ask one of the preselected questions. A discussion guide helps the leader ensure that the topic will be thoroughly examined.

Procedures for Large-Group Involvement. With small groups of up to ten members, all members have a chance to participate actively throughout the decision making process (Hare 1976, pp. 230–231). When the number of group members is large, however, it becomes difficult for everyone to participate actively. For example, what does a curriculum director do when there is an important curriculum decision to make involving over a hundred teachers? What does a school principal do when there is an important rescheduling decision to make that involves a faculty of seventy persons? Seventy-five to a hundred teachers sitting in a cafeteria to discuss an issue would be an exercise in folly. At best, only a few brave souls would speak up, and the leader would have no sense of what others thought. If the leader truly wants the involvement of all members in making a decision, then tightly planned procedures are necessary. With all the procedures about to be described, faculty should clearly understand the decision-making method to be used for the final decision (majority vote, consensus, frequencies, and so on).

Three different procedures will be explained. An example involving a staff of seventy-five teachers brought together for the purpose of deciding on how to allocate the use of six new microcomputers in the high school resource center will be used. All three methods are based on breaking the entire group into subgroups of seven to twelve and having a representative committee of one member from each subgroup. Please refer to Figure 18-4 as the three procedures are explained.

Procedure A, postrepresentational, begins with step 1. The leader convenes the entire group and explains the task and procedures to be used and the method of decision making. Step 2 is assigning the seventy-five faculty members to seven subgroups of ten to eleven members each. The leader should have decided on assignments of subgroups according to logical criteria (grade level, content field, or years of teaching experience). Grouping can be made horizontally (teachers of the same grade, content field, or teaching experience) or vertically (teachers from different grade levels, content fields, or years of teaching experience). The subgroups are assigned to discuss the topic, make recommendations, and select a representative both to report the group's position and

Figure 18-4 Three procedures for large-group decision making

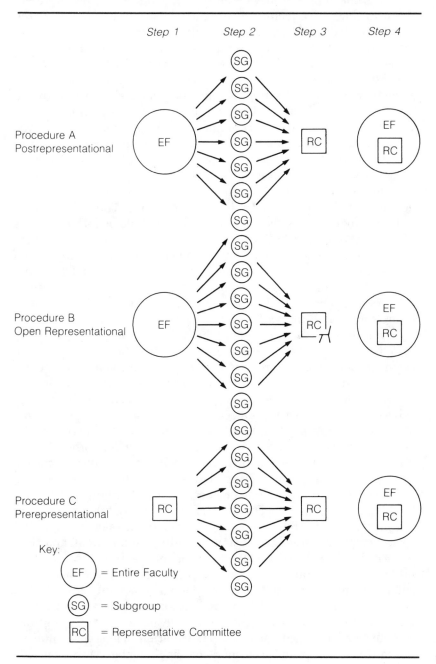

Step 1   *Step 2*   *Step 3*   *Step 4*

Procedure A
Postrepresentational

Procedure B
Open Representational

Procedure C
Prerepresentational

Key:

(EF) = Entire Faculty

(SG) = Subgroup

|RC| = Representative Committee

to be a member of the representative committee. After the subgroup meeting, the representatives report orally on their subgroup's position to the entire faculty. After each subgroup has reported, the entire faculty recesses. In step 3 the representative committee, consisting of the seven representative members, meet on their own to recommend or decide the use of the microcomputers. In step 4 the entire faculty reconvenes to hear the representative committee's recommendation or decision. Again, the leader should have made clear at the beginning whether the representative group would come to the faculty with a recommendation or a decision. If it was to be a recommendation, the entire faculty would vote on the proposal; if it was to be a decision, the entire faculty would listen to the decision.

The advantages of the postrepresentative procedure is that a decision can be made after only a few meetings. The disadvantage is that subgroup members might feel that hidden influences are affecting the representative committee. Since most faculty members (in the example, sixty-eight out of seventy-five) are omitted from the representative committee meeting, speculation might abound about what transpires in the representative group. However, since each faculty member helped to choose the representatives, trust in their work should prevail.

Procedure B, open representation, is similar to procedure A except that an open chair or open forum is added to the representative committee. This procedure provides an opportunity for every faculty member to have input throughout the decision-making process. Step 1 is an explanation to the entire faculty of the task. Step 2 involves subgroup meetings with the election of a representative and a report of the subgroup's position to all faculty. Step 3 is a meeting of the representative committee with an invitation for any other faculty member to attend and participate. The representative committee deliberates in an open meeting. Times are built into the meeting for the use of an open chair or open forum where outside faculty might make comments. The open chair is at the table of the representative committee. An outside member can take the seat and speak for a certain length of time (usually two minutes), and then must relinquish the seat. Outside members are limited to a certain number of appearances. An open forum is similar except that an outside member does not physically have to move to a chair. He or she can raise his or her hand and speak when called on. Certain times at the beginning, middle, and closing of the meeting are established for outside-member participation. The representative committee can then consider outside-member contributions throughout their deliberations. In step 4 the representative committee makes its recommendation or decision to the entire group.

The advantage of open representation is the elimination of suspicion. All members, whether representatives or not, can be involved. A faculty member cannot rationally complain that he or she was excluded from the process. The open chair or forum invites participation but does not require it. Those faculty members who are indifferent about the decision or trust the representative group or have other priorities are under no pressure to attend. On the other hand, those faculty members who care intensely or are distrustful have an opportunity to participate. For these various reasons, it is important to schedule the representative group meetings at a time that is convenient for all faculty members. (Releasing seven representatives from teaching duties for a 11:00 A.M. meeting and calling it an open meeting is not good enough.) The disadvantage of open representation is duration. Allowing input from other members throughout the process will slow down the proceedings of the representative groups. The leader might consider the tradeoff. Is it more important to have some involvement for a quicker decision or greater involvement for a slower decision?

Procedure C, prerepresentational, is the quickest of all but is predicated on the greatest amount of trust between faculty and leader. It begins with a selected representative group *before* the entire faculty convenes. In step 1 the leader selects a seven-member committee that he or she believes best represents the entire faculty. The representative committee meet on their own to develop tentative recommendations to the entire faculty. In step 2 the representative committee report their tentative recommendations to the entire faculty for the purpose of gathering reactions. Reactions are gathered by each member of the representative committee sitting with a subgroup of faculty. The subgroups, having just heard the representative committee's report, can now tell the representative member what they think. The representative member takes careful notes and at the conclusion of the subgroup meeting summarizes the reactions and tells the subgroup that he or she will personally give those reactions to the representative committee at their next meeting. In step 3 the representative committee reconvenes by themselves, listens to the report of each subgroup's reactions, and then decides whether to revise, change, or keep the original recommendation. In step 4 the representative committee gives its recommendation (to be voted on) or decision (to be implemented) to the entire faculty.

The critical element in procedure C is the leader's selection of the representative committee. The leader might be open to the criticism that the representative committee was selected on the basis of allegiance to the leader's own views and that the process was therefore manipulated. However, if faculty trust the leader's motives and understand the criteria for selection of the committee, the procedure should be effective.

The three procedures are alternative ways to have large-group involvement on important decisions. The task has to be important, of concern, and affect each person in order to justify such involvement. If the task is not important, if persons are indifferent and the effect will be minimal, the leader should not subject the faculty to such procedures. Decisions of lesser importance should be made in less involving ways. As a rule of thumb, decisions no one cares about should be made by the leader, decisions that already have been made by superordinates should simply be reported, and decisions that concern and affect some and not others should be made by those concerned and affected. The use of any of these large-group procedures should be reserved for only the most crucial decisions of broad impact.

Summary

This chapter examined the knowledge and skills needed to help professional groups develop. Particular emphasis was put on the supervisor's role in terms of behaving, confronting dysfunctional members, resolving conflict, and preparing for meetings.

The theme of looking at professional groups in a developmental manner should be familiar by now. As a group works together, the leader needs to practice skills that enable the group to become more cohesive, responsible, and autonomous. Eventually the leader would hope to lessen his or her own control and influence so that the group becomes a wise and autonomous body.

EXERCISES

Academic

1. Assume you are the leader of a group that is very person-oriented but is routinely failing to attend to tasks for which it is responsible. Assume further that you have determined that the roles of initiator-contributor, coordinator, orienter, and energizer

are missing and that their absence is largely responsible for the group's failure to attend to assigned tasks. Write a paper explaining what steps you can take to make sure these task roles become present.

2. Assume you are the leader of a group that is generally functioning well but contains a blocker and a recognition-seeker, each of whom is reducing the effectiveness of the group. Write a paper discussing plans for dealing individually with each of these group members to eliminate or reduce their dysfunctional behaviors.

3. Summarize three small-group research studies. Include a discussion of the purpose, participants, methodology, results, and conclusions of each study. Analyze the findings in terms of whether they are congruent with information presented in this chapter.

4. Assume you have been charged with leadership of a meeting at which a department/team of nine teachers will decide on a new textbook series to be used by those teachers. (You may decide the subject area and grade or age levels for which the text is to be used.) Prepare a written plan for leading the group meeting. Include a general format, an agenda, your plan for opening the meeting, and a discussion guide with preselected questions.

5. Assume you have been assigned to organize a meeting of 130 teachers who are to decide on a proposal to adopt a building-wide system of discipline. Write a paper discussing the procedure and specific strategies you will use in facilitating a group decision on the proposal.

Field

1. Record and analyze an audiotape of yourself leading a group decision-making process. Determine any leadership deficiencies you exhibited during the discussion. Was there a lack of pre-planning for the meeting? Was your leadership lacking in facilitation of task or person behaviors? Did you fail to deal effectively with a dysfunctional member? Did you fail to handle conflict properly? Based on your analysis, prepare a self-improvement plan to be followed in a second group session. If possible, analyze an audiotape of a second meeting to see if you improved your leadership in the selected areas.

2. Assign task, people, and dysfunctional roles to various members of a simulated group decision-making meeting. After the sim-

ulation, allow each member of the group to express personal reactions to the behaviors of the various role players. Hold a group discussion on how each member affected the group's effectiveness.

3. Hold a one-to-one meeting with a dysfunctional group member of a real group that you lead. The conference should aim to improve that individual's in-group behavior. Write a summary of the conference and its results.

4. Prepare for and lead a real-life small-group meeting. Prepare a written evaluation of your small-group leadership.

5. Prepare for and lead a large-group decision-making process, using one of the procedures for large-group involvement discussed in this chapter. Write a report on the success of the process.

Developmental

1. Using knowledge and skills you have acquired in group development, continue to facilitate long-range development of a group of which you are a leader or member.

2. Begin an in-depth study of one of the following areas:
   a. Small-group research
   b. Group counseling skills
   c. Leadership style
   d. Organizational management
   e. Group discussion/interaction

3. Begin a file of group development activities. Each group activity can be summarized on an index card and classified according to categories that are useful for you.

REFERENCES

Bales, R.F. 1953. The equilibrium problem in small groups. In T. Parsons, R.F. Bales, and E.A. Shils (Eds.), *Working papers in the theory of action*. Glencoe, Ill.: Free Press, pp. 111–161.

Benne, D.D., and Sheats, P. 1948. Functional roles of group members. *Journal of Social Issues* 4(2):41–49.

Brandt, R. 1987. On cooperation in schools: A conversation with David and Roger Johnson. *Educational Leadership* 45(3):14–19.

Corey, G., and Corey, M. 1982. *Groups: Process and practice.* Monterey, Calif.: Brooks/Cole, pp. 39–47.

Gordon, T. 1980. *Leadership effectiveness training—L.E.T.* New York: Bantam Books, Chapter 9.

Hare, A.P. 1976. *Handbook of small group research,* 2nd ed. New York: Free Press, pp. 230–231.

————. 1982. *Creativity in small groups.* Beverly Hills, Calif.: Sage, pp. 17–53.

Hersey, P., and Blanchard, K.H. 1969. Life-cycle theory of leadership. *Training and Development Journal* 23(5):26–34.

————. 1988. *Management of organizational behavior: Utilizing human resources,* 5th ed. Englewood Cliffs, N.J.: Prentice-Hall.

Johnson, D.W., and Johnson, R.T. 1987a. *Joining together: Group theory and group skills,* 3rd ed. Englewood Cliffs, N.J.: Prentice-Hall.

————. 1987b. Research shows the benefits of adult cooperation. *Educational Leadership* 45(3):27–30.

Kemp, C.G. 1970. *Perspectives on the group process: A foundation for counseling with groups,* 2nd ed. Boston: Houghton Mifflin.

Little, J.W. 1982. Norms of collegiality and experimentation: Workplace conditions of school success. *American Educational Research Journal* 19(3):325–340.

Slavin, R.E. 1987. Cooperative learning and the cooperative schools. *Educational Leadership* 45(3):7–13.

Chapter 19

Action Research: The School as the Center of Inquiry

> Why should our schools not be staffed, gradually if you will, by scholar-teachers in command of the conceptual tools and methods of inquiry requisite to investigating the learning process as it operates in their own classrooms? Why should our schools not nurture the continuing wisdom and power of such scholar-teachers? [Schaefer 1967, p. 5.]

Thus were the questions raised by James Schaefer more than two decades ago in *The School as the Center of Inquiry*. Those questions have been posed from time to time, and different eras of school reform have either responded or chosen to ignore them. The progressive era from the 1920s to the early 1940s and the open education era from the mid-1960s to the early 1970s were times of responsiveness. Since then, the potential of teachers and supervisors as investigators of school improvement has largely been ignored. A noted exception has been the Institute for Research on Teaching at Michigan State University which incorporated practicing teachers as scholars in research. At that time, "the idea of teachers as researchers of practice was foreign and novel. Skeptics outnumbered the enthusiasts. Now the reverse is true" (Gross 1986). Consistent with the renewed attention to school practitioners as researchers of instruction has been the inauguration and growth of North American journals edited, written, and published by practitioners (*Teacher as Researcher* and *Democratic Schools*, both established in 1986). Furthermore, numerous coalitions, networks, and programs of schools and districts began in the 1980s, committed to the concept of teachers and administrators as site-based scholars in the investigation of instructional improvement. This flurry of activity is derived from a concept of inquiry that is often referred to as *action research*. In this chapter, action research as the integrating task for instructional improvement will be examined. A brief history will be given, examples of individual teachers and schools will be explained, and a procedure for making decisions about school-wide action research will be illustrated.

Action Research: The Concept

The famous social scientist, Kurt Lewin, devoted his career to studying democracy and the relationships of individuals within groups. His contributions ushered in the school of gestalt psychology, group dynamics, and the concept of action research. He argued that social research should be based on the actions groups take to improve their conditions. Social research should not focus on controlled experiments, removed from real conditions. As people plan changes and engage in real activities, fact finding should determine whether success is being achieved and whether further planning and action are necessary (Lewin 1948, p. 206).

Stephen Corey applied Lewin's concept of action research to education. He argued that traditional research is done mainly by researchers outside the public school and has little influence on school practice. Corey wrote (1953, p. 9):

> Learning that changes behavior substantially is most likely to result when a person himself tries to improve a situation that makes a difference to him . . . when he defines the problem, hypothesizes actions that may help him cope with it, engages in these actions, studies the consequences, and generalizes from them, he will more frequently internalize the experience than when all this is done for him by somebody else, and he reads about it. . . . The value of action research . . . is determined primarily by the extent to which findings lead to improvement in the practices of the people engaged in the research.

Thus action research in education is study conducted by colleagues in a school setting of the results of their activities to improve instruction. Although an individual teacher can conduct action research, in most cases it is best done as a cooperative endeavor by faculty attempting to improve on a common instructional concern. Action research implies that the practitioners are the researchers. The objectivity and rigor of research methodology can be questioned by classical researchers, but the benefits of the process for students and teachers seem to outweigh the loss of experimental purity.

How Is Action Research Conducted?

There is little mystery to the process of action research, whether conducted individually, as a small group, or in an entire school. First, there is a goal identification phase—collecting baseline information and determining goals and objectives that are worthy of instructional improvement. Second, there is a planning (or treatment) phase, which results in an action plan of specific activities to be performed, time lines, resources needed, and further data to be collected. Third is an evaluation phase of collecting, assessing, and interpreting the data in light of the stated goals and objectives. Fourth is a phase of revising and modifying the original goals, objectives, and activities based on the analysis and interpretation of results.

If these four phases sound suspiciously similar to the development of action plans with individual teachers in Chapter 15 (direct assistance), you have won the first round of the supervision concentration game. The aim of direct assistance to teachers is to promote increased thought, choice, and responsibility in individual teachers, and this can be done through cycles of classroom action research. The supervisor's role is to determine what type of assistance the individual teacher needs (directive informational, collaborative, or nondirective), depending on the developmental levels of the teacher with respect to the particular topic.

Likewise, curriculum development, staff development, and group development tasks are focused on collective action research; the supervisor chooses an appropriate entry strategy for working with an action research team. The choice of interpersonal approach is shown in Table 19-1.

Based on characteristics of teachers, including their ability to think abstractly about instructional problems, their commitment to making changes, their experience with instructional change, and their expertise with instruction, the supervisor determines a general interpersonal approach. He or she might choose to be nondirective by using behaviors of listening, reflecting, clarifying, and encouraging and allow teachers to make their own decisions. The supervisor might choose to be collaborative by stressing behaviors of presenting, problem solving, and negotiating, thus aiming for a mutual, democratic decision. He or she might choose to be directive informational by presenting, problem solving, and directing the teachers by framing the alternatives. A comprehensive, action research team approach might consist of the steps explained in the next few paragraphs.

Table 19-1   Choosing an interpersonal approach

Interpersonal Behaviors	Decision
Nondirective: listening reflecting clarifying encouraging	high teacher/low supervisor
Collaborative: presenting problem solving negotiating	equal teacher/equal supervisor
Directive informational: presenting problem solving directing alternatives	low teacher/high supervisor
Characteristics of teachers Abstraction Commitment Experience Expertise	

First, the team conducts a needs assessment of faculty and collects baseline data to determine common goals for improvement of instruction.

Techniques for conducting a needs assessment can be chosen from the following list:

• Eyes and ears

• Official records

• Third-party review

• Written open-ended survey

• Check and ranking lists

• Delphi

(Explanations of each assessment technique can be found in Chapter 12).

Second, the team brainstorms activities that will cut across supervision tasks. The team can respond to these four questions corresponding to supervisory tasks:

1. What type and frequency of direct assistance must be provided to teachers to reach our instructional goals?

2. What is the necessary curriculum development, in terms of course content, curriculum guides, lesson plans, and instructional materials, to reach our instructional goals?

3. What staff development and in-service education opportunities, such as lectures, workshops, demonstrations, courses, and visits, need to be provided for faculty to reach our instructional goals?

4. What meetings and discussions need to be arranged as part of group development for faculty to share and reach our instructional goals?

These tasks of supervision are explained in Chapters 15, 16, 17, and 18.

Third, the team makes a plan relating activities to goals. Techniques for writing plans are as follows:

- Listing of activities with items and person(s) responsible
- Simple flow chart
- Management by objectives (MBO)
- Gant chart
- Program evaluation and review techniques (PERT)
- Planning, programming, budgeting system (PPBS)

A description of each planning device can be found in Chapter 12.

Fourth, the team determines ways to observe the progress of the action plan as it is implemented in classrooms. Observations can be made with the use of the following instruments:

- Categorical frequency
- Physical indicator
- Performance indicator
- Visual diagramming
- Space utilization
- Detached open-ended narrative
- Participant open-ended observation
- Focused questionnaire
- Educational criticism

Use of these instruments is explained in Chapter 13.

Sixth, the team chooses a research and evaluation design that will enable them to analyze data, determine whether objectives have been met, and decide what further changes need to be made. Choices can be made from these designs:

- Qualitative
- Correlational
- Experimental
- Quasi-experimental
- Cybernetic
- Self-study

To understand the uses of each design, refer to Chapter 14.

Action Research:
Vehicle for a Cause beyond Oneself

Action research is used in many schools under various names, ranging from "organizational development committees," to "leadership councils," to "quality circle groups." Regardless of the name, action research is a wonderful vehicle for bringing together individual teachers' needs with organizational goals to achieve a cause beyond oneself.

Previously, each task of supervision (direct assistance, curriculum development, staff development, and group development) was discussed separately. In reality, any effort to improve instruction must relate each task to the others. It is time to soften the boundaries between the tasks and show how action research can be the vehicle for their integration.

Action research is focused on the need to improve instruction, as perceived by the faculty. As instructional improvements are identified, faculty and supervisor plan related activities to be implemented in each of the tasks of supervision (see Figure 19-1).

Think of action research as a huge meteor falling into the middle of the supervision ocean. As it hits, it causes a rippling of water that activates the four seas of direct assistance, staff development, curriculum development, and group development. The rippling of water continues to increase in force until a giant wave gathers and crashes onto all instructional shores, sweeping away the old sand of past instructional failures and replacing it with the new sand of instructional improvement. Stepping away from the beach, let's look at some examples of action research related to supervisory activities.

Examples of Action Research

Figure 19-2 (pages 399–402) is an excellent example of action research in an individual classroom conducted by teachers (Joossens and Tierney 1987).

Figure 19-1   Action research as the core of related supervisory activities

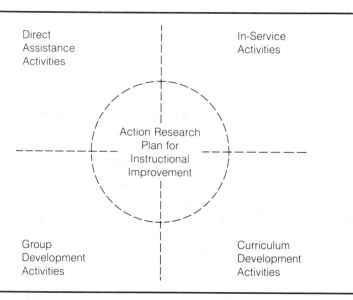

There are virtually no limits to instrutional topics for action research. The basic question to be answered is, "Are students better off as a result of instructional changes?"

Action research at the school level can be seen in various cases. Using the *Effective School Battery* (Gottfredson 1985), five middle/junior and high schools in Maryland choose to measure themselves on scales of teacher reports of safety, morale, planning and action, smooth administration, pro-integration attitudes, and job satisfaction, as well as student reports of safety, respect for students, fairness of rules, clarity of rules, attachment to school, and belief in rules (Hollifield 1986). They use the scores of the survey assessment with other data about students and parents to set goals, objectives, and action plans for the year, and then reassessment is conducted to determine whether improvement has occurred. Some of the participants' reactions were recorded by Hollifield (1986): "First time in the 23 years that I've been here that I've seen anything like this. . . . It helps you see your school as an outsider might see it" (p. 4). A participant from one school said that after the initial shock on seeing the results of teachers' attitudes towards students, "We were no longer surprised. We had a lot [of teachers] who believed strongly that if the kids don't want to learn, then the heck with them" (p. 7). A participant from a third school remarked, "The results were eye opening. . . . We thought we were better than

Figure 19-2 Classroom research using the graphic organizer in English

---

Need

To aid student motivation in the last quarter of the year. To increase student ability to read books above the reading level with some independence. To develop a positive attitude toward reading.

Experimental Classes

32 students were designated in the eleventh grade regular level English classes. For the most part, they were not college bound and had expressed little interest in reading stories or novels. Their average DRP score was 72, but 10 of the students had a DRP score below 60. The literature textbook is designated by the College Board as being 61 DRP.

Action Plan

A generic plan of an interactive lesson [Illustration 1 on page 402] was followed by the Reading Resource Specialist and the participating English teacher to execute the study of novels and short stories during the fourth quarter. The most important step was the first—creating the graphic organizer. Conferences were held between RRS and teacher to identify the key concepts and vocabulary and then make a structured overview which could be shared with the students at the outset of the lesson. The emphasis was to be placed on student-centered, interactive lessons with little emphasis on handouts.

Data Collection

Five methods of Data Collection were agreed upon between the teacher and RRS. First, the third quarter grades were to be compared to the fourth quarter grades. Second, the students were to take the Mikulecky Behavioural Reading Attitude Measure to determine the attitude toward reading in general. The teacher was reluctant to agree to this because she had found in the past that the nearer the end of school came, the more the students tended to resist reading of any kind. Third, DRP scores from the pre- and post-tests would be compared. Fourth, videotaping would be done to determine through observation the level of student interaction. And fifth, comments and observations of students would be noted.

Figure 19-2 (continued)

Implementation of the Strategy

The RRS and the English teacher worked together closely in implementing the 6 generic steps of an interactive lesson. The teacher was aware that her traditional approach to classroom management would change with more emphasis on interaction between student, teacher and text. The novel that was studied during this period was *The Pearl*. The Structured Overview was left on the board from the outset, and the students all took notes as they brainstormed and discussed the concepts and vocabulary and generated study questions. Videotapes were made of the lessons using the steps.

Evaluation

At the end of the 10 weeks the students again took the two tests to determine if any growth had been made. Using an assignment of 5 points for each positive response on the Mikulecky Behavioural reading Attitude Measure, the students improved from 61 to 66. The DRP test results averaged 72 in pre-testing and 76 in post-testing (instructional level), which is an average year's growth.

Students were taped going through Steps I, II, and III. Their interaction with the teacher is clearly visible and the implementation of the strategies is easy to follow.

Most important, however, was that the grades of fourth quarter were better than third quarter. The students' average for third was 75 and for fourth the average was 81. To improve during fourth quarter is a difficult goal, and the students were pleased.

Students made comments about the increased interaction and preparation for reading: "I really wanted to read the book so that I could learn how Kino was like I am about greed."

"I understood the book and stories we read because we had plenty of time to discuss what we already knew about the big idea (concept)."

"Copying down what we come up with is a lot better than copying down what the teacher says or draws on the board for us."

"I like to think my ideas are important. That is what I like best about Miss Tierney's new way of teaching."

Conclusion

The strategies used in implementing the 10-week study proved very successful for the students and met the needs iden-

Figure 19-2 (continued)

tified. A drawback was found that more time is spent by the teacher in organizing the lesson. However, less time is actually spent getting the students to understand the concepts because they are involved in the process of learning!

The teacher was delighted that the students reacted positively to being more directly involved in the lessons. When she first started the interactive lessons, she found that the students wanted to quit doing the brainstorming and vocabulary discussions and categorizing so that they could READ THE BOOK! It concerned her at first, but then she realized that the students had never asked to be alone to start reading anything on their own.

The Attitude Inventory revealed that even unmotivated students can become more excited about reading.

The videotapes have been shown during several presentations and are used in Apopka High School's Interdisciplinary Workshops to show other teachers how the strategies they are learning can be applied to a sequential unit.

The 6-step Interactive Lesson has been adapted by many of the Apopka High School teachers and many are learning to use the graphic organizer. It is proving valuable to have a success story to share.

Apopka's Steps
for
an Interactive,
Student-Centered Lesson

1. Teacher-made Graphic Organizer

   - Key Concepts
   - Key Vocabulary
   - Structured Overview

2. Brainstorming/Predicting

3. Categorizing Words

4. Student-Generated Questions for Study Guide

5. Synthesized Information

   - Lecture/Notetaking
   - Text
   - Small/Large Group Discussion
   - Student-Generated Structured Overviews

6. Review

Figure 19-2 (continued)

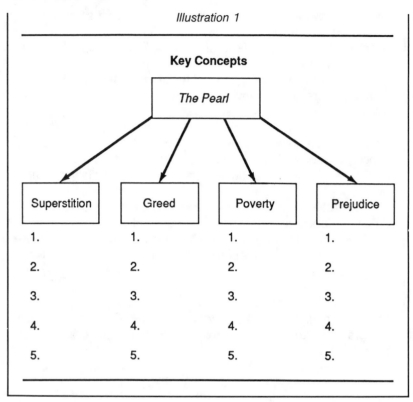

Illustration 1

Key Concepts

The Pearl

Superstition	Greed	Poverty	Prejudice
1.	1.	1.	1.
2.	2.	2.	2.
3.	3.	3.	3.
4.	4.	4.	4.
5.	5.	5.	5.

Source: Joosens and Tierney, Classroom research using the graphic organizer in English, in *Teacher as Researcher*, Vol. 2, No. 2 (June 1987), pp. 4–5. Reprinted with permission of the publisher.

the results indicated. . . . We thought students had better feelings about the school" (p. 13).

The fifth school was a high school with a 99 percent black population, 85 percent on free lunch, and only 15 percent who went on to further education. The school staff was surprised to find that many more students had aspirations to pursue higher education. In one year's time the school made progress toward meeting each of the six standards it had set. Teacher attendance rose from 45 percent to above 90 percent; student attendance increased from 89 percent to 96 percent; math scores increased by 11 percent; reading by 5 percent; and parent ratings and student ratings of school increased above the school's target (p. 18). Hollified noted that the ultimate measure of improved school climate in a high school might be the serendipitous finding that the doors were put back in the rest rooms!

In Newark, New Jersey (Azumi 1987), teams from each school

consisting of three teachers, one administrator, and one parent were established in 1985. Each team served as catalyst for school-wide change. The teams eventually expanded in composition and numbers. They conducted needs assessments, devised action plans, and assessed their progress. A study of all fifty-four elementary schools after a two-year implementation period found that most of the schools indicated improvement in at least one area. (p. 13). Azumi cautioned that two years may be too short a time to be sure of the effects of school improvement and that study of these schools over three to five years will provide more conclusive results.

Parkay (1986) wrote about the dramatic improvement in two inner-city Miami elementary schools involved in a model for school improvement based on organizational development and problem-solving. The model is based on the work of Joyce, Hersh, and McKibbin (1983).

1. A shared understanding of what school improvement means.

2. Emphasis on developing the total school so that it becomes more effective instead of meeting specific research-based critieria for effectiveness.

3. The expectation of a commitment to improvement and growth by school and district staff, with the school as the unit of change and the classroom as the unit of influence.

4. Participatory processes for assessment, problem solving, decision making, and evaluation according to the criteria of effective schools.

5. An organizational structure that includes clear leadership, a team approach, and school-wide responsibilities with clearly defined roles for all staff members.

6. Training for roles and responsibilities that includes theory, modeling, practice, structured feedback, and support through coaching or on-site follow-up.

7. Ownership of and continuous sharing of the results of the on-going school improvement process.

The results of both school improvement projects (one entitled Project Pride and the other Champions of Excellence) were remarkable. "After nearly two years of school improvement work, both schools reported increased student achievement, attendance, and involvement. In addition, teachers demonstrated a strong commitment to professional growth, and many reported a renewed zest for teaching." (Parkay 1986, p. 10). Furthermore, one of these schools was selected as one of the top ten schools in the county.

For each of you, there are examples closer to home in which individual teachers, department and grade-level teams, and schools have come together to assess, plan, act, and reassess their effects on behalf of students. (You could contact the National Network of Successful Schools, listed in the References for this chapter.) Cases can be found that are as ordinary as a school improving discipline and cooperative behavior of students, or as extraordinary as creating an entirely new school curriculum. For example, a local elementary school in Georgia had been committed to mastery learning and had experienced considerable student success. However, teachers expressed concern about the lack of consistent classroom and school rules and enforcement procedures. The principal agreed to form a representative committee composed of seven teachers. The action research committee met and, with input from the entire faculty and administration, developed a set of common expectations for students and enforcement procedures for classroom teachers, specialists, lunchroom monitors, bus drivers, and principals. At the same time, in-service activities aimed at improving teacher management methods were arranged. Teachers altered the curriculum by teaching students the new rules and procedures. They met as a group on an ongoing basis to brainstorm and problem solve further improvements. Supervisors and peers observed each other and provided feedback on progress. The committee collected information on teachers' perceptions of improved student behavior, decreases in referrals to the principal's office, amount of time for classroom instruction, and improved student achievement. The committee conducted a simple pre- and posttest evaluation four weeks and then three months after the new procedures had been implemented. The results showed major improvement. The committee decided to keep the new policies in effect and to continue monitoring progress.

As a further example, long-term action research was conducted over several years by the faculty of the Annehurst (Ohio) school. A leadership committee of teachers worked with their school principal and several university consultants to improve school-wide instruction over a period of three and a half years. The objective of the action project was to individualize instruction, to provide multilevel and varied materials suitable for each student, and to implement team teaching (Mills 1981). The product of the project has been the creation by the faculty of a widely acclaimed curriculum, the Annehurst Curriculum Classification System (Frymier 1977). The evaluation of student progress since implementation of the action plan had shown a major increase in student achievement for over six years (Cornbleth 1981).

The attention given to effective and successful schools has been a stimulant to action research in schools. Brookover's studies of improving schools (Brookover et al. 1979), Edmond's studies of effective schools (1979), the study by Rutter et al. of effective high schools (1979), Little's study of successful schools (1982), Berman and McLaughlin's study of successful program implementation (1978), the Phi Delta Kappa Commission on Schools with Good Discipline (Wayson et al. 1982), and Rosenholtz's (1985) and Parkey and Smith's (1983) review of the effective-schools literature have all reported the collective participation of faculty in planning action research as a characteristic of successful schools.

Lezotte (1986) states that the school effectiveness research has given impetus to school improvement programs as a form of action research. School improvement should include *a focus on teaching and learning, evidence, and analysis of evidence.* The strategic unit of change should be the individual school, with collaboration among principal, teachers, central office personnel and parents.

Shared Governance for Action Research

A shortcoming of earlier studies of school improvement and action research has been the lack of descriptions of how individual schools or districts went about the process of change (Fullan 1985, p. 398). Achieving "a cause beyond oneself" in pursuing collaborative and collective instructional goals for students sounds admirable, but how does a supervisor initiate and sustain such efforts? What follows is one explanation, using case studies from the demonstration public schools that are part of the Program for School Improvement (PSI) at the University of Georgia. The model of shared governance and school-wide instructional change has been adapted and used in elementary, middle, and secondary schools in Georgia, South Carolina, Vermont, Michigan, and the United States Department of Defense Dependent Schools in Europe.

Premises

Three declarative premises underlie shared governance. Those premises are:

1. Every professional in the school who so desires can be involved in making decisions about school-wide instructional improvements.

2. Any professional in the school who does not desire to is not obligated to be involved in making decisions about school-wide instructional improvements.

3. Once a decision is made about school-wide instructional improvements, all staff must implement the decision.

Thus an individual can choose to be or not to be part of the decision-making process. However, once decisions are made, all individuals must implement the agreed-upon actions. Operationalizing these premises allows a school to move forward with people who are interested in participating without forcing any individual who is not interested into a corner. Afterwards, an individual who did not wish to participate in making decisions has no grounds for complaint about decisions about school-wide instructional actions. Perhaps when the next issue, concern, or topic is brought up for school-wide action, nonparticipants who have been disgruntled with previous decisions will have a renewed interest in participating.

Principles

The principles in operating shared governance for instructional improvement are:

1. *One person, one vote.* Each representative has the same rights, responsibilities, and equal vote as any other representative. Each teacher who sits on the representative school-wide council has the same vote as the school principal or any other administrator or formal supervisor. This means, in practical terms, that an individual administrator or supervisor cannot get his or her own way with decisions about instructional improvement, just as a single teacher representative cannot get his or her own way. Decisions are made by the group, so expertise, influence, and credibility are more important than power and authority.

2. *Limit decisions to school-wide instruction within the control and sphere of responsibility of the school.* Action research and shared governance involves the core of a school's existence: curriculum and instruction, or teaching and learning. Areas for decision making should be school-wide and instructional. Issues of day-to-day administration, contracts, school board policies, other schools, and personnel are not the concerns of shared governance for school-wide action research. The scope of concerns for deliberations, decisions, and actions is always grounded in the question: "What should *we* be doing *here* with *our* school to improve learning for *our* students?"

This is not to dismiss the influence on student learning of external policies and operations, nor is it to suggest that changes to improve conditions for students should not be pursued at levels beyond the school. It is simply to suggest that unless a school has a clear, streamlined mechanism for keeping the focus on creating a dialogue about instruction within the school, shared governance will often dissipate into a depository of complaints about noninstructional concerns. Time and energy spent on complaining or proposing what other schools, parents, central office, and school board should do (which the individual school has no legal or direct control over) take time and energy away from instructional changes that *can* be made. (Talking about others can be an excuse for not talking about ourselves.)

3. *Authentic feedback necessitates small groups.* To call a faculty meeting with a large staff for the intended purpose of an open, freewheeling discussion of ideas, opinions, and positions is at best misguided, if not outright manipulative. Large meetings result in input from the most confident, the loudest, and the most powerful persons—who are not necessarily the wisest, most insightful, or most interested persons. A true forum for intellectual discourse is a small group (ideally, seven to eleven members); therefore, shared governance in large schools must operate in small groups.

Operational Model

The work of Schmuck, Runkel, Arends, and Arends (1977) has provided the basis for an operational model for shared governance, action research, and school improvement which uses the premises of individual choice of involvement and implementation by all and the principles of one-person, one-vote, focus on teaching, and small groups. One particular version of this model that I have been using with schools with be discussed here (see Glickman 1989; Glickman and Wright 1986). Many schools use comparable models of operation and have their own specific versions. The goal is not to advocate a particular model of shared governance, but rather to achieve the premises and principles of shared governance and action research, leading to a purposeful, collective, and thoughtful school—a school that is the center of inquiry.

The Formal Groups.   Shared governance in this model involves three groups (see Figure 19-3). *The executive council* is a seven-to-eleven-member body, consisting of a majority of teachers with administrators. Teachers could be chosen from among grade-level heads, team leaders, department heads, and union representatives, they could be elected at large from the faculty, or some combination of election and appointment could be used. They hold a term of at least three years and move off the council at staggered times. Teachers serve as chairperson and co-chairperson of the executive council. The principal is a member of the committee with the same rights and responsibilities as any other member. The executive council's responsibility is solely for acting on and monitoring school-wide instructional improvement recommendations. *The council does not*

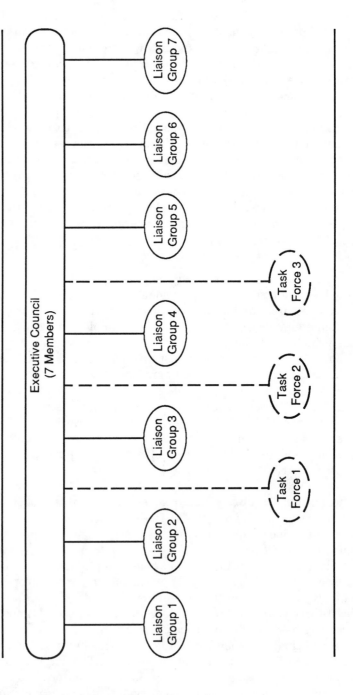

Figure 19-3 Action research as the core of related supervisory activities

make recommendations; it is an approving board. Recommendations must come from task force groups within the school. The executive council does not involve itself in administrative matters, community relations, school board policies, personnel matters, or issues that are departmental in nature. It acts upon instructional improvement recommendations that the faculty has the legal power to carry out. This differentiation between instructional and administrative responsibilities helps avoid problems that can arise from delving into matters beyond the school's own control.

Liaison groups are formal groups set up as communication links between the faculty and executive council concerning needs, reactions, opinions, and ideas about school-wide instruction. The liaison groups meet formally only two or three times a year, but they are an important unit for considering the faculty's ideas and opinions about assessing instructional goals and responding to proposed recommendations. For example, in the case of a school with fifty teachers, there could be seven liaison groups consisting of approximately seven faculty members each. An alphabetized list of all faculty names is gathered and each person is assigned a number from one to seven. All 1's go to liaison group 1, all 2's go to liaison group 2, and so forth. This assignment procedure ensures that members in each liaison group come from various departments and grade levels. Each liaison group is a microcosm of the entire school. One executive council member is assigned to each liaison group and serves as the liaison group's representative to the council. The executive council member can (a) call the liaison group together from time to time for a brief meeting to review a specific recommendation under executive council consideration, (b) gather written opinions about a particular proposal, or (c) simply drop by and talk to the various liaison group members.

Task forces are the last groups shown in Figure 19-3. These ad hoc task groups of volunteers are formed after the executive council has solicited feedback from all the liaison groups about perceived school-wide instructional needs and reviewed any existing data on school-wide instruction. The executive council then targets priority instructional areas for the next one to three years. School-wide priorities might be such matters as increasing instructional time, coordinating curriculum, improving student attitudes, teaching higher-order thinking, increasing student success rates, improving school discipline, improving school and classroom climate, improving the quality of feedback to students, or improving test scores.

Once the needs for improvement have been selected by the executive council, ad hock task force groups are formed by recruiting volunteers who have an interest in and a commitment to the particular topic. At least one executive council member serves on each task force, but this person normally does not serve as chair of the task force. The task force volunteers meet, review their task, select their own chairperson, schedule meetings, and set a time line for making a final recommendation for school-wide action to the executive council. Depending on the topic, one task force might meet three times over three weeks to make a recommendation, whereas another task force might meet every other week for five months before making a recommendation.

Decision-Making Procedures. When the task force is ready to make a recommendation, it makes its report in three parts: (1) goals and objectives, (2) action plan (What will be done, by whom, and when?), (3) evaluation (How will the success of actions be known?) The executive council discusses the recommendations and either makes an immediate decision to approve (most councils use a consensus vote to approve a first-time recommendation) or, without the required vote, tables the recommendation until the next meeting. During the interim, the executive council members can discuss the recommendation and check with their respective liaison groups to gather input from the entire faculty. At the next meeting, a second vote can be taken. (Most councils use a two-thirds majority vote to approve a tabled recommendation.) By the second vote, the council will have a good sense of total faculty receptivity and the chances of successful implementation.

Implementation. After a decision has been made, the executive council (with the task force) announces the approved plan to the school. The task force then disbands, and the executive council implements the plan. It becomes the responsibility of the executive council (including the principal) to enforce the school-wide decisions and to monitor and evaluate the results.

Personal Examples of School-Based Action Research Plans

To provide some insight into the developmental nature of organizations (their receptivity and focus of concern with instructional improvement) and the use of action research to integrate the other tasks of supervision—direct assistance, curriculum development, staff development, and group development—let me highlight two schools that I have personally worked with over an extended period of time. Oglethorpe County High School is located in a rural, economically disadvantaged community. It has used shared governance and action research since 1983. The first year of its operation, the executive council targeted task force groups on the topics of (1) coordinating academic clubs throughout the school and (2) a policy for smoking in the teacher's lounge. The latter topic hardly appeared to be an instructional concern! Yet the faculty was convinced that since the only meeting place for teachers to talk about instruction was the faculty lounge, and there was disagreement about smoking there, this topic was related to the success of the instructional improvement process. There was no lack of volunteers to serve on the smoking task force—seventeen in all. (Volunteers for the task force on coordinating academic clubs were four!) The school faculty was initially skeptical of shared governance— "just another fad" or administrative ploy. However, the smoking lounge task force met several times, with much debate and conflict, and finally made a recommendation that was approved by the school council. Suddenly, new policies were explained, established, and enforced throughout the school, not by administrative decree but by a democratic process. Everyone in the school then realized that the decision-making process was for real and to be taken seriously. The academic club task force struggled with goals, objectives, and actions and finally recommended such simple but important actions as expanding club offerings, drawing up a master schedule to avoid time conflicts, and recruiting more students to participate. These approved recommendations become the law of the land.

Five years later, from these auspicious beginnings, every teacher had served on a task force, and shared governance had dealt with improved achievement, student study skills, reporting procedures, and (most notably) reducing the student dropout rate. The latter task involved integrated staff development for all teachers in communicating with troubled students; curriculum revisions, including alternative teaching strategies and materials for disengaged students; and group development activities in which teachers meet in small groups to discuss ways to help individual students who have been found to be in immediate need of help. The results were a decrease of 50 percent in the dropout rate over a two-year period and the implementation of a totally teacher-developed, interdisciplinary team-teaching curriculum for teaching high school subjects, without fifty-minute periods, extending into educational settings beyond the school. Each ensuing year, the topics and plans have become increasingly complex and profound. It all started with smoking in the teachers' lounge.

Fowler Drive Elementary School (Clarke County, Georgia) is a school of approximately 900 students, racially mixed, drawn from an urban environment, and with a high proportion of "at-risk" students. For several years the school has operated on the principles and premises of shared governance and action research, keeping as its goal the successful education of *all* students. They break down data to compare educational progress by sex, race, and socioeconomic level. Study groups and task forces target interventions to improve attitudes, thinking, and achievement of particular groups of students. Plans have increasingly integrated the tasks of supervision.

The first-year focus was on in-service education conducted by external trainers on children's stages of learning. The following year, teachers assumed responsibility for conducting facets of the in-service to include cognitive monitoring and piloting a direct-assistance peer-coaching program. The third year the plan included curriculum development in mediating the existing basal reading series with a whole-language approach, incorporating greater direct assistance by expanding peer coaching, and implementing monthly group development activities based on a blueprint for action to help minority students. Teachers and administrators develop the action research plans, arrange and conduct in-service education, revise the curriculum, and do the evaluation of the impact of the plan on students and staff. The results have been improved student attitudes towards learning, maintenance of achievement levels, substantial increase in student promotion rates, and statistically significant gains in measures of teachers' conceptual thinking.

These are two good schools, striving to be better; there are many more such schools throughout the country. You might work in one and know of other examples. Why is it that such elementary, middle, and senior high schools—which, according to most research on schools, should be stagnant and recalcitrant to change—are not? Many of these good schools are situated in conservative, fiscally poor communities and lack the advantages of dealing with the children of highly educated parents. These teachers should be "stressed out," "burnt out," and full of "despair" and "helplessness." But they are not. In fact, they willingly increase work for themselves, and each roadblock or failure in helping students succeed makes them want to work harder. Why do they do this? The pay is not great, the facilities not luxurious, the community not gushing in recognition or praise. One of these principals remarked to me, "If I ever asked teachers to do what they are requiring themselves to do, I'd be lynched." So why do they work harder and smarter?

Because it's their school, their students, their goals, and their decisions—nobody else's! These good schools are not utopias. Nor are they maverick organizations, without limitations and responsibilities to regulatory agencies. They are different because those who have responsibilities for supervision of instruction have squarely placed the practice of inquiry and decision making about instruction as central to the work of teachers.

Conclusion: Focus, Structure, and Time for Development

Supervision provides a focus, structure, and time for teachers to be engaged in dialogue, debate, research, decisions, and actions about instruction. Without focus, teachers will not discuss teaching, because it has not been an accepted norm for discussion in most schools. Without structure, there are no clear apparatus, procedures, and rules for how decisions are made and implemented. Without time, there is no functional or symbolic expression that teachers have the capacity to make collective and wise instructional decisions on behalf of students. Although examples have been given at the school level, the same applications of shared governance and action research (with curriculum and instruction) can be made at the district level.

As Carlson and Matthes (1987) state, a major pitfall in school improvement is "ignoring the effects of different organization life stages on cultural issues." Edelfelt (1983) and Sohns (1984) have noted that organizations, like individuals, are at different stages of development, proceed at different rates, and are vulnerable to external forces. The fifteen years of site-based governance of schools in Salt Lake City (McLeese and Malen 1987) provide an excellent example of how faculty committees have grown from advisory to decision making; from concerns that were teacher-centered and of a physical and maintenance nature (the smoking in the teachers' lounge) to concerns that have become student-centered and of a curricular and instructional nature. The developmental progression is not linear, and it's fragile, but action research is predicated on shared governance as the essence of professional work. The local unit must determine where the point of entry should be, where the initial focus should be, and how those in supervision should work with teachers to increase collective choice, thought, and action. The overall goal, however, remains the same: the school as the center of inquiry.

EXERCISES

Academic

1. Assume you have been assigned the task of speaking in favor of a proposal to provide funding for action research at the next school board meeting. Write your speech, telling how you and your staff will carry out such research and what the benefits will be. To attempt to convince the school board, include in your speech references to sources other than this book.

2. Describe two action research projects that have been reported in the literature and not discussed in this book.

3. Select an objective for instructional improvement that can be adapted to action research. Based on that objective, prepare a written plan for an action research project. Make sure that procedures for conducting action research listed in this chapter are addressed in your plan.

4. Briefly describe an action research project that might be carried out by a small group of teachers facilitated by a supervisor. Next, describe the knowledge and skills the supervisor would need in order to lead the group successfully in the action research. Rely on previous chapters of this book for your answer.

5. Create a model for evaluating action research projects. Components of the model should provide for evaluation of needs assessment, objectives, planning and sequencing of activities, implementation of activities, measurement techniques, and data analysis. Each component should be accompanied by critical questions to be asked concerning the appropriate phase of the action research project.

Field

1. Plan and carry out a short-term, individual action research project. Report on the action research, its results, your conclusions, and your recommendations.

2. Observe, evaluate, and report on an action research project currently being carried out in a school setting. Include a discussion of whether all four tasks of supervision have been integrated in the action research.

3. Describe an instructional improvement recently introduced in a school with which you are familiar. Suggest how the innovation could have been tried out as action research before being fully implemented. Your suggested plan should meet all the require-

ments (necessary procedures, integrated supervision tasks) for authentic action research.

4. Determine an instructional improvement that would benefit a school with which you are familiar. Suggest how each of the four tasks of supervision would be met in relation to your instructional improvement objective:

   a. What direct assistance would have to be provided to facilitate the instructional improvement?

   b. What curriculum development would have to be made?

   c. What staff development activities would be necessary?

   d. What types of group development would faculty need?

5. Interview faculty and supervisors of a clearly successful school to determine whether action research is carried out in that school. If so, do faculty members participate collectively in planning for action research? What is the mechanism for such participation (curriculum council, research committees, circle groups)? What are some examples of action research that have been carried out?

   If the selected school does not conduct action research, are teachers allowed opportunities for professional interaction, discussion of ideas for instructional improvement, and reflective and collective thinking? If so, how are such opportunities provided?

   Prepare a report on your interviews.

Developmental

1. Volunteer to supervise or participate in a long-range group action research project within an educational setting.

2. Take advantage of future opportunities to hold discussions with those involved in school action research. Such discussions can help you generate your own ideas for action research projects and effective supervision of action research.

3. Continue to explore the literature and research on action research. Begin a file of articles appropriate for sharing with educators interested in action research.

REFERENCES

Azumi, J.E. 1987. Effective schools characteristics, school improvement and school outcomes: What are the relationships? Paper presented to the annual meeting of the American Educational Research Association, Washington, D.C., April.

Berman, P., and McLaughlin, M.W. 1978. *Federal programs supporting educational change*, Vol. 8: *Implementing and sustaining innovations*. ED 159-289. Santa Monica, Calif.: Rand Corp.

Brookover, W., Beady, C., Flood, P. Schweiter, J., and Wisenbaker, J. 1979. *School social systems and students' achievement: Schools can make a difference*. New York: Praeger.

Carlson, R.V., and Matthes, W.A. 1987. "Good" rural schools: An organizational-cultural perspective. Paper presented at the annual meeting of the American Educational Research Association, Washington, D.C., April.

Corey, S. M. 1953. *Action research to improve school practices*. New York: Teachers College, Columbia University.

Cornbleth, C. 1981. Curriculum materials can make a difference. *Educational Leadership* 38(7):567–568.

Edelfelt, R.A. 1983. In-service education: Moving from professional development to school improvement. *Urban Educator* (Winter).

Edmond, R. 1979. Effective schools for the urban poor. *Educational Leadership* 37(1):15–24.

Frymier, J.R. 1977. *Annehurst curriculum classification systems: A practical way to improve instruction*. West Lafayette, Ind.: Kappa Delta Pi.

Fullan, M. 1985. Change processes and strategies at the local level. *Elementary School Journal* 85(3):391–421.

Glickman, C.D. 1989. *Shared governance at Ogelthorpe County High School*. Athens, Ga.: Monographs in Education.

Glickman, C.D., and Wright, L.V. 1986. Decision making in schools. In P.R. Burden (Ed.), *Establishing career ladders in teaching: A guide for policy makers*. Springfield, Ill.: Charles C. Thomas, pp. 111–129.

Gottfredson, C. 1985. *Effective school battery: User's manual*. Odessa, Fla.: Psychological Assessment Resources.

Gross, S. (Ed.). 1986. Teacher collaboration: New partnership to attack old problems. *Communication Quarterly* 9(1):1–4. (Institute for Research on Teaching).

Hollifield, J.H. 1986. How schools react to assessment data. Presentation to the annual meeting of the American Educational Research Association, San Francisco, April.

Joossens, and Tierney, 1987 Classroom research using the graphic organizer in English. *Teacher as Researcher* 2(2):4–5.

Joyce, B., Hersh, R., and McKibben, M. 1983. *The structure of school improvement.* New York: Longman, 1983.

Lewin, K. 1948. *Resolving social conflicts.* New York: Harper and Brothers.

Lezotte, L. W. 1986. School effectiveness, reflections, and future directions. Presentation to the annual meeting of the American Educational Research Association, San Francisco, April.

Little, J.W. 1982. Norms of collegiality and experimentation: Workplace conditions of school success. *American Educational Research Journal 19*(3):325–340.

McLeese, P., and Malen, B. 1987. Site based governance: The Salt Lake City experience 1970–1985. Paper presented to the annual meeting of the American Educational Research Association, Washington, D.C., April.

Mills, T. 1981. The development of Annehurst School. *Educational Leadership 38*(7):569.

National Network of Successful Schools. Susan Mundry, 290 South Main Street, Andover, Mass. 01810.

Parkay, F.W. 1986. Implementing research on school effectiveness: Two inner-city case studies. Paper presented to the annual meeting of the American Educational Research Association, San Francisco, April 20.

Parkey, S.C., and Smith, M.S. 1983. Effective schools—A review. *Elementary School Journal 83:*427–452.

Rosenholtz, S.J. 1985. Effective schools: Interpreting the evidence. *American Journal of Education 93*(3):352–388.

Rutter, M., Maughan, B., Mortimore, P., Ouston, J., and Smith, A. 1979. *Fifteen thousand hours: Secondary schools and their effects on children.* Cambridge, Mass.: Harvard University Press.

Schaefer, R. 1967. *The school as the center of inquiry.* New York: Harper and Row.

Schmuck, R.A., Runkel, P., Arends, J.H., and Arends, R.I. 1977. *The second handbook of organizational development in schools.* Palo Alto, Calif.: Mayfield.

Sohns, M.L. 1984. School readiness for staff development. Unpublished manuscript, Government Center, Hanford, Calif.

Wayson, W.W., DeVoss, G.G., Kaeser, S.C., Lasley, T., and Pinnel, G.S. 1982. *Handbook for developing schools with good discipline.* Bloomington, Ind.: Phi Delta Kappa.

PART V CONCLUSION

The purpose of Part V was to make instructional improvement and school success a realistic goal. We have looked at the five tasks of supervision that have direct impact on instructional improvement: direct assistance, staff development, curriculum development, group development, and action research. Emphasis was given on how the use of each task can unite teacher needs with organizational goals (see Figure V-1).

We were able to use prerequisites of knowledge, interpersonal skills, and technical skills to function in the realm of supervision and apply it to the five tasks. Chapter 15 on direct assistance examined clinical procedures for observations, peer supervision, accessibility, arranged time, delegation, and separating direct assistance from formal evaluation. Chapter 16 looked at staff development in terms of research findings of successful in-service, teacher concerns, conceptual and psychological states of teachers, and experience impact of activities. Chapter 17 on curriculum development examined varying formats for writing curriculum, the range of developers of curriculum, and degree of teacher involvement. Chapter 18 on group development studied the supervisor's role in the group with attention to task and person behaviors, confronting dysfunctional members, resolving conflict, preparing for meetings, and lessening leadership control as the group becomes cohesive. Finally, Chapter 19 on action research showed how teachers can become researchers on their own instructional problems. Such research integrates the four previous supervisory tasks and unifies teacher needs with organizational goals to promote collective action.

Figure V-1 Supervision for successful schools

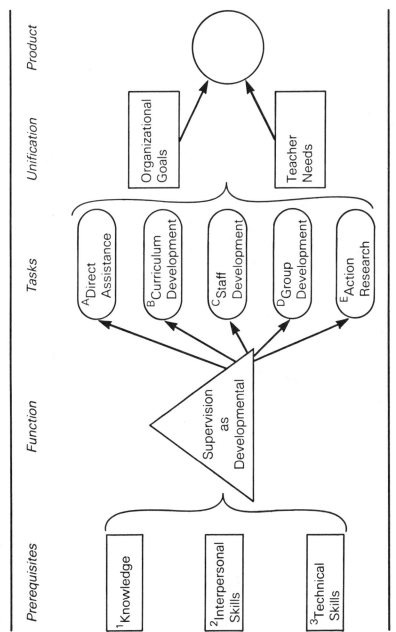

| Prerequisites | Function | Tasks | Unification | Product |

Prerequisites:
- ¹Knowledge
- ²Interpersonal Skills
- ³Technical Skills

Function:
- Supervision as Developmental

Tasks:
- ᴬDirect Assistance
- ᴮCurriculum Development
- ᶜStaff Development
- ᴰGroup Development
- ᴱAction Research

Unification:
- Organizational Goals
- Teacher Needs

PART VI

FUNCTION OF SUPERVISION

Introduction

Chapter 2 introduced five research-based propositions about supervision:

- Proposition 1: *Supervision can enhance teacher belief in a cause beyond oneself.*
- Proposition 2: *Supervision can promote teacher sense of efficacy.*
- Proposition 3: *Supervision can make teachers aware of how they complement each other in striving for common goals.*
- Proposition 4: *Supervision can stimulate teachers to plan common purpose and actions.*
- Proposition 5: *Supervision can challenge teachers to think abstractly about their work.*

Chapter 3 looked at the obstacles to supervision. Those obstacles were listed as three propositions:

- Proposition 1: *Supervision cannot rely on the existing work environment of schools to stimulate instructional improvement.*
- Proposition 2: *Supervisors cannot assume that all teachers are reflective, autonomous, and responsible for their own development.*
- Proposition 3: *Supervisors will have to redefine their responsibilities—from controllers of teachers' instruction to involvers of teachers in decisions about school instruction.*

Chapter 4 detailed the need for looking at teachers in a developmental manner and proposed the following:

- Proposition 1: *Supervision, to be effective, must be a function that responds to the developmental stages of teachers.*
- Proposition 2: *Supervision, to be effective, must be a function that responds to adult life transitions of teachers.*

Finally, Chapter 5 concluded Part II (prerequisite knowledge) with propositions about supervisory beliefs and actions:

- Proposition 1: *Supervisors should use a variety of practices that emanate from various philosophical and belief structures with developmental directionality in mind.*
- Proposition 2: *As supervisors gradually increase teacher choice and control over instructional improvement, teachers will become more abstract and committed to improvement, and a sense of ethos or a cause beyond oneself will emerge.*

The subsequent parts of the book explained the technical and interpersonal skills a supervisor needs to carry out the five tasks of supervision. Each task of supervision was carefully outlined with respect to how its delivery to teachers could help them move toward higher stages of professional development and collective action. This final part will examine the meaning of the function of development as it applies to supervision for school success.

Chapter 20

Development and School Success

The major thesis of this book has been that supervision must be viewed and applied as a developmental function for school success. By way of conclusion, this chapter will summarize what is meant by development and school success. There are two possible meanings of development that are complementary and of equal importance.

The first meaning of development as a supervisory function is the use of instructional-change strategies that move from persuasive to facilitative.

The second meaning of development as a supervisory function is the determination of supervisory intervention according to individual and group characteristics of teachers.

Let's take a closer look at both of these meanings.

Developmental View of Change Strategies for Instructional Improvement

Zaltman and Duncan (1977) identify four strategies that a change agent can use with a target group. The strategies are labeled *power, persuasive, reeducative,* and *facilitative.*

Power strategy is the use of formal authority and control over the target group to force them to change according to the agent's plan. The change agent can use rewards, negative reinforcements, or punishment to achieve compliance.

Persuasive strategy is the use of logic and wisdom to convince the target group that change needs to be made according to the change agent's plan. The agent appeals to the target group's common sense and emotions to achieve their following.

Reeducative strategy is the use of new information provided by the change agent to the target group for the group to determine their own plan. The agent asks the group to rethink what they currently do based on ideas, opinions, and facts not previously considered.

Facilitative strategy is the delivery of resources by the change agent to the target group after the group has determined its plan. The agent serves as a helper in terms of supplying goods, giving technical services, and removing obstacles from the path of the target group's plan.

With these change strategies, we can see how moving from power to facilitative strategies moves the locus of control for the plan of action from the change agent to the target group. A power strategy is a plan the agent forces on the group. A persuasive strategy is a plan by the agent that depends on the group's willingness to follow. A reeducative strategy gives the target group control over the plan based on the agent supplying new information. A facilitative strategy gives complete control to the group to plan, with the agent assisting in the implementation.

Technical skills for supervision can be used in any of the four change strategies, but should they be used? One can use skills of planning and assessing, observing, researching, and evaluating to coerce, persuade, reeducate, or facilitate teachers. Power strategies have little place in public education that undergirds a democratic society. The use of power in public education is simply wrong. Furthermore, even if power were not wrong, in such a loosely coupled institution as school, implementation cannot be constantly monitored and will not work. What is appropriate in schools is the use of persuasive, reeducative, and facilitative change strategies used with the aim of increasing teachers' control over instructional improvement.

Thus three change strategies may be considered as developmental or growth-oriented. Over time, persuasive strategies should be replaced by reeducative strategies, which should in turn be replaced by facilitative strategies. The inner strategies for each task of supervision can be viewed in a similar developmental manner (see Table 20-1).

A change strategy for a group of teachers who have little experience working with each other and are characterized by low abstraction and commitment would be *persuasive*. Direct assistance would be furnished by directive, informational interpersonal behavior by the supervisor. Staff development would focus on demonstration of skills, with the emphasis on explanation, workshop practice, and described personal benefits. Curriculum development would be primarily *imitative*, characterized by externally developed and prescribed curriculum. Group development would have a supervisor assuming the *selling* posture by providing a high task

Table 20-1   Developmental directionality: Change strategies with the tasks of supervision

| | Change Strategy | | |
	Persuasive	Reeducative	Facilitative
Direct assistance	Directive informational	Collaborative	Nondirective
Staff development	Demonstration of skills	Application of skills	Refining skills
Curriculum development	Imitative	Mediative	Generative
Group development	Selling	Participating	Delegating
Action research	Supervisor leadership	Shared leadership	Teacher leadership
Task of supervision			

and high person orientation. Action research would be *led* by the *supervisor*, with teachers' input into a plan for instructional improvement.

A change strategy for a group of teachers who have worked together and possess moderate or mixed degrees of abstraction and commitment would be a *reeducative* strategy. Direct assistance would be provided via collaborative supervisory interpersonal skills. Staff development would emphasize *application of skills*, with classroom practice, observation, and peer supervision. Curriculum development would be *mediative*, characterized by a team of teachers led by district specialists revising and adapting existing curriculum. Group development would have supervisor leadership, characterized by *participating* with teachers in the structure and content of meetings. Action research would be *shared* between supervisor and teacher in determining future instructional improvements.

A change strategy for an experienced, highly abstract and committed faculty would be *facilitative*. Direct assistance would be given through *nondirective* interpersonal behaviors of the supervisor. Staff development would be centered on *refining skills* through modification of existing classroom practice by teams of teachers engaged in brainstorming and problem solving. Curriculum development would be *generative*, characterized by teachers creating their own curricula with the resource assistance of specialists. Group development would be approached by a supervisor as *delegating* the structure and content of the meetings to teachers. In the same manner, action research would come from the *lead-*

ership of the teachers, in which they would plan, act, research, and use the supervisor as a consultant.

A supervisor uses his or her own knowledge about self, characteristics of faculty, and skills for planning supervisory tasks to determine the change strategy to use. There exists no scientific precision or algorithm for determining a faculty's level of experience, abstraction, and commitment. Supervision for successful schools is a developmental function that increases teachers' choices, stimulates teachers' thinking, and encourages collective action—a cause beyond oneself. Thus one meaning of supervision as development is the strategic movement from persuasive to reeducative to facilitative change. The other meaning of supervision as development is responding to teachers as growing, dynamic professionals.

Developmental View of Teachers

Previous chapters have shown that teachers' thinking, concerns, and commitments change over their careers. The changes are not linear or monolithic (Datan, Rodeheaver, and Hughes 1987); there are regressions and recyclings. Advances in one area of instructional improvement proceed at a different pace from the progress in other areas. Yet optimal career development of teachers shows movement from egocentric to altruistic concerns and from concrete to abstract thinking. The most successful schools are characterized by teachers who can think in complex and differentiated ways and who view instruction as a team or school-wide effort. Common cause, common action, challenging ideas, professional talk, and visibility of effort are components of the concept of a cause beyond oneself as the key to successful schools. One simple point of this book is that most teachers do not enter a school with the optimal collective capacity to think and act. A cause beyond oneself is not inherent in schools; most often, the norms of the work environment of schools and the established career patterns of teaching work against such development. For teachers to achieve higher stages of professional development, the supervisor must respond to the individuals' and the group's present stage and alter the work environment in ways that stimulate, challenge, and provide options for them. Therefore the second meaning of development is to view teachers as growing adults who will become more professional and successful as they are provided with a work environment that demands choice, autonomy, dialogue, and reflection.

Current Concerns with Teaching: Within and Without

Our times have witnessed considerable national concern with upgrading the teaching profession. Among the results have been (1) providing college scholarships to attract more intelligent and achievement-minded students into teacher education, (2) raising teacher salaries to compare more favorably with salaries in private industries, and (3) creating financial career ladders to pay teachers substantially higher salaries when they achieve certain plateaus (Darling-Hammond and Berry 1988). The aim of these actions is to attract and keep more capable people in the profession by providing financial incentives. Such increases are long overdue. Teaching should be a more extrinsically rewarded profession. At the same time, national concern has resulted in more legislated requirements for schools. The result has been that even with more financial benefits, teachers' morale and satisfaction has been seriously eroded. Changing the outer conditions for teachers without making subsequent changes in the internal conditions in their work life will not substantially improve instruction. Improving the external conditions without improving the internal conditions is like baking a loaf of bread and having a beautiful, smoothly textured crust, only to bite into a moldy and unmixed core. Obviously, the teaching profession should be satisfying from both within and without.

The Carnegie Foundation survey of 13,500 teachers, directed by Ernest Boyer, addressed these internal conditions (Boyer 1988):

> What the data shows is that teachers feel largely bypassed in the process. Regulations have added more paperwork and the bureaucracy has increased. Teaching conditions have gotten worse. And in the process, morale has gone down.

John Goodlad, upon completing the most comprehensive study of schools ever undertaken in the United States, concluded (Goodlad 1984, pp. 193–194):

> In general the practicing teacher—to the degree we can generalize from our findings—functions in a context where the beliefs and expectations are those of a profession but where the realities tend to constrain, likening actual practice to a trade. ... a question arises as to whether the circumstances can be made conducive to developing in all teachers the behavior a profession entails. By its very nature a profession involves both considerable autonomy in decision making and knowledge and skills developed before entry and then honed in practice. The teachers in our sample, on the whole, went into teaching because of those inherent profes-

sional values. However, they encountered in schools many realities not conducive to professional growth.

Boyer and Goodlad, two of our most distinguished educators, have concluded from their research that the work environment of schools is not conducive to the professional development of teachers and to the success of schools. Only when supervisors attend to individual differences in teachers and improve what Boyer (1983, p. 159) refers to as "the intellectual climate of the school" will teachers become more abstract in their thinking and committed to improving instruction for students.

Only we, as supervisors, can improve the internal conditions of schools. Many supervisors have made their schools centers of teacher inquiry, autonomy, and dialogue. There is certainly enough information available about supervision, interpersonal skills, technical skills, tasks, the nature of change, and the psychology of individual and group development to make all our schools better places. The door for improving internal conditions will never close; it's simply a matter of whether or not we care to step in and make a difference.

The Role of Supervision and Supervisor

This book began by defining the key to successful schools as instructional supervision that fosters teacher development by promoting greater abstraction, commitment, and collective action. The aim of supervision is to bring faculty together as knowledgeable professionals working for the benefit of all students. The role of supervision is to change the attitude of many schools that a classroom is an island unto itself to an attitude that faculty is engaged in a common school-wide instructional task that transcends any one classroom—a cause beyond oneself.

Supervisors—whether they be building-level persons such as school principals, department heads, or instructional lead teachers or master teachers; district personnel such as assistant superintendents, curriculum directors, subject area specialists, or consultants; or school-level generalists (early childhood, elementary, middle school, or secondary)—can play an important part in improving schools. The critical tasks for such improvement are direct assistance, curriculum development, staff development, group development, and action research. Each of these tasks can be planned to enhance teacher development and collective action. District-wide and building-level supervisors can work together to implement such plans. An instrument that shows how a school or district can assess its current supervisory practice can be found in Appendix C. Rarely can one person do it all, but in almost any situation, supervisors concerned with instructional improvement can begin. We know that school success can be achieved when supervisors attend to those tasks that enable teachers to develop individually and collectively (Pratzner 1984).

What Is School Success?

Ironically, the definition of school success has been left to the end of this book. This has been done with a purpose, however. The rationale for a school faculty making its own collective definition of school success should be apparent. In referring to studies of successful schools to support many of the propositions of this book, I mentioned schools that were achieving what they had set out to do, regardless of what those goals were. Some schools prioritize academic learning and achievement as their criteria for success. Some prioritize creativity and self-directed learning. Other schools prioritize problem solving, community involvement, and social cooperation as their criteria for success. Many schools want it all: They want to be successful in academics, creativity, self-directed learning, problem solving, community involvement, and social cooperation (Goodlad 1984, pp. 33–60). Although I personally prefer schools that strive to have it all, that decision should be a local school matter. It is in the clarity of common purpose that action to improve instruction takes place.

With an understanding of what is meant by improved instruction and school success, we can fill in the remaining circle on the diagram of supervision for successful schools that has served as the map of this book (see Figure 20-1).

EXERCISES

Academic

1. Find in the literature a description of an educational leader who has turned an unsuccessful school into a successful one. Which of the change strategies discussed in this chapter did the supervisor use? Report on actions related to each of the five tasks

Figure 20-1 Supervision for successful schools

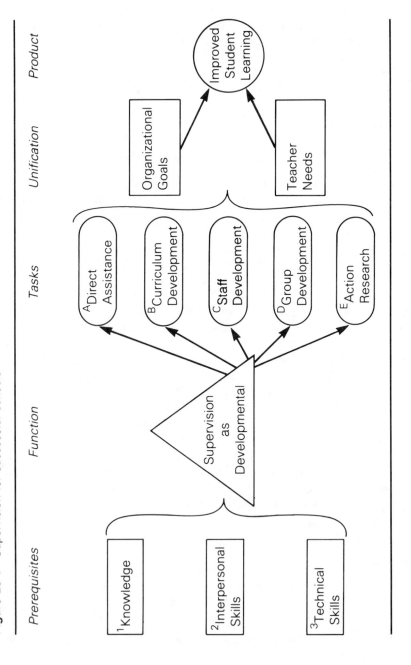

Prerequisites   *Function*   *Tasks*   *Unification*   *Product*

of supervision that he or she carried out while turning the school around.

2. If Boyer (1983, 1988) or Goodlad (1984) were asked to write a three-page paper on "What Makes Effective and Successful Schools," what would each of them say in his essay? Assume the role of one of these authors and, on the basis of reading their studies, write such a paper.

3. Prepare a report comparing and contrasting conclusions and recommendations found in the national study *A Nation at Risk: The Imperative for Educational Reform* (U.S. Department of Education 1983) with the views of this book on steps needed to improve the quality of education in our schools.

4. Prepare a report on recent efforts by individuals and groups outside of education and government to provide concrete assistance to education and educators. What have they proposed, and what is being done?

5. Diagram your own model for effective supervision. Provide a written explanation of each component of your model. Explain the scope, arrangement, sequence, and relationship of model components.

Field

1. Attempt to carry out one (or more) of the tasks of supervision, and use change strategy (persuasive, reeducative, or facilitative) appropriate for the teacher(s) you are working with. Report on your efforts and results.

2. Interview a supervisor on practical problems that must be considered to bring about change within a typical public school system. Prepare a report on your interview. Include your own ideas on how appropriate knowledge, skills, roles, functions, processes, tasks, and strategies discussed in this book can be applied to overcome or reduce problems described by the interviewee.

3. Prepare a photo or written essay about schools, students, teachers, and supervisors that has as its theme "A Cause beyond Oneself" and that reflects the meaning this book attaches to this phrase. Share the essay with others.

4. Paint or sculpt a work of art that symbolizes the developmental function of educational supervision. Share the work of art with those interested in supervision as a developmental function.

5. Create a collage in which the key ideas of the text are represented. Share the collage with others who have read this text.

Developmental

1. Begin a file of newspaper, magazine, and journal articles describing ideas and efforts of individuals and organizations both in and outside of education for achieving success in education.
2. Use selected readings from other texts on educational supervision to compare authors' ideas on specific issues you consider crucial to your own education and development in supervision.
3. Use opportunities as they arise to test out this book's ideas on supervision within your own particular work setting. Through such exploration, determine which of the proposals and suggestions are of most value to your own development and that of others.

REFERENCES

Boyer, E.L. 1983. *High school: A report on secondary education in America.* New York: Harper & Row.

―――. 1988. *Report card on school reform: The teachers speak.* Princeton, N.J.: Carnegie Commission for the Advancement of Teaching.

Darling-Hammond, L., and Berry, B. 1988. *The evolution of teacher policy.* Santa Monica, Calif.: Rand Center for Policy Research in Education.

Datan, N., Rodeheaver, D., and Hughes, F. 1987. Adult development and aging. *Annual Review of Psychology 38*:153–180.

Goodlad, J.I. 1984. *A place called school: Prospects for the future.* New York: McGraw-Hill.

Pratzner, F.C. 1984. Quality of school life: Foundations for improvement. *Educational Researcher 13*(3):20–25.

U.S. Department of Education. 1983. *A nation at risk: The imperative for educational reform.* Washington, D.C.: U.S. Department of Education.

Zaltman, G., and Duncan, R. 1977. *Strategies for planned change.* New York: Wiley.

Chapter 21

Supervision and Reform: At Last, Sam and Samantha's Time?

I had a reunion with an old friend—hurried discussions about shared events, catching up on family and lost acquaintances, tales about sitting in graduate school classes, and the two of us laughing as old pictures were brought out. Each picture spins more stories, more laughter, and more reminiscing about the two years that we taught and lived in the same community. Dinner is over, and the two of us remain seated in our chairs. I start thinking of how Sam and I began teaching together twenty years ago—bright-faced twenty-two-year-olds, eager to save the world. He had come from the Southwest, from a large farming family; I had come from the Northeast, from a suburban clan near a major city. That first year, we were joined by Samantha, from the West Coast, a former Peace Corps volunteer. Besides being new, transplanted, and eager to be teachers, the three of us had little common history. We were of different races, different religions, and different backgrounds. But we became fast friends, teaching in the same school in a small, rural community in the Southeast. We made naive and tactless blunders with school administrators and community officials, but we also made some heartfelt connections with our junior high school students and parents. Twenty years ago, it was obvious that Sam and Samantha were talented eductors. Students clamored to be with them, and their students learned! They taught in unconventional and boisterous ways, but everyone in the school—old-time teachers, administrators, students, and parents—concurred that these two could teach.

After dinner, we discussed the different paths taken by the three of us. Samantha moved with her husband (and dogs) to upstate New York and became a career teacher in a village elementary school. On occasions when I've been to New York state, people who know of Samantha have told me that her classroom exploits have become almost legendary. As for Sam, he's still in the same community, teaching in the same school district where we all began.

He switched to the high school in 1973 and has been there since. Like Samantha, he is a career teacher. As for me, I moved back to New England to teach, then became a school principal, and eventually moved into university work, first in Ohio and now in Georgia.

Later that evening our conversation became quite serious as we discussed education and the current impact of reform. I was somewhat taken aback as Sam mentioned his views:

> I've been teaching for twenty years now, and I can't remember all the "reforms" I've been through. I'm not sure that I can take another one! It seems that every three years someone—whether it's a new hotshot superintendent, the state department, the governor, or a university professor—comes up with some great new idea of how American education is to be saved. What happens is that I and my colleagues become the punching bag recipients of someone else's plan.
>
> Why is it so hard for people outside of the classroom, including you folks from the university, to understand that we teachers know at least as much if not more about our students, teaching, and ways to improve as you do? To be blunt, I've seen these ideas come and go. Each reform dumps more work on us, and we're still left with our 125 students a day, working under the same conditions that I had twenty years ago. Each new idea that comes down from on high doesn't improve my teaching—it often takes away from my teaching! Today I'm being forced to teach in ways that I know are not in the best interest of students.

I listened carefully to Sam because he was telling me almost verbatim the sentiments expressed by scores of other teachers whom I highly respect. I had read of research surveys showing that teachers as a group have had it up to their ears with paperwork, lesson alignment, teaching to test objectives, and being monitored and evaluated according to how closely they follow a lockstep sequence of instruction (Boyer 1988). Somehow, hearing these remarks from Sam meant more to me than survey statistics. I knew him as a friend first, then as a teacher, and he wasn't a doomsayer or a radical. He was a sensible, sane, reserved person who cared about his students. Sam never looked for ways to make his job easier; he looked for ways to do more for his students. When he spoke to me, friend to friend, I knew that he meant what he was saying about educational reform. His was not a union tactic or a special interest plea. If Samantha had been with us, I suspect that she would have concurred with Sam's sentiments, in language more forceful and colorful.

Several months later, after talking with more teachers and administrators throughout the United States and Canada, working with our demonstration school projects in Georgia, reading articles and attending conferences with education policy analysts such as Arthur Wise (1988), Larry Cuban (1987), Susan Rosenholtz (1988), and Michael Kirst (1987), I began to understand the critical juncture of school reform in the 1990s. It has to do with whether or not, at last, it is Sam and Samantha's time. If so, supervision will become the function in schools that brings Sam and Samantha into the process of decision making about teaching. If not, supervision will remain what it has "usually been about: status, authority, and the peculiar evil of silence" (Glickman 1988). If supervision and reform remain as they have been in the 1980s, you can throw this book away or file it under science fiction. However, if it is Sam and Samantha's time, this book might help turn rhetoric into reality for the improvement of schools.

Two Reform Movements

The first reform movement, called legislated learning (Wise 1987), began in the early 1970s as part of school accountability, competency-based education, performance contracting, and a neo-scientific view that research could uncover scientific principles and elements of effective schools and effective teaching. If students were not learning, and if schools were not improving, it was because educators in the schools were not following the best available scientific evidence. The spate of reports in the early 1980s, which painted a bleak picture of public education and student achievement in comparison to other industrialized countries, added fuel to a scientific, reductionist view of reform—the need for installing "best practice" into the schools. In 1983 *A Nation at Risk* deplored the mediocrity of education and stated unequivocally that schools as they exist have done a ruinous job to the economy and society. An "unfriendly nation" wishing to undermine the United States could not have done more thorough damage than we have done in our schools. Such inflammatory language propelled legislative initiatives into an array of requirements, enacted through the prodding of governors throughout the land. The banner words for legislative learning were "academic excellence" (Kirst 1987). Schools were to become centers of excellence and have excellent education! This was to be accomplished by the states (via their respective departments of education) taking control over local schools through "standards" and "requirements." Statewide curriculum, statewide tests, statewide teacher evaluation, statewide promotion and retention policies, and statewide mentor career ladder plans were enacted (Cornett 1987).

To be sure, such renewed interest in education created benefits. More equitable funding formulae, improved salaries, scholarships and career incentives, and facility upgrades were some of the positives. But *"legislated learning" and "academic excellence" reflected an essentialist, top-down reform movement that viewed teachers and administrators as the problem, rather than the solution to poor schools.* The feeling was that schools, when left to local educators and local boards, could not be trusted. Since the early 1970s, there has been a steady increase in regulations and a tightening of external controls over school operations. The typical procedure for determining solutions to school improvement has been to appoint a state blue-ribbon commission consisting of political and corporate leaders, with only token representation from educators. The commission then listens to research experts, develops a list of requirements for schools, and has the list revised and approved by the state legislature, signed by the governor, and enforced by the state department of education. Every three to five years, when education results are publicized as still unsatisfactory, another round of legislated learning occurs, with the establishment of the next blue-ribbon commission.

The second reform movement that has more recently emerged is entitled *"empowerment"*; the banner that flies over it has the words" *"restructuring schools"* (Pipho 1988; Sergiovanni and Moore 1989). For various reasons, some having to do with increased dissatisfaction with the results of legislated learning, some with a lack of state money to fund legislated mandates, and some with a political climate shifting toward concern with the issues of poverty and disenfranchisement, there is a different experimental and pragmatic view of school reform: *Local teachers and administrators are the solution, rather than the problem in school reform.* Schools need to be deregulated so as to give local educators the maximum flexibility to address the unique educational and instructional concerns of the students and community.

This bottom-up view of school reform, wherein the district and state become providers of resources, money, and knowledge to the local schools to facilitate the school's own instructional decisions, is an attempt to promote variety rather than uniformity of practices across schools and districts. The premise is that there are not and never can be scientifically validated best practices of supervision and teaching. Rather, best practice must be derived from what is best for students—by those teachers closest to them. Reports by the Carnegie Forum (1986) and the Holmes Group (1986) have stimulated much discussion about a bottom-up, grass-roots approach to school improvement, whereby teachers are the primary instructional decision makers in the school. The principal is not seen as the sole instructional leader, but rather as the leader of instructional leaders. Teachers are jointly responsible for supervision of the instructional tasks in a school—direct assistance, staff development, curriculum development, group development, and action research. Examples of second-wave reform are the Washington State Schools for the Twenty-First Century Program, the Massachusetts Carnegie School Program, the National Coalition of Essential Schools, the National Network for Educational Renewal, the Georgia Program for School Improvement, the National Education Association's Mastery in Learning Project, the American Federation of Teachers' Research-into-Practice Practitioners Network, and the Association of Supervision and Curriculum Development's Consortium of Restructured Schools.

The tension in education, at this writing, is that there are two totally contradictory reform movements going on at the same time. Education is at a crossroads. The legislated learning movement is nearing a possible culmination point (in some states, there simply isn't much more that can be legislated, short of hiring full-time inspectors for each school); the empowerment movement gaining momentum. Educators are hearing two different messages. One says, "You have district and state requirements you must comply with!" The other says, "You are the professionals—do what you think is best; we'll work with you." No wonder educators are a bit schizophrenic at this time!

Whether education reform will remain primarily legislative or tilt more towards empowerment has much to do with the initiatives and preparation of those in instructional leadership roles. Empowerment meets with the overwhelming approval of most educators, but if it is to succeed, many issues, nuisances, and perils must be personally and professionally confronted and resolved. If the function of supervision is to empower teachers rather than enforce their compliance, we must be fully aware of the revolutionary changes this entails in terms of ways of thinking about ourselves, teachers, and schools. We also need to consider the transitional steps necessary to move from external control and uniformity of practice to informed, school-based decision making, internal control, and divergence of practice.

Reform One—The Answers;
Reform Two—The Questions

As Cuban (1987) has noted, most reform efforts do not fundamentally alter the prevailing organization, scheduling, curriculum, or structure of teaching. Legislative learning reforms have tended to add more to what is already taking place. Certain and uniform answers to reform are readily proposed by laypersons and embraced by the public because they fit into the public's (and our) notions of teaching and schools. The practices that are proposed, passed, and regulated to improve schools are said to be "scientifically derived," "research-based," and "proven" answers that will work if only local schools will implement them correctly. However, these answers consist largely of doing more of what is currently being done. Most legislated reforms enact

- More direct teacher-centered instruction
- More homework
- More standardization and restrictions of the curriculum
- More testing of students
- More alignment of lesson plans with test objectives
- More uniform, lockstep retention policies
- More and tighter evaluation of teachers

As such practices are implemented over a period of time, and noticeable improvements in student achievement, success, and attitude are not forthcoming, the next blue-ribbon commission, state superintendent, or district central office superintendent comes forth with a further plan to tighten, standardize, and demand more of what has previously not worked. As Plank (1987) observed, legislative reform answers tend to "reinforce rather than challenge the present structure . . . (and) have ensured that the main consequence has been further homogenization . . . among schools both across and within states" (pp. 16–17). The troublesome point is that as such practices fail to improve learning for students, the answer has been to enforce more of what is not working.

For example, there have been only slight gains in basic-skills achievement in the past decade, according to a national survey (Carnegie Forum 1988). The Education Testing Service (1986), in reviewing three National Assessment of Educational Progress Surveys, reported:

> Evidence is mounting that Americans are not learning to read and write with more than "surface understanding" whether . . . fourth-grade . . . or young adults, their ability to dissect ideas and defend positions is limited.

Furthermore, 700,000 functionally illiterate adults continue to graduate each year, and another 700,000 students drop out of school. The dropout rate in the United States remains alarmingly high. "Since 1980, the national figure for all students has declined from 76 percent high school graduation to 73 percent. The unintended fallout from ... excellence state reforms undoubtedly will cut the number even further" (Hodginson 1985, p. 13).

Why has legislated reform, based on applying more of the same, persisted at a time when evidence indicates little progress and when recent research indicates that successful schools are not a template of homogeneous, standardized, and conventional practice? Legislative, top-down reform depends on authorities having the right answers and getting Sam and Samantha to do it right!

Empowerment reform raises the possibility that authorities do not know all the answers and allows school practitioners to work out their own solutions. Empowerment reform asks questions that defy the conventional norms, structures, and pat answers of schools. Among the questions to be wrestled with by empowered professionals are:

- Why have grade levels?
- Why have grades?
- What is the best curriculum?
- What are the best locations for education in and out of schools?
- Why teach six and one-half hours, five days a week? Why fifty-minute periods of time?
- Why subjects? Why not integrated projects?
- Why not portfolios of work for student evaluation?
- Why textbooks?
- Why one teacher, one classroom?
- Why Carnegie units?

Such questions of uncertainty challenge the fundamental structure of schools.

Shanker, commenting on the reason for the poor higher-order thinking skills of students, says that "it is the way schools are pretty universally structured now, that not all kids can sit still and listen to somebody for five or six hours each day" (Association for Supervision and Curriculum Development 1988, p. 6). Shanker's comment echoes a conception of education that has been largely lost in the legislated reform of our schools. According to Piaget,

> The goal of intellectual education is not to know how to repeat or retain ready-made truths. ... It is in learning to master the truth by oneself at the risk of losing a lot of time and going through all the roundabout ways that are inherent in real activity [1973, p. 106].

Some of you may take such asking of questions as heresy, while others may work in schools where such questions are routinely raised and answered. Schools that are empowered often do not look like the public's conventional image of schools. The questions are not meant to shock—simply to indicate that empowerment reform opens the boundaries of acceptable practice. With excitement come discomfort, dissent, controversy, challenge, and at times fright.

Let's take such a mundane convention as a school lunchroom as an example. Students wait in line with their trays, receive their food, and sit at an institutional-type table. Virtually every school operates within this convention. Why? There are a few schools where lunch is an aesthetic, pleasant learning experience, with piped-in music, white tablecloth, and family-style serving. Most summer camps operate this way; why don't more schools? It doesn't cost more, except for washing the tablecloths, so why not? Likewise, there are a few high schools in the country that don't use Carnegie units or fifty-minute class periods; why aren't there more? There are elementary programs that don't use basal reader textbooks, don't have grade levels, don't use standardized text, and are very successful. Why aren't there more? There are school districts that don't evaluate teachers according to six or seven elements of effective instruction; some evaluate according to three elements—"due regard," "due process," and "due diligence." Why aren't there more? Because we are rarely challenged to raise questions about conventional practices, so that new possibilities can emerge. The point of empowerment reform is not that conventional answers should be rejected and that all schools should innovate. The point is that when schools are not regulated by the outside, all instructional practices are fair game for discussion and action.

Are we willing to identify, ask, and act upon such questions? Do we want the power to do so? This is not an idle question, because in doing so, the locus of accountability and responsibility changes.

Rhetoric or Reality of Restructuring

Educators, like all people, are intrigued and flattered when they are viewed as the source of control in an improvement effort. We may think of empowerment as the heady nectar of beauty and strength, but when the "rubber hits the road" and states begin to give districts the opportunity to restructure their schools, will we do it? Some schools initiate and fight for restructuring in their districts, while other schools passively accept and complain about external mandates. When restrictions are lessened and schools are given more freedom, many schools will probably "talk a good game" but stay within the same conventions. To be honest, if history is any guide, most people in controlling positions in schools and districts would rather complain about the current system of education than do something about it (Cuban 1984; Reid 1987).

To put ourselves "at risk" by taking responsibility for change is another matter altogether. What will it mean to prepare ourselves for *true* improvement of schools? I say *true* because schools will not improve until teachers—the people closest to students—are given the choice and responsibility to make collective, informed decisions about teaching practice. The arena of choice, responsibility, and decision making may be small and restrictive for some staffs to begin with, but the direction should be to enlarge choice, responsibility, and decision making over time. This is the *only* way supervision will improve instruction on a large and long-term scale. Supervision must shift decision making about instruction from external authority to internal control. As long as decisions are made by authorities away from those who teach, we will have dormant, unattractive work environments that will stymie the intellectual growth of teachers and the intellectual life of students. Legislative answers can never work entirely, because teachers are the heart of teaching. Without choice and responsibility, they will comply, subvert, or flee, and motivation, growth, and collective purpose will remain absent (see Lutz and Lutz 1987). What motivates people to work harder and smarter is not money but rather a work environment "that lets [professionals] make decisions and nurtures a free exchange of ideas and information" (Harris Survey 1988).

Now that the rhetoric of restructuring schools, empowerment, school councils, and strategic, school-based decision making is upon us, the next decade will reveal whether we are only flirting or ready to make a profound commitment to improving schools.

A Profession Based on Uncertainty

One wonders how good a law firm would be if it were given manuals on how to apply the law, were told precisely how much time to spend on each case, were directed how to govern its internal affairs, and had no say whatever in who the partners were. Teaching often lacks a sense of ownership, a sense among the teachers working together that the school is theirs, and that its future and their reputation are indistinguishable. Hired hands own nothing, are told what to do, and have little stake in their enterprises. Teachers are often treated like hired hands. Not surprisingly, they often act like hired hands [Sizer 1984, p. 184].

A profession is marked by its ability to make decisions about problematic situations that defy prior technical prescriptions. Members must bring their own background, training, and skills to bear on the problem and devise, improvise, and revise strategies along the way (Schon 1987). Education is a tremendously complex, fragile, and uncontrollable enterprise. Teaching systems cannot ride roughshod over students; understanding students must determine teaching practices. Consequences can be anticipated but not known until actions are taken (Smith and Blase 1987). Supervision of instruction cannot be a system that rides herd over teachers; understanding teachers must determine supervisory practices.

Not all teachers, administrators, and schools are ready for shared governance. In some schools, opening the faculty for empowerment would be like opening the door of a cage containing birds who have had their wings clipped for years. Pushing them out the door won't help them fly! Letting the feathers grow back gradually while enlarging the cage and adding more perches will help them relearn the skills of flying. When they are ready, the door is opened and a new world is revealed. So it is with schools!

What a restructured school will look like is difficult to say. We won't know until we are in the midst of doing it. The path is uncertain, full of risks and danger. However, we can prepare for successful explorations by finding the perches in our schools and enlarging the cage of choice and responsibility for decision making. It's not good enough to say that we want empowerment while continuing to reinforce top-down bureaucratic structures. "Nor is it good enough . . . for nominally accepting one educational philosophy and accommodating ourselves in practice to another. It is a challenge to understand the task of reorganization courageously and to keep at it persistently" (Dewey 1916, p. 137).

Will we make mistakes? Of course! Parents and communities will need to be brought along as vital stakeholders in the process. Misunderstandings, setbacks, and controversy need to be anticipated, and the information gained from such difficulties should be used in each subsequent decision. Accountability of results will be essential. Schools will have to determine and evaluate the impact on students. Will each program be successful? Of course not! We will have to learn from failure as well as from success in developing future programs. Will all teachers and administrators be eager to participate? No, we will have to move with the movers and keep access and information open to the resisters. We will have to listen carefully to the resistance to understand and check our directions.

State requirements will be lessened, but will they go away? No! Community expectations for schools will exist. Legal parameters for public schools, within a democratic society, will remain in place. School boards will remain the legal entity for district policies. Resources of time, money, personnel, and materials will remain finite. Anarchy should not be the condition of schools; neither should prescriptive mandates void of choice. Freedom in a democracy is choice within boundaries, and our schools should be models of democracy.

Finally, who will be accountable for the results? When the choice and responsibility for decision making rests squarely with the staff in the schools, it will no longer be sufficient to say that the school is accountable to the community or to the state. Educators will have to be accountable to themselves. By taking on choice, responsibility, and the ensuing accountability for decisions, schools will be moral institutions (Wynne 1987).

Stupidity and Betterment

Is it desirable to move from an era of legislative, top-down reform to an era of grass-roots, bottom-up reform? Will all schools make improvements? Will shared leadership solve nagging concerns? Will innovation be practical and valuable? My answer is that more schools will improve than won't. Shared leadership will propel more schools than not into purposeful actions. More innovations will be successful than not. However, it's not a utopia! Some teachers and administrators will abuse such freedom and make their own jobs easier, to the detriment of students. Other schools will talk about improvement and do little. Some schools will make minor changes for the advantage of students. Many schools will unleash the unfulfilled wisdom and potential of their staffs to infuse learning with excitement and relevance. The pivotal question is whether schools as a whole will be further ahead by decentralizing decisions about supervision, curriculum, and instruction than they would be by keeping such decisions centralized, uniform, and mandated. I'm not naive—there are admittedly some sick schools where such decentralization will feed back into an unsavory protectionism that is harmful to students. In such cases, external authorities will need the legal right to step in with mandates. On the whole, however, education will be improved by increasing the arena of decision making for those who teach—for the simple reason that teachers are not stupid!

What it finally comes down to is a judgment by those in positions of control about the wisdom of teachers. Aubrey Finch, a high school principal who has been practicing shared instructional governance with his staff since 1983, was challenged at a conference by another principal: "How can you be one vote among equals with your staff on instructional decisions? How can you afford to lose a decision that you oppose? Aren't you the legal authority of your school? Doesn't your school board, like mine, put your neck in the noose if things go awry at your school?" Finch, without hesitation, replied, "My teachers aren't stupid. In fact, many of them know quite a bit more about teaching than I do. Yes, my board holds me responsible. I'd rather have a decision by a collection of wise people than one by me. But if your teachers are stupid and you are smarter than they are, don't involve them in decision making" (Glickman 1989).

That is the keystone of this book: one's view of teachers. If they are viewed as stupid, and those with formal authority see themselves as wiser and superior, teachers will continue to be treated as deskilled workers following prescriptive mandates. If, on the other hand, teachers are viewed as wise, with the potential to be wiser, those who hold formal authority will treat them as colleagues and participants in the intellectual journey of bettering instruction.

Sam and Samantha taught with me twenty years ago. Now I have a position with public status, a degree of fame, and some credibility: a university professor who has written six books and given numerous keynote addresses to national forums. But I don't come close to possessing the wisdom that Sam and Samantha have about their teaching, their schools, their students, and their communities. Furthermore, I do not have the intensity of care that Sam and Samantha have for their students and for instruction in their schools. Simply put, Sam and Samantha are not stupid! They are not only wiser than I am on many matters; they are probably as wise as, if not wiser than, their department heads, supervisors, principals, central office directors, and state officials. It is amazing that they have persevered for so long in schools where they are viewed as persons who are neither capable nor inclined to participate in decisions about teaching and learning.

Sam and Samantha are like most teachers, caring and wise, with untapped potential for making schools what they truly can be—educative settings. Can we acknowledge that teachers possess expertise, knowledge, and concern, and that they will show a far greater sense of purpose ("a cause beyond oneself") when decisions are made *with* rather than *at* them? At last, is it time for teachers to be equals, rather than perfunctory advisors in the remaking of education? Is it Sam and Samantha's time?

REFERENCES

Association for Supervision and Curriculum Development. 1988. Restructured schools: Frequently involved, rarely defined. *ASCD Update 30*(1):6.

Boyer, E. 1988. *Report on school reform: The teachers speak.* New York: Carnegie Foundation for the Advancement of Teaching.

Carnegie Forum on Education and The Economy Task Force on Teaching as a Profession. 1986. *A nation prepared: Teachers for the 21st century.* New York: Carnegie Forum on Education and the Economy.

Cornett, L. 1987. More pay for teachers and administrators who do more: Incentive pay programs, 1987. *Career Ladder Clearinghouse* (December):1–27.

Cuban, L. 1984. *How teachers taught: Constancy and change in American classrooms, 1890–1980.* New York: Longman.

———. 1987. The district superintendent and the restructuring of schools. Paper presented to the Conference on Restructuring Schooling for Quality Education, San Antonio, Tex., August.

Dewey, J. 1916. *Democracy and education.* New York: Macmillan.

Educational Testing Service. 1987. Learning to be literate. *ETS Developments 33*(1):2.

Glickman, C.D. 1988. Supervision and the rhetoric of empowerment: Silence or collision? *Action in Teacher Education 10*(1): 11–15.

———. 1989. *The story of Ogelthorpe County High School.* Athens, Ga.: Monographs in Education.

Harris Survey. 1988. Rating the work place. Cited in the *Burlington* (Vermont) *Free Press,* July 23, 1988, 18a.

The Holmes Group. 1986. *Tomorrow's teachers.* East Lansing, Mich.: The Holmes Group.

Hodginson, H.L. 1985. All one system: *Demographics of education— Kindergarten through graduate school.* Washington, D.C.: Institute for Educational Leadership.

Kirst, M.W. 1987. Rethinking who should control our schools. Paper presented to the Conference on Restructuring Schooling for Quality Education, San Antonio, Tex., August.

Lutz, F.W., and Lutz, S.B. 1987. Reforming rural education: A look from both ends of the tunnel. Paper presented at the annual meeting of the American Educational Research Association, Washington, D.C., April.

National Commission on Excellence in Education. 1983. *A nation at risk: The imperative for educational reform.* Washington, D.C.: U.S. Government Printing Office.

Piaget, J. 1973. *To understand is to invent: The future of education.* New York: Viking Press.

Pipho, C. 1988. Restructured schools: Rhetoric on the rebound? *Kappan 69*(10):710–711.

Plank, D.W. 1987. Why school reform doesn't change schools: Political and organizational explanations. Paper presented at the annual meeting of the American Educational Research Association, Washington, D.C., April.

Reid, W.A. 1987. Institutions and practice: Professional education reports and the language of reform. *Educational Researcher 16*(8):10–15.

Rosenholtz, S. 1988. Improving the quality of work life in teaching. Paper presented to the Conference on Restructuring from Within: The Next Reform Agenda for School Improvement, Athens, Ga., June.

Schon, D.A. 1987. *Educating the reflective practitioner.* San Francisco: Jossey-Bass.

Sergiovanni, T.J., and Moore, J.H. 1989. *Schooling for tomorrow: Directing reforms to issues that count.* Boston: Allyn and Bacon.

Sizer, T. 1984. *Horace's compromise: The dilemma of the American high school.* Boston: Houghton Mifflin.

Smith, J., and Blase, J. 1987. Educational leadership as a moral concept. Paper presented at the annual meeting of the American Educational Research Association, Washington, D.C., April.

Wise, A.E. 1987. The teacher as professional: Policy implications for quality schooling. Paper presented at the Conference on

Restructuring Schooling for Quality Education, San Antonio, Tex., August.

———. 1988. The two conflicting trends in school reform. Legislated learning revisited. *Kappan* 69(5):328–333.

Wynne, E. 1987. Schools as morally governed institutions. Paper presented at the annual meeting of the American Educational Research Association, Washington, D.C., April.

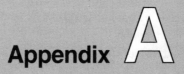

Appendix A

What Is Your
Educational Philosophy?

Instructions

Please check the answer under each item that best reflects your thinking. You may also want to check more than one answer for any one of the questions.

1. What is the essence of education?
   A. The essence of education is *reason* and *intuition*.
   B. The essence of education is *growth*.
   C. The essence of education is *knowledge* and *skills*.
   D. The essence of education is *choice*.

2. What is the nature of the learner?
   A. The learner is an experiencing organism.
   B. The learner is a unique, free choosing, and responsible creature made up of intellect and emotion.
   C. The learner is a rational and intuitive being.
   D. The learner is a storehouse for knowledge and skills, which, once acquired, can later be applied and used.

3. How should education provide for the needs of man?
   A. The students need a passionate encounter with the perennial problems of life; the agony and joy of love, reality of choice, anguish of freedom, consequences of actions and the inevitability of death.
   B. Education allows for the needs of man when it inculcates the child with certain esential skills and knowledge which all men should possess.

Source: "What is Your EP: A Test Which Identifies Your Educational Philosophy," by Patricia D. Jersin, appears in *Clearing House* Vol. 46, January 1972, pp. 274–278. Reprinted by permission of Fairleigh Dickinson University. (You may note that Jersin has identified four philosophies. Since educational *practice* is reflected in three, I would subsume her philosophies in this way—Perennialism (belief in changeless knowledge) grouped with Essentialism, Progressivism as Experimentalism, and Existentialism as itself.)

C. The one distinguishing characteristic of man is intelligence. Education should concentrate on developing the intellectual needs of students.

D. Since the needs of man are variable, education should concentrate on developing the individual differences in students.

4. What should be the environment of education?

A. Education should possess an environment where the student adjusts to the material and social world as it really exists.

B. The environment of education should be life itself, where students can experience living—not prepare for it.

C. The environment of education should be one that encourages the growth of free, creative individuality, not adjustment to group thinking nor the public norms.

D. Education is not a true replica of life, rather, it is an artificial environment where the child should be developing his intellectual potentialities and preparing for the future.

5. What should be the goal of education?

A. Growth, through the reconstruction of experience, is the nature, and should be the open-ended goal, of education.

B. The only type of goal to which education should lead is to the goal of truth, which is absolute, universal, and unchanging.

C. The primary concern of education should be with the development of the uniqueness of individual students.

D. The goal of education should be to provide a framework of knowledge for the student against which new truths can be gathered and assimilated.

6. What should be the concern of the school?

A. The school should concern itself with man's distinguishing characteristic, his mind, and concentrate on developing rationality.

B. The school should provide an education for the "whole child," centering its attention on all the needs and interests of the child.

C. The school should educate the child to attain the basic knowledge necessary to understand the real world outside.

D. The school should provide each student with assistance in his journey toward self-realization.

7. What should be the atmosphere of the school?

A. The school should provide for group thinking in a democratic atmosphere that fosters cooperation rather than competition.

    B. The atmosphere of the school should be one of authentic freedom where a student is allowed to find his own truth and ultimate fulfillment through non-conforming choice making.

    C. The school should surround its students with "Great Books" and foster individuality in an atmosphere of intellectualism and creative thinking.

    D. The school should retain an atmosphere of mental discipline, yet incorporate innovative techniques which would introduce the student to a perceptual examination of the realities about him.

8. How should appropriate learning occur?

    A. Appropriate learning occurs as the student freely engages in choosing among alternatives while weighing personal responsibilities and the possible consequences of his actions.

    B. Appropriate learning takes place through the experience of problem-solving projects by which the child is led from practical issues to theoretical principles (concrete-to-abstract).

    C. Appropriate learning takes place as certain basic readings acquaint students with the world's permanencies, inculcating them in theoretical principles that they will later apply in life (abstract-to-concrete).

    D. Appropriate learning occurs when hard effort has been extended to absorb and master the prescribed subject matter.

9. What should be the role of the teacher?

    A. The teacher should discipline pupils intellectually through a study of the great works in literature where the universal concerns of man have best been expressed.

    B. The teacher should present principles and values and the reasons for them, encouraging students to examine them in order to choose for themselves whether or not to accept them.

    C. The teacher should guide and advise students, since the children's own interests should determine what they learn, not authority nor the subject matter of the textbooks.

    D. The teacher, the responsible authority, should mediate between the adult world and the world of the child since immature students cannot comprehend the nature and demands of adulthood by themselves.

10. What should the curriculum include?

    A. The curriculum should include only that which has survived the test of time and combines the symbols and ideas of literature, history, and mathematics with the sciences of the physical world.

B. The curriculum should concentrate on teaching students how to manage change through problem solving activities in the social studies . . . empirical sciences and vocational technology.

C. The curriculum should concentrate on intellectual subject matter and include English, languages, history, mathematics, natural sciences, the fine arts, and also philosophy.

D. The curriculum should concentrate on the humanities; history, literature, philosophy, and art—where greater depth into the nature of man and his conflict with the world are revealed.

11. What should be the preferred teaching method?

A. *Projects* should be the preferred method whereby the students can be guided through problem-solving experiences.

B. *Lectures, readings,* and *discussions* should be the preferred methods for training the intellect.

C. *Demonstrations* should be the preferred method for teaching knowledge and skills.

D. *Socratic dialogue* (drawing responses from a questioning conversation) should be the preferred method for finding the self.

Scoring the Test

This test is self-scoring. Circle the answer you selected for each of the questions checked on the test (Table A-1). Total the number of circles below each column.

Table A-1   What is your EP?

	Progressivism	Perennialism	Essentialism	Existentialism
1	B	A	C	D
2	A	C	D	B
3	D	C	B	A
4	B	D	A	C
5	A	B	D	C
6	B	A	C	D
7	A	C	D	B
8	B	C	D	A
9	C	A	D	B
10	B	C	A	D
11	A	B	C	D

Implications

The four answers selected for each of the questions in this multiple-choice test represent positions on educational issues being taken by hypothetical advocates of the major educational philosophies heading each column—Progressivism, Perennialism, Essentialism, and Existentialism. If, in scoring your test, you find that a majority of your choices, no matter how much doubling up of answers, falls in a single column, you are selecting a dominant educational philosophy from among the four. For example, if you find your totals: Progressivism (9), Perennialism (1), Essentialism (3), and Existentialism (2); your dominant educational philosophy as determined by this test would be *Progressivism* (9 out of 15 choices being a majority). If you discover yourself spread rather evenly among several, or even all four, this scattering of answers demonstrates an eclectic set of educational values. Indecisiveness in selecting from the four positions could indicate other values and beliefs not contained within one of these major educational systems.

In all formal systems of philosophy, an important measure of the system's validity is its consistency. Your consistency in taking this test can be measured by comparing the answer you selected for item #1 that identifies *essence* with your other answers. The more of the remaining 10 responses you find in the same column where you circled item #1, the more consistent you should be in your educational philosophy. The fewer of the other 10 responses in the same column as item #1, the more you should find your responses contradicting one another—a problem inherent in eclecticism. Again, keep in mind, lack of consistency may also be due to valuing another set of educational beliefs, consistent in themselves, but not included as one of the possible systems selected for representation here.

Appendix B

Skill Practices Using Nondirective, Collaborative, and Directive Informational Approaches

B1: Directions for All Skill Practices

1. Each conference will have the same identical three phases.

Phase One: Goal Identification.

Gathering information and descriptions of situation
Finding a focus for improvement
Stating a goal

Phase Two: Plan.

Exploring alternative actions
Anticipating consequences for various alternatives
Selecting and specifying those actions likely to achieve the goal
Writing the plan

Phase Three: Critique.

Supervisor asking for feedback on his or her behaviors
Discussing ways the supervisor could improve further conferences
with supervisee

2. Each conference will produce a simplified plan of action to include

I. Goal to be achieved

II. Specific actions to be taken

(A more detailed plan could include objectives, activities, resources, and evaluation.)

3. Each skill practice should be a *real* conference dealing with an *actual* professional concern, problem, or situation that the supervisee wishes to act upon and that is *within* his or her control to do something about. Situations that are dependent on actions by persons outside of the supervisees' sphere of influence should not be used in these skill practices.

4. An authentic and original plan that will be implemented should be the outcome of the conference. Once again, supervisor and supervisees are not pretending to be somebody else—they are to be themselves, engaged in real professional discussion about goals and actions.

5. The only difference is that one person is responsible for conducting the conference according to a particular approach. The person conducting the conference is called the supervisor, responsible for moving through the three phases and seeing that an action plan is derived. The supervisee is the person who comes to the conference with a professional goal or concern for which he or she wishes to establish a plan.

6. At the conclusion of each skill practice, it is illuminating to ask the *supervisees,* in writing, to rate the value of their plans (how good is the plan for reaching your goal) on a scale from one (not of value) to ten (of great value) and then, also in writing, to describe with three adjectives the personal experience of having a (nondirective, collaborative, or directive informational) approach used. Ask the supervisor to describe with three adjectives the personal experience of using a (nondirective, collaborative, or directive informational) approach. Each person should write independently, and then the instructor can solicit responses to each question with the entire group. Some fascinating discussions about the use and misuse of a particular approach usually ensue, with an opportunity at the end to compare all three approaches.

7. Each skill practice session will need about thirty to forty minutes for the actual conference and twenty to thirty minutes for debriefing—a total of fifty to seventy minutes for each approach.

8. It might help to reproduce the skill practice guides on the next two pages as overheads. Explain the approach to be used, ask

CONFERENCES

GOAL IDENTIFICATION PHASE
Information & Descriptions

Focus on Improvement

Goal Statement

PLAN PHASE
Alternative Actions

Consequences

Selecting & Specifying

Writing Plan

CRITIQUE PHASE
Feedback on Supervisor's Behaviors

Feedback on Ways to Improve Next Conference

WRITTEN ACTION PLAN

Goal Statement

Actions to be Taken

1.

2.

3.

Signed _____

_____

participants to pair off, designate supervisor and supervisee, and time (announcing start and stop) through each step of the conference.

B2: Nondirective Skill Practice

Directions: Review Chapter 7. (Remember that the supervisor's responsibility is to facilitate the supervisee's own thinking and decision making and not to impose his or her own ideas.)

I. Goal Identification Phase
   A. Supervisor begins, "Could you explain the current concern that you need to take action?"
      Supervisee talk   3 minutes
      Paraphrase by supervisor   45 seconds
      Accuracy of paraphrase
      (check by supervisor)   30 seconds
   B. Supervisor asks questions to gather further information—2 minutes.
   C. Supervisor states perceived goal and checks for accuracy. Supervisor writes goal on first part of plan—3 minutes.

II. Plan Phase
   A. Supervisor asks supervisee to brainstorm possible alternative actions (at least three)—5 minutes.
   B. Supervisor asks supervisee to weigh pros and cons of alternatives—3 minutes.
   C. Supervisor asks, "What will you do?" Paraphrase: "Then I understand you will. . . ."—2 minutes.
   D. Supervisor now writes a plan of action as dictated by supervisee (make sure actions are clear and specific)—3 minutes.

III. Critique Phase—3 minutes
   A. Supervisor asks, "What feedback can you give me on how I conducted this conference?"
   B. Supervisor asks, "What might we do next time to make these observations and conferences more helpful?"
   C. Supervisor summarizes what he or she has learned, for use in later conferences.

B3: Collaborative Skill Practice

Directions: Review Chapter 8. (Remember that the supervisee and supervisor have equal influence in determining the goal and plan. So as not to exert undue influence, the supervisor should allow the supervisee to lead first in each phase of the conference. Before beginning, they should pick a topic of concern that is of mutual interest.)

I. Goal Identification Phase

    A. *Describe the situation* (both parties). Supervisor asks supervisee to explain the current situation that he or she wishes to improve. Supervisor paraphrases and checks for accuracy, and then explains how he or she sees the situation, asks for a paraphrase, and gives feedback on accuracy—7 minutes.

    B. *Further information.* Supervisee asks questions of supervisor and supervisor asks questions of supervisee, to gather further information to determine a common goal—5 minutes.

    C. *State goal.* Supervisor states the common goal, checks for accuracy and agreement, and writes it down on the first part of the plan—2 minutes.

II. Plan Phase

    A. *Brainstorm possible actions* (let supervisee lead). Supervisor asks supervisee to brainstorm 3 to 5 possible alternative actions and then offers his or her own possibilities of actions—2 minutes.

    B. *Ask questions and discuss consequences.* Supervisor and supervisee question each other about consequences of various proposed actions and look for commonalities and differences—5 minutes.

    C. *Negotiate.* Supervisor and supervisee determine actions that they both agree will help reach the goal—2 minutes.

    D. *State a jointly agreed action.* Supervisor and supervisee specify the agreed upon actions so that each knows exactly:
Who will do what?
How will it be done?
When will it be done?
When will it be reviewed?—3 minutes.

    E. *Write plan.* Supervisor writes the agreed-upon actions in the plan. (No action is recorded unless both parties fully agree to it.)—5 minutes.

III. Critique Phase—3 minutes

    A. Supervisor asks, "What feedback can you give me on how I conducted this conference?"

    B. Supervisor asks, "What might we do next time to make these observations and conferences more helpful?"

    C. Supervisor summarizes what he or she has learned, for use in later conferences.

B4: Directive Informational Skill Practice

Directions: Review Chapter 9. (Remember that the supervisor is the source of information and direction in developing the plan. In this case, the supervisor does not have prior information about the situation or possible goals, so he or she gathers feedback to identify the goal. Eventually, the supervisor will provide the arena of choice for the supervisee in developing the final plan.)

I. Goal Identification Phase
   A. Supervisor tells supervisee, "Describe to me the situation that you are facing"—3 minutes.
   B. Supervisor asks for additional information about the situation—2 minutes.
   C. Supervisor asks questions to understand the supervisee's goal—2 minutes.
   D. The supervisor states his or her understanding of the goal and asks supervisee to react to the statement—1 minute.
   E. Supervisor writes statement of goal—1 minute.

II. Plan Phase
   A. After writing the goal, the supervisor thinks of possible actions and says, "Based on my experience (knowledge), I believe that you might do the following. . . ." The supervisor gives at least three specific actions and reviews the anticipated consequences of using each action—4 minutes.
   B. Supervisor asks supervisee to respond to the proposed actions: "What do you think?"—2 minutes.
   C. After hearing the supervisee's response, the supervisor now modifies, revises, or expands the alternatives and directs the choices. "These appear to be realistic actions that you might take. You could do the following . . . ." Supervisor then asks "Which one of these make the most sense to you?" and "Which will you use?"—4 minutes.
   D. After the supervisee makes his or her choices, the supervisor affirms, "I understand that you will do . . ." and writes actions on plan—4 minutes.

III. Critique Phase—3 minutes
   A. Supervisor asks, "What feedback can you give me on how I conducted this conference?"
   B. Supervisor asks, "What might we do next time to make these observations and conferences more helpful?"
   C. Supervisor summarizes what he or she has learned, for use in later conferences.

Appendix C

Assessing School-Based Supervisory Practices for Promoting Instructional Improvement

Directions: For each item, please circle a number in the right column to indicate the degree to which the item describes the current supervisory practice in your school(s):

1. Definitely false
2. More false than true
3. More true than false
4. Definitely true

   I. In the area of direct personal support in my school(s), leadership personnel provide:

   A. Assistance with identifying and obtaining resources for instruction — 1 2 3 4

   B. Demonstration of teaching techniques in the classroom — 1 2 3 4

   C. Consultation on instructional problems and concerns — 1 2 3 4

   D. Conferences to schedule and plan observations — 1 2 3 4

   E. Observations of classes for assistance in improving instruction (not for evaluation) — 1 2 3 4

   F. Conferences after observations to discuss and analyze the lesson observed — 1 2 3 4

Source: Jean W. Jones, A data collection system for describing research-based supervisory practices for promoting instructional improvement in a local school district. Ed.D. dissertation, University of Georgia, 1986. Reprinted by permission of the author.

G. Opportunities to analyze teaching with
   audio or videotape   1 2 3 4
H. Opportunities to observe and discuss classes
   taught by other teachers   1 2 3 4
I. Genuine concern for teachers and students   1 2 3 4
J. Supportive and helpful assistance   1 2 3 4
K. Stimulation to think consciously about
   teaching skills   1 2 3 4

II. In my school(s), leadership personnel assist
teachers with:
A. Planning appropriate learning objectives   1 2 3 4
B. Designing appropriate instructional
   activities   1 2 3 4
C. Developing remedial and enrichment
   activities   1 2 3 4
D. Developing activities for daily review and
   diagnosis   1 2 3 4
E. Developing strategies for student team or
   group learning   1 2 3 4
F. Developing learning activities for students
   who finish early   1 2 3 4
G. Evaluating student progress   1 2 3 4
H. Interpreting and using test scores from
   standardized or criterion-referenced tests   1 2 3 4
I. Organizing and arranging the space and
   materials for instruction   1 2 3 4
J. Increasing and maintaining student
   academic engagement time   1 2 3 4
K. Stimulating learner interest during lesson
   presentation   1 2 3 4
L. Managing student behavior (discipline)   1 2 3 4
M. Clarifying classroom rules and procedures
   for students   1 2 3 4
N. Giving clear directions and preparing for
   transitions in the classroom   1 2 3 4
O. Using questioning techniques with students   1 2 3 4
P. Involving all students during guided
   practice to increase success on objectives   1 2 3 4
Q. Providing students with corrective feedback
   and praise   1 2 3 4

III. Structured learning opportunities such as
workshops, in-service activities, or staff
development programs in my school(s) include:

A. Active support and clear direction by
   leadership personnel   1 2 3 4
B. Opportunities for collaborative planning of
   in-service activities   1 2 3 4
C. In-service activities that are consistent with
   clearly defined goals for instructional
   improvement   1 2 3 4
D. Activities that present information or skills
   that have been shown to be effective   1 2 3 4
E. Presentation of information and skills that
   are practical and useful   1 2 3 4
F. Activities that are well organized and
   carefully developed   1 2 3 4
G. Program leaders who have credibility and
   expertise   1 2 3 4
H. Formal opportunities to learn, solve
   problems, and interact with small groups or
   teams   1 2 3 4
I. Programs that extend over several sessions   1 2 3 4
J. Presentations by a combination of
   instructional techniques   1 2 3 4
K. Presentation of information or skills through
   modeling or demonstrations (live or taped)   1 2 3 4
L. Planned opportunities to discuss usefulness
   of information or skills and to share
   instructional ideas   1 2 3 4
M. Opportunities to apply and practice
   information or skills by direct experience
   during workshop or teaching situations   1 2 3 4
N. Opportunities for observation and objective
   feedback between sessions to promote
   acquisition of information or skill   1 2 3 4
O. Observations by leadership personnel to see
   if skills or information presented in in-
   service programs are being used   1 2 3 4
P. Access to materials and resource people to
   help implement a program after formal in-
   service presentations have been completed   1 2 3 4

IV. Are there additional ways in which leadership
    personnel can support teachers in increasing
    and maintaining instructional effectiveness?
    Please comment:

Name Index

Subject Index

Abstract thinking, 22, 49, 54–56, 60–63, 68, 70, 94, 290, 300, 317–318, 319, 322, 323, 327, 333, 356, 358, 394, 425, 426, 428
Action research, 4, 5, 7, 22, 45, 49, 67, 279, 392–413, 418, 425, 428, 437
  defined, 393
  design, 396–397
  evaluation phase, 394
  examples of, 397–405, 410–413
  goal identification phase, 394
  planning phase, 394, 396
  shared governance, 405–410, 411, 413, 442, 443
Adult development, 7, 13, 14, 40, 45–57, 65–69, 70, 176, 178–187, 203, 317–318, 319, 332 (*see also* Life-span transitions; Motivation)
  cognitive, 46, 55, 56–57, 290
  conceptual, 47, 52, 54, 317–318, 319
  crystallized learning, 47, 56
  defined, 46
  fluid learning, 47
  moral development, 47–48, 64, 178, 179, 338–339
  personality (ego) development, 47, 49, 53–54, 55, 56, 64
  stages, 46
Annehurst Curriculum Classification System, 404
Assessment, 7, 53, 57, 204–208, 211–212, 334, 395, 460–462
  cognitive dissonance, 116–117
  defined, 204
  Delphi technique, 215, 395
  methods, 212–215
  of needs, 212–215, 220, 262, 334, 395
  open-ended survey, 213, 395
  organizational, 211–212
  ranking list, 213–215, 395
  of self, 113–116
  third-party review, 213, 395
  of use of time, 205–208

Bloom's taxonomy, 347–348

Categorical frequency observation instruments, 230–232, 237, 248, 396
Clinical supervision, 280–291
  analysis, 281–283
  critique, 285
  interpretation, 281–283
  observation, 281
  peer coaching, 285–291
  preconference, 281, 285
  postconference, 283–285
Collaborative approach, 108, 109, 111, 112, 116, 117, 136–149, 175, 176, 188, 189, 283, 394, 457–458
  defined, 108
  with groups, 141–144
  with individuals, 137–141
  issues in, 144–146
  scenarios, 136, 141–142
  when to use, 146–147, 191
Collaborative supervision, 88, 103, 116, 117
  defined, 88
Common cause among school staff, 9, 19, 20, 22, 34, 40, 45, 57, 67, 94, 204, 254, 279, 327, 358, 366, 397, 426, 428, 429, 445
Curriculum, 3, 15, 18, 21, 24, 28, 35, 55, 58, 61, 78, 253, 340–343, 356, 358–360, 404, 411, 412
  Annehurst Curriculum Classification System, 404
  defined, 343
  effect of reforms on, 358–360
  "teacher-proof," 340–343
Curriculum development, 4, 5, 7, 20, 22, 45, 49, 67, 204, 212–221, 279, 338–363, 394, 396, 397, 418, 424, 425, 428, 437
  behavioral-objective format, 343–345, 348, 350, 357
  Bloom's taxonomy, 347–348
  conceptual mapping format, 346–347, 348, 357
  formats, 343–347
  integrating format, 355–356
  levels of, 350–351
  loosely coupled organizations, 340–341